Garden
Flowers

THE COMPLETE BOOK OF
Garden Flowers

How to grow over 300 of the best performing varieties

SERIES EDITOR   GRAHAM STRONG

MEREHURST

Merehurst Ltd, Ferry House, 51-57 Lacy Road, Putney, London SW15 1PR

CONTENTS

GROWING ANNUALS

Annuals are perhaps the easiest plants you will ever grow. Yet their ease of growth in no way detracts from their ability to provide colour in the garden, in some cases virtually all-year-round. Whether your garden is large, small, or you work within the confines of just a small patio, annuals are plants for you.

Miracles are happening in our gardens every day, but perhaps the greatest 'miracle' in which we can take part is growing plants from seeds. Nothing is quite as amazing, or as humbling, as seeing a fully-grown plant, which started life as a tiny seed, burst into flower and create a riot of colour just a few months after it was sown. Some annuals need no more care than simply scattering the seeds over the surface of the ground and 'raking' them in using your fingertips – others demand only that they are sown to the correct depth and then given room to grow as they develop. By their very nature, many annuals produce brilliant results even in the poorest of soils. So get some seed catalogues, visit the local garden centre, and start performing your own garden miracles with the easiest plants on earth!

LEFT: Annuals like these purple violas and white-flowered lobularia (alyssum) can be sown directly into the soil where you want them to flower, in criss-crossing patterns as here.

ABOVE: Rudbeckia or coneflower is available in a wide range of sizes, and provides valuable colour in late summer.

MANY ANNUALS THRIVE in some of the most inhospitable parts of the garden. These portulacas or sun flowers are perfectly at home growing on a rockery with very little soil for their roots — they are just as suited to light, sandy soils and make good summer bedding plants.

WHAT ARE ANNUALS?

Virtually all annuals are raised by sowing seeds, either in early spring under cover (in a heated greenhouse, conservatory or on the kitchen windowsill), or directly into prepared soil outdoors. Some annuals are so adaptable that you only need sow them once – from then on these so-called 'self-seeders' regularly drop seeds into the soil which then 'come up', or germinate, of their own accord. In many ways these 'hardy annuals' do a better job at sowing than we do – finding just the right spot for perfect growth – often in places we might never dream of actually sowing seeds, such as between the cracks in paving stones and in the gravel of driveways.

At the other extreme are annuals which need to be started into growth long before the warmer days of spring arrive outdoors. The so-called 'half-hardy' annuals are those plants which are damaged by frosts, but which perform brilliantly during the summer months. For these you must be able to provide suitable growing conditions, especially at sowing time, when temperature is all-important for actually getting the seeds to come up. In some cases, such as with ricinus, the castor oil plant, it is grown as a half-hardy annual, even though it is by nature a shrub, which in its native habitat would, like the shrubs in our gardens, eventually form a large plant. Petunias are another example of a half-hardy annual which is really a perennial plant, and quite capable of surviving the winter if potted-up and kept protected in a cold but 'frost-free' place overwinter. It helps to understand what the terms mean when growing annuals as you will come across them all the time in catalogues and on the back of seed packets.

HARDY ANNUALS

The easiest of all annuals to grow, sow hardy annuals exactly where you want the plants to flower. Many hardy annuals do not like root disturbance, so bear this in mind.

They are given their ideal planting distances by gradually 'thinning out' as the young plants grow – all this means is carefully removing a few plants every few weeks in spring, to give those left behind more room to develop. By early summer this thinning should be complete, and plants can be left to produce flowers. Hardy annuals are not affected by low temperatures, and many, like calendula, the pot marigold, are sown and germinate outdoors in September for strong plants with earlier flowers the following spring. Most self-seeders belong to this group.

HALF-HARDY ANNUALS

As already mentioned, these plants are not able to withstand frost or freezing temperatures and must be raised from seed every season, often starting in late winter and very early spring. Many half-hardy annuals are actually 'perennials' – plants which keep growing year after year, but which are better-suited to our needs when grown as strong, young plants every season. Half-hardy annuals are only planted (or moved outdoors if grown in containers) when spring frosts are finished. The exact timing of this depends on the actual area you garden in, but this book gives sowing/planting times for average conditions in the middle of Britain. At the other end of the season, the first autumn frosts will flatten most half-hardy annuals, and they can be removed for composting.

HARDY BIENNIALS

A biennial is simply a plant which straddles two growing seasons before it produces its show of flowers or foliage. A good example is cheiranthus, or wallflower, which is sown outdoors in early summer. The young leafy plants are grown on, then lifted and planted in October where you want flowers the following spring. Think of hardy biennials as annuals with a 'foot' in two seasons – instead of producing their flowers or leaves all within what we think of as 'summer', they get going in one season, spend the winter building up speed, then go all out for flowering the next spring and summer. Biennials are especially useful for filling any 'gaps' between late spring and early summer, and many such as sweet William are easy and worthwhile plants for cut flowers.

BUYING SEEDS

Growing from seed is addictive – once you have sampled one seed catalogue you will certainly want more. You can buy annual seeds by sending for them by post or a home delivery service, by visiting garden centres or the gardening section of do-it-yourself stores, or, increasingly, by buying them with your other shopping at the supermarket.

The choice will always be greater in catalogues, but the more limited range that you might find in garden centres can actually be more helpful. The seed packets here are guaranteed to be colourful, giving encouragement to the beginner. Some mail order seed companies pack in plain, information-only packets for mail order – this is no reflection on the quality of the seeds, but they do lack inspiration! Bright, colourful packets are a great help when planning a colour-themed display with annuals, so do not be afraid to play around with a handful of packets until you get a good balance or contrast of colours just to your liking.

If you do buy seeds from garden centres and similar outlets, always avoid any packets that are faded, yellow, and have obviously been exposed to the sun, as the results are likely to be disappointing.

SEED PACKETS

Remember that seeds are alive, and need looking after to keep them in tip-top condition until sowing. Inside most seed packets you will find another, smaller packet made of foil. Seeds are sealed inside this inner packet in a kind of 'suspended animation' which preserves them until the foil seal is broken. This is when the normal ageing processes of the seed begins. Where this type of storage is not vital for success, seeds are simply found sealed within the outer paper packet. Foil packets should not be opened until the time of sowing for best results. On most packets the inspiration on the front is backed-up by full growing instructions on the reverse. The better packets give sowing times, expected flowering period, and alternative sowing times in autumn. Keep seed packets after sowing – along with catalogues they build up into an invaluable reference library which you can refer to as and when necessary. Always keep seeds in a cool, dry, frost-free place.

YOUNG PLANTS

Many half-hardy annuals included in this book can also be bought in spring and summer as 'young plants', and this is stated, where relevant, in the paragraph 'features' for each of the 90 annuals covered. The term 'young plant' covers anything from ready-germinated trays of small seedlings to a large plant, perhaps in flower, growing in a 9cm (3½in) pot which you will find for sale in garden centres. Buying young plants simply means that a lot of the work in raising the plants from seed has been done for you by the grower – which has advantages and disadvantages. Young plants are a great help if you do not have facilities for raising seeds or enough space, and they are often delivered ready to go straight into containers. The range compared to the number of varieties available from seed is limited, although this is always improving. You pay for convenience – seed raising is usually cheaper than buying in young plants.

WHAT CAN GO WRONG?

Yellow leaves
● Seedlings are being grown too cold in the early stages or plants may have been planted outdoors too early.
● Plants may need feeding – water thoroughly with an all-purpose liquid or soluble plant food, wetting the leaves at the same time to act as a foliar feed.

Curled or distorted leaves
● Look for clusters of aphids attacking flower buds and the youngest leaves at the shoot tips. Rub them off with your fingers or use a spray containing permethrin.
● Drift from weedkillers can cause this problem, so take great care if you are treating a lawn for weeds using a hormone weedkiller – avoid days when there is any breeze, and keep well away from bedding displays.

Holes and silvery trails on/in leaves
● Slugs and snails will eat most annual plants and are a particular threat in late spring and early summer, especially after rain when the air is warm and moist. They leave silver slime-trails on the soil and on plants where they have been feeding. Chemical slug pellets can be scattered sparingly among plants or an unbroken ring of sharp grit 5cm (2in) wide can be used as a physical deterrent on smaller areas. Another option is to check plants at night and pick off slugs and snails while they feed, dropping them into salty water.

White 'powder' on leaves
● Powdery mildew affects many annuals but not usually until late summer. This disease is not a serious threat and treatment is not needed.

Seedlings indoors suddenly collapse and fall over
● 'Damping off' disease can attack annual seedlings, and is a particular problem if the compost becomes too wet. Always use clean pots for sowing and fresh compost. If it does attack, water lightly with a copper-based fungicide and resow to play safe.

Leaf edges chewed
● Various caterpillars will attack annuals and can soon strip leaves bare. Pick them off by hand or use a spray containing permethrin, wetting both sides of the leaves with a strong jet from the sprayer.

Plants cut off at ground level
● Cutworms can sever newly planted bedding plants outdoors causing a sudden wilting and yellowing of plants under attack. Search around in the soil and the greenish-brown caterpillars are easily found and destroyed.

Creamy-white grubs eating roots
● Vine weevil grubs can cause severe damage to container plants. Never re-use old compost, and if you find grubs, treat all pots with biological control or a chemical based on phenols as a drench.

Orange marigolds, red and orange nasturtiums, asters and brown-coned rudbeckia intermingle forming a colour co-ordinated annual border.

One of the wisest approaches is to decide carefully just what you feel you can achieve with your existing facilities. If your 'propagator' (somewhere that plants are raised from seeds in the early stages) is just the kitchen windowsill, then buying half-hardy annuals in as young plants might be the best option. These small plug plants are delivered in mid-spring and can be potted up and grown on on the windowsill or even next to the glass in an unheated conservatory. This cuts out the often tricky job of germinating the seeds to begin with, but means you can still grow the plants you really want. And of course there is nothing to stop you sowing hardy annuals straight into the soil outdoors at the right time.

If you are more restricted, say to just a small patio or balcony, young plants might be the whole solution – larger plants are delivered (or can be bought) in late spring and early summer and these can be planted straight into containers and hanging baskets without growing on. Even then there is nothing to stop you scattering a few seeds of malcolmia, Virginian stock, in the top of your patio pots for some quick and scented flowers!

Most seed catalogues and specialist young plant suppliers carry extensive and informative sections on young plants, and they are well worth getting hold of. Pay particular attention to 'last order dates' – these are the cut-off points for placing young plant orders and many start to appear even as early as January and February.

ANNUALS IN CONTAINERS

A container in the broadest gardening sense is anything capable of holding compost and supporting plant growth –

this could be a 9cm (3½in) diameter plastic plant pot to a large terracotta trough or tub. Whatever you use, it must have some form of drainage, and this is usually through holes in the base. Moulded plastic containers often have no preformed holes and so you must drill these before planting up. Waterlogged compost kills plant roots and the whole plant will soon die.

For most purposes a good 'multipurpose' compost serves all of an annual plant's needs – from sowing to growing on and finally being planted up. Most multipurpose composts are based on peat with plant nutrients and other materials such as water-storing granules and 'wetters' (allowing dried-out compost to be re-wetted) already added. An increasing number of composts available are based on recycled materials, and the coir-based ones are improving constantly. A few specific plants do prefer a soil-based compost, such as the 'John Innes' types, both for sowing and growing – details of these are given under 'growing method' where relevant. Always buy fresh bags of compost in spring, avoiding any that are over-heavy and wet, or split with green algae growing in them, or faded and past their sell-by date!

There is no reason why hardy annuals cannot be used for container growing – the fact that many are usually sown direct into the soil is not a problem. Simply sow them in small pots or multi-cell trays (plastic trays where the area is divided into individual units or 'cells') at the same times as recommended for outdoor sowing, and plant into your containers during spring. Where appropriate under each plant entry, varieties suited to containers are given – these are usually dwarfer versions of taller varieties, and the range is increasing all the time. Half-hardy annuals offer great scope for container growing, for the reasons already discussed.

SOWING ANNUALS

Annual seeds are either sown indoors or outdoors. Those sown outdoors are the easiest – they need no extra warmth or heat, just sow them in a patch of well-prepared ground and thin to give them space as they grow. Sowing depth will depend on the size of the seed, but it is essential to work the soil using a rake (or your fingers in a small area) so it is fine and crumbly to at least 2.5cm (1in) deep.

Seed can then be simply scattered over the soil and raked in, or sown in seed drills – these are simply grooves made in the soil with the head of a rake, the edge of a piece of wood, a length of bamboo cane or even the side of your hand. Whichever you use, just press the edge into the soil to make a groove of the right depth. Then sprinkle the seeds thinly along the drill, by rubbing them between your finger and thumb. Once finished, soil is moved back over the seeds with a rake or by lightly brushing the flat of your hand over the sown area. Take care not to disturb the sown seeds, and label with the variety and date sown. If you are sowing a large area with a variety of hardy annuals, or planning a mixture of hardy and half-hardy varieties, mark the sown patches with boundaries of light-coloured sand – a traditional but still effective way of seeing just where you have been! By sowing in short drills within these marked areas it is easy to tell the annuals from the weeds because they come up in rows.

Indoors, half-hardy annuals are sown ideally in a heated propagator with temperature control, and this piece of 'kit' is virtually essential when raising plants like pelargoniums (bedding geraniums) and begonias – both of which need high, constant, temperatures. Otherwise a brightly lit windowsill in a warm kitchen will work wonders – many half-hardy annuals are very undemanding once they have come up, and if not kept over-wet will grow steadily even in quite cool conditions.

Narrow 'windowsill propagators' are available which have a heated base and allow you to move pots on and off as seedlings appear – these are invaluable if you plan to do a lot of seed-raising. For all the plants in this book a 9cm (3½in) diameter pot is sufficient for the germination of an average packet of half-hardy annual seeds. If you raise half-hardy annuals remember that they will not be able to go out until after the last spring frosts. You can sow many plants later than the 'ideal' times – this book describes the optimum sowing times unless otherwise stated – and to plan for a later display of flowers with the advantage of them being easier to raise and look after a little later in the spring season.

SOIL PREPARATION

All that annuals need to grow well is soil that has had plenty of 'organic matter' added before sowing or planting, and this is best done by digging it in thoroughly the previous autumn or in early spring. Suppliers of manure take some tracking down these days, so using home-made compost (or leaf mould) is a better option. Whatever you use, it must be dark, well-rotted, and thoroughly broken down. Organic matter is vital for improving the soil's ability to hold onto moisture at the height of summer, and also supplies some plant foods. To take proper care of feeding, scatter pelleted poultry manure over the area 2–3 weeks before sowing/planting and rake it in. This should provide ample nutrients for the rest of the summer.

THINNING OUT

'Thinning out' or 'thinning' means allowing enough room for plants to develop fully. This is most important with hardy annuals – as young seedlings grow larger some are gradually removed to leave room for those left behind. Make sure you put your fingers on the soil when pulling plants out or there is a risk the plants you leave behind will be uprooted. Water well after thinning to settle seedlings back in. Thinning can start when plants are just 2.5cm (1in) tall and is usually finished by early summer. Autumn-sown annuals should be thinned in spring, in case some plants are lost during the winter months.

GROWING ON

Once seedlings have been transplanted (moved) to either individual pots or cell trays, they are 'grown on'. This stage lasts until they are finally hardened off before planting out outdoors or in pots. During growing on, make sure plants do not dry out, space them out (if pot-grown) as they develop, and keep an eye out for pests and diseases. Some plants (like thunbergia, black-eyed-Susan) benefit from being potted on when their roots fill the pot.

HARDENING OFF

Toughening plants raised indoors ready for outdoor conditions is vital if they are not to suffer a growth 'check' when you put them out. Few of us have (or have the room for) the traditional 'coldframe' which was the classic way of hardening off. These days we can make use of garden fleece, which is much easier, and just as effective. From mid-May onwards plants can be stood outside on warm days, in a sunny spot. For the first week bring them in at night, then leave them out, but covered with fleece at night. Gradually, unless frost is forecast, the fleece can be left off even at night, but replaced during frosty spells. By early June, plants will be hardened off and ready to plant.

PLANTING

Whether you are planting in beds or containers, water the pots/trays the night before to soak the roots. Planting can be done with a trowel – or even by hand on light soils. Using your hands is certainly the best way of planting up containers and hanging baskets. Never plant the base of plants deeper than they were growing originally, firm well, and water. Keep labels with plants for future reference, and note the planting date on the label as well.

WATERING

Lack of water causes many hardy annuals to flower and then quickly die. When the soil feels dry, enough water should be given so that it really gets down to the roots – the soil should feel moist at least 15cm (6in) down. Use a trowel and check that this is happening. Containers need much more care as they rely solely on you for their water. Choosing a compost containing water-storing crystals provides the best insurance. Do not overwater early on or roots may rot, but check them at least every other day and never allow them to dry out.

FEEDING

By mixing slow-release fertiliser granules with the compost before planting you can take care of feeding for the whole season – you just need to water. Outdoors, bedding displays will benefit from liquid feeding every 2–4 weeks. Many hardy annuals need no extra feeding and actually thrive on poor, hungry soils.

USING ANNUALS IN YOUR GARDEN

With annuals the sky really is the limit. You can choose to grow just hardy or half-hardy annuals, a mixture of both, or you can be more adventurous and put them to work for you in a wide range of garden situations. Or, of course, you could just leave them to do their own thing!

Once you have annuals in your garden you will never want to be without them. Self-seeding annuals like limnanthes and nigella will want to do their own thing and grow where they fall, while others such as lavatera and ricinus are put to much better use by carefully planning where they will grow. You can find a spot for annuals in every garden, and sometimes they can even help you out of a tight corner! What better plants could you ask for?

ABOVE: The delicately veined flower of agrostemma, the corncockle, an easily-grown hardy annual that is sown outdoors in spring where you want it to flower.

AS EDGING PLANTS these Begonia semperflorens *are a good choice – being of even height they are good for growing in lines.*

BEDDING SCHEMES

We see annuals used in bedding schemes almost every day of our lives, on traffic roundabouts, in public parks, and in each others gardens. The 'scheme' part of the phrase comes from the fact that many of these flashy, colourful displays are pre-planned and in many ways made-to-measure. If that is the effect you are after, then you must do your homework. The 'structure' of a basic bedding scheme is quite simple – you have tall plants in the centre of the bed, and the shortest plants around the edge. In between are plants in a range of sizes and with varying growth habits, which fill the space between the tallest and the shortest. Bedding schemes can be as simple, or as elaborate, as you like. The key points to remember are to work out which plants are going where, how many you need, and of course, whether they are suited to being grown together.

HARDY ANNUAL SCHEMES

Creating a show using just hardy annuals is both very easy and tremendous fun. The sheer range of hardy annual varieties is enormous and it is easy to be spoilt for choice. You can go out and sow an entire bed with hardy annuals at one go, then sit back and wait for the seedlings to come up. All you need to do then is keep down annual weeds (all perennial weeds should be removed before sowing), thin out every few weeks until early summer, push in twiggy

THIS SUMMER BEDDING SCHEME features zinnias in the centre of the bed (with variegated tradescantia creeping through) then scarlet salvias, dropping down to the pink fluffy heads of ageratum, the floss flower, below.

supports for taller, straggly plants and enjoy the show. The best effect is from bold groups of colour, so sow in patches at least 60cm (2ft) across. Sow roughly circular areas as a fool-proof guide, although interweaving shapes can create some dramatic effects, with different plants merging as they grow into each other. Take a tip from the traditions of the past and mark out the sown areas with sand, just so you know what is where, and label each patch, or mark the varieties clearly on a sketch plan if you have one. Using just hardy annuals means there is no need for heating early in the season, and no crisis when growing space runs short. Many hardy annuals can also be sown in autumn, usually September, to grow through the winter and then give a early performance the following spring.

CARE-FREE HARDY ANNUALS

What could be better than a plant you only buy once, but will then always have many of? It sounds too good to be true but that is just what you get with a great many hardy annuals – the self-seeders that arrive in a packet and then spread to all their favourite spots. We have to thank the origins of many of these plants for their valuable qualities. Agrostemma, the corncockle, for example, was once a common weed of cornfields, and many other care-free annuals like it thrive on the poorest and hungriest of soils. These plants will tell you where they prefer growing by seeding themselves there, and they will need no more

attention other than being pulled out when they get too dominant or invasive in areas set aside for more carefully planned activities. Calendula, centaurea, eschscholzia, papaver and tropaeolum are all good examples of care-free annuals.

BORDER FILLERS

With the sudden loss of a favourite plant your dreams of a 'perfect' border can soon evaporate, and this is where annuals can get you out of a tight spot. Any spare patch of ground can be sown, or planted, with annuals, which will grow quickly to fill any gaps. You might even scatter seeds in amongst perennial plants and let them get on with it. Lunaria, honesty, is quite at home growing amongst spring-flowering perennial euphorbias, the purple lunaria flowers making a good contrast with the pale yellow-green euphorbias. For a touch of the tropical, ricinus, the castor oil plant, is unbeatable, with its large, exotic-looking leaves in a range of colours. Sunflowers (helianthus) are always a good bet for some instant colour when needed, and the newer dwarf varieties like 'Pacino' are easy to grow in pots for planting out as and when their bright flowers are called for to perk up flagging borders.

ABUTILON
Flowering maple

ABUTILON *has a distinct 'exotic' look with its hanging, bell-like flowers that are either single or bicoloured, as seen here.*

BEING A SHRUB, *abutilon can be kept from year to year in a frost-free greenhouse and planted outdoors in mixed borders in summer.*

FEATURES

A deciduous tender shrub that is easy to raise from seed sown in spring, with maple-like leaves and showy, hanging, bell-shaped flowers in a wide range of colours. Plants make bushy growth, and are useful in summer bedding schemes and for patio containers sited in a warm spot, but they must be protected from frost. Abutilon can be kept in a conservatory or frost-free greenhouse in winter and will flower throughout spring and summer. Plants grow to 60–90cm (2–3ft) tall. Varieties such as *Abutilon pictum* 'Thompsonii', with variegated leaves, are available from garden centres as young plants in spring; these can be potted up, grown on and then planted outdoors after the last frosts.

ABUTILON AT A GLANCE

A deciduous shrub grown as a summer bedding and container plant, with bell-like flowers. Frost hardy to –5ºC (23ºF).

JAN	/	
FEB	sow	
MAR	pot up	
APR	pot on	
MAY	harden off/plant	
JUN	flowering	
JULY	flowering	
AUG	flowering	
SEPT	flowering	
OCT	/	
NOV	/	
DEC	/	

RECOMMENDED VARIETIES

Abutilon hybrids:
  'Large Flowered Mixed'
  'Mixed Colours'

CONDITIONS

Aspect Grow in full sun in borders or on a south-facing patio. In southern areas plants grown against a south-facing wall in well-drained soil will often survive mild winters outdoors without protection.

Site Mix plenty of rotted manure/compost into soil before planting, and use multipurpose compost in containers. Soil should be well-drained but moisture-retentive for best results.

GROWING METHOD

Sowing In February, sow in 9cm (3½in) diameter pots, cover seed with its own depth of multipurpose compost, and keep at 21ºC (70ºF) in light. Seedlings appear over 1–2 months so check regularly. When plants are 5cm (2in) tall, pot up into 9cm (3½in) pots and grow on. Plant out in early June after the last frosts.

Feeding Apply liquid feed weekly. Mix slow-release fertiliser granules with container compost.

Problems Use sprays containing pirimicarb for aphids, malathion for mealy bugs and bifenthrin for red spider mite, or, on plants growing in conservatories, use natural predators.

FLOWERING

Season Flowers appear all summer outdoors, and some may appear year-round on indoor plants and those grown in southerly, mild areas, especially near the coast.

Cutting Not suitable.

General Plants can be potted up before frosts and kept indoors. Increase favourites by taking cuttings in spring, rooting them on a windowsill or in a heated propagator.

AGERATUM

Floss flower

AGERATUM FLOWERS are carried on neat-growing plants and are good for 'cooling down' other plants with bright flowers.

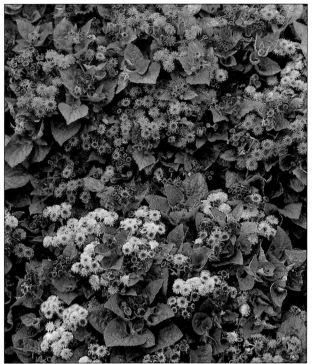

MODERN VARIETIES of ageratum for bedding produce masses of flowers which gradually rise above the leaves as they open.

FEATURES

Ageratum, a half-hardy annual, has fluffy long-lived flowers in blue, pink, white and bicolours such as blue-white. Use dwarf varieties for edging, as they grow up to 15cm (6in). Tall varieties are used in borders and for cutting, growing to 75cm (2½ft). Use for bedding/containers. Available as young plants.

CONDITIONS

Aspect   Needs full sun and a sheltered position.

AGERATUM AT A GLANCE

A half-hardy annual grown for its fluffy flowers, ideal for edging, bedding, containers and cutting. Frost hardy to 0°C (32°F).

		RECOMMENDED VARIETIES
JAN	/	*Ageratum houstonianum:*
FEB	sow	**For bedding**
MAR	sow	'Adriatic'
APR	grow on	'Bavaria'
MAY	plant	'Blue Champion'
JUN	flowering	'Blue Mink'
JULY	flowering	'Pink Powderpuffs'
AUG	flowering	'White Blue'
SEPT	flowering	'Capri'
OCT	/	'White Hawaii'
NOV	/	**For cutting**
DEC	/	'Blue Horizon'

Site   Prefers well-drained soil enriched with rotted manure or compost well ahead of planting. In containers use multipurpose compost and ensure that there is good drainage.

GROWING METHOD

Sowing   Sow seeds in 9cm (3½in) pots in February/March and just cover, and keep at 21°C (70°F). Seedlings appear after a week and can be moved to cell trays of multipurpose compost when two leaves are developed. Harden off and plant outside after frosts, spacing tall varieties 30–40 cm (12–16in) apart, dwarf varieties 10–15cm (4–6in) apart.

Feeding   Apply liquid feed fortnightly to maintain strong growth, or mix slow-release fertiliser with compost before planting up.

Problems   Ageratum can suffer from root rot so grow in well-drained containers on heavy clay soils, and avoid getting the compost too wet.

FLOWERING

Season   Flowers appear all summer until the first frosts. Regular dead-heading, especially after heavy rain, will prolong flowering and often encourage a second 'flush' of colour.

Cutting   Tall varieties are suitable for cutting.

AFTER FLOWERING

General   Remove plants when past their best, usually after the first sharp frosts of autumn.

AMARANTHUS

Love-lies-bleeding

SOME AMARANTHUS produce masses of copper-crimson leaves in summer and red flower spikes. They make good pot plants.

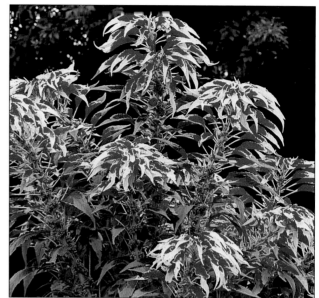

'JOSEPH'S COAT', 60cm (2ft) tall, has striking gold and crimson upper leaves, and green-yellow lower leaves marked with brown.

FEATURES

Amaranthus is grown for its colourful, exotic-looking foliage and its, spikey, erect or drooping tassels of blood-red, green, golden-brown, purple or multi-coloured flowers up to 45cm (18in) long. Leaves can be red, bronze, yellow, brown or green, depending on the variety grown. Size ranges from 38cm (15in) to 1.2m (4ft) tall. Use plants as pot plants, in patio containers and as dramatic centrepieces in summer bedding displays. Superb used cut for fresh or dried flower arrangements indoors.

CONDITIONS

Aspect Full sun and shelter is essential for success.
Site Soil should be well-drained, with plenty of

rotted compost or manure added. Varieties of *Amaranthus caudatus* will also succeed on thin, dry soils. Use multipurpose compost in containers and pots. In northern areas grow in 20–25cm (8–10in) diameter pots in the greenhouse or conservatory. Tall growing varieties may need staking.

GROWING METHOD

Sowing Sow seeds in March at 21°C (70°F) in 9cm (3½in) diameter pots of multipurpose compost, just covering the seed. Seeds germinate in 7–14 days or sooner, and should be transplanted into cell trays or 9cm (3½in) diameter pots of multipurpose compost. Plant outside after the last frosts in late May/early June, 30–90cm (1–3ft) apart and water.
Feeding Feed weekly from early summer onwards with general-purpose liquid feed. In containers, mix slow-release fertiliser with compost before planting, and feed every two weeks with half-strength liquid feed as well.
Problems Aphids can feed on the colourful leaves and build up into large colonies unless caught early. Use a spray containing permethrin.

FLOWERING

Season Foliage is colourful from early summer onwards, and is joined by flowerheads and then colourful seedheads later on.
Cutting Varieties grown for their flowers can be cut and used fresh, while seedheads can be left to develop, then cut and dried for indoor use.

AFTER FLOWERING

General Remove plants when past their best.

AMARANTHUS AT A GLANCE

A half-hardy annual grown for its leaves and flowers for bedding, containers and for drying. Frost hardy to 0°C (32°F).

		RECOMMENDED VARIETIES
JAN	/	*Amaranthus caudatus:*
FEB	/	'Green Thumb'
MAR	sow	'Viridis'
APR	transplant	*Amaranthus cruentus:*
MAY	transplant	'Golden Giant'
JUN	flowering	'Split Personality'
JULY	flowering	'Ruby Slippers'
AUG	flowering	*Amaranthus hybridus:*
SEPT	flowering	'Intense Purple'
OCT	flowering	*Amaranthus tricolor:*
NOV	/	'Aurora Yellow'
DEC	/	'Joseph's Coat'

ANTIRRHINUM

Snapdragon

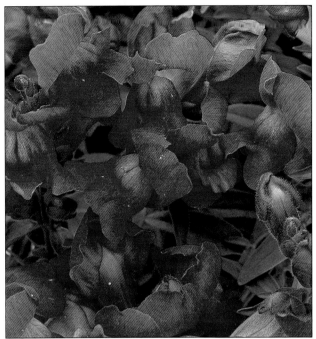

OLDER VARIETIES of snapdragon like this actually have flowers that 'snap' when squeezed. This trick is not found in newer types.

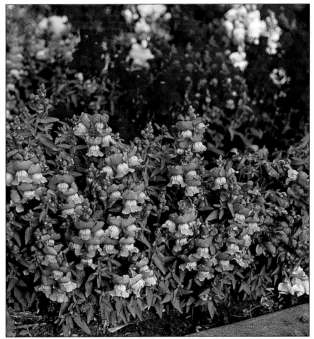

DWARF VARIETIES reaching just 15cm (6in) are colourful for bed edges and have bushy growth without the need for pinching out.

FEATURES

Antirrhinums fall into three groups: tall varieties up to 1.2m (4ft) for cutting; 'intermediates' for bedding, 45cm (18in); dwarf varieties for edging/containers, 30cm (12in). Colour range is wide, and includes bicolours, and doubles. Flowers of older varieties open when squeezed at the sides, hence the name 'snapdragon'. Grow as a half-hardy annual. Available as young plants.

CONDITIONS

Aspect   Must be in full sun all day.

ANTIRRHINUM AT A GLANCE

A half-hardy annual grown for its tubular flowers, used for containers, bedding displays and cutting. Frost hardy to 0°C (32°F).

		RECOMMENDED VARIETIES
JAN	/	*Antirrhinum majus:*
FEB	sow	**For containers**
MAR	sow	'Lipstick Silver'
APR	grow on	'Magic Carpet Mixed'
MAY	plant	'Tom Thumb Mixed'
JUN	flowering	**For bedding**
JULY	flowering	'Brighton Rock Mixed'
AUG	flowering	'Corona Mixed'
SEPT	flowering	'Sonnet Mixed'
OCT	/	**For cutting**
NOV	/	'Liberty Mixed'
DEC	/	

Site   Soil must be very well-drained but have plenty of rotted compost or manure dug in before planting. In containers use multipurpose compost and ensure good, free drainage.

GROWING METHOD

Sowing   Sow in February/March and barely cover the very fine seed. Use 9cm (3½in) pots of multipurpose compost and keep in light at 18°C (64°F). Seedlings appear after a week and can be transplanted to cell trays when two young leaves have developed. Plant outside after hardening off following the last frosts, 15–45cm (6–18in) apart depending on the variety. Those grown for bedding purposes should have the growing tip pinched out when 15cm (6in) tall to encourage bushy growth.

Feeding   Liquid feed plants in beds with a hand-held feeder fortnightly. Mix slow-release fertiliser with container compost before planting up.

Problems   Seedlings are prone to 'damping off' so water pots with a copper-based fungicide. Plants suffer with rust disease. Grow a 'resistant' variety such as 'Monarch Mixed' or use a spray containing penconazole at regular intervals.

FLOWERING

Season   Flowers appear all summer and should be removed as they fade to keep buds coming.

Cutting   Tall varieties are excellent as cut spikes.

AFTER FLOWERING

General   Pull plants up when they are over.

ARCTOTIS
African daisy

AFRICAN DAISIES should be pinched out when they are 12.5cm (5in) tall to encourage branching and masses of summer flowers.

WHEN PLANTED in groups of 3–6 plants, arctotis will form spreading clumps in sunny, south-facing borders and on banks.

FEATURES

African daisy is a perennial grown as a half-hardy annual for its flowers in shades of pink, red, yellow, gold, white and even blue, often with darker centre. Plants reach 45cm (18in) in height and have attractive silvery leaves. Use in bedding or as a container plant. Flowers are good for cutting.

CONDITIONS

Aspect   Must have full sun all day long for the flowers

ARCTOTIS AT A GLANCE

A half-hardy annual grown for its flowers, used in bedding, containers and as a cut flower. Frost hardy to 0°C (32°F).

		RECOMMENDED VARIETIES
JAN	/	*Arctotis hybrida:*
FEB	sow	'Harlequin'
MAR	sow	'Special Hybrids Mixed'
APR	transplant	'Treasure Chest'
MAY	transplant	'T&M Hybrids'
JUN	flowering	
JULY	flowering	*Arctotis hirsuta*
AUG	flowering	
SEPT	flowering	*Arctotis venusta*
OCT	/	
NOV	/	
DEC	/	

Site
to stay open and give the best display, so choose a south-facing border, patio or bank. Soil must be well-drained but moisture-retentive, so work in rotted compost before planting. In containers use multipurpose compost and ensure drainage by adding a 5cm (2in) layer of gravel or polystyrene chunks.

GROWING METHOD

Sowing
Sow in February/March in small pots of multipurpose compost, just covering the seed, and keep at 18°C (64°F). Seedlings appear in 2–3 weeks and are transplanted individually into 9cm (3½in) pots. Grow on, harden off at the end of May before planting after frosts, spacing plants 30–45cm (12–18in) apart.

Feeding
Extra feeding is rarely necessary but container-grown plants benefit from liquid feed every two weeks. Avoid getting the compost too wet, especially in cooler, wet spells.

Problems
Grows poorly on heavy, badly drained soils. Plants in containers must receive full sun.

FLOWERING

Season   Flowers from early summer onwards.
Cutting   A useful but short-lived cut flower.

AFTER FLOWERING

General
Pot up before frosts and keep dry and frost-free over winter. Take and root cuttings in spring.

BEGONIA
Begonia

FOR BEDDING DISPLAYS in partial shade few plants can equal the mixed varieties of Begonia semperflorens, *seen here.*

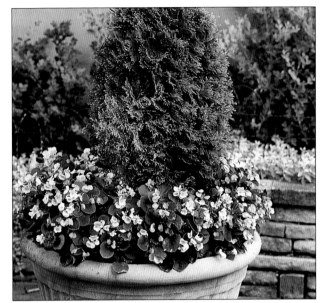

IN CONTAINERS begonias give a show from early summer, and you can choose dark-leaved types for specific colour schemes.

FEATURES

Excellent for bedding and containers, begonias have fleshy green or bronze leaves and flowers in many colours, and are grown as half-hardy annuals. 'Fibrous' rooted varieties of *Begonia semperflorens* grow up to 20cm (8in), have many small flowers and do well in shaded spots. 'Tuberous' rooted types reach 25cm (10in) tall with fewer but larger flowers up to 10cm (4in) across. Trailing varieties are also available for hanging baskets, reaching 30–60cm (1–2ft). Flowers are in mixed or single colours. A wide range of all types are available as young plants.

CONDITIONS

Aspect   Will succeed best in partial shade with at least

Site   some protection from direct hot sun. Soil should be very well prepared with plenty of rotted manure or compost mixed in. Begonias produce masses of fine feeding roots. Plants do not like very heavy clay soils that stay wet for long periods, so grow in containers if necessary, using multipurpose compost when potting up in spring.

GROWING METHOD

Sowing   Sow January/February. Seed is as fine as dust, so mix with a little dry silver sand and sow on the surface of 9cm (3½in) pots of seed compost based on peat or coir. Stand the pot in tepid water until the compost looks moist. Keep at 21°C (70°F) in a heated propagator in a light spot, and carefully transplant seedlings to cell trays when they have produced several tiny leaves. Seed raising is a challenge so consider growing from young plants. Plant outdoors after the last frosts in early June, 15–20cm (6–8in) apart depending on variety.

Feeding   Water regularly in dry spells and liquid feed bedding displays every 2–3 weeks, or mix slow-release fertiliser with compost first.

Problems   Overwatering causes root rot and death. Remove faded flowers, especially in wet spells.

FLOWERING

Season   Flowers from early summer until frost.
Cutting   Not suitable as a cut flower.

AFTER FLOWERING

General   Varieties that form round tubers can be potted up in autumn, dried off and then grown again the following spring.

BEGONIA AT A GLANCE

A half-hardy annual grown for its flowers and green/bronze foliage, useful for bedding/containers. Frost hardy to 0°C (32°F).

JAN	sow
FEB	sow
MAR	transplant
APR	grow on
MAY	harden off
JUN	flowering
JULY	flowering
AUG	flowering
SEPT	flowering
OCT	/
NOV	/
DEC	/

RECOMMENDED VARIETIES

Begonia semperflorens:
'Ambassador Mixed'
'Cocktail Mixed'
'Pink Sundae'
Tuberous varieties
'Non-Stop Mixed'
'Non-Stop Appleblossom'
'Pin-Up'
Trailing varieties
'Illumination Mixed'
'Show Angels Mixed'

BELLIS
Daisy

VARIETIES OF BELLIS differ greatly. Some have small flowers with yellow centres, or the whole flower is a mass of fine petals.

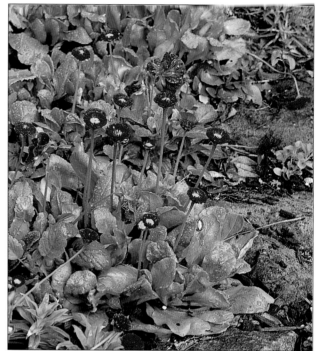

AFTER THE SPRING SHOW is over bellis can be replanted on rockeries where it will grow as a perennial in spreading clumps.

FEATURES

All varieties of bellis are related to garden daisies, and are perennials grown as hardy biennials. Use in spring bedding and containers, with bulbs like tulips. Plants are spreading, 10–20cm (4–8in) high, with white, pink, red or bicoloured double or 'eyed' flowers. Petals can be tubular, or fine and needle-like. Available as young plants.

CONDITIONS

Aspect   Needs a sunny, warm spot to encourage early

Site   flowers when grown for spring displays.
Most soils are suitable, but adding well-rotted manure or compost before planting increases plant vigour and flower size. In containers use multipurpose compost and make sure the container is very free draining.

GROWING METHOD

Sowing   Sow seed outdoors in May/June in fine soil in drills 1cm (½in) deep. Keep well-watered and when plants are large enough, space small clumps out in rows, 10–15cm (4–6in) apart. Alternatively, pot up into 9cm (3½in) pots. Grow on during the summer, then water, lift carefully and plant out in beds or containers in autumn, spacing 15–20cm (6–8in) apart.

Feeding   Liquid feed can be given every 2–3 weeks in spring when growth starts, but avoid feeding in winter, and take special care not to overwater containers or plants will rot off.

Problems   Bellis is trouble-free.

FLOWERING

Season   Flowers appear from early spring into summer. Removal of faded flowers helps prolong flowering and reduces self-seeding.

Cutting   Can be used in small spring posies.

AFTER FLOWERING

General   Plants are removed to make way for summer bedding and can be either discarded or replanted and left to grow as perennials.

BELLIS AT A GLANCE

A perennial grown as a biennial for spring bedding displays and used with bulbs in patio containers. Frost hardy to –15°C (5°F).

		RECOMMENDED VARIETIES
JAN	/	
FEB	flowering	*Bellis perennis:*
MAR	flowering	**Small flowers**
APR	flowering	'Carpet Mixed'
MAY	flowers/sow	'Medici Mixed'
JUN	sow	'Pomponette Mixed'
JULY	grow on	'Pomponette Pink
AUG	grow on	Buttons'
SEPT	grow on	**Large flowers**
OCT	plant	'Blush'
NOV	/	'Giant Flowered Mixed'
DEC	/	'Goliath Mixed'
		'Habanera Mixed'

BRACHYSCOME
Swan river daisy

SWAN RIVER DAISIES produce mounds of small, daisy-like flowers in profusion throughout the summer months.

FOR MIXED SHADES and 'eyes' of different colours choose an up-to-date variety of Brachyscome iberidifolia *such as 'Bravo Mixed'.*

FEATURES

Brachyscome is covered in mounds of daisy flowers, and is good in beds and in hanging baskets and patio containers. It makes an effective edging plant where it can develop unhindered without being crowded out by more vigorous plants. Leaves are light green and feathery with a delicate appearance. Plants grow 23cm (9in) tall with a similar spread. Choose single colours or mixtures.
Brachyscome can be planted in May before the last frosts, and will tolerate short dry spells. A half-hardy annual, also seen as 'brachycome'.

CONDITIONS

Aspect   Choose a south-facing position in full sun.

BRACHYSCOME AT A GLANCE

A half-hardy annual grown for its daisy-like flowers, useful for bedding, baskets and containers. Frost hardy to 0°C (32°F)

		RECOMMENDED VARIETIES
JAN	/	
FEB	/	*Brachyscome iberidifolia:*
MAR	sow	'Blue Star'
APR	sow/transplant	'Bravo Mixed'
MAY	plant outdoors	'Mixed'
JUN	flowering	'Purple Splendour'
JULY	flowering	'White Splendour'
AUG	flowering	
SEPT	flowering	
OCT	/	
NOV	/	
DEC	/	

Site   Choose a warm, sheltered spot away from wind. Brachyscome likes rich, well-drained soil, with plenty of rotted compost or manure added. Use multipurpose potting compost in containers.

GROWING METHOD

Sowing   Sow in March and April in 9cm (3½in) diameter pots, just covering the seeds, and germinate at 18°C (64°F). Seedlings emerge within three weeks. Transplant into cell trays of multipurpose compost, and plant out in beds 23–30cm (9–12in) apart.

Feeding   Liquid feed each week outdoors. Add slow-release fertiliser granules to container compost, and also liquid feed every two weeks in summer. Avoid overwatering, especially in dull, wet spells or plants may rot off.

Problems   Support floppy plants with small twigs. Avoid planting among large, vigorous container plants that will swamp low growers and cast them in shade at the height of summer. Control slugs with pellets or set slug traps in bedding displays.

FLOWERING

Season   Flowers appear all summer and are faintly scented – this is best appreciated by growing them at nose height in hanging baskets, flower bags and windowboxes.

Cutting   Not suitable.

AFTER FLOWERING

General   Remove when flowers are over and add to the compost heap or bin.

BRASSICA

Ornamental cabbage and kale

ORNAMENTAL KALES help pack a punch in the garden during autumn with their bright leaves that deepen in colour when the temperature falls below 10°C (50°F). Plants grown in containers should be kept in a sheltered spot during spells of severe winter weather.

FEATURES

Ornamental cabbages and kales are grown for colourful autumn and winter foliage, growing 30–45cm (12–18in) tall and wide. Use for bedding or large pots. Leaf colour is pink, rose or white and improves with temperatures below 10°C (50°F). Damage is caused by severe frost. Available as young plants.

CONDITIONS

Aspect   Needs full sun to develop good colour.

BRASSICA AT A GLANCE

A hardy annual grown for its brightly coloured leaves which last from autumn until spring. Frost hardy to –15°C (5°F).

		RECOMMENDED VARIETIES
JAN	leaves	**Cabbages**
FEB	leaves	'Delight Mixed'
MAR	leaves	'Northern Lights'
APR	leaves	'Ornamental Mixed'
MAY	leaves	'Tokyo Mixed'
JUN	sow	
JULY	sow	**Kales**
AUG	grow-on	'Nagoya Mixed'
SEPT	plant	'Red & White Peacock'
OCT	leaves	'Red Chidori'
NOV	leaves	
DEC	leaves	

Site   Enrich soil with rotted compost or manure ahead of planting. Adding lime will improve results on acid soils. Avoid spots exposed to driving winter winds. Plant up containers using multipurpose compost making sure pots and tubs are free draining.

GROWING METHOD

Sowing   Seed is sown in June/July in 9cm (3½in) pots of multipurpose compost and kept out of the sun. Large seedlings appear after a week and are transplanted to individual 9cm (3½in) pots. Grow these on outdoors, watering frequently, and then plant out in beds or in containers in early autumn where the display is required.

Feeding   Give a high-potash liquid feed fortnightly throughout the summer months. Tomato food is suitable and encourages leaf colour.

Problems   Cabbage caterpillars will also attack ornamental varieties and kales. Pick off by hand or use a spray containing permethrin.

FLOWERING

Season   Plants are at their best in autumn and early winter. Any surviving the winter will produce tall clusters of yellow flowers in spring.

Cutting   Whole heads makes a striking, unusual element in winter flower arrangements.

AFTER FLOWERING

General   Remove in spring or if killed by frosts.

BROWALLIA

Bush violet

BROWALLIA FLOWERS have an almost crystalline texture when lit by the sun. They appear in masses on rounded plants, and at the height of summer can almost completely hide the leaves. Seen here are the varieties 'Blue Troll' and 'White Troll'.

FEATURES

Browallia takes its common name from its violet-blue flowers which have a pale 'eye'. White flowered varieties and mixtures are available. Plants grow up to 30cm (12in) and are suitable for containers and baskets, and in warmer areas, bedding. Varieties of *Browallia speciosa* are grown as half-hardy annuals and can also be used as indoor pot plants.

CONDITIONS

Aspect   Needs a warm, sheltered spot in sun.

BROWALLIA AT A GLANCE

A half-hardy annual grown for its blue, white or pink flowers, useful for bedding/container planting. Frost hardy to 0°C (32°F).

		RECOMMENDED VARIETIES
JAN	/	*Browallia speciosa:*
FEB	sow	**Blue flowers**
MAR	sow	'Blue Troll'
APR	grow on	'Blue Bells'
MAY	plant	'Starlight Blue'
JUN	flowering	
JULY	flowering	
AUG	flowering	**White flowers**
SEPT	flowering	'White Troll'
OCT	/	
NOV	/	**Blue/pink/white flowers**
DEC	/	'Jingle Bells'

Site   Browallia does not tolerate poor drainage, and on heavy soils should only be grown as a container plant, using multipurpose compost. Otherwise, mix in well-rotted compost or manure several weeks before planting out.

GROWING METHOD

Sowing   For summer bedding sow the seed on the surface of 9cm (3½in) pots of multipurpose compost in February/March. Keep at 18°C (64°F) and do not let the surface dry out. Seedlings appear in 2–3 weeks and should be transplanted to individual cell trays or 7.5cm (3in) pots. Harden off at the end of May and plant in early June. For flowering pot plants seed can be sown in the same way until June.

Feeding   Give plants a liquid feed fortnightly or, in containers and windowboxes, mix slow-release fertiliser with the compost first.

Problems   Aphids sometimes attack the soft leaves so use a spray containing permethrin if they appear.

FLOWERING

Season   Flowers appear from early summer onwards and continue until the first frosts. Take off faded flowers regularly to encourage buds.

Cutting   Not suitable as a cut flower.

AFTER FLOWERING

General   Plants die when frosts arrive. Pot plants indoors can be kept going indefinitely.

CALCEOLARIA

Slipper flower

THE HOT COLOURS OF THE 'SUNSET' strain of calceolaria excel outdoors and combine well with marigolds.

FEATURES

Only a few varieties of calceolaria are suitable for outdoors; these are different to the indoor pot type. By nature shrubs, they are grown from seed each year as hardy annuals and are useful for bedding and containers. None grow more than 40cm (16in) tall and wide.

CONDITIONS

Aspect Needs full sun or part shade.

CALCEOLARIA AT A GLANCE

A half-hardy annual, calceolaria is used for bedding and containers, with bright flowers. Frost hardy to 0°C (32°F).

		RECOMMENDED VARIETIES
JAN	sow	Calceolaria hybrids:
FEB	sow	'Little Sweeties Mixed'
MAR	transplant	'Midas'
APR	grow on	'Sunshine'
MAY	harden off	'Sunset Mixed'
JUN	flowering	
JULY	flowering	
AUG	flowering	
SEPT	flowering	
OCT	/	
NOV	/	
DEC	/	

Site Slipper flowers thrive in moist soil where their roots stay as cool as possible. Mix in well-rotted compost or manure before planting and use a peat- or coir-based multipurpose compost for filling containers.

GROWING METHOD

Sowing The fine seed can be sown on the surface of peat- or coir-based multipurpose compost in a 9cm (3½in) pot, January–March, at a temperature of 18°C (64°F). Keep in a bright place. Seedlings appear in 2–3 weeks and can be transplanted to cell trays, then hardened off and planted after frosts, 15–30cm (6–12in) apart, or used with other plants in containers.

Feeding Liquid feed every 3–4 weeks or mix slow-release fertiliser with compost before planting.

Problems Slugs will eat the leaves of young plants in wet spells during early summer. Protect plants with a barrier of grit or eggshell or scatter slug pellets sparingly around plants.

FLOWERING

Season Plants will flower from early summer until frosts. Take off dead flowers weekly.

Cutting A few stems can be taken but avoid damaging the overall shape and appearance of the plant.

AFTER FLOWERING

General Remove plants in autumn when finished.

CALENDULA
Pot marigold

MIXED VARIETIES of calendula offer a wide colour range, most commonly shades of orange and yellow as seen here.

CALENDULA is a bushy plant producing masses of summer flowers – the edible petals can be scattered on summer salads.

FEATURES

Also known as English marigold, calendula is a fast-growing, hardy annual with daisy-type flowers in shades of yellow, orange, red, pinkish and even green. Flowers can be fully double while others have a distinct darker 'eye'. The edible petals can be used in salads. Perfect for a cottage garden bed or border, and very easy to grow, the large curled seeds are sown straight into the soil outdoors. Plant size ranges from 30–70cm (12–28in) tall and wide.

CONDITIONS

Aspect   Needs full sun to succeed.
Site   Does well even in poor soil, which can actually increase the number of flowers. Add rotted organic matter to the soil ahead of planting time to improve results. Calendula does not do well on heavy, badly drained soils, so grow in containers under these conditions.

GROWING METHOD

Sowing   March to May or August/September are the sowing periods. Sow the large seeds direct into finely raked moist soil where you want plants to flower, in drills 1cm (½in) deep, and cover. Thin out as seedlings grow so that plants are eventually spaced 25–30cm (10–12in) apart. Autumn-sown plants flower earlier the following year. If flowers for cutting are required sow seed thinly in long rows.

Feeding   Liquid feed once a month to encourage larger blooms. Use a feed high in potash to encourage flowers rather than leafy growth – tomato fertilisers are a good choice.

Problems   The leaves are prone to attack by aphids causing twisting and damage. Use a spray containing permethrin, but avoid eating flowers. Powdery mildew can affect leaves in late summer but is not worth treating – pick off the worst affected leaves and compost them.

FLOWERING

Season   Flowers appear in late spring on plants sown the previous autumn, and from early summer on spring-sown plants. Removal of faded blooms will keep up a succession of flowers.

Cutting   Good as a cut flower – cutting helps to keep flowers coming. Cut when flowers are well formed but before petals open out too far.

AFTER FLOWERING

General   Pull up after flowering. Will self-seed if a few heads are left to ripen fully and shed seeds.

CALENDULA AT A GLANCE

A hardy annual for growing in beds and borders and a useful cut flower in many shades. Frost hardy to –15°C (5°F).

		RECOMMENDED VARIETIES
JAN	/	*Calendula officinalis:*
FEB	/	'Art Shades Mixed'
MAR	sow	'Fiesta Gitana Mixed'
APR	sow	'Greenheart Orange'
MAY	thin out	'Kablouna Lemon Cream'
JUN	flowering	'Kablouna Mixed'
JULY	flowering	'Orange King'
AUG	flowers/sow	'Pacific Beauty'
SEPT	flowers/sow	'Pink Surprise'
OCT	/	'Princess Mixed'
NOV	/	'Radio'
DEC	/	'Touch of Red Mixed'

CALLISTEPHUS
China aster

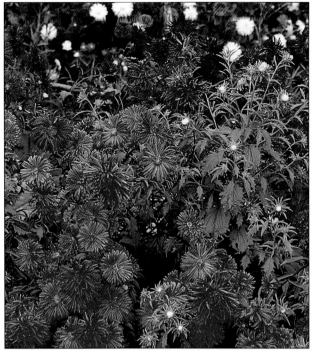

CHINA ASTERS with their large, showy and often double flowers can be used as summer bedding plants for massed displays.

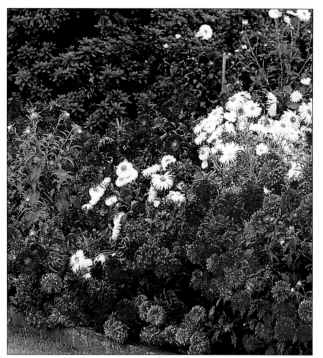

AS A CUT FLOWER callistephus is unrivalled for producing long-lasting blooms in late summer when other flowers are past their best.

FEATURES

China asters are half-hardy annuals and are not to be confused with the perennial asters or Michaelmas daisies. Grow as bedding, as cut flowers, and in large pots. Flowers come in a wide range from narrow, quill-like petals to bicolours, and also single shades. Size ranges from 20–90cm (8–36in) tall, depending on the variety. Available as young plants.

CONDITIONS

Aspect   Must have a warm spot in full sun all day.

CALLISTEPHUS AT A GLANCE

A half-hardy annual grown for its flowers, used in bedding, containers and as a cut flower. Frost hardy to 0°C (32°F).

		RECOMMENDED VARIETIES
JAN	/	*Callistephus chinensis:*
FEB	/	'Apricot Giant'
MAR	sow	'Dwarf Comet Mixed'
APR	sow	'Matsumoto Mixed'
MAY	plant	'Moraketa'
JUN	flowering	'Milady Mixed'
JULY	flowering	'Ostrich Plume Mixed'
AUG	flowering	'Red Ribbon'
SEPT	flowering	'Teisa Stars Mixed'
OCT	flowering	
NOV	/	
DEC	/	

Site   Plants need well-drained soil with added organic matter such as rotted manure or compost dug in before planting. If grown in containers use multipurpose compost with slow-release fertiliser granules mixed in.

GROWING METHOD

Sowing   Sow in March/April in 9cm (3½in) pots of compost and keep at 16°C (61°F). Seedlings appear after a week and can be transplanted to cell trays and grown on. Plant in late May, plants are not damaged by the last frosts. Seed can also be sown direct into the ground in late April and May. Plant 20–60cm (8–24in) apart.

Feeding   Water regularly and give plants in containers a general liquid feed every two weeks. In beds feed when you water with a hand-held feeder.

Problems   Aphids cause the leaves to distort which can affect flowering. Use a spray containing dimethoate. If plants suddenly collapse and die they are suffering from aster wilt and should be removed with the soil around their roots and put in the dustbin. Avoid growing asters in that spot and try 'resistant' varieties.

FLOWERING

Season   Early summer to early autumn.
Cutting   An excellent and long-lasting cut flower.

AFTER FLOWERING

General   Remove plants after flowering and compost any that do not show signs of wilt disease.

CAMPANULA

Canterbury bells

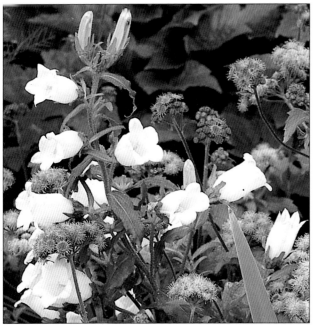

THE BELL-LIKE flowers of Campanula medium give it its common name of Canterbury bells. It is seen here growing with ageratum.

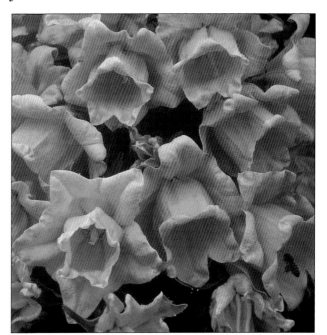

WHEN CANTERBURY BELLS display this characteristic 'saucer' behind the cup-shaped bloom, they simply ooze charm.

FEATURES

Canterbury bells are best in massed plantings in mixed borders and are good for cutting. Dwarf varieties can be used for bedding and in containers. The large, bell-like single or double flowers are blue, pink, mauve or white, on stems 60–90cm (2–3ft) high, rising from large clumps. Usually grown as a hardy biennial, the dwarf variety 'Chelsea Pink' is grown as an annual, flowering three months after sowing in February. Stake tall plants.

CONDITIONS

Aspect   Grow in an open spot in full sun.

CAMPANULA AT A GLANCE

A hardy biennial grown for bedding and for the tall flower spikes that are ideal for cutting. Frost hardy to −15°C (5°F).

JAN	/	
FEB	/	
MAR	/	
APR	sow	
MAY	sow	
JUN	flowers/sow	
JULY	flowering	
AUG	flowering	
SEPT	flowering	
OCT	plant	
NOV	/	
DEC	/	

RECOMMENDED VARIETIES

Campanula medium:
Tall varieties
  'Calycanthema Mixed'
  'Cup and Saucer Mixed'
  'Rosea'
  'Single Mixed'

Shorter/dwarf varieties
  'Bella Series'
  'Bells of Holland'
  'Chelsea Pink'
  'Russian Pink'

Site   Plenty of well-rotted manure or compost dug into the soil produces strong growth. Requires good drainage but the soil should retain moisture and not dry out completely. In containers use multipurpose compost.

GROWING METHOD

Sowing   Sow the fine seed from April–June outdoors, or in small pots of multipurpose compost. Just cover the seed. Either transplant seedlings to 30cm (12in) apart or pot up individually into 9cm (3½in) pots. Grow on through the summer and plant during autumn in groups of 3–5, spacing plants 30cm (12in) apart. Flowers will appear the following summer.

Feeding   Give a monthly liquid feed, starting a few weeks after transplanting or potting up and make sure potted plants do not dry out. Scatter a general granular fertiliser over beds in spring to keep growth strong and encourage flowers.

Problems   Slugs will eat the crowns of plants in early summer, especially after rain, so scatter slug pellets or use a physical barrier like grit.

FLOWERING

Season   Flower spikes appear from early summer onwards. A second 'flush' of flowers is possible if all stems are cut to the ground when faded.

Cutting   Good cut flower so grow extra plants of a tall variety in rows just for cutting.

AFTER FLOWERING

General   Remove plants after the flowering season and add them to the compost heap or bin.

CATHARANTHUS
Madagascar periwinkle

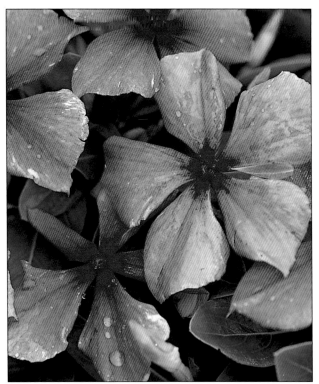

THE FAMILIAR FLOWERS of Catharanthus roseus look similar to those of its close relative the hardy vinca.

FOR BEDDING DISPLAYS catharanthus is available in mixed colours which often contain flowers with darker 'eyes' as seen here.

FEATURES

Varieties of *Catharanthus roseus* have pink/rose, mauve or white flowers, often with a deeper centre. Plants are spreading, growing to 25–40cm (10–16in), and suitable for massed bedding displays or pots indoors. Grow as a half-hardy annual.

CONDITIONS

Aspect Needs full sun to succeed outdoors.

CATHARANTHUS AT A GLANCE		
A half-hardy annual grown for its bright flowers and ideal for use in containers on a warm sunny patio. Frost hardy to 0°C (32°F).		
JAN	/	**RECOMMENDED VARIETIES**
FEB	/	*Catharanthus roseus:*
MAR	sow	'Apricot Delight'
APR	transplant	'Pacifica Red'
MAY	harden off/plant	'Peppermint Cooler'
JUN	flowering	'Pretty In... Mixed'
JULY	flowering	'Tropicana Mixed'
AUG	flowering	'Terrace Vermillion'
SEPT	flowering	
OCT	/	
NOV	/	
DEC	/	

Site Needs good drainage but enrich the soil with well-rotted manure or compost before planting. For containers use multipurpose compost with extra slow-release fertiliser mixed in before planting up.

GROWING METHOD

Sowing Sow seed in March/April in 9cm (3½in) pots of multipurpose compost and lightly cover. Keep at 18°C (64°F) in a light spot and transplant seedlings when they are 2.5cm (1in) tall, into cell trays. Keep in a warm greenhouse or warm spot indoors and do not get the compost too wet. Harden off in late May and plant 20–30cm (8–12in) apart in their final positions or use in containers.

Feeding In bedding displays, apply a liquid plant food monthly to keep plants growing vigorously throughout the summer months.

Problems Overwatering and wet soil/compost can lead to rotting. If red spider mite attacks the leaves use a spray containing bifenthrin.

FLOWERING

Season Flowers appear throughout the summer.

Cutting Not suitable for cutting.

AFTER FLOWERING

General Remove plants after the first autumn frosts and use for composting.

CELOSIA
Prince of Wales' feathers

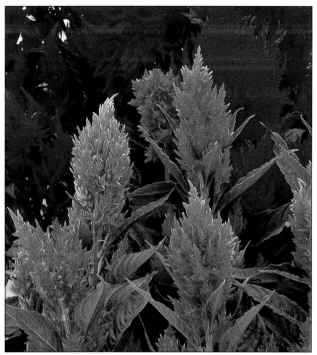

THE FEATHERY FLOWERS of celosia are made up of masses of smaller flowers, and have a distinctive, plume-like shape.

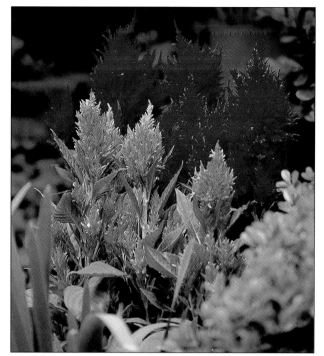

THE BRILLIANT PLUMES of cockscomb always look best in patio pots and containers when planted together in groups of 4–6 plants.

FEATURES

Also known as Prince of Wales' feathers, celosia or cockscomb has plume-like or crested flowers (shown left) ranging in colour from deep crimson to scarlet, orange and yellow. Tall forms grow to 75cm (30in), the dwarf forms to 25–30cm (10–12in). Grow it as a half-hardy annual and use in bedding or as a striking plant for containers. Good for cutting.

CONDITIONS

Aspect   Must have a sunny, warm spot to do well.

CELOSIA AT A GLANCE

A half-hardy annual grown for its feathery, plume-like flower-heads in a range of colours. Frost hardy to 0°C (32°F).

JAN	/	
FEB	sow	**RECOMMENDED VARIETIES**
MAR	sow	**Plumed**
APR	pot on	*Celosia argentea:*
MAY	harden off/plant	'Kimono Mixed'
JUN	flowering	'Dwarf Geisha'
JULY	flowering	'Century Mixed'
AUG	flowering	'New Look'
SEPT	flowering	*Celosia spicata:*
OCT	/	'Flamingo Feather'
NOV	/	**Crested**
DEC	/	*Celosia cristata:*
		'Jewel Box Mixed'

Site   Needs well-drained soil that has been enriched with well-rotted manure or compost. Good soil preparation is essential to ensure strong plants and large flowerheads. Plant up containers using multipurpose compost

GROWING METHOD

Sowing   Celosias dislike having their roots disturbed so sow 2–3 seeds per cell in a multi-cell tray using multipurpose compost, in February/March. Keep at 18°C (64°F) and when the seedlings appear after 2–3 weeks, remove all but the strongest. Carefully pot the young plants on into 9cm (3½in) pots, then harden off for two weeks before planting after the last frosts. Plant without damaging the roots, 15–30cm (6–12in) apart, and water.

Feeding   Feed bedding monthly with liquid feed. Mix slow-release fertiliser with the compost before planting up containers.

Problems   Wet, cold soil/compost can cause rotting of the roots, so avoid heavy soils and grow in pots.

FLOWERING

Season   Flowers appear throughout summer.

Cutting   May be used as a cut flower for unusual indoor decoration. Cut some plumes and hang them upside down in a dry, airy place for later use in dried flower arrangements.

AFTER FLOWERING

General   Remove plants after the first frosts of autumn.

CENTAUREA
Cornflower

CORNFLOWERS should have pale, fading flowers removed regularly. For indoor use cut the stems when the buds are still closed.

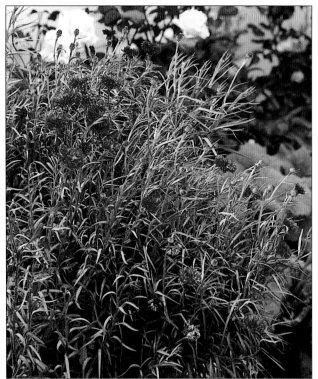

GROWN IN GROUPS like this, cornflowers will support each other quite naturally. In windy spots push twigs in between plants.

FEATURES

Cornflower, *Centaurea cyanus* is, one of the easiest hardy annuals to grow and can be used in bedding, containers and for cut flowers. Other than blue, there are mixtures available and single colours such as the 'Florence' types in red, pink and white, reaching 35cm (14in) tall. Taller varieties like 'Blue Diadem' are best for cutting. Regular removal of dead flowers is essential to prolong flowering and to stop plants from becoming shabby.

CENTAUREA AT A GLANCE

A hardy annual grown for its 'cottage garden' type flowers in various colours, useful for cutting. Frost hardy to −15°C (5°F).

		RECOMMENDED VARIETIES
JAN	/	*Centaurea cyanus:*
FEB	/	**Short varieties**
MAR	sow	'Florence Blue'
APR	thin out	'Florence Mixed'
MAY	flowering	'Florence Pink'
JUN	flowering	'Florence Red'
JULY	flowering	'Florence White'
AUG	flowering	'Midget Mixed'
SEPT	flowers/sow	**Tall varieties**
OCT	/	'Blue Diadem'
NOV	/	'Black Ball'
DEC	/	

CONDITIONS

Aspect Needs full sun all day.
Site Must have very well-drained soil, but no special soil preparation is necessary. Staking is necessary when grown in windy situations, but the plants are self-supporting when they are planted in groups. For container growing use multipurpose compost.

GROWING METHOD

Sowing Sow seed in spring where plants are to flower in short rows 1cm (½in) deep and about 30cm (12in) apart. Thin out so plants are finally 7.5–15cm (3–6in) apart. This can also be done in late September for stronger plants and earlier flowers, but leave thinning out until the following spring. Can also be sown in pots and transplanted to cell trays for plants to use in patio containers.
Feeding Extra feeding is usually unnecessary.
Problems White mildew affects leaves but is not serious.

FLOWERING

Season Summer until early autumn.
Cutting Cut before the petals open out too far.

AFTER FLOWERING

General Remove plants once flowering is finished. Plants self-seed if they are left in the ground.

CHEIRANTHUS
Wallflower

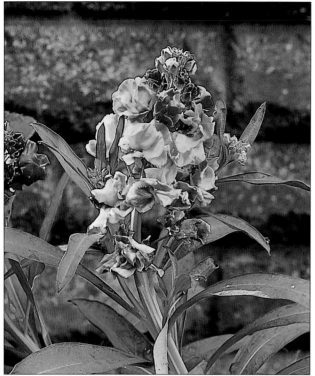

THE INTENSE COLOURS of wallflowers are only matched by their strong, lingering scent which is best on warm, still days.

'IVORY WHITE' is a useful single-coloured variety of Cheiranthus cheiri *for bedding schemes which are colour-themed.*

FEATURES

Wallflowers have fragrant flowers of yellow, brown, cream, red and orange and are grown for their sweet spring scent. These hardy biennials grow between 20–45cm (8–18in) depending on variety, and are available as mixed or single colours. Plants are used for bedding but may also be used in patio containers, where they can be moved near doors and windows when in bloom. Ready-grown plants can be bought in early autumn.

CHEIRANTHUS AT A GLANCE

With its bright flowers and strong scent, this biennial is useful for spring bedding and for containers. Frost hardy to –15°C (5°F).

JAN	/	
FEB	flowering	RECOMMENDED VARIETIES
MAR	flowering	*Cheiranthus cheiri:*
APR	flowering	**Tall**
MAY	sow	'Blood Red'
JUN	sow	'Cloth of Gold'
JULY	thin out	'Harlequin'
AUG	grow on	**Medium**
SEPT	grow on	'My Fair Lady Mixed'
OCT	plant	'Vulcan Improved'
NOV	/	**Dwarf**
DEC	/	'Prince Mixed'
		'Tom Thumb Mixed'

CONDITIONS

Aspect Grow in full sun for the best scent.
Site Must have very well-drained soil. Add lime before planting to reduce the effect of clubroot disease. Use multipurpose compost in containers and windowboxes. Avoid spots exposed to winter winds and move containers to shelter during severe winter weather.

GROWING METHOD

Sowing Sow May/June outdoors in rows 30cm (12in) apart and 1cm (⅓in) deep. As plants grow, thin them to 30cm (12in) apart, and pinch when 7.5cm (3in) tall to make growth bushy. Can also be sown in pots and transplanted into 9cm (3½in) pots. Plant in October in beds or containers. When lifting plants keep as much soil on the roots as possible.

Feeding Give a liquid feed monthly during summer.
Problems Avoid growing in soil known to be infected with clubroot disease, or raise plants in pots using multipurpose compost.

FLOWERING

Season Late winter through to spring.
Cutting Cut stems last well in water.

AFTER FLOWERING

General Remove plants in late spring after flowering.

CLEOME
Spider flower

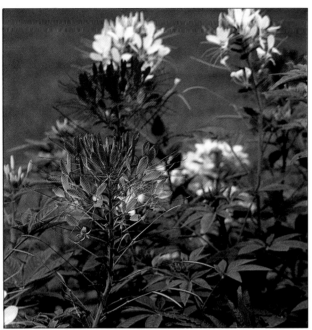

SPIDER FLOWERS are available as single colours or mixed. The popular 'Colour Fountains Mixed' is seen here in a summer border.

THE EXOTIC FEEL that cleome adds to the garden can be used to best effect on a warm patio where their scent lingers in still air.

FEATURES

The spider-like flowers of *Cleome spinosa*, in pink, white or rose, have narrow petals with long stamens. They appear all summer up and down the length of the stem. These large half-hardy annuals grow to 1.5m (5ft) tall with a single stem, and with lobed leaves. Plant at the back of borders or use them as central 'dot' plants in large tubs for an 'exotic' feel. Look out for the thorny stems and pungent leaves.

CONDITIONS

Aspect   Needs full sun and a sheltered position to achieve maximum height during the summer.

CLEOME AT A GLANCE

A half-hardy annual grown for its exotic flowers and ideal as a centrepiece for bedding/containers. Frost hardy to 0°C (32°F).

		RECOMMENDED VARIETIES
JAN	/	
FEB	sow 🕊	*Cleome spinosa:*
MAR	sow 🕊	**Mixed colours**
APR	grow on 🕊	'Colour Fountain Mixed'
MAY	harden off/plant 🕊	
JUN	flowering 🌼	**Single colours**
JULY	flowering 🌼	'Cherry Queen'
AUG	flowering 🌼	'Helen Campbell'
SEPT	flowering 🌼	'Pink Queen'
OCT	/	'Violet Queen'
NOV	/	
DEC	/	

Site   Needs good drainage but tolerates a wide range of soils. For best results improve soil by digging in rotted manure or compost, and use multipurpose compost with slow-release fertiliser added when planting containers. Stems are generally strong enough that they can be grow without extra support.

GROWING METHOD

Sowing   Sow seeds in 9cm (3½in) pots of multipurpose compost in February/March and keep at 18°C (64°F). Seedlings appear after two weeks and are transplanted to 9cm (3½in) pots, grown on in a warm greenhouse or conservatory. Pot on into 12.5cm (5in) pots in early May, and harden off before planting after the last frosts.

Feeding   Feed plants in beds fortnightly with liquid feed from a hand-held applicator. Don't allow the compost in containers to become over-wet.

Problems   Aphids attack young plants and cause twisted growth. Check under the leaves regularly and use a spray with permethrin if necessary, making sure the spray gets under the leaves.

FLOWERING

Season   The long flowering period extends throughout summer and well into mild autumns. The long thin seed pods give it a real 'spidery' look.

Cutting   Useful as a cut flower, but watch the spines.

AFTER FLOWERING

General   Remove plants after flowering, but wear gloves for protection as the stems are spiny.

CONSOLIDA
Larkspur

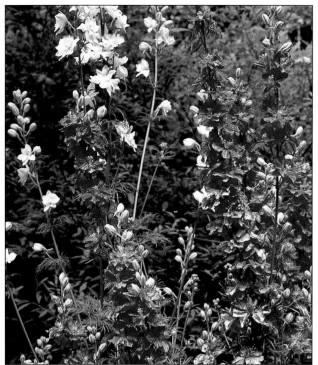

LARKSPUR IS DOUBLY useful as a cut flower because the spikes can be dried and used for dried flower arrangements.

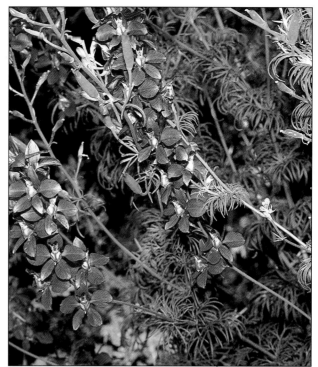

FINELY DIVIDED LEAVES are characteristic of Consolida ajacis, *while flowers can be single, as here, or double, in various colours.*

FEATURES

Consolida ajacis, larkspur, is related to delphinium but is not as tall and is grown as a hardy annual. Ideal for a 'cottage garden' border, larkspur grows up to 90cm (3ft) tall and has spikes of pink, white, red, blue and violet single or double flowers, with finely cut leaves. Good for cutting. Seeds are poisonous.

CONDITIONS

Aspect   Grow in a sunny, open spot.

CONSOLIDA AT A GLANCE

A hardy annual grown for its spikes of bright flowers which are useful for borders and cutting. Frost hardy to −15°C (5°F).

JAN	/	
FEB	/	
MAR	sow	
APR	thin out	
MAY	thin/flowers	
JUN	flowering	
JULY	flowering	
AUG	flowering	
SEPT	flowers/sow	
OCT	/	
NOV	/	
DEC	/	

RECOMMENDED VARIETIES

Consolida ajacis:
Tall, for cutting
  'Earl Grey'
  'Frosted Skies'
  'Giant Imperial Mixed'
  'Hyacinth Flowered Mixed'
Short, for bedding
  'Dwarf Hyacinth Flowered Mixed'
  'Dwarf Rocket Mixed'

Site
Soil can be enriched with manure or compost well ahead of planting, but it must be well-drained. Plants will also grow well on thin and hungry soils. Plants should support each other as they grow and not need artificial support. Use taller varieties at the back of borders.

GROWING METHOD

Sowing
Sow direct where the plants are to grow for best results, in short rows 1cm (½in) deep, in either March or September. Expect seedlings to appear in 2–3 weeks. Thin plants out as they grow so they are eventually 7.5–15cm (3–6in) apart depending on the variety.

Feeding   Extra feeding is not necessary.

Problems
Slugs eat young seedlings so scatter slug pellets around plants or protect them with a 5cm (2in) wide barrier of sharp grit.

FLOWERING

Season
Flowers appear from spring onwards on autumn-sown plants, June onwards from spring sowings. Removing faded flower spikes will encourage more flowers.

Cutting
An excellent cut flower. Cut long stems and scald ends before soaking in cool water.

AFTER FLOWERING

General
Leave a few plants to die down naturally and self-seed into the soil, otherwise pull up when finished and use for composting.

COREOPSIS
Tickseed

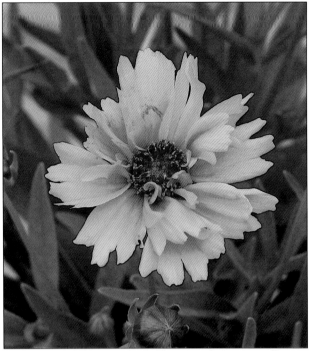

'EARLY SUNRISE' is a semi-double variety of coreopsis usually treated as an annual, growing 45cm (18in) tall and good for cutting.

COREOPSIS CAN FORM very large clumps. It gets its common name 'tickseed' from seeds which look like small bugs.

FEATURES

Coreopsis make good garden plants with single and double flowers in yellow, red and mahogany tones, growing 25–90cm (10–36in) tall depending on the variety. Some bedding varieties are perennials but are best grown as hardy or half-hardy annuals from a spring sowing. Dwarf varieties are used in patio pots.

CONDITIONS

Aspect   For best results grow in full sun.
Site   Tolerates poor soil, but soil which has been enriched with rotted manure/compost ahead of planting time will give stronger plants. In containers use multipurpose compost. Taller varieties should not need support if planted in groups so plants support each other.

COREOPSIS AT A GLANCE

A perennial grown as both as a hardy or half-hardy annual for its yellow to mahogany flowers. Frost hardy to –15°C (5°F).

JAN	/	
FEB	sow	
MAR	sow	
APR	transplant	
MAY	harden-off/plant	
JUN	grow on	
JULY	flowering	
AUG	flowering	
SEPT	flowering	
OCT	flowering	
NOV	/	
DEC	/	

RECOMMENDED VARIETIES

Coreopsis tinctoria:
'Mahogany Midget'
'T&M Dwarf Mixed'
'T&M Originals Mixed'

Coreopsis grandiflora:
'Early Sunrise'
'Gold Star'
'Mayfield Giant'
'Sunburst'

GROWING METHOD

Sowing   Sow seed February/March in 9cm (3½in) pots of multipurpose compost, just cover, and keep at 16°C (61°F). Transplant into cell trays, harden off for two weeks in late May and plant out after the last frosts. Seed can also be sown straight outdoors in May/June but expect later flowers continuing into the autumn.
Feeding   Should not need extra feeding if soil is well prepared. Add slow-release fertiliser to compost when planting up containers.
Problems   Slugs and snails will eat seedlings in spring during wet spells so protect with slug pellets.

FLOWERING

Season   The flowering period lasts throughout summer, especially if spent flowers are regularly removed from the plants.
Cutting   Tall varieties can be used as cut flowers. Pick when flowers have opened fully but the petals are still fresh looking.

AFTER FLOWERING

General   Perennial varieties such as 'Mayfield Giant' and 'Sunrise' can be lifted in autumn and planted in permanent border positions.

COSMOS
Cosmos

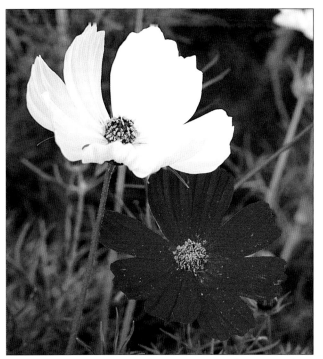

'SENSATION MIXED' is a tall-growing (90cm/3ft) cosmos with single flowers of red, pink, white and shades in between.

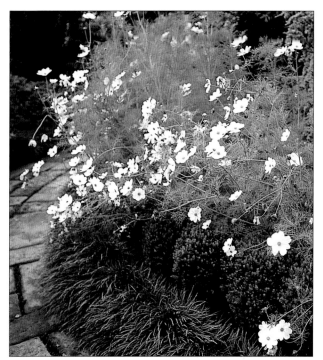

DURING THE SUMMER varieties of Cosmos bipinnatus *grown in borders form masses of feathery leaves topped by flowers.*

FEATURES

Cosmos, with their finely cut, feathery foliage and large daisy-type flowers grow up to 1.5m (5ft) tall, but shorter varieties are available and can be used in containers. Varieties of *Cosmos bipinnatus* have red, pink, purple or white flowers, while yellow, orange and scarlet are available in varieties of *Cosmos sulphureus*. Cosmos is grown as either a hardy or a half-hardy annual, and is an excellent choice for a cottage garden style border. 'Seashells' has tubular 'fluted' petals, and the taller varieties such as 'Sensation Mixed' are good for cutting.

COSMOS AT A GLANCE

A hardy or half-hardy annual grown for its large daisy-like flowers. For borders, pots and cutting. Frost hardy to 0°C (32°F).

JAN	/	
FEB	/	
MAR	sow	
APR	sow/transplant	
MAY	sow/plant	
JUN	flowering	
JULY	flowering	
AUG	flowering	
SEPT	flowering	
OCT	/	
NOV	/	
DEC	/	

RECOMMENDED VARIETIES

Cosmos bipinnatus:
 'Daydream'
 'Gazebo'
 'Picotee'
 'Seashells/Sea Shells'
 'Sensation Mixed'
 'Sonata Mixed'
Cosmos sulphureus:
 'Ladybird Mixed'
 'Ladybird Scarlet'
 'Sunny Red'

CONDITIONS

Aspect Needs full sun to flourish.
Site Well-drained soil is essential for success, and good results are guaranteed on light and slightly hungry soils. Pea sticks or twiggy shoots may be needed for support in exposed spots. Any multipurpose compost will give good results in patio pots and containers.

GROWING METHOD

Sowing Raise plants by sowing in March at 16°C (61°F). Sow the long thin seeds in 9cm (3½in) pots of multipurpose compost, then transplant to cell trays and grow on. Harden off at the end of May before planting after frosts, or sow in April/May directly into the ground where plants are to grow. Final spacing between plants should be 15–45cm (6–18in) depending on the variety grown.
Feeding Generally not necessary.
Problems Slugs will eat young seedlings outdoors so protect with slug pellets.

FLOWERING

Season Flowers appear from early summer onwards.
Cutting The taller varieties are ideal as cut flowers. Ensure regular removal of faded flowers.

AFTER FLOWERING

General Pull up plants when frosted, but leaving a few to die off will ensure some self-sown seedlings.

DAHLIA
Bedding dahlia

BEDDING DAHLIAS usually come in mixed colours. By planting time you can usually separate plants by flower colour.

'DOUBLE DELIGHT MIXED' is a popular bedding variety ideally suited for growing in patio containers, reaching 45cm (18in) tall.

FEATURES

Seed-raised bedding dahlias are close cousins of the 'border' dahlia grown from tubers. A wide range is available, the dwarfer types growing only 30cm (12in) tall. Flower colour is varied and some like 'Redskin' also have bronze leaves. Grow as half-hardy annuals, and use for bedding displays, patio containers and even windowboxes. Choose from single, double or decorative 'collarette' type flowers. Widely available as young plants.

CONDITIONS

Aspect   Bedding dahlias need full sun all day.
Site   Dig in large amounts of decayed manure or compost at least two or three weeks before planting. Soil must be well-drained but moisture-retentive. For containers use multipurpose compost with added slow-release fertiliser granules to keep growth strong through the summer months.

GROWING METHOD

Sowing   Sow seed February/March in 9cm (3½in) pots and just cover. Water and keep at 16°C (61°F) in a light spot. Transplant seedlings when big enough to handle into individual 9cm (3½in) pots and grow on. Harden off at the end of May and plant in early June when all frosts are over, spacing plants 15–30cm (6–12in) apart.
Feeding   Water and liquid feed once a week, depending on the soil and weather conditions. Continue watering regularly throughout the season.
Problems   Dahlia leaves are eaten by slugs so protect with slug pellets. Flowers may be chewed by earwigs – to catch them fill upturned pots with straw and support these on canes amongst the flowers. Powdery mildew can affect leaves in late summer but is not serious.

FLOWERING

Season   The main show is from midsummer onwards lasting well into autumn until the first frosts.
Cutting   Taller varieties of bedding dahlias make useful and long-lived cut flowers.

AFTER FLOWERING

General   Remove plants when the leaves turn black and collapse. Fleshy tubers of favourite plants can be stored dry and frost-free over the winter.

DAHLIA AT A GLANCE

A half-hardy annual grown for its pretty flowers and an ideal summer bedding or container plant. Frost hardy to 0°C (32°F).

Month	Activity	Recommended Varieties
Jan	/	
Feb	sow	**Dahlia hybrids:**
Mar	sow	**Taller varieties**
Apr	transplant/grow	'Collarette Dandy'
May	harden off/plant	'Coltness Hybrids Mixed'
Jun	flowering	'Pompon Mixed'
July	flowering	**Shorter varieties**
Aug	flowering	'Diablo Mixed'
Sept	flowering	'Dwarf Double Delight'
Oct	flowering	'Dwarf Amore'
Nov	/	'Figaro Mixed'
Dec	/	'Redskin'

DIANTHUS BARBATUS
Sweet William

THE IMPACT OF SWEET WILLIAMS comes from their massed heads of small flowers which often have attractive 'picotee' edges.

STRONG SCENT is a characteristic of Dianthus barbatus *varieties and makes this an ideal plant for cutting in bunches in early summer.*

FEATURES

Sweet Williams are varieties of *Dianthus barbatus* and have flowers in pink, white, red, burgundy and bicolours, on large rounded heads. Individual flowers often have darker central 'eyes'. Plants have clumping growth up to 45cm (18in), while dwarf forms grow to just 15cm (6in). The flowers appear from spring into early summer and are scented and ideal for cutting. Easily grown from seed as a hardy biennial, and useful for bedding schemes and as blocks of spring colour in mixed borders. Some less common varieties like 'Sooty' have dark, almost black flowers.

DIANTHUS AT A GLANCE

A summer-sown biennial grown for its large heads of scented flowers in spring and early summer. Frost hardy to −15°C (5°F).

		RECOMMENDED VARIETIES
JAN	/	*Dianthus barbatus:*
FEB	/	**Tall varieties**
MAR	/	'Auricula-Eyed Mixed'
APR	flowering	'Forerunner Mixed'
MAY	flowers/sow	'Gemstones'
JUN	flowers/sow	'Harlequin'
JULY	flowering	'Monarch Mixed'
AUG	grow on	**Dwarf varieties**
SEPT	grow on	'Dwarf Mixed'
OCT	plant	'Indian Carpet Mixed'
NOV	/	
DEC	/	

CONDITIONS

Aspect   Grow sweet Williams in full sun.
Site   Needs well-drained soil that has been limed before planting, and has had plenty of rotted compost mixed in several weeks before.

GROWING METHOD

Sowing   Sow the fine seed in rows outdoors, 1cm (½in) deep and just cover, in May/June. Transplant the seedlings so they are in rows 15cm (6in) apart and pinch out the growing tips to make them bushy. Water regularly throughout the summer months, and then lift and plant in their flowering positions in October, keeping the roots intact. For cut flowers only, the plants can be left growing in rows.
Feeding   Liquid feed monthly during the summer.
Problems   Poor drainage during winter can kill plants. If leaves are attacked by rust disease try a spray containing the fungicide penconazole.

FLOWERING

Season   Flowers appear from late spring to early summer and it is possible to get a second 'flush' if all the stalks are cut hard back after the first flowers have faded.
Cutting   An excellent cut flower, and ideal for making into a rounded 'posy'.

AFTER FLOWERING

General   Pull plants up when they are past their best, or leave some to develop into bigger clumps.

DIANTHUS CHINENSIS
Chinese pink

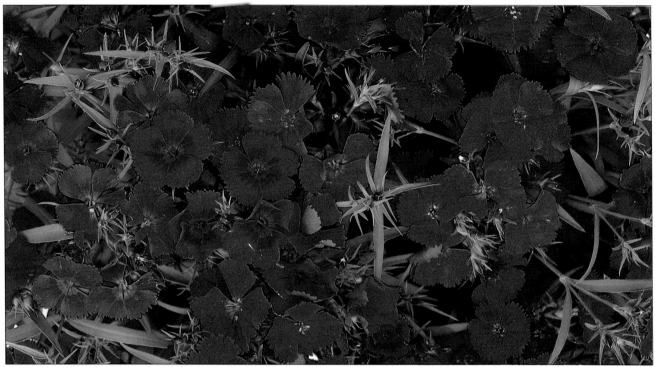

AS CONTAINER PLANTS Chinese pinks are perfect as neat edging plants, all growing to the same height. They are also valuable as colourful fillers and effectively bridge the gap between taller plants in the centre of large tubs and trailing plants falling over the edges.

FEATURES

Growing 20–30cm (8–12in) high, varieties of *Dianthus chinensis* are suitable for massed planting, edging garden beds, or for use in troughs or pots. Chinese pink is grown as a half-hardy annual although it is fully hardy outdoors. Flower are red, pink or white with only slight scent. Available as young plants.

CONDITIONS

Aspect   Needs full sun to flower at its best.

DIANTHUS AT A GLANCE

A hardy annual grown for its small brightly coloured 'pink' type flowers, used in bedding/pots. Frost hardy to –15°C (5°F).

JAN	/	
FEB	/	
MAR	sow	
APR	transplant	
MAY	harden off/plant	
JUN	flowering	
JULY	flowering	
AUG	flowering	
SEPT	flowering	
OCT	/	
NOV	/	
DEC	/	

RECOMMENDED VARIETIES

Dianthus chinensis:
'Baby Doll Mixed'
'Black & White Minstrels'
'Double Gaiety Mixed'
'Princess Mixed'
'Raspberry Parfait'
'Snowfire'
'Strawberry Parfait'
'T&M Frosty Mixed'

Site   Needs well-drained soil, but dig in plenty of well-rotted manure or compost when preparing beds. Lime can be added to the soil before planting and raked in. Containers must have very good drainage.

GROWING METHOD

Sowing   Sow seeds in 9cm (3½in) pots of multipurpose compost in March, just cover, and keep at 15°C (60°F) in a light place. When seedlings are 2.5cm (1in) tall, transplant to cell trays and grow on with some protection (a cold-frame is suitable). Harden off at the end of May and plant out in beds or containers.

Feeding   Do not overwater – a good weekly watering should be sufficient, and feed with liquid feed every 2–3 weeks. Plants in containers need no extra feeding if slow-release fertiliser is added.

Problems   Overwatering will cause yellowing of the leaves and rotting off at soil/compost level.

FLOWERING

Season   Plants come into flower from early summer onwards and will continue until autumn if dead flowerheads are removed regularly.

Cutting   Taller varieties can be used as cut flowers, but choose a variety known for its scent such as 'Double Gaiety Mixed'.

AFTER FLOWERING

General   Remove plants when finished and compost.

DOROTHEANTHUS
Mesembryanthemum or Livingstone daisy

LIVINGSTONE DAISIES set beds alight with colour on bright sunny days when the flowers open fully. Planted 15cm (6in) apart each way they soon knit together to create a tapestry of colour, and look especially at home when creeping amongst pieces of stone on a sunny rock garden.

FEATURES

Mesembryanthemum, also known as Livingstone daisy, is ideal for planting on dry, sunny banks, on rockeries, and in pots of free-draining compost. It has a spreading habit, but is only 15cm (6in) tall at most. The fleshy leaves have a crystalline texture with bright, daisy-like flowers in many shades. Grow as a half-hardy annual. All varieties of *Dorotheanthus bellidiformis* have the habit of closing their flowers in dull and wet spells of weather, opening again in bright sunshine.

DOROTHEANTHUS AT A GLANCE

A half-hardy, spreading annual grown for its daisy-like flowers which open fully in sunshine. Frost hardy to 0°C (32°F).

		RECOMMENDED VARIETIES
JAN	/	*Dorotheanthus bellidiformis:*
FEB	/	'Gelato Pink'
MAR	sow	'Harlequin Mixed'
APR	sow/transplant	'Lunette' ('Yellow Ice')
MAY	plant/harden off	'Magic Carpet Mixed'
JUN	flowering	'Sparkles'
JULY	flowering	
AUG	flowering	
SEPT	flowering	
OCT	/	
NOV	/	
DEC	/	

CONDITIONS

Aspect   Needs full direct sun all day and will perform even better on a south-facing sloping bank.

Site   Needs very well drained soil, with no special soil preparation necessary as plants grow better on light, sandy and hungry soils. If grown in containers used soil-based compost and mix with fifty per cent grit for good drainage.

GROWING METHOD

Sowing   Sow seed in a 9cm (3½in) pot of soil-based seed compost in March and barely cover. Keep at 18°C (64°F) in a light spot. When seedlings are large enough transplant to cell trays of soil-based potting compost and grow on. Harden off at the end of May for two weeks and plant after the last frosts 15cm (6in) apart.

Feeding   Extra feeding is unnecessary and produces leaves at the expense of flowers. Take care not to overwater in beds or pots or plants will rot.

Problems   Slugs will attack the fleshy young leaves so scatter slug pellets after planting out.

FLOWERING

Season   Flowers appear from midsummer onwards. Remove faded flowers to encourage more.

Cutting   Not suitable for cutting.

AFTER FLOWERING

General   Pull up and compost when finished.

ESCHSCHOLZIA
California poppy

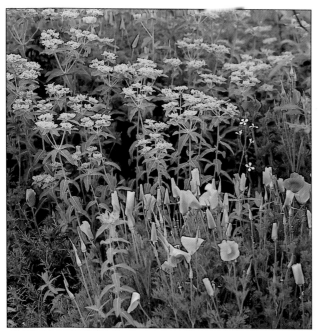

AUTUMN SOWING of eschscholzia will produce early spring flowers around the same time as this bright green Euphorbia polychroma.

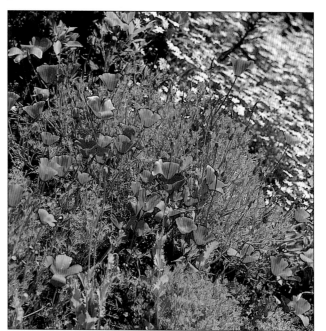

DRY, HOT, SUN-BAKED banks are perfect for California poppies, where conditions are very like those of their native America.

FEATURES

The bright flowers and finely divided blue-green foliage of the California poppy are best in large drifts, although it grows well even in cracks in paving and in gravel, and thrives on dry soils in full sun. Varieties of *Eschscholzia californica* have flowers in yellow, cream, pink/beige, apricot and scarlet. They grow 30cm (12in) tall and wide. Grow as a hardy annual, sowing where plants are to flower. Very easy to grow and quickly self-seeds.

CONDITIONS

Aspect   Eschscholzia thrives in hot, sun-baked spots

ESCHSCHOLZIA AT A GLANCE

A hardy annual grown for its bright poppy-like flowers and ideal for light, dry soils and along paths. Frost hardy to –15ºC (5ºF).

JAN	/	
FEB	/	
MAR	sow	
APR	thin out	
MAY	thin out	
JUN	flowering	
JULY	flowering	
AUG	flowering	
SEPT	flowers/sow	
OCT	/	
NOV	/	
DEC	/	

RECOMMENDED VARIETIES

Eschscholzia californica:
  'Apricot Bush'
  'Apricot Chiffon'
  'Apricot Flambeau'
  'Dalli'
  'Mission Bells Mixed'
  'Prima Ballerina'
  'Rose Bush'
  'Thai Silk Mixed'
Eschscholzia lobbii:
  'Moonlight'

Site   where other annuals struggle to grow. Must have full sun and likes it hot.
Poor light soil often gives the best results, as long as drainage is good. No special soil preparation is necessary, and avoid adding compost or manure which encourages leafy growth at the expense of flowers.

GROWING METHOD

Sowing   Sow in March or September outdoors where plants are to flower as it dislikes being transplanted. Spread seed thinly in short drills 1cm (½in) deep and cover. Thin seedlings as they grow to allow 7.5–15cm (3–6in) between plants. Water thoroughly after thinning to settle plants back in.

Feeding   Except in spells of drought, watering is not necessary, and extra feed is not required.

Problems   No particular problems.

FLOWERING

Season   Long flowering period through the spring and summer months if faded flowers are removed.

Cutting   Use as a cut flower, although flowers close at night. Cut long stems and place in water immediately to just below the flower buds.

AFTER FLOWERING

General   Often self-seeds, so seedlings can be expected the following season. These will appear in cracks in paving, along paths and drives and in gravel, where they are perfectly at home in dry, poor soil conditions.

EUPHORBIA
Snow-on-the-mountain

THE COLOUR of snow-on-the-mountain comes from the white-edged leaves and this becomes more intense near the tops of the plants.

WHEN GROWN IN POTS Euphorbia marginata *can be planted in mixed borders in groups of 3–5 plants for cool splashes of colour.*

FEATURES

Commonly known as snow-on-the-mountain, *Euphorbia marginata* is grown for its attractive leaves. The flowers are insignificant, but the leaves have an edging of white. Plants grow 60–90cm (2–3ft) tall and are used in annual or mixed borders. Grow as a hardy annual. The milky sap is poisonous.

CONDITIONS

Aspect Needs to be grown in the open in full sun.

EUPHORBIA AT A GLANCE	
A hardy annual grown for its attractive leaves which are streaked and edged with white. Frost hardy to –5°C (23°F).	
JAN /	RECOMMENDED VARIETIES
FEB /	*Euphorbia marginata:*
MAR sow	'Summer Icicle'
APR thin out	
MAY thin out	
JUN flowering	
JULY flowering	
AUG flowering	
SEPT flowering	
OCT /	
NOV /	
DEC /	

Site Does not tolerate poor drainage and succeeds best on light and slightly hungry soils – sandy soils give good results. Add very well-rotted organic matter before planting to help retain soil moisture.

GROWING METHOD

Sowing Sow seed during March direct into the ground where plants are to grow, which avoids root disturbance as they develop. Make short drills 1cm (½in) deep and scatter seed thinly, then cover. Plants are gradually thinned out so that final spacing is 15–30cm (6–12in) by early summer. In exposed gardens short twigs can be used as supports. Alternatively, sow in pots in a coldframe and transplant to cell trays, planting out in May.

Feeding Grows well without extra feeding.
Problems Trouble-free.

FLOWERING

Season From early summer onwards.
Cutting Foliage may be used in arrangements but stems must be burnt or scalded to stop the milky sap bleeding. Wear gloves to avoid getting the irritant sap on skin.

AFTER FLOWERING

General Remove plants in late summer and autumn when they are past their best, but leave a few to die down and self-seed into the soil.

GAZANIA
Gazania

GAZANIA flowers often have striking darker markings toward their centres.

IN MILD SEASIDE GARDENS it is worth leaving gazanias out during the winter months as they often survive unharmed and will give an early show of flowers the following spring.

FEATURES

Gazanias come in an amazing range of brilliant colours from pastel pinks to cream, strong reds and mahogany. Modern varieties with striped petals are very eye-catching. All have contrasting 'eyes' to the flowers. Gazanias are grown as half-hardy annuals from spring-sown seeds and used in beds and patio pots. Flowers tend to close up in dull weather, but newer varieties like 'Daybreak Bright Orange' stay open longer. They grow up to 30cm (12in) tall and wide and thrive in seaside gardens.

CONDITIONS

Aspect   For the flowers to open reliably gazanias must be grown where they get baking sun all day.

GAZANIA AT A GLANCE

A half-hardy annual grown for its bright flowers that open fully in sun. Use in beds and containers. Frost hardy to −5°C (23°F).

		RECOMMENDED VARIETIES
JAN	/	*Gazania rigens:*
FEB	/	'Chansonette'
MAR	sow	'Chansonette Pink
APR	transplant	Shades'
MAY	harden off/plant	'Daybreak Bright
JUN	flowering	Orange'
JULY	flowering	'Daybreak Red Stripe'
AUG	flowering	'Harlequin Hybrids'
SEPT	flowering	'Mini Star Mixed'
OCT	/	'Sundance Mixed'
NOV	/	'Talent'
DEC	/	

Site   Needs well-drained soil that is not too rich or leafy growth is the result. Light sandy soils give the best results. If growing in patio containers, choose clay pots or troughs and use a soil-based compost with extra sharp grit mixed in to ensure good drainage at all times.

GROWING METHOD

Sowing   Seed is sown in March at 20°C (68°F) in a heated propagator, in 9cm (3½in) pots. Just cover the seeds and keep in a light spot. Seedlings appear in 1–2 weeks and can be transplanted when large enough into cell trays. Grow on in a greenhouse or conservatory, then harden off and plant in late May, spacing plants 30cm (12in) apart. In mixed containers make sure they are not shaded out by other plants growing nearby.

Feeding   Only water when the soil or compost becomes dry, and stand patio pots under cover during prolonged spells of summer rain.

Problems   No real problems, but slugs may attack leaves in wet weather, so protect with slug pellets.

FLOWERING

Season   The flowering period lasts throughout summer if dead flowers and their stalks are removed.

Cutting   Flowers are not suitable for cutting.

AFTER FLOWERING

General   Favourite plants can be lifted, potted up and kept dry in a frost-free greenhouse over winter. Cuttings can be taken in spring and new plants grown on for planting out.

GODETIA
Godetia

FOR A RAINBOW of summer colour sow a mixed variety of godetia that includes shades of rose, pink and white flowers.

AT ITS PEAK godetia is smothered in masses of bright flowers with large petals that have a texture similar to crepe paper.

FEATURES

Godetia is available in a wide range of varieties and many colours. This hardy annual can be spring- or autumn-sown, the latter giving earlier flowers on bigger plants. Size ranges from 20–90cm (8–36in), with the taller varieties being ideal for cutting. Don't fuss over godetia – the best flowers are produced on slightly hungry, dry soils.

GODETIA AT A GLANCE

Grown for its bright single or double flowers, this hardy annual can be spring- or autumn-sown. Frost hardy to −15°C (5°F).

Jan	/	
Feb	/	
Mar	sow	
Apr	sow	
May	thin out	
Jun	flowering	
July	flowering	
Aug	flowering	
Sept	flowers/sow	
Oct	/	
Nov	/	
Dec	/	

RECOMMENDED VARIETIES

Godetia hybrids:
Tall varieties
  'Duke of York'
  'Grace Mixed'
  'Schamini Carmine'
  'Sybil Sherwood'
Dwarf varieties
  'Charivari'
  'Lilac Pixie'
  'Precious Gems'
  'Salmon Princess'

CONDITIONS

Aspect   Needs an open position in full sun.
Site   Needs perfect drainage, but not rich soil.

GROWING METHOD

Sowing   Sow where plants are to grow, just covering the seeds in shallow drills 15cm (6in) apart during March/April, or during September. Thin seedlings until they are 15–30cm (6–12in) apart depending on variety. Do not thin autumn-sown plants until the following spring to allow for winter losses.
Feeding   Not needed, or excessive leafy growth results.
Problems   Overwatering quickly causes root rot then collapse and death of plants.

FLOWERING

Season   Flowers appear from May onwards on plants sown the previous autumn. Spring-sown plants start flowering from June.
Cutting   Excellent cut flower, especially if the taller varieties such as 'Schamini Carmine' and 'Grace Mixed' are grown in rows.

AFTER FLOWERING

General   Remove plants when flowering is over. A few can be left to self-seed onto the soil.

GOMPHRENA

Globe amaranth

'STRAWBERRY FIELDS' is a large-growing variety of gomphrena with red flowers 5cm (2in) across, on stems 75cm (30in) tall.

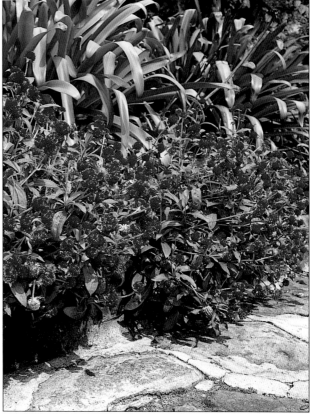

GLOBE AMARANTH makes a good edging for paths – choose one of the lower-growing varieties such as 'Gemini Mixed' at 60cm (2ft).

FEATURES

Also commonly known as bachelor's buttons, gomphrena is a half-hardy annual growing 30–75cm (12–30in) tall depending on the variety. Its rounded heads of purple, pink, white, red and mauve flowers are used in bedding displays and for cutting and drying. 'Strawberry Fields' has bright red flowers.

GOMPHRENA AT A GLANCE

A half-hardy annual grown for its clover-like flowerheads, used in bedding and for cutting. Frost hardy to 0°C (32°F).

JAN	/	
FEB	/	
MAR	sow	
APR	transplant	
MAY	harden off/plant	
JUN	flowering	
JULY	flowering	
AUG	flowering	
SEPT	flowering	
OCT	/	
NOV	/	
DEC	/	

RECOMMENDED VARIETIES

Gomphrena globosa:
  'Buddy'
  'Full Series'
  'Gemini Mixed'
  'Globe Amaranth'
  'Qis Mixed'

Gomphrena hybrid:
  'Strawberry Fields'

CONDITIONS

Aspect   Must have a sunny spot.
Site   Needs well-drained soil enriched with rotted manure or compost.

GROWING METHOD

Sowing   Sow in March in 9cm (3½in) pots of multipurpose compost, just covering the seeds (soaking for a few days before helps germination). Keep at 18°C (64°F) in a warm, dark place such as an airing cupboard and check regularly – seedlings appear in about two weeks. Transplant into cell trays, grow on under cover, harden off in late May, and plant out after frosts, 25–30cm (10–12in) apart.
Feeding   Give an all-purpose liquid feed monthly.
Problems   No special problems affect gomphrena.

FLOWERING

Season   Flowers appear from midsummer to autumn.
Cutting   Used fresh as a cut flower, but can also be dried in late summer by hanging upside down in a warm, dry, airy place.

AFTER FLOWERING

General   Pull up in autumn and use for composting.

GYPSOPHILA

Baby's breath

CLOUDS OF SMALL FLOWERS are produced on annual gypsophila all summer if a few seeds are sown at two-week intervals from April until early June. For cut flowers grow plants in a spare corner because they look bare once you begin to regularly remove stems.

FEATURES

Hardy annual varieties of *Gypsophila elegans* grow up to 60cm (2ft) tall and wide with many-divided stems bearing small, dainty pink, white or rose flowers. It is widely used in flower arranging and as a 'foil' for other plants in summer bedding schemes. The dwarf-growing *Gypsophila muralis* 'Garden Bride', at 15cm (6in), is ideal for baskets and containers.

CONDITIONS

Aspect   Grow gypsophila in full sun.

GYPSOPHILA AT A GLANCE

Gypsophila is a hardy annual grown for tall, much branching stems of flowers, for beds/cutting. Frost hardy to –15°C (5°F).

		RECOMMENDED VARIETIES
JAN	/	
FEB	/	*Gypsophila elegans:*
MAR	/	'Bright Rose'
APR	sow	'Colour Blend'
MAY	thin out	'Covent Garden'
JUN	flowering	'Kermesina'
JULY	flowering	'Monarch White'
AUG	flowering	'Rosea'
SEPT	flowers/sow	'Snow Fountain'
OCT	/	'White Elephant'
NOV	/	*Gypsophila muralis:*
DEC	/	'Garden Bride'

Site
Rotted compost or manure should be dug in before planting, for strong plants and better flowers, but the soil must also be well-drained. Varieties grown in baskets and containers will succeed in any multipurpose compost.

GROWING METHOD

Sowing
Seeds can go straight into the ground where plants will grow and flower. Sow in short drills 1cm (½in) deep in April, then thin to finally leave plants 10–15cm (4–6in) apart to give each other support and allow room to grow. September sowing produces stronger plants with earlier flowers the following spring – do not thin out until after winter.

Feeding
Feeding is not generally necessary if the soil has been well prepared beforehand. In dry spells give the soil a thorough soaking, and do not let containers dry out.

Problems
Gypsophila is trouble-free, but young plants are prone to rotting off on heavy soils.

FLOWERING

Season
Flowers appear from June onwards on spring-sown plants, several weeks earlier on those sown the previous autumn.

Cutting
Excellent when cut and an ideal 'filler' to marry together other flowers in a wide range of floral arrangements.

AFTER FLOWERING

General   Pull up plants and use for composting.

HELIANTHUS
Sunflower

SUNFLOWERS *have a central 'disc' which eventually becomes the fat seedhead in autumn and makes useful food for the birds.*

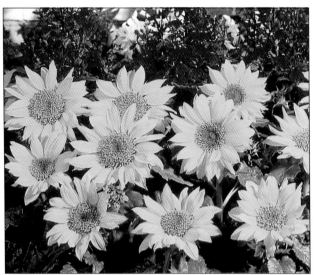

'PACINO' *is a modern variety of* Helianthus annuus, *small enough to be used in patio pots, growing to only 45cm (18in) tall.*

FEATURES

Sunflowers range in height from 45cm (18in) up to 5m (15ft) depending on the variety grown. They can be used in bedding, in patio containers, as cut flowers, or can be grown as traditional 'giants' to several metres (feet) tall. Plants produce single or multi-flowered heads and the colour range is enormous. 'Teddy Bear' has furry, double flowers. Annual sunflowers are fully hardy and flower from mid-summer onwards. Certain varieties such as 'Prado Sun & Fire' have been bred to be pollen-free and these are ideal for use as indoor cut flowers. Seedheads left in the garden in autumn provide food for birds.

CONDITIONS

Aspect   Must have an open position in full sun.

HELIANTHUS AT A GLANCE

A hardy annual grown for its large flowers on both dwarf and tall plants; some are ideal for cutting. Frost hardy to –15°C (5°F).

		RECOMMENDED VARIETIES
JAN	/	*Helianthus annuus:*
FEB	/	**Tall varieties**
MAR	sow	'Italian White'
APR	thin out	'Pastiche'
MAY	support	'Velvet Queen'
JUN	flowering	**For containers**
JULY	flowering	'Big Smile'
AUG	flowering	'Pacino'
SEPT	flowering	**Double flowers**
OCT	/	'Orange Sun'
NOV	/	'Sungold Double'
DEC	/	'Teddy Bear'

Site   Tolerates most soil conditions but soil enriched with plenty of manure or compost makes growth both rapid and vigorous, producing the largest flowerheads. Plants grown in groups in borders tend to support each other, but in exposed spots tie tall varieties to a cane. Use multipurpose compost mixed with slow-release fertiliser for planting up patio containers and windowboxes.

GROWING METHOD

Sowing   Seeds are large and easy to handle – sow three seeds outdoors where plants are to grow in March, removing all but the strongest when 15cm (6in) tall. Can also be sown three seeds to a 9cm (3½in) pot of compost and treated in the same way. Pot-grown plants can be kept outdoors and planted when the roots fill the pot. Spacing depends on the variety grown.

Feeding   Extra feeding is not usually needed but keep plants well watered in long dry spells.

Problems   Slugs and snails can attack young plants cutting them off at ground level, so protect with slug pellets or a barrier of sharp grit.

FLOWERING

Season   Throughout summer and early autumn.

Cutting   A very good cut flower but use a heavy vase or add some weight to the bottom of it to prevent it toppling over. Pollen-free varieties should be grown if allergies are a known problem.

AFTER FLOWERING

General   Leave the seedheads as bird food during autumn and winter, and then dig out the extensive roots. Sunflower roots can help break-up and loosen heavy, compacted soils.

HELICHRYSUM
Strawflower

FOR DRYING cut helichrysum before the flowers reach this stage, while the petals are still curved inwards (bottom right).

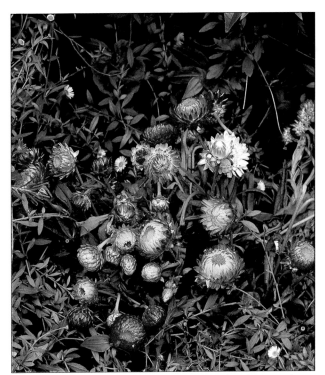

PAPER DAISIES ARE APT to be rather leggy, but the range of flower colours can be stunning, as shown here.

FEATURES

Varieties of strawflower come from *Helichrysum bracteatum*, with plants growing 15–60cm (6–24in) tall. They are among the easiest annuals to grow for dried flowers, with double blooms in many colours, and petals that feel straw-like. Dwarf varieties make long-lasting container plants. A half-hardy annual.

CONDITIONS

Aspect   Must have a warm spot in full sun.

HELICHRYSUM AT A GLANCE

A half-hardy annual grown for its long-lasting dried flowers, and also used in bedding and containers. Frost hardy to 0°C (32°F).

JAN	/	
FEB	/	
MAR	sow	
APR	transplant/grow	
MAY	harden off/plant	
JUN	flowering	
JULY	flowering	
AUG	flowering	
SEPT	flowers/cutting	
OCT	flowers/cutting	
NOV	/	
DEC	/	

RECOMMENDED VARIETIES

Helichrysum bracteatum:
Tall varieties
  'Drakkar Pastel Mixed'
  'Monstrosum Double Mixed'
  'Pastel Mixed'
  'Swiss Giants'
Dwarf varieties
  'Bright Bikini'
  'Chico Mixed'
  'Hot Bikini'

Site   Needs very well-drained soil that has been enriched with rotted compost or manure. If growing in containers use multipurpose compost and add slow-release fertiliser. Tall varieties will need staking as they develop.

GROWING METHOD

Sowing   Sow seeds in March in 9cm (3½in) pots of multipurpose compost and germinate at 18°C (64°F). Transplant seedlings to cell trays when large enough and grow on, then harden off at the end of May and plant 15–60cm (6–24in) apart depending on the variety. Seed can also be sown direct into short drills in the soil during May and the young plants gradually thinned to the planting distances above. In containers pack 2–3 plants together in groups to get a good block of flower colour.

Feeding   Helichrysum grows well without extra feeding, but water container-grown plants regularly.

Problems   By late summer the leaves are often attacked by mildew, but it is not worth treating.

FLOWERING

Season   Flowers appear from early to midsummer.

Cutting   Pick the flowers when the petals are still incurved. Hang the bunches upside down in a dry, airy place to dry out. Long-lasting.

AFTER FLOWERING

General   Cut what you want and then pull up.

HELIPTERUM

Everlasting daisy

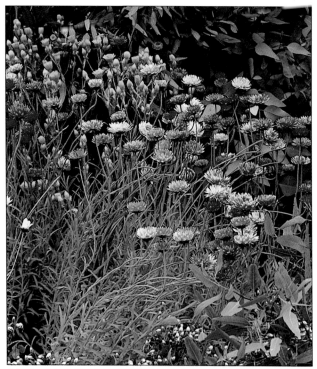

WHEN PLANTS REACH this stage of growth the entire plant can be harvested and hung up to dry. Individual stems are then cut off.

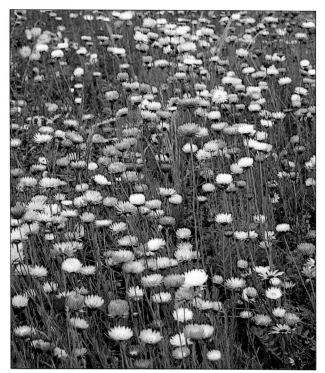

THINNING PLANTS to 15–30cm (6–12in) apart helps them support each other. The flowers have a distinct rustle in a breeze.

FEATURES

The papery flowers of everlasting daisies come mainly in pinks and white. They grow 30–45cm (12–18in) tall, and can be used in bedding or cut for dried flower arrangements. In catalogues they are also found listed under acrolinium and rhodanthe. Hardy annual.

CONDITIONS

Aspect These Australian natives need full sun.
Site Helipterum must have perfectly drained soil and does not require special preparation – the best results are obtained on thin and hungry soils which mimic the plant's natural growing conditions. Sheltered hot-spots are best.

HELIPTERUM AT A GLANCE

A half–hardy annual grown for its pinkish, 'papery' flowers that are good for cutting and drying. Frost hardy to 0°C (32°F).

		RECOMMENDED VARIETIES
JAN	/	
FEB	/	**Helipterum hybrids:**
MAR	/	'Bonny'
APR	sow	'Double Mixed'
MAY	sow/thin	'Goliath'
JUN	flowering	'Pierrot'
JULY	flowering	'Special Mixed'
AUG	flowers/cutting	
SEPT	flowers/cutting	
OCT	/	
NOV	/	
DEC	/	

GROWING METHOD

Sowing Sow seeds direct into the soil in short drills 1cm (½in) deep and 15cm (6in) apart in April and May. Thin the seedlings as they grow, so plants are eventually 15–30cm (6–12in) apart by early summer. Water only during long dry spells, but this is not necessary once flower buds begin to appear.

Feeding Do not feed.

Problems Plants fail on heavy, wet soils that are slow to warm up in spring, so try growing them in raised beds which have better drainage.

FLOWERING

Season Although the plants flower for only a brief spell the effect is long-lasting because of their 'everlasting' nature.

Cutting Ideal as cut, dried flower. For the best results cut off whole plants when most of the flowers are still just opening out, and hang upside down in a dry, airy place.

AFTER FLOWERING

General Plants sometimes self-seed. Any plants not lifted for drying are pulled up in autumn and added to the compost heap.

IBERIS
Candytuft

CANDYTUFT is available in a wide range of colourful mixtures. Each 5cm (2in) wide 'flower' is actually a mass of smaller flowers.

ALL SORTS OF COLOURS appear in varieties of Iberis umbellata, *including white as seen here. The flowers have a sweet fragrance.*

FEATURES

Very decorative plants that grow no more than 30cm (12in) tall, varieties of *Iberis umbellata,* a hardy annual, have sweet-scented flowers in white, pink, mauve, red and purple. They produce good results even in poor soils and quickly self-seed so you get new plants springing up every year, which are at home growing in-between paving and in gravel drives. The best plants with the most flowers come from sowing in early spring.

CONDITIONS

Aspect Iberis prefers an open spot in full sun.
Site Although it is happy in poor soil, adding rotted manure or compost before planting will help keep moisture in and reduce the need for extra watering during summer.

IBERIS AT A GLANCE

Iberis is a hardy annual grown for its heads of bright, scented flowers which are used in bedding. Frost hardy to −15°C (5°F).

		RECOMMENDED VARIETIES
JAN	/	
FEB	/	*Iberis umbellata:*
MAR	sow	'Dwarf Fairy Mixed'
APR	sow	'Fantasia Mixed'
MAY	thin out	'Flash Mixed'
JUN	flowering	'Spangles'
JULY	flowering	
AUG	flowering	
SEPT	sow	
OCT	/	
NOV	/	
DEC	/	

GROWING METHOD

Sowing Seed is sown outdoors in March/April where the plants are to flower. Mark out circular patches of ground with sand and make short parallel drills 1cm (½in) deep inside the circle, spaced 15cm (6in) apart. Sow the seeds thinly in these drills and cover with fine, raked soil. Seedlings appear in 2–3 weeks and should be thinned out so they are eventually 7.5–15cm (3–6in) apart by early summer. Can also be sown in September for earlier flowers.

Feeding Extra feeding is not necessary. Watering in early summer will stop plants flowering prematurely before they achieve a good size.

Problems Being relatives of brassicas like cabbage, they can suffer from clubroot disease. Treatment is not worthwhile, but to continue to enjoy candytuft where clubroot is present, sow a pinch of seed in 9cm (3½in) pots of multi-purpose compost in early spring and plant out clumps in early summer. Disease-free roots will support the plants and let them flower.

FLOWERING

Season Flowers will appear from early summer.
Cutting Good cut flower. Flowers that are well formed but not over-mature should last well if picked early in the day and immediately plunged into water to soak before arranging.

AFTER FLOWERING

General Plants can be cut down after flowering, given a good soak with liquid feed, and they will usually produce a second 'flush' of flowerheads several weeks later. Candytuft self-seeds very easily so leave a few plants to die away naturally and scatter their seeds. Seed can also be collected for sowing the following spring.

IMPATIENS
Busy lizzie

VIGOROUS AND LARGE-FLOWERED, 'Accent Mixed' will carpet the ground in borders or fill containers in sun or shade.

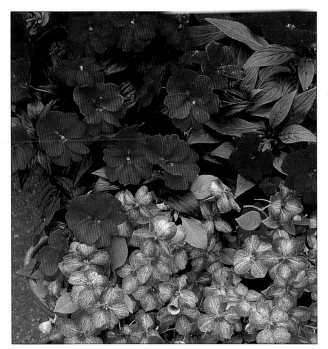

NEW GUINEA busy lizzies can be successfully combined with smaller flowered varieties like this delightful 'Mosaic Lilac'.

FEATURES

Impatiens perform well in sun or shade and a huge range is available. Use in bedding, tubs, windowboxes, hanging baskets and flower bags. As well as busy lizzies, there are also the larger 'New Guinea' types (30cm/12in), and the 'balsams', with bushy growth (25cm/10in). Busy lizzies grow from 15–30cm (6–12in) tall and wide depending on variety. All impatiens are half-hardy annuals, and raising from seed requires some care. Widely available as young plants by mail order, they can also be bought ready-grown in spring. Flowers can be single or double in mixed or various colours.

IMPATIENS AT A GLANCE

A half-hardy annual grown for its flowers for bedding, containers and hanging planters. Frost hardy to 0°C (32°F).

JAN	/	
FEB	sow	
MAR	sow	
APR	grow on	
MAY	harden/plant	
JUN	flowering	
JULY	flowering	
AUG	flowering	
SEPT	flowering	
OCT	flowering	
NOV	/	
DEC	/	

RECOMMENDED VARIETIES

Busy lizzies:
  'Accent Mixed'
  'Bruno'
  'Mosaic Rose'
  'Super Elfin Mixed'
New Guinea impatiens:
  'Firelake Mixed'
  'Spectra'
  'Tango'
Impatiens balsamifera:
  'Tom Thumb Mixed'

CONDITIONS

Aspect Will succeed in full sun or moderate shade.
Site Soil should have rotted manure or compost mixed in before planting, and should be well-drained. Avoid planting in windy spots. In containers and baskets use multipurpose compost with slow-release fertiliser added.

GROWING METHOD

Sowing In late February/March sow seeds onto a fine layer of vermiculite in 9cm (3½in) pots of seed compost. Tap to settle but do not cover. Seal in a clear plastic bag or put in a heated propagator, in a bright place at 21–24°C (70–75°F). Seedlings appear in 2–3 weeks and are transplanted to cell trays when 2.5cm (1in) tall. Grow on, then harden off and plant out after frosts, 15–30cm (6–12in) apart.
Feeding Apply liquid feed weekly to beds or containers using a hand-held feeder.
Problems Damping off disease attacks seedlings. Use clean pots, fresh compost and treat with a copper-based fungicide if seedlings collapse.

FLOWERING

Season Flowers appear on young plants before planting and then throughout summer. Take off dead flowers to keep new ones coming.
Cutting Not suitable as a cut flower.

AFTER FLOWERING

General Remove when plants are past their best.

IPOMOEA
Morning glory

'HEAVENLY BLUE' morning glory never looks better than when scrambling through a host plant like this apple.

FEATURES

Look under ipomoea or morning glory in seed catalogues to find varieties of this stunning climber. Most familiar is sky-blue flowered 'Heavenly Blue'; others are red, pink, white, mauve, chocolate, one is striped, and 'Murasaki Jishi' is double-flowered. Average height is 3–4m (10–12ft). Plants will climb fences and other plants. For patios grow 3–4 plants in a 30cm (12in) pot up a wigwam of 1.5m (5ft) canes. A half-hardy annual with flowers mostly 7.5cm (3in) across. Seeds are poisonous.

IPOMOEA AT A GLANCE

A half-hardy annual climber grown for its trumpet-shaped flowers which open in the morning. Frost hardy to 0°C (32°F).

JAN	/	
FEB	/	
MAR	/	
APR	sow	
MAY	grow on	
JUN	plant	
JULY	flowering	
AUG	flowering	
SEPT	flowering	
OCT	/	
NOV	/	
DEC	/	

RECOMMENDED VARIETIES

Ipomoea hybrids:
'Cardinal'
'Chocolate'
'Early Call Mixed'
'Flying Saucers'
'Grandpa Otts'
'Heavenly Blue'
'Mini Sky–Blue'
'Murasaki Jishi'
'Platycodon Flowered White'

CONDITIONS

Aspect Must have full sun all day.
Site Mix rotted compost with soil before planting. In containers use multipurpose compost with slow-release fertiliser added. All ipomoeas must have shelter from wind, and must have support for their twining stems.

GROWING METHOD

Sowing Soak the seeds in warm water the night before sowing, then sow one to a 9cm (3½in) pot, 2.5cm (1in) deep, in April. Keep in a temperature of at least 21°C (70°F) and put in bright light when the big pink seedlings come up 1–2 weeks later. Keep warm and grow on, potting on into 12.5cm (5in) pots when the roots fill the pot. Support shoots with short stakes. Gradually harden-off in late May, planting out or into containers in early June.
Feeding Feed monthly with a high-potash tomato food.
Problems Seedlings will turn yellow if they are kept too cold in the early stages. Red spider mite feeds on leaves – use a spray containing bifenthrin.

FLOWERING

Season Summer.
Cutting Unsuitable for cutting.

AFTER FLOWERING

General Use for composting when finished.

KOCHIA
Summer cypress

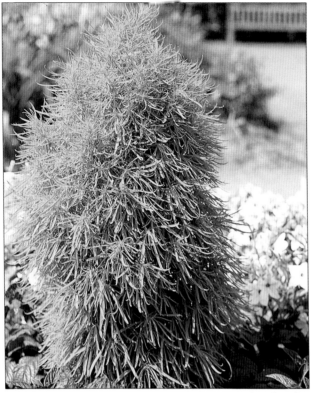

SUMMER CYPRESS is so-called because it resembles a dwarf conifer in colour and shape. In early autumn plants turn bright red.

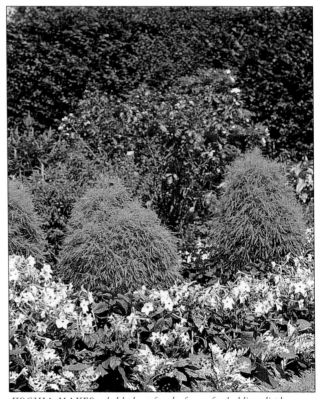

KOCHIA MAKES a bold plant for the focus of a bedding display – seen here with pink nicotianas and silver-leaved senecio.

FEATURES

Summer cypress is a bushy half-hardy foliage annual that grows up to 90cm (3ft) high with soft, light-green feathery foliage forming an upright cone- or dome-shape. 'Trichophylla' has narrow leaves and looks similar to a dwarf conifer in summer, turning to a fiery bronze red in autumn, hence its other common name of burning bush. Grow in groups of 2–3 or singly as the centrepiece of a bedding scheme.

KOCHIA AT A GLANCE

A half-hardy annual grown for its light-green leaves on bushy plants which turn red in autumn. Frost hardy to 0ºC (32ºF).

		RECOMMENDED VARIETIES
JAN	/	*Kochia scoparia:*
FEB	sow	'Trichophylla'
MAR	sow	
APR	grow on	
MAY	harden off/plant	**For all-green leaves**
JUN	leaves	'Evergreen'
JULY	leaves	
AUG	leaves	
SEPT	leaves	
OCT	leaves	
NOV	/	
DEC	/	

CONDITIONS

Aspect Needs full sun to get the best leaf colour.

Site Grows on most soils but must be well-drained. Add manure/compost before planting.

GROWING METHOD

Sowing Sow February/March on the surface of a 9cm (3½in) pot of moist multipurpose compost but do not cover. Keep at 16ºC (61ºF) in a bright spot, and expect seedlings in 2–3 weeks. When large enough, transplant to 9cm (3½in) pots of multipurpose compost and grow on, hardening off in late May and planting outdoors after the last frosts. Space plants at least 60cm (2ft) apart to allow room for development. They can also be planted in rows as a temporary and unusual summer 'hedge'.

Feeding Water thoroughly in early summer for 2–3 weeks after planting. Extra feeding is not essential to get good results.

Problems No particular problems.

FLOWERING

Season Not grown for flowers but leaves.

Cutting Unsuitable for cutting.

AFTER FLOWERING

General Pull up and compost in autumn.

LATHYRUS

Sweet pea

SWEET PEAS are perhaps the easiest and most rewarding of cut flowers you can grow. Choose a variety known for its fragrance.

CLIMBING VARIETIES of Lathyrus odoratus *make useful 'living screens' in summer with the added benefits of colour and scent.*

FEATURES

Varieties of *Lathyrus odoratus*, or sweet pea, occupy several pages in seed catalogues, but there are two basic groups – the tall climbers reaching 2–2.5m (6–8ft), used as cut flowers and for screening, and dwarf 'patio' varieties reaching up to 90cm (3ft) which are used in bedding, baskets and containers. Not all sweet peas have good scent, so check before buying seeds, and choose a fragrant mixed variety for a range of flower colours, which can be white, pink, red, mauve, orange or blue, as well as many with picotee and other patterns. Sweet peas are easily-grown hardy annuals.

CONDITIONS

Aspect Grow in full sun.

LATHYRUS AT A GLANCE

A hardy annual climber producing often strongly-scented flowers which are ideal for cutting. Frost hardy to –15°C (5°F).

		RECOMMENDED VARIETIES
JAN	/	*Lathyrus odoratus:*
FEB	/	**Tall, fragrant varieties**
MAR	sow	'Bouquet Mixed'
APR	grow on	'Great Expectations'
MAY	plant	'Old Fashioned Mixed'
JUN	flowering	'Old Spice Mixed'
JULY	flowering	**Dwarf/patio varieties**
AUG	flowering	'Explorer'
SEPT	flowering	'Fantasia Mixed'
OCT	sow	'Jet-Set Mixed'
NOV	/	'Knee-High'
DEC	/	

Site Needs well-drained soil packed with organic matter. Add compost or rotted manure the autumn before sowing or planting. Climbing varieties need canes, bean netting, fences or other supports to grow through. Use multipurpose compost for planting up baskets and patio containers.

GROWING METHOD

Sowing Seeds can be sown individually in 9cm (3½in) pots in February/March and germinated in a coldframe, cold porch, or even outdoors in a spot sheltered from rain. Nick or file the tough seed coat until a pale 'spot' appears, then sow 2.5cm (1in) deep in soil-based seed compost. Pinch out the growing tips when plants are 7.5cm (3in) tall to encourage sideshoots to grow. Grow outside, then plant out in May, 30cm (12in) apart for climbers, and 15–30cm (6–12in) apart for patio varieties used in baskets and containers.

Feeding Plants benefit from a monthly feed with liquid tomato food. Water thoroughly in dry spells.

Problems Mice will dig young seedlings up so set traps. Powdery mildew can attack leaves in the summer – use a spray containing sulphur.

FLOWERING

Season Seed can also be sown in October, and plants overwintered for flowers from early summer. Spring-sown plants flower from June.

Cutting Cut when the first few flowers on the stalk are opening and stand up to their necks in water.

AFTER FLOWERING

General Cut off at ground level in autumn so the nitrogen-rich roots rot down in the soil.

LAVATERA
Annual mallow

'SILVER CUP' is one of the most popular varieties of annual mallow, with rose-pink flowers up to 12.5cm (5in) across.

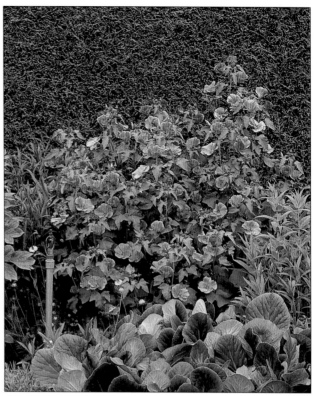

IN MIXED BORDERS annual mallow can be sown direct into open patches of soil, for mounds of colour from mid to late summer.

FEATURES

White, rose, pink and red flowers with a silky sheen are characteristic of annual mallow. Plants grow between 60–120cm (2–4ft) depending on variety, and bloom continuously from mid-June onwards. Use them as the centrepiece in summer bedding schemes or grow in large blocks in annual borders. An easily-grown hardy annual that is also useful as a cut flower.

LAVATERA AT A GLANCE

A hardy annual grown for its large, colourful summer flowers on bushy plants 60–120cm (2–4ft) tall. Frost hardy to –15°C (5°F).

		RECOMMENDED VARIETIES
JAN	/	
FEB	/	*Lavatera trimestris:*
MAR	sow	'Beauty Mixed'
APR	sow/thin out	'Dwarf White Cherub'
MAY	sow/thin out	'Loveliness'
JUN	flowering	'Mont Blanc'
JULY	flowering	'Mont Rose'
AUG	flowering	'Parade Mixed'
SEPT	flowering	'Pink Beauty'
OCT	/	'Ruby Regis'
NOV	/	'Silver Cup'
DEC	/	

CONDITIONS

Aspect   Must have full sun all day.
Site   Lavatera needs good drainage but not rich soil – plants flower better if the ground is hungry, making them good plants for light sandy soils. They do well in seaside gardens.

GROWING METHOD

Sowing   Seed is sown outdoors March–May, and earlier sowings mean earlier flowers. Mark out circles 60cm (2ft) or more across, then sow seed in short drills 1cm (½in) deep. Once seedlings appear thin them out gradually so they are 30–60cm (1–2ft) apart by early summer. Growing this way creates a roughly circular block of colour, which can be used as the centrepiece of a bedding scheme using annuals.
Feeding   Feeding is not necessary. Water thoroughly in early summer during long dry spells.
Problems   Sometimes killed suddenly by soil fungal diseases – grow in a new spot the next season.

FLOWERING

Season   Summer.
Cutting   Grow a few plants just for cut stems.

AFTER FLOWERING

General   Leave a few plants to self-seed, then pull up.

LIMNANTHES

Poached egg flower

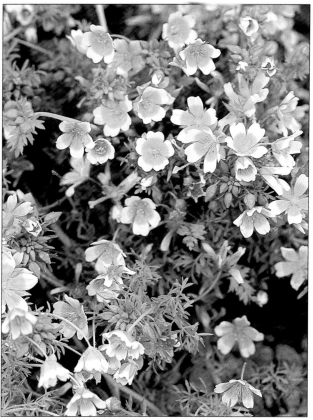

POACHED EGG FLOWER *has 2.5cm (1in) wide flowers like tiny eggs in early summer, and attractive, divided, fern-like leaves.*

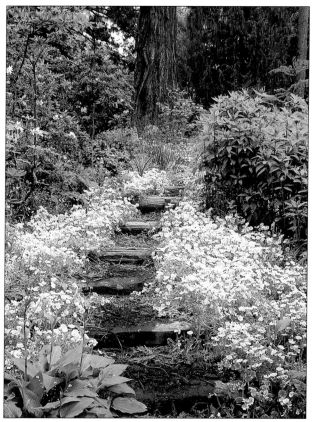

THE SEEDS OF LIMNANTHES *go everywhere after flowering and seem to enjoy spreading along path edges in particular.*

FEATURES

Limnanthes douglasii has cup-shaped white flowers with bright yellow centres, which explains its common name of poached egg flower. Plants grow to 15–23cm (6–9in) in height and have a spreading habit. A hardy annual, it self-seeds very easily and keeps on coming. Grow in annual beds, along path edges and among other plants in borders.

LIMNANTHES AT A GLANCE

A hardy annual which quickly self-seeds, producing masses of yellow/white flowers in summer. Frost hardy to –15°C (5°F).

JAN	/	RECOMMENDED VARIETIES
FEB	/	*Limnanthes douglasii*
MAR	sow	
APR	sow/thin	
MAY	sow/thin	
JUN	flowering	
JULY	flowering	
AUG	/	
SEPT	sow	
OCT	/	
NOV	/	
DEC	/	

CONDITIONS

Aspect   Prefers full sun and an open situation.
Site   Needs moisture-retentive soil with rotted organic matter mixed in well ahead of sowing.

GROWING METHOD

Sowing   Spring or autumn are the sowing times. Sow from March to May or in September. Either sow seed in short drills 1cm (½in) deep or mark areas of soil, scatter the seed over the surface and rake in. Seedlings appear after 1–2 weeks and should be thinned out so they are about 7.5–15cm (3–6in) apart, although this is not too critical. If sowing in autumn do not thin until spring in case of winter losses.

Feeding   Feeding is not necessary, but water thoroughly in dry spells during early summer.

Problems   No special problems.

FLOWERING

Season   Overwintered plants flower from late spring depending on the weather, and are very attractive to bees and beneficial garden insects.

Cutting   Not suitable for cutting.

AFTER FLOWERING

General   Pull plants up as soon as they are over.

LIMONIUM
Statice

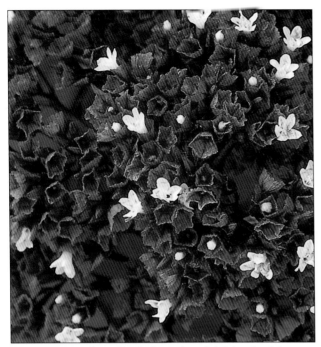

LONG AFTER the small pale flowers have faded the colourful papery bracts are still going strong, and they keep their colour when dried.

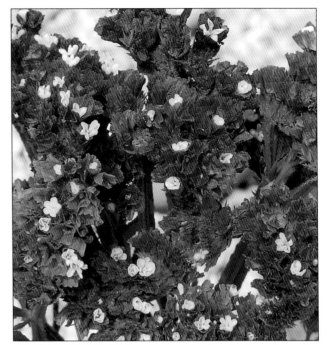

'PURPLE MONARCH' is a classic strain of statice for cutting and drying. It grows to 60cm (24in).

FEATURES

Annual varieties of *Limonium sinuatum* grow up to 90cm (3ft) tall and have peculiar winged stems. The actual flowers are small, but statice is grown for its papery bracts of purple, white, pink, apricot, yellow, rose or blue, which persist all summer, and can be used as a cut and dried flower. A half-hardy annual which is used solely for cutting, or in the case of the short varieties as a bedding/container plant.

CONDITIONS

Aspect   Grow in full sun in an open position.

LIMONIUM AT A GLANCE

A half-hardy annual grown for its heads of brightly coloured bracts used for bedding and drying. Frost hardy to –5°C (23°F).

		RECOMMENDED VARIETIES
JAN	/	*Limonium sinuatum:*
FEB	sow	**Tall varieties**
MAR	sow/transplant	'Art Shades Mixed'
APR	grow on	'Forever Mixed'
MAY	grow on/harden	'Forever Moonlight'
JUN	plant/grow	'Sunburst Mixed'
JULY	flowering	'Sunset Mixed'
AUG	flowers/cutting	**Short varieties**
SEPT	flowers/cutting	'Biedermeier Mixed'
OCT	/	'Petite Bouquet'
NOV	/	
DEC	/	

Site   Must have very well-drained soil, and is quite happy in sandy, light soils that are on the 'hungry' side. If growing dwarf varieties for containers use multipurpose compost. Statice does exceedingly well in seaside gardens.

GROWING METHOD

Sowing   Sow seed in February/March in a 9cm (3½in) pot of multipurpose compost and keep at 18°C (64°F). Transplant to cell trays, grow on, then harden off in late May and plant after the last frosts 15–45cm (6–18in) apart. If growing for cut flowers, seed can be sown outdoors in rows from early May, 1cm (½in) deep and thinned to similar spacings.

Feeding   Does not need regular feeding, but water well if dry straight after planting out.

Problems   Plants may rot on heavy, wet soils, and powdery mildew can attack the leaves in late summer, but this is rarely serious.

FLOWERING

Season   Long flowering period throughout summer.

Cutting   Ideal cut flower. Can be used fresh, or cut and dried by hanging bunches upside down in a dry airy place. Cut when the flowerheads are showing maximum colour. Dried flowers retain their colour well over a long period.

AFTER FLOWERING

General   Pull plants up and compost once all the flowers have been cut or have gone over.

LINARIA
Toadflax

WHEN SOWN IN BOLD PATCHES varieties of Linaria maroccana *soon knit together to produce a tapestry of colour if one of the mixtures such as 'Fairy Bouquet' is grown. Clumps can also be carefully lifted and planted into patio pots in late spring and early summer.*

FEATURES

Linaria is commonly known as toadflax and has dainty little flowers like tiny snapdragons in a wide colour range including white, cream, yellow, red, blue and pink. Plants grow 23–60cm (9–24in) and are good massed in drifts in annual borders, or used as fillers in mixed border plantings. Most annual toadflax are varieties of *Linaria maroccana*. A hardy annual that can be sown direct outdoors.

LINARIA AT A GLANCE

A hardy annual grown for its spikes of pretty flowers like small snapdragons appearing in summer. Frost hardy to −15°C (5°F).

		RECOMMENDED VARIETIES
JAN	/	
FEB	/	*Linaria anticaria*
MAR	sow	
APR	sow/thin out	*Linaria maroccana:*
MAY	sow/thin out	'Fairy Bouquet'
JUN	thin/flowers	'Fantasia Blue'
JULY	flowering	'Fantasia Mixed'
AUG	flowering	'Fantasia Pink'
SEPT	flowering	'Northern Lights'
OCT	/	
NOV	/	*Linaria reticulata:*
DEC	/	'Crown Jewels'

CONDITIONS

Aspect Needs a warm, sunny spot.
Site Well-drained soil enriched with manure or compost ahead of planting is essential. Very good plants can be grown on light, sandy soils.

GROWING METHOD

Sowing Seeds are best sown in short drills 1cm (½in) deep March–May. Mark the sowing areas with a ring of light-coloured sand and label if sowing more than one annual in the same bed. The seedlings will appear in rows and can be told from nearby weed seedlings quite easily. Thin the seedlings out so they are finally 10–15cm (4–6in) apart by early summer. Alternatively, leave them to grow as small clumps of 4–6 plants every 30cm (12in) or so.
Feeding Feeding is rarely needed but water well after the final thinning if the soil is dry.
Problems No special problems.

FLOWERING

Season Flowers appear early to mid summer.
Cutting Not usually used for cutting.

AFTER FLOWERING

General Leave a few plants to die down and self-seed. Others can be pulled up and composted.

LOBELIA
Lobelia

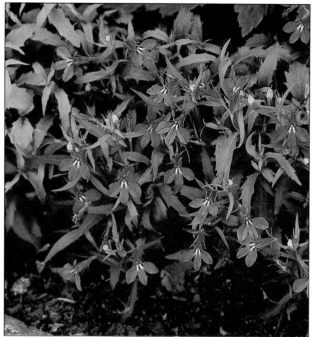

LOBELIA FLOWERS are tubular with a large lower 'lip' divided into three rounded lobes. Dark flowers have pale throats.

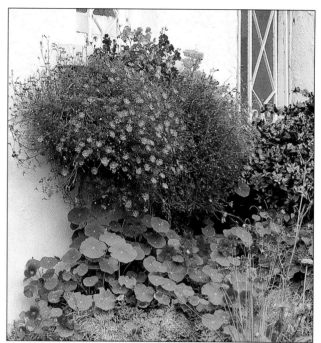

IN THIS HANGING BASKET lobelias mingle with begonias and brachyscome, and bright red nasturtiums creep up from below.

FEATURES

Choose the bushier 'edging' varieties for bedding schemes and the 'trailers' for hanging baskets, flower bags and containers. Flower colour ranges from white through pink, mauve and white to blue, and striking two-toned varieties like 'Riviera Blue Splash' are also available. Edgers grow 10–15cm (4–6in) tall, trailers up to 45cm (18in) long when well fed, and plants have a similar spread. Varieties of *Lobelia erinus* are available as single or mixed colours, and modern coated seed makes sowing much easier. A range of varieties are available as young plants by mail order. Half-hardy.

LOBELIA AT A GLANCE

A half-hardy annual used as an edging plant or a trailing plant for baskets, with many small flowers. Frost hardy to 0°C (32°F).

		RECOMMENDED VARIETIES
JAN	sow 🌱	*Lobelia erinus:*
FEB	sow/transplant 🌱	**Edging varieties**
MAR	sow/transplant 🌱	'Cambridge Blue'
APR	grow on 🌱	'Crystal Palace'
MAY	harden off/plant 🌱	'Mrs Clibran Improved'
JUN	flowering 🌸	'Riviera Lilac'
JULY	flowering 🌸	**Trailing varieties**
AUG	flowering 🌸	'Cascade Mixed'
SEPT	flowering 🌸	'Fountains Mixed'
OCT	/	'Regatta Mixed'
NOV	/	'String of Pearls Mixed'
DEC	/	

CONDITIONS

Aspect　Flowers best when grown in full sun.
Site　Enrich soil with rotted compost or manure before planting. Drainage must be good, but lobelia must also have adequate moisture all through the season. For baskets and containers use multipurpose compost and add slow-release fertiliser granules before planting up.

GROWING METHOD

Sowing　Sow January–March in a 9cm (3½in) pot of multipurpose compost. Sow the tiny seeds evenly over the surface but do not cover, and put in a well-lit spot at 18°C (64°F). When the seedlings form a green 'mat', carefully tease them apart into small clumps of 4–6, and transplant each clump to one unit of a multi-cell tray. Grow on, harden off in late May and plant after frosts.

Feeding　Feed fortnightly with high-potash liquid feed, and never allow the plants to dry out.

Problems　Trouble-free, but if seedlings keel over in spring water with copper-based fungicide.

FLOWERING

Season　Flowers appear from June onwards.
Cutting　Not suitable for cutting.

AFTER FLOWERING

General　Go over plants with shears when they look untidy and water with liquid feed – this encourages more flowers. Compost in autumn.

LOBULARIA

Alyssum

ALYSSUM IS COMPACT and this makes it the ideal edging plant to fill in between other summer bedders. Flowers smell of honey.

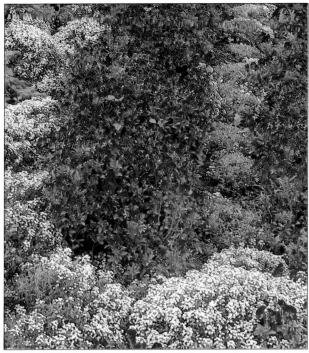

'CARPET OF SNOW' is used here in a bed to create living lines and patterns around slightly taller plants such as these violas.

FEATURES

Lobularia maritima, alyssum, has masses of tiny flowers in various colours in round heads; white, pink, lavender and purple. All varieties smell sweetly of honey, although you need to get up close. None grow more than 15cm (6in) high, making alyssum ideal as an edging plant, but it is also useful for planting in pots, troughs and hanging baskets.

CONDITIONS

Aspect   Grow alyssum in a spot receiving full sun.

LOBULARIA AT A GLANCE

A low-growing hardy annual for edging summer bedding schemes, with honey-scented flowers. Frost hardy to −15°C (5°F).

JAN	/	RECOMMENDED VARIETIES
FEB	sow	*Lobularia maritima :*
MAR	sow/transplant	'Aphrodite'
APR	sow/grow on	'Creamery'
MAY	sow/harden off	'Easter Basket Mixed'
JUN	flowering	'Easter Bonnet'
JULY	flowering	'Golf Mixed'
AUG	flowering	'Golf Rose'
SEPT	flowering	'Little Dorrit'
OCT	/	'Rosie O'Day'
NOV	/	'Snow Carpet'
DEC	/	'Snow Crystals'

Site   Must have well-drained soil and adding rotted organic matter helps retain soil moisture. For baskets and patio containers plant using multipurpose potting compost.

GROWING METHOD

Sowing   Alyssum grown for bedding and containers is best raised in early spring. Sow a whole packet of seeds in February/March in a 9cm (3½in) pot of multipurpose compost, and just cover. When seedlings are 1cm (½in) tall split up into small clumps of 4–6 seedlings and transplant each to individual units of a multi-cell tray. This is especially useful to get a good spread of different flowers colours when growing a mixed variety. Grow on and harden off in late May before planting out. Seeds can also be sown direct into the soil in an annual border during April/May 1cm (½in) deep.

Feeding   Extra feeding is unnecessary.

Problems   Look out for slugs which will attack newly-planted alyssum, especially after rain.

FLOWERING

Season   Flowers often appear before planting and until late summer – clip them over with shears and water well to encourage a second flush.

Cutting   Not suitable as a cut flower.

AFTER FLOWERING

General   Seeds will self-sow very easily, and come up the following spring. Compost when finished.

LUNARIA
Honesty

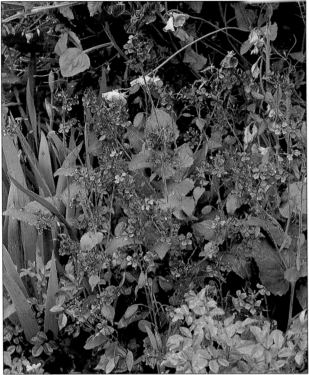

THE SEEDHEADS of Lunaria annua *are sought after for dried flower arrangements. Here they are still in the green stages of growth.*

'ALBA VARIEGATA' has leaves splashed with creamy-white and also white flowers. It adds easy and quick colour to spring borders.

FEATURES

Honesty, *Lunaria annua*, a hardy biennial is also known as the money plant because of its large circular, smooth, silvery seedheads that resemble coins. It grows up to 90cm (3ft) tall and is a plant that is best left to do its own thing, self-seeding very quickly, and thriving under dry hedges where most plants will not grow, and will seed into mixed borders. Flowers are purple or white and appear in early spring, and variegated varieties are available.

LUNARIA AT A GLANCE

A hardy biennial grown for its pretty purple/white flowers followed by large silvery seedheads. Frost hardy to −15°C (5°F).

JAN	/	
FEB	/	
MAR	sow/flowers	
APR	thin/flowers	
MAY	thin/flowers	
JUN	flowering	
JULY	/	
AUG	/	
SEPT	/	
OCT	/	
NOV	/	
DEC	/	

RECOMMENDED VARIETIES

Lunaria annua:
 'Fine Mixed'
 'Mixed'

Variegated leaves
 'Variegata'

White flowers
 'Alba Variegata '

CONDITIONS

Aspect Succeeds in sun or the shade cast by hedges and large shrubs.
Site Thriving in poor soils, plants grow larger still if they are sown into soil that has been improved with rotted manure or compost, and produce the best seedheads for drying.

GROWING METHOD

Sowing Mark out patches using sand and sow the large seeds 2.5cm (1in) deep in short drills, with 5–7.5cm (2–3in) between each seed in March. Seedlings are quick to appear and can be thinned or left to develop as they are. Next spring look out for seedlings and move them when small to where you want plants to grow.
Feeding Needs no extra feeding or watering.

FLOWERING

Season Flowers from early spring to early summer.
Cutting Can be cut for flowers but some must be left to set seed if you want the large, silvery heads.

AFTER FLOWERING

General Cut when the seedheads are mature and dry, on a warm day, and hang upside-down in a dry, airy place until you can carefully remove the outer skin of the pod. Leave a few plants to die down naturally and self-seed.

LUPINUS
Annual lupin

SHORTER AND SQUATTER than their perennial cousins, annual lupins can create a sea of colour when sown in large drifts like this. As the flowers fade the spikes should be removed completely with secateurs to divert energy into new flowers rather than seed pods.

FEATURES

By growing annual lupins from seed you can enjoy the features of their perennial relatives without giving up too much space in the garden. Annual lupins are smaller, growing between 30–90cm (1–3ft) tall, but have very colourful spikes in mixed shades and also striking single colours such as the blue-flowered *Lupinus texensis*. Hardy annuals. Seeds and plants are poisonous if eaten.

LUPINUS AT A GLANCE

A hardy annual grown for its spikes of colourful and spicey-scented flowers during summer. Frost hardy to –15°C (5°F).

		RECOMMENDED VARIETIES
JAN	/	**Lupinus hybrids:**
FEB	/	'Biancaneve'
MAR	/	'New White'
APR	sow	'Pink Javelin'
MAY	thin out	'Pixie Delight'
JUN	flowering	'Sunrise'
JULY	flowering	**Yellow flowers**
AUG	flowering	*Lupinus luteus*
SEPT	flowering	**Blue flowers**
OCT	/	*Lupinus texensis*
NOV	/	*Lupinus varius*
DEC	/	

CONDITIONS

Aspect Needs full sun.
Site Well-drained, light soil is best for annual lupins, but mix in rotted manure or compost.

GROWING METHOD

Sowing The large seeds can go straight into the ground in April, but to ensure germination the tough seed coat must be nicked with a sharp knife or rubbed down with a file until the pale inside just shows. Next, soak the seeds on wet tissue paper and sow when they have swollen up, 7.5–15cm (3–6in) apart and 5cm (2in) deep, where you want plants to grow. Thin seedlings to 15cm (6in) apart when well established. To grow in pots do the same, sowing one seed to a 9cm (3½in) pot, then plant out.
Feeding Lupins need no extra feeding.
Problems Fat green lupin aphids can kill entire plants, so use a spray containing permethrin.

FLOWERING

Season Flowers appear from midsummer.
Cutting Cut when some buds at the base of the flower spike are fully open.

AFTER FLOWERING

General Cut off to leave the nitrogen-rich roots to rot in the ground, and compost the tops.

MALCOLMIA

Virginian stock

PINK IS JUST one of the colours found in Virginian stocks. Expect reds, yellows and whites from a variety like 'Fine Mixed'.

JUST FOUR WEEKS after sowing plants will be in flower. Malcolmia maritima thrives in the thin light soils of seaside gardens.

FEATURES

Keep a packet of Virginian stock, *Malcolmia maritima* seed to hand at all times and sow a pinch of seeds every two weeks in gaps and under windows – plants will flower just a month later. They grow 15–20cm (6–8in) high with small, single, four-petalled, sweetly scented flowers in red, mauve, pink, yellow and white from June–September. They can also be sown into patio tubs. Hardy annual.

MALCOLMIA AT A GLANCE

Hardy annual grown for its pink, red, yellow or white flowers. Flowers a month after sowing. Frost hardy to –15°C (5°F).

		RECOMMENDED VARIETIES
JAN	/	*Malcolmia maritima:*
FEB	/	'Fine Mixed'
MAR	sow	'Mixed'
APR	sow/flowers	
MAY	sow/flowers	
JUN	sow/flowers	
JULY	sow/flowers	
AUG	sow/flowers	
SEPT	sow/flowers	
OCT	sow	
NOV	/	
DEC	/	

CONDITIONS

Aspect   Prefers full sun but tolerates some shade.
Site   Will grow on most soils but needs good drainage to do well.

GROWING METHOD

Sowing   Seed can literally be scattered in small patches 30cm (12in) across on the soil where you want flowers and mixed in using your fingertips, or it is simply scattered along the cracks in paths and driveways, from March onwards, and repeated every few weeks all through the summer. Mark sown areas in borders with a label or circle of light-coloured sand. Seedlings soon come up and there is no need to bother with thinning. For early flowers the following spring sow in October.

Feeding   Not necessary.
Problems   Trouble-free.

FLOWERING

Season   Expect flowers all summer long with repeat sowings.
Cutting   Unsuitable as a cut flower.

AFTER FLOWERING

General   Pull up as soon as the plants are over, and resow. Self-sown seedlings soon appear.

MATTHIOLA

Brompton stock

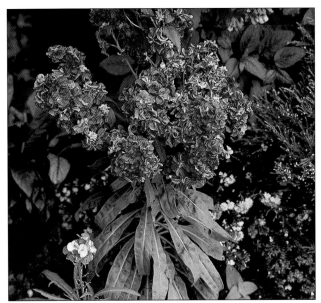

WHEN BEDDED-OUT in spring Brompton stocks provide an early splash of colour and fill the air with scent on warm days.

FLOWER COLOUR varies, and it should be possible to see the colour in the flower buds before you plant, ensuring an even display.

FEATURES

The sweetly scented flowers of Brompton stocks are held above the grey-green leaves on plants up to 45cm (18in) tall. There is a full range of pastel colours with some stronger purples, crimson and magenta as well; the flowers are double. Derived from *Matthiola incana*, Brompton stocks are lovely in massed spring plantings, giving off a delicious strong fragrance. They are grown as biennials.

CONDITIONS

Aspect   Need full sun and a sheltered position.
Site   Must have well-drained soil. Incorporate rotted manure or compost into the soil a few weeks before planting. Tall varieties will need short stakes to prevent their flowers flopping.

MATTHIOLA AT A GLANCE

A hardy biennial sown in summer for strongly-scented pink flowers the following spring. Frost hardy to −15°C (5°F).

		RECOMMENDED VARIETIES
JAN	grow on 🌱	*Matthiola incana:*
FEB	plant 🌱	'Brompton Mixed'
MAR	plant 🌱	'Brompton Dwarf Mixed'
APR	flowering 🌸	'Spring Flowering Mixed'
MAY	flowering 🌸	
JUN	sow 🌱	
JULY	sow/transplant 🌱	
AUG	transplant 🌱	
SEPT	grow on 🌱	
OCT	grow on 🌱	
NOV	grow on 🌱	
DEC	grow on 🌱	

GROWING METHOD

Sowing   June/July is the time to sow seed, in a 9cm (3½in) pot of multipurpose compost. When the seedlings are large enough, transplant one seedling to a 9cm (3½in) pot of multipurpose compost, water well and grow on. Later, pot on into 12.5cm (5in) pots. When the first frosts arrive take the young plants into a coldframe, cold greenhouse or porch, standing them outside during mild spells all through the winter months. Keep on the dry side and only water when they wilt. Plant out from February onwards when the soil is workable, or pot on into large pots and grow in a cool conservatory or porch with canes for support.

Feeding   Do not feed until 2–3 weeks before planting out, then give a general purpose liquid feed.

Problems   Cabbage butterflies will lay eggs on the young plants in late summer and the caterpillars can strip leaves, so use a spray containing permethrin, or pick them off by hand.

FLOWERING

Season   Brompton stocks will fill beds and borders with colour and scent during April and May, weather permitting. They perform best in calm, mild spells with plenty of sunshine. While most plants will have double flowers, there may be singles which can be put to one side, planted separately, and used for cutting.

Cutting   A good cut flower. Scald stems after picking and change vase water every couple of days.

AFTER FLOWERING

General   Dig plants up when the show is over and prepare the ground for summer bedding plants. Add to the compost heap/bin.

MIMULUS
Monkey flower

MONKEY FLOWERS have blooms which are face-like and marked with intricate patterns and spotting. They are good for shade.

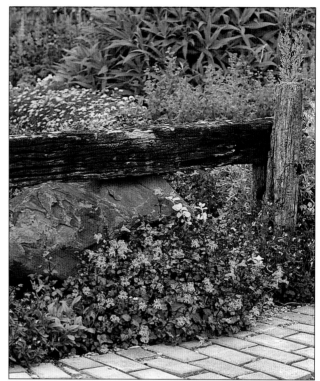

PLANT MIMULUS along the edges of a path. Monkey flowers will bloom in just nine weeks.

FEATURES

Mimulus or monkey flower is grown as a half-hardy annual and is useful for summer bedding and containers, with bright flowers in a range of colours, mainly red and orange, on plants 30–45cm (12–18in) tall and wide. It is very useful for growing in shaded and wet spots.

CONDITIONS

Aspect   Will grow in sun or shade.

MIMULUS AT A GLANCE

Grown as a half-hardy annual for bedding, windowboxes and hanging baskets. Colourful flowers. Frost hardy to –15ºC (5ºF).

JAN	/	RECOMMENDED VARIETIES
FEB	sow	**Mimulus hybrids:**
MAR	sow/transplant	'Calypso'
APR	grow on	'Extra Choice Mixed'
MAY	grow on/harden	'Magic Ivory'
JUN	flowering	'Magic Pastels Mixed'
JULY	flowering	'Malibu'
AUG	flowering	'Malibu Orange'
SEPT	flowering	'Malibu Sunshine'
OCT	/	'Queen's Prize Mixed'
NOV	/	'Sparkles'
DEC	/	'Viva'

Site   Needs moist soil so dig in plenty of rotted organic matter well ahead of planting. Use a peat- or coir-based multipurpose compost for growing mimulus in containers. Add slow-release fertiliser granules when planting.

GROWING METHOD

Sowing   Sow in 9cm (3½in) pots in February/March, barely covering the fine seed. Keep at 12ºC (54ºF) in bright light and expect seedlings after about two weeks. When large enough transplant to cell trays and grow on until the end of May, then harden off and plant from mid-May onwards, 15–30cm (6–12in) apart, or in groups of 2–3 in troughs and pots.

Feeding   Feed monthly with liquid feed and ensure that containers never dry out or flowering will be reduced and plants damaged.

Problems   If slugs attack plants growing in shaded areas protect with slug pellets or scatter sharp grit to make a physical barrier. Container-grown plants suffer in excessive heat so move them to a position where they are out of midday sun.

FLOWERING

Season   Summer, from June onwards.
Cutting   Not suitable for cutting.

AFTER FLOWERING

General   Pull up and compost when finished.

MOLUCCELLA
Bells of Ireland

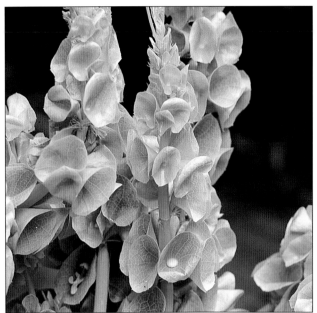

THE FLOWERS OF Moluccella laevis *are actually small, pale, and found in the centre of each of the showier bell-like bracts.*

MOLUCCELLA is ideal for use in mixed borders to add a welcome touch of vivid green. Sow in patches 60cm (2ft) across.

FEATURES

A half-hardy annual, also known as shell flower, moluccella is very lightly scented, and produces 60–90cm (2–3ft) tall spikes in summer. It has small flowers surrounded by the more obvious and showy bell- or shell-like apple-green bracts. You can grow moluccella in flower beds and mixed borders, but its main value is as a cut flower, either fresh or dried. It is long-lasting when dried in late summer, the green spikes gradually fade from green to pale brown through autumn and into winter.

CONDITIONS

Aspect   Needs an open spot in full sun.

MOLUCCELLA AT A GLANCE

A half-hardy annual grown for its tall spikes of green bracts which are used for drying. Frost hardy to 0°C (32°F).

		RECOMMENDED VARIETIES
JAN	/	*Moluccella laevis*
FEB	sow	
MAR	sow	
APR	transplant/grow	
MAY	plant/sow	
JUN	flowering	
JULY	flowering	
AUG	flowering	
SEPT	flowers/cutting	
OCT	/	
NOV	/	
DEC	/	

Site   Must have good drainage, and working rotted manure or compost into the ground before sowing or planting helps. Avoid exposed, windy spots or the tall stems may be flattened.

GROWING METHOD

Sowing   Either sow seed in 9cm (3½in) pots of multipurpose compost in February/March at 18°C (64°F), or sow directly in the soil where they are to grow in late April and May. Gradually thin out so plants are spaced 30–40cm (12–16in) apart. Plants raised under cover are hardened off before being planted.

Feeding   If organic matter has already been added to the soil, extra feeding is not necessary, but keep plants well watered during long dry spells.

Problems   Seeds can sometimes be slow and difficult to germinate, so put them in the bottom of a refrigerator for two weeks before you sow, to 'chill' them, then sow in pots as described above and expect seedlings in 2–3 weeks.

FLOWERING

Season   Even after the actual flowers have faded the green bracts go on providing colour and interest until they are cut for drying.

Cutting   Ideal as a cut flower, used fresh or dried. Cut when flowers are well formed. Leaves can be removed to display the green bracts better. The stems dry to a light brown colour.

AFTER FLOWERING

General   Remove roots once stems have been harvested, but leave a few behind to develop on the plant and finally shed seeds, which will self-sow.

MYOSOTIS

Forget-me-not

FORGET-ME-NOTS flower from early spring after growing slowly during the winter months. Flowers often have yellow 'eyes'.

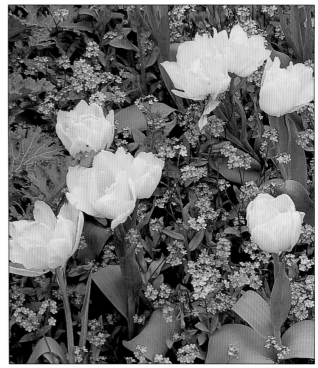

'MONTE CARLO' early double tulips rising up through a haze of forget-me-nots is a springtime classic that is seldom bettered.

FEATURES

Forget-me-nots are useful spring bedding plants, producing swathes of pink, blue or white flowers from April onwards. They go well with bulbs like tulips which push up through the myosotis flowers. Grow as a hardy biennial and use shorter varieties such as 'Blue Ball', reaching 15cm (6in), in winter and spring patio containers. None grow more than 30cm (12in) tall, and these are the ideal choice for spring bedding displays. Available by mail order in autumn as ready-grown young plants.

MYOSOTIS AT A GLANCE

A hardy biennial grown for its small flowers which appear in masses from early spring. Frost hardy to −15°C (5°F).

		RECOMMENDED VARIETIES
JAN	/	*Myosotis sylvatica:*
FEB	/	'Blue Ball'
MAR	/	'Carmine King'
APR	flowering	'Compindi'
MAY	flowers/sow	'Indigo'
JUN	sow	'Light Blue'
JULY	grow on	'Music'
AUG	grow on	'Rosylva'
SEPT	grow on	'Royal Blue'
OCT	plant	'Spring Symphony Mxd'
NOV	/	'Victoria Mixed'
DEC	/	

CONDITIONS

Aspect — Full or dappled sunlight is suitable.

Site — Responds well to soil with plenty of rotted compost or manure mixed in that holds plenty of moisture. When planting containers in autumn ensure good drainage and use a multipurpose compost.

GROWING METHOD

Sowing — Seed is sown direct into the ground May–July, in drills 1cm (½in) deep. Thin seedlings as they develop so plants are eventually 7.5–15cm (3–6in) apart, keep weed free and water copiously in dry spells. Plant into their flowering positions/containers in October and water to settle in.

Feeding — Do not feed after planting in autumn, but scatter a general granular fertiliser around plants in spring as they show signs of growth.

Problems — Powdery mildew can affect leaves but this is generally not worth treating.

FLOWERING

Season — From late winter to early summer.

Cutting — Not suitable for cutting.

AFTER FLOWERING

General — Remove plants to make way for summer bedding, but if you leave a few to die down they will self-sow into the soil.

NEMESIA
Nemesia

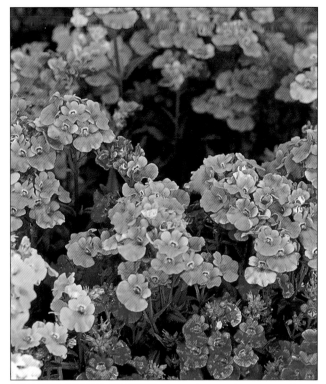

THE TWO-LIPPED FLOWERS of nemesias come in an array of colours and they all have patterns deep in the flower's 'throat'.

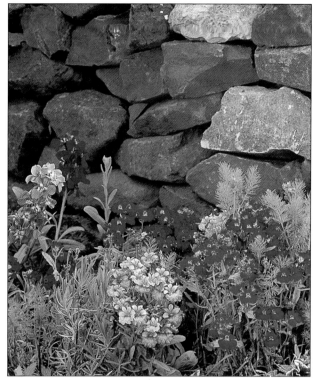

NEMESIAS CARRY THEIR flowers in large, almost flattish heads with individual flowers pointing off in all directions.

FEATURES

No varieties of *Nemesia strumosa* grow more than 30cm (12in) high making them ideal for beds and containers. Grown as a half-hardy annual, flowers can be single colours or bright and varied mixtures. Good as edging for troughs and windowboxes. Very easy to grow.

CONDITIONS

Aspect   Must have full sun to grow successfully.

NEMESIA AT A GLANCE

A half-hardy annual grown for its pretty lipped flowers, used for bedding and patio containers. Frost hardy to 0ºC (32ºF).

		RECOMMENDED VARIETIES
JAN	/	*Nemesia strumosa:*
FEB	/	**Mixed colours**
MAR	sow	'Carnival Mixed'
APR	sow/transplant	'Pastel Mixed'
MAY	harden off/plant	'Sparklers'
JUN	flowering	'Tapestry'
JULY	flowering	**Single colours**
AUG	flowering	'Blue Gem'
SEPT	flowering	'Fire King'
OCT	/	'KLM'
NOV	/	'National Ensign'
DEC	/	

Site   In containers use multipurpose compost with slow-release fertiliser mixed well in. Soil with plenty of organic matter dug in well ahead of planting gives good results, and must be well-drained.

GROWING METHOD

Sowing   Raise plants by sowing in small pots of soil-based seed compost starting in March/April (and repeating every few weeks for a succession of flowers), just covering the seeds. Keep at 15ºC (60ºF) in a light place, and transplant to cell trays when seedlings are large enough to handle. Grow on and harden off in late May before planting after the last frosts, 15–30cm (6–12in) apart. In containers make sure they are not swamped.

Feeding   Give a liquid feed to plants grown as bedding every two weeks, with a hand-held feeder. Regular watering in dry spells is vital.

Problems   Plants may rot off in heavy, wet soils.

FLOWERING

Season   For more flowerheads, pinch out growing tips of plants when they are 10cm (4in) high.

Cutting   Not suited to cutting.

AFTER FLOWERING

General   Pull plants up when finished – this is quite often as they have a short flowering period.

NEMOPHILA
Baby blue eyes

NEMOPHILA MENZIESII *flowers are a brilliant sky-blue with a distinctive paler 'eye', carried over bright green feathery leaves.*

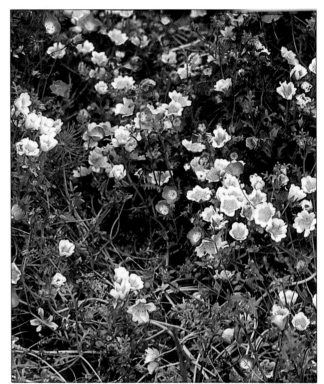

NEMOPHILA *can be grown with other hardy annuals such as limnanthes, the poached egg flower, for a striking colour combination.*

FEATURES

Nemophila is an easy annual sown in autumn or spring. Flowers are sky-blue, white, or black/white. Plants grow to 20cm (8in) high, with feathery leaves and a carpeting habit. Use them in borders, on rockeries and around the edge of containers and windowboxes.

CONDITIONS

Aspect   Needs full sun or part shade to succeed.

NEMOPHILA AT A GLANCE

A hardy spreading annual grown for its flowers for beds, rockeries and container edges. Frost hardy to –15ºC (5ºF).

JAN	/	
FEB	/	
MAR	/	
APR	sow	
MAY	flowers/sow	
JUN	flowering	
JULY	flowering	
AUG	flowering	
SEPT	flowers/sow	
OCT	/	
NOV	/	
DEC	/	

RECOMMENDED VARIETIES

Nemophila menziesii:
(Also listed as *N.insignis*)
  'Baby Blue Eyes'
  'Penny Black'
  'Snowstorm'

Nemophila maculata:
  'Five Spot'

Site   Needs well-drained soil, but mix in well-rotted organic matter before sowing to retain moisture. Nemophila will thrive in most multipurpose composts used in containers.

GROWING METHOD

Sowing   Sow seeds straight into the soil in autumn or spring, in drills 1cm (½in) deep. Seeds sown in autumn will produce young plants which survive the winter and flower earlier. Gradually thin plants out so they are 7.5–15cm (3–6in) apart as flowers appear.

Feeding   On well-prepared soil feeding is unnecessary, although large beds can be fed monthly with a general liquid feed applied through a hand-held feeder. Keep plants watered in dry spells or they may quickly die off.

Problems   Aphids can attack the soft leaves, so use a spray containing permethrin.

FLOWERING

Season   On autumn-sown plants flowers appear from early spring to the first frosts, but appear slightly later on spring-sown plants.

Cutting   Not suitable for use as a cut flower.

AFTER FLOWERING

General   Leave plants to set seed and die back before removing – nemophila self-seeds and plants will appear on their own each spring.

NICOTIANA
Tobacco plant

'DOMINO SALMON PINK' is a popular variety of nicotiana because of its striking colour and sheer flower power. Here in a bedding display it covers the ground and produces tubular, salmon-pink flowers non-stop through the summer. It is also useful for containers.

FEATURES

Not grown for tobacco but for their tubular flowers. Choose from dwarf modern varieties growing 30cm (1ft) tall with upward-facing flowers, for bedding and containers, to *Nicotiana sylvestris* at 1.5m (5ft) for large borders – plant it behind other plants and especially against a dark evergreen background so that the large leaves as well as the flowers are shown off to best effect. Some release scent in the evening, so plant near doors and windows, or grow a few in large tubs that can be moved into the house or conservatory on a warm summer evening. Flowers can be pink to lime-green. A half-hardy annual. Widely available as young plants in a good selection of varieties.

NICOTIANA AT A GLANCE

A half-hardy annual grown for it colourful and often scented flowers, used in bedding/containers. Frost hardy to 0°C (32°F).

JAN /	RECOMMENDED VARIETIES
FEB /	
MAR sow 🖎	*Nicotiana sanderae:*
APR transplant/grow on 🖎	'Domino Mixed'
MAY harden off/plant 🖎	'Domino Salmon Pink'
JUN flowering 🌿	'Havana Appleblossom'
JULY flowering 🌿	'Hippy Mixed'
AUG flowering 🌿	'Lime Green'
SEPT flowering 🌿	'Merlin Peach'
OCT /	
NOV /	*Nicotiana langsdorfii*
DEC /	*Nicotiana sylvestris*

CONDITIONS

Aspect Full sun or light shade. The flowers stay open longer in sun.

Site Grow in well-drained, moisture retentive soil with rotted manure/compost mixed in. For container growing use multipurpose compost.

GROWING METHOD

Sowing Use 9cm (3½in) diameter pots of multipurpose compost, sow the fine seed on the surface in March, but do not cover, and keep in a light place at 21°C (70°F). Tiny seedlings emerge within three weeks. Transplant to cell trays of multipurpose compost or into 9cm (3½in) diameter pots when each young plant has developed 3–4 small leaves. Grow on and harden off in late May, then plant after the last frosts in your area, 30–45cm (12–18in) apart depending on the variety grown.

Feeding Liquid feed weekly outdoors. Add slow-release fertiliser granules to container compost before planting.

Problems Use a spray containing pirimicarb for aphids. Destroy plants attacked by virus, showing any puckered and mottled leaves

FLOWERING

Season Flowers all summer. Nip off dead flowers.
Cutting Not suitable.

AFTER FLOWERING

General Remove plants after first frosts. It is possible to collect seed from *Nicotiana sylvestris* which can then be sown the following spring.

NIGELLA

Love-in-a-mist

'MISS JEKYLL' with semi-double blue flowers is a reliable variety of
Nigella damascena. *Each flower has a feathery 'collar'.*

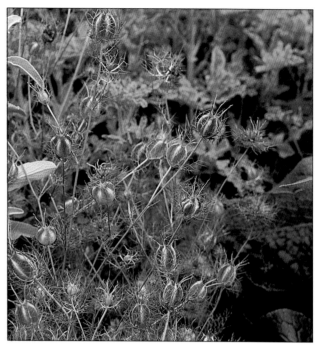

AFTER THE FLOWERS come the curiously attractive seedheads that
give the plant its other common name, devil-in-a-bush.

FEATURES

Love-in-a-mist has fine, feathery leaves, with a
fringe of foliage surrounding and slightly
veiling each of the flowers, hence its common
name. When the spiky seed pods appear it is
also called devil-in-a-bush. Flowers are blue,
pale and deep pink, white or purple. Nigella
grows 45cm (18in) tall and is good for big
drifts in beds or for cutting. Hardy annual.
The variety 'Transformer' has novel seed pods.

CONDITIONS

Aspect   Give it a sunny spot in an open position.

NIGELLA AT A GLANCE

A hardy annual grown for its flowers and its attractive, inflated
seed pods which can be dried. Frost hardy to –15°C (5°F).

JAN	/	
FEB	/	
MAR	sow	
APR	flowers/thin	
MAY	flowering	
JUN	flowering	
JULY	flowering	
AUG	flowering	
SEPT	flowers/sow	
OCT	/	
NOV	/	
DEC	/	

RECOMMENDED VARIETIES

Nigella damascena:
  'Dwarf Moody Blue'
  'Miss Jekyll'
  'Miss Jekyll Alba'
  'Mulberry Rose'
  'Oxford Blue'
  'Persian Jewels'
  'Shorty Blue'

Nigella orientalis:
  'Transformer'

Site   Needs good drainage but isn't too fussy about
soils – rotted organic matter may be dug in
ahead of planting, but this is not essential, and
good results can be had on quite thin, poor
soils as long as it is grown in full sun.

GROWING METHOD

Sowing   Sow in March or September, in short drills
1cm (½in) deep. Thin plants as they grow so
there is about 15–20cm (6–8in) between them
as they begin to produce flower buds. Leave
thinning of autumn-sown plants until spring
in case there are winter losses. Plants can also
be raised in cell trays, sowing 2–3 seeds per
tray and removing all but the strongest
seedling – nigella does not like disturbance.

Feeding   Does not need extra feeding during summer.

Problems   Plants are trouble free.

FLOWERING

Season   Autumn-sown plants flower from late spring,
spring-sown from early summer.

Cutting   Delightful cut flower. Remove foliage from
lower part of stalk to prolong flower life.

AFTER FLOWERING

General   The inflated seed pods that form are useful in
dried flower arrangements. Pick stems after
pods have dried on the plant and hang upside
down in a warm, airy place. Nigella self-seeds
prolifically and will produce masses of
seedlings the following spring. Dead plants
can be pulled up and composted.

OSTEOSPERMUM
Osteospermum

OSTEOSPERMUM flowers are at their best in full sun in an open situation.

CREATE A CARPET OF OSTEOSPERMUM BEDDING in early summer which will continue to flower in flushes until the first frosts. Remember to propagate fresh plants each year.

FEATURES

Many varieties of osteospermum can be bought in spring as young plants, but others can be grown from seed and treated as half-hardy annuals. Growing from seed is a cost-effective way of raising large numbers of plants quickly. Favourite plants can be potted-up in autumn and kept in a well-lit frost-free place over winter, then increased by cuttings in spring. In mild areas plants will often survive the winter outdoors and carry on producing a few flowers except in severe spells. In some catalogues it is listed as dimorphotheca. Plants can grow 30–75cm (12–30in) tall.

CONDITIONS

Aspect Must have full, baking sun for best results.

OSTEOSPERMUM AT A GLANCE

A hardy/half-hardy annual grown for its brightly-coloured daisy-like flowers that appear all summer. Frost hardy to –5°C (23°F).

		RECOMMENDED VARIETIES
JAN	/	**Osteospermum hybrids:**
FEB	/	'Gaiety'
MAR	sow	'Giant Mixed'
APR	sow/transplant	'Glistening White'
MAY	harden off/plant	'Ink Spot'
JUN	flowering	'Potpourri'
JULY	flowering	'Salmon Queen'
AUG	flowering	'Starshine'
SEPT	flowering	'Tetra Pole Star'
OCT	flowering	
NOV	/	
DEC	/	

Site Is not fussy about soil but it must be very well-drained. A sheltered spot with the sun beating down all day is ideal. Plants also perform well in containers and these should be sited in full sun facing south if possible. Use multipurpose compost.

GROWING METHOD

Sowing March/April is the time to sow, sowing seed thinly in 9cm (3½in) diameter pots of soil-based seed compost, and just covering. Germinate at 18°C (64°F) in a bright spot. Seedlings are transplanted to cell trays or individual 9cm (3½in) pots when large enough to handle. Harden off for two weeks and start planting from mid-May onwards.

Feeding Water well to establish and then water only in long spells of hot, dry weather. Extra feeding is unnecessary, but container-grown plants will benefit from occasional liquid feeds given for the benefit of other plants.

Problems Aphids can attack the leaves, flower stalks and buds so choose a spray containing permethrin and wet both sides of the leaves.

FLOWERING

Season Flowers appear from early summer onwards with a peak later on when temperatures reach their highest.

Cutting Flowers are unsuitable for cutting.

AFTER FLOWERING

General After the main flowering give plants an overall clipping to tidy them up and maintain compact growth. Lift and pot favourite plants and keep frost-free over winter.

PAPAVER NUDICAULE
Iceland poppy

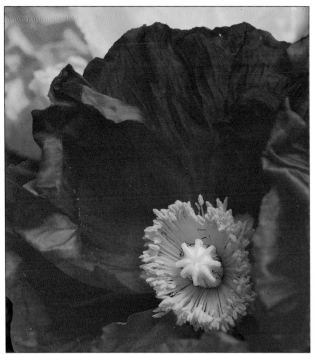

ICELAND POPPY has petals with the texture of crepe paper and a velvety sheen. The centre of the flower is a mass of yellow stamens.

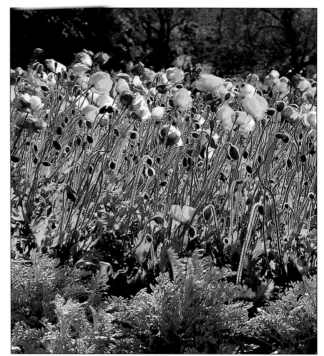

THEIR TALL STEMS mean the flowers of Papaver nudicaule *waft gently in the breeze, and look good like this, massed in bedding.*

FEATURES

Varieties of *Papaver nudicaule* are available in a wide range of colours and range from 25–75cm (10–30in) tall depending on variety. They can be treated as either half-hardy annuals or hardy biennials sown in summer or autumn. Tall varieties are used for cutting. Plants sown early flower from April onwards.

CONDITIONS

Aspect   Can be grown in cool and warm areas.
Site   Poppies need well-drained but moisture-

retentive soil with plenty of rotted organic matter added ahead of planting or sowing.

GROWING METHOD

Sowing   Sow seed outdoors April–June or in September. Scatter the seed thinly along shallow drills 1cm (½in) deep, and rake over with fine soil. Thin out when seedlings are 5cm (2in) high, so that the spacing is ultimately at about 15–30cm (6–12in) intervals by October. Do not disturb the fine roots when thinning out, and always water when finished to settle plants back in. Thin autumn-sown poppies in spring in case of winter losses. For earlier flowers sow in pots at 15°C (60°F) in February and grow in cell-trays, planting in late May.

Feeding   Extra feeding not needed.
Problems   Autumn-sown plants may rot off in heavy soils, so sow in cell trays and keep dry in a coldframe over winter, planting out in spring.

FLOWERING

Season   Flowers appear during early summer and should be picked off as they fade.
Cutting   Excellent cut flower. Pick when buds are just opening. Singe stem ends before arranging.

AFTER FLOWERING

General   Leave a few plants to self-seed, but otherwise pull up after the flowers are finished.

PAPAVER AT A GLANCE

A hardy biennial (or half-hardy annual) grown for its large showy flowers which appear in summer. Frost hardy to –15°C (5°F).

		RECOMMENDED VARIETIES
JAN	/	*Papaver nudicaule:*
FEB	/	**Biennials**
MAR	/	'Large Flowered Special
APR	sow 🌿	Mixture'
MAY	flowers/sow 🌿	'Meadow Pastels'
JUN	flowers/sow 🌿	'Red Sails'
JULY	flowering 🌸	'Wonderland Mixed'
AUG	flowering 🌸	
SEPT	flowers/sow 🌸	**Half-hardy annuals**
OCT	plant 🌿	'Summer Breeze'
NOV	/	
DEC	/	

PAPAVER RHOEAS

Shirley poppy

THE UNOPENED BUDS of Shirley poppies gradually rise up from amongst the leaves before bursting open as the petals unfurl.

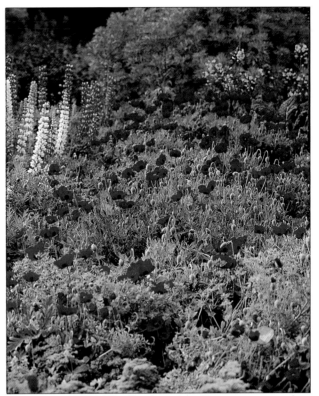

WHEN ALLOWED TO self-seed, poppies will come up amongst other plants. Unwanted plants are very easily pulled out.

FEATURES

Shirley poppies, varieties of *Papaver rhoeas*, generally grow to about 60cm (2ft) high, have a very delicate appearance and come in a wide range of colours including pastels. There are single or double varieties and they look effective in large drifts, but can also be sown in patches 30–60cm (1–2ft) across and used as fillers in mixed borders. Each flower can be 7.5cm (3in) across. A hardy annual.

PAPAVER AT A GLANCE

Shirley poppies are hardy annuals sown in spring or autumn and grown for their large flowers. Frost hardy to –15°C (5°F).

		RECOMMENDED VARIETIES
JAN	/	*Papaver rhoeas:*
FEB	/	'Angels Choir Mixed'
MAR	sow	'Angel Wings Mixed'
APR	sow/thin	'Mother of Pearl'
MAY	flowers/sow	'Selected Single Mixed'
JUN	flowering	'Shirley Double Mixed'
JULY	flowering	'Shirley Single Mixed'
AUG	flowering	
SEPT	flowers/sow	
OCT	/	
NOV	/	
DEC	/	

CONDITIONS

Aspect   Avoid any shade and grow in full sun.
Site   Must have very well-drained soil. Rotted compost or manure should be added to the soil a few weeks before sowing.

GROWING METHOD

Sowing   The fine seed can either be scattered on the soil and simply raked in, and the area marked with a circle of sand, or it can be sown in short 1cm (½in) deep drills. March–May and September are the sowing times. Gradually thin out the seedlings until they are 30cm (12in) apart, but avoid transplanting as they dislike disturbance. If sowing in autumn leave thinning until the following spring in case of winter losses.
Feeding   Extra summer feeding is not required, but water thoroughly should plants start to wilt.
Problems   Trouble-free.

FLOWERING

Season   Autumn-sown plants flower from late spring onwards, while spring-sown flower in summer.
Cutting   Suitable as a cut flower if stems are scalded before arranging.

AFTER FLOWERING

General   Leave a few plants to die down and self-seed.

PELARGONIUM
Bedding geranium

DARK ZONED LEAVES and an enticing range of single and two-tone flower colours are characteristic of 'Avanti Mixed'.

YOU MAY BE SURPRISED to see an ivy-leaved geranium as good as 'Summertime Lilac' coming true from seed.

FEATURES

Better known as geraniums, seed-raised pelargoniums are available with large bright flowerheads for bedding, and also as trailing 'ivy-leaved' types. Seeds are sown January/February and need warmth to succeed, so consider buying them as young plants delivered ready-grown in spring. Varieties for bedding and patio containers grow no more than 30cm (1ft), while ivy-leaved types can spread and trail up to 60cm (2ft). Flowers may be single colours or mixtures – the new 'ripple' varieties are eye-catching. Plant 30–60cm (1–2ft) apart. All are half-hardy annuals.

PELARGONIUM AT A GLANCE

Half-hardy annuals grown for their flowers and also the attractive ivy-like foliage of some varieties. Frost hardy to 0°C (32°F).

JAN	sow	
FEB	sow	
MAR	transplant	
APR	pot on	
MAY	harden off/plant	
JUN	flowering	
JULY	flowering	
AUG	flowering	
SEPT	flowering	
OCT	/	
NOV	/	
DEC	/	

RECOMMENDED VARIETIES

Pelargonium hybrids:
For bedding
'Avanti Mixed'
'Raspberry Ripple'
'Ripple Mixed'
'Sensation Mixed'
'Stardust Mixed'
'Video Mixed'
Ivy-leaved varieties
'Summertime Lilac'
'Summer Showers'

CONDITIONS

Aspect Must be grown in full sun.
Site Well-prepared soil with rotted compost or manure mixed in gives best results. Soil must be well-drained, and when planting up containers use multipurpose compost with slow-release fertiliser mixed in. Bedding geraniums do well in terracotta containers.

GROWING METHOD

Sowing Sow January/February in a heated propagator in a guaranteed temperature of 18°C (64°F). Seedlings appear in 2–3 weeks and can be transplanted to 7.5cm (3in) pots or cell trays of multipurpose compost. Plants must have good light and a temperature of 16–18°C (61–64°F) to grow well. Pot on into 10–12.5cm (4–5in) diameter pots, harden off in late May and plant out after the last frosts.
Feeding Liquid feed bedding plants every 2–3 weeks.
Problems Heavy wet soils can lead to rotting of the stems, so grow in containers. Snap off faded flowerheads to avoid grey mould.

FLOWERING

Season Flowers appear from early summer onwards.
Cutting Not suitable.

AFTER FLOWERING

General Pull up and compost. Favourite plants can be kept dry and frost-free over winter.

PETUNIA
Petunia

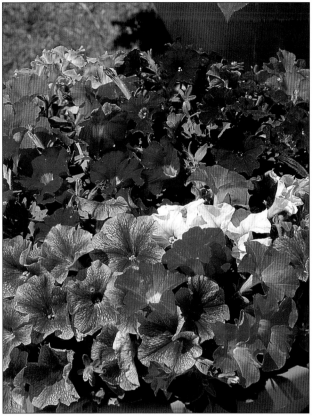

'FANTASY MIXED' is the latest in a new range of 'milliflora' petunias with 2.5cm (1in) flowers, ideal for containers and baskets.

MULTIFLORA PETUNIAS such as 'Summer Morn Mixed' have 5cm (2in) flowers and are suited to large patio tubs and bedding.

FEATURES

Petunias come in a wide range of different types depending on whether they are raised from seed or bought as young plants. Most petunias are perennials grown as half-hardy annuals. Seed-raised varieties fall into the following groups: Millifloras – small flowers 2.5cm (1in) across on compact mounds, for containers and hanging baskets; Multifloras – plenty of 5cm (2in) wide flowers on bushy plants. For bedding and patio containers, with good weather resistance; Floribundas – intermediate in size between multifloras and grandifloras with 7.5cm (3in) flowers; Grandifloras – large trumpet-like 12.5cm (5in) flowers which can bruise in heavy rain and are best for containers in a sheltered position. These all grow 23–30cm (9-12in) tall and can spread up to 60cm (2ft), and are also available as double-flowered varieties. Plant 23–30cm (9–12in) apart. Flower colour varies from single shades to striped, picotee and other variations. Many seed-raised varieties are also widely available as young plants.

An increasing number of petunias are only available as young plants, setting no seed. These are suited to container growing, and include many large double-flowered 'patio' varieties such as 'Able Mabel' and the vigorous Surfinias which can trail to 1.2–1.5m (4–5ft) – see page 78.

PETUNIA AT A GLANCE

A half-hardy annual grown for all-round use in summer bedding, hanging baskets and containers. Frost hardy to 0°C (5°F).

		RECOMMENDED VARIETIES
JAN	sow	*Petunia hybrida:*
FEB	sow	**Millifloras**
MAR	sow/transplant	'Fantasy Mixed'
APR	pot on/grow on	**Multifloras**
MAY	harden off/plant	'Celebrity Bunting'
JUN	flowering	'Summer Morn Mixed'
JULY	flowering	**Floribundas**
AUG	flowering	'Mirage Mixed'
SEPT	flowering	'Niagara Mixture'
OCT	/	**Grandifloras**
NOV	/	'Daddy Mixed'
DEC	/	'Lavender Storm'

CONDITIONS

Aspect Choose a sunny, south-facing situation for petunias in beds and containers.

Site Avoid spots exposed to wind which damages

PETUNIA 'ABLE MABEL' is the first of a revolutionary new type of double-flowered 'patio' petunia available only as young plants.

the flowers. Light, free-draining soil with rotted compost/manure mixed in is best. In containers use multipurpose compost.

GROWING METHOD

Sowing Sowing can take place January–March where a temperature of 21°C (70°F) is possible. Sow onto the level surface of a 9cm (3½in) pot of multipurpose compost, but do not cover seeds, and keep in the light. Seedlings will appear inside two weeks, and should be transplanted to cell trays of multipurpose compost when large enough. Pot on into 9cm (3½in) diameter pots, grow-on and harden off before planting out in early June.

Feeding Give a weekly liquid feed with a high-potash fertiliser to encourage flowers. Mix slow-release fertiliser granules with container compost.

Problems Slugs eat leaves in wet weather – use pellets or slug traps. Plants with mottled, crinkled leaves affected by virus should be destroyed.

FLOWERING

Season Flowers appear all summer. Pick off dead flowers regularly.

Cutting Not suitable.

AFTER FLOWERING

General Remove when flowers end.

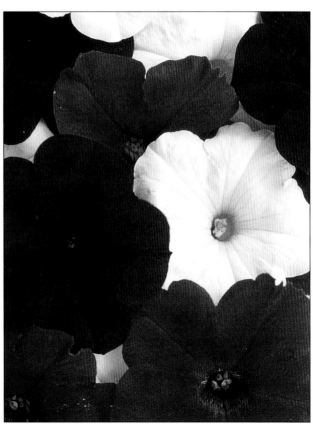

FOR A TOUCH OF the patriotic, 'Celebrity Bunting' is a stunning multiflora variety with blend of red, white and blue flowers.

PHLOX

Annual phlox

'TWINKLE MIXED' is a striking variety of annual phlox growing around 15cm (6in) tall with star-like flowers in various shades.

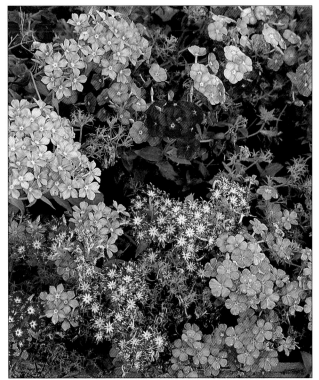

THE FLOWERS OF annual phlox open at their peak to make rounded heads of colour that can completely fill summer containers.

FEATURES

Annual phlox are versatile plants which can be used for bedding, containers and as unique cut flowers. They are half-hardy annuals, growing between 10–45cm (4–18in) tall depending on the variety – taller are better for cutting. Flower colour ranges from the blue of 'Bobby Sox' to the varied shades of 'Tapestry' which is also scented. Several varieties are now available as young plants by mail order. Flowers are long-lived and plants are easy to care for.

PHLOX AT A GLANCE

A half-hardy annual grown for its heads of colourful flowers, for bedding, containers and for cutting. Frost hardy to –5°C (23°F).

JAN	/	
FEB	sow	
MAR	sow/transplant	
APR	grow on	
MAY	harden off/plant	
JUN	flowering	
JULY	flowering	
AUG	flowering	
SEPT	flowering	
OCT	/	
NOV	/	
DEC	/	

RECOMMENDED VARIETIES

Phlox drummondii:
  'African Sunset'
  'Bobby Sox'
  'Bright Eyes'
  'Brilliant'
  'Cecily Old & New Shades'
  'Double Chanel'
  'Phlox of Sheep'
  'Tapestry'
  'Tutti-Frutti'
  'Twinkle Mixed'

CONDITIONS

Aspect   Needs full sun.

Site   Needs well-drained soil with manure or compost mixed in to improve moisture holding. Phlox grow well in multipurpose compost used to fill summer containers.

GROWING METHOD

Sowing   Sow seed in February/March in 9cm (3½in) pots of multipurpose compost, keep at 18°C (64°F), and expect seedlings in 1–3 weeks. Transplant to cell trays or 9cm (3½in) pots, pinch out the tips when 7.5cm (3in) high, and grow on until late May, then harden off and plant after the last frosts in your area.

Feeding   Add slow-release fertiliser granules to compost before planting containers, which should be sufficient. Plants in beds can be given a liquid feed every 2–3 weeks in summer.

Problems   Plants will struggle on heavy soils in a cold spring so delay planting until warmer weather.

FLOWERING

Season   Flowers appear all summer until frosts.

Cutting   Tall varieties are good for cutting and some like 'Tapestry' have a strong, sweet scent.

AFTER FLOWERING

General   Pull up after flowering and compost them.

PORTULACA

Sun plant

DOUBLE-FLOWERED mixed varieties of portulaca come in a wide range of colours, but attractive single colours are also available.

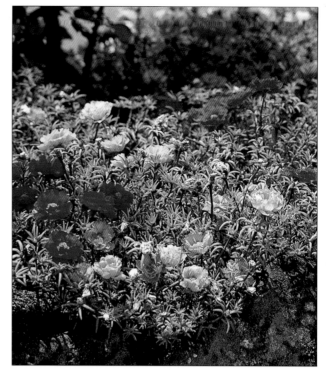

SUN PLANTS can survive the winter in mild seaside gardens, and thrive in the well-drained soil of rockeries.

FEATURES

Commonly known as sun plant, portulaca grows 15cm (6in) high with a spreading habit and succulent leaves. The 5cm (2in) flowers open in sun, although modern varieties open even on dull days. It thrives in poor, dry soils and is easily ruined by too much coddling. A half-hardy annual, for beds, pots and rockeries.

CONDITIONS

Aspect   A hot, sunny position gives the best plants.

PORTULACA AT A GLANCE

Portulaca is a half-hardy annual grown for summer flowers, and gives good results even on thin soils. Frost hardy to 0°C (32°F).

JAN	/	
FEB	/	
MAR	sow	🌱
APR	sow	🌱
MAY	harden off/plant	🌱
JUN	flowering	🌸
JULY	flowering	🌸
AUG	flowering	🌸
SEPT	flowering	🌸
OCT	/	
NOV	/	
DEC	/	

RECOMMENDED VARIETIES

Portulaca grandiflora:
'Cloudbeater Mixed'
'Double Mixed'
'Kariba Mixed'
'Patio Gems'
'Sundance'
'Sundial Mango'
'Sundial Mixed'
'Sundial Peppermint'
'Swanlake'

Site   Unless soil is very well drained plants are prone to rotting. Otherwise plants grow and flower well even where the soil is quite poor – particularly in seaside gardens – as they are adapted to live on little water. Grow them on their own in patio containers, using soil-based potting compost mixed fifty-fifty with sharp grit. Do not feed, and water only when plants start to wilt. Place pots in blazing sunshine.

GROWING METHOD

Sowing   Sow seeds in March/April in 9cm (3½in) pots of soil-based seed compost and germinate at 18°C (64°F) in good light. Keep the seedlings on the dry side and transplant to cell trays of soil-based compost with grit added. Grow on, harden off in late May and plant after frosts, watering in well, then only when plants wilt.

Feeding   Feeding portulaca is not necessary.

Problems   Seedlings will 'damp off' if the compost is kept too wet. If they do fall over, water the pots lightly with a copper-based fungicide.

FLOWERING

Season   Flowers appear throughout summer and into early autumn.

Cutting   Not suitable.

AFTER FLOWERING

General   Pull plants up after the first autumn frosts and add their fleshy remains to the compost heap.

PRIMULA
Polyanthus

Not an F1 hybrid strain, but 'Giant Superb Mixed' polyanthus are tough, large-flowered and full of character.

F1 'Crescendo Mixed' exhibit the clearer, more uniform colours of a highly bred strain, but seed is more expensive.

FEATURES

Polyanthus, a hybrid type of primula, is perfect in patio pots or mass planted in the garden for a stunning spring display. Its very brightly coloured flowers up to 5cm (2in) across, on stems 15–30cm (6–12in) tall, rise from neat clumps of bright green, crinkled leaves. A hardy perennial, it is grown as a hardy biennial for spring bedding and containers. Widely available as young plants.

CONDITIONS

Aspect Grows in full sun or light shade under trees.
Site Needs well-drained soil but with plenty of organic matter mixed in to help retain moisture – plants do not like to be bone dry at any stage while growing. For containers use multipurpose compost with gravel or chunks of polystyrene put in the base.

GROWING METHOD

Sowing Polyanthus seed can be tricky to germinate, and the most important rule is not to keep it too warm. Sow in 9cm (3½in) pots of peat-based seed compost from March–July, barely cover, then stand outside in a covered, shaded spot out of the sun. Seedlings will appear 2–3 weeks later. Transplant to cell trays or 9cm (3½in) pots of peat-based potting compost and, pot on into 12.5cm (5in) pots when roots are well developed. Grow during the summer in a shaded spot and do not let them dry out. Plant out in October where flowers are required the following spring, in beds or containers with bulbs and other plants.
Feeding Feed fortnightly with liquid feed in summer.
Problems Slugs can devour leaves so use slug pellets. Never bury the crowns or plants may rot.

FLOWERING

Season Flowers appear earlier in mild winters and carry on throughout spring.
Cutting Charming in spring posies.

AFTER FLOWERING

General Polyanthus taken from spring displays can be planted in borders where they will form large clumps and flower regularly every spring.

PRIMULA AT A GLANCE

A hardy biennial grown for its bright spring flowers for use in bedding and containers. Frost hardy to –15°C (5°F).

JAN	/	
FEB	flowering	RECOMMENDED VARIETIES
MAR	flowers/sow	**Primula hybrids:**
APR	flowers/sow	'Crescendo Mixed'
MAY	flowers/sow	'Dobies Superb Mixed'
JUN	sow/grow	'Giant Superb Mixed'
JULY	sow/grow	'Gold Lace'
AUG	grow	'Harlequin Mixed'
SEPT	grow	'Heritage Mixed'
OCT	plant	'Large Flowered Mixed'
NOV	/	'Pacific Giants Mixed'
DEC	/	'Spring Rainbow Mixed'
		'Unwins Superb Mixed'

RANUNCULUS
Persian buttercup

DOUBLE FLOWERS are characteristic of Ranunculus asiaticus varieties, and are all clear and bright as in this yellow-flowered plant.

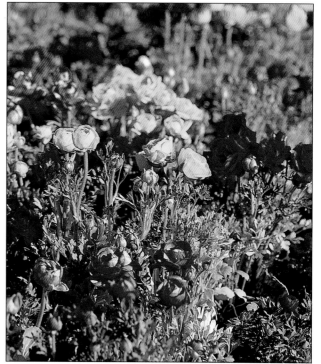

YOU CAN PLANT ranunculus in beds in spring when the worst of the winter is over, where they will give a bright show of colour.

FEATURES

Hardy varieties of *Ranunculus asiaticus* are sown in late summer and autumn for flowers during winter and spring. Seed-raised plants reach around 20–25cm (8–10in) tall. Flowers are double. Young plants are sometimes offered in spring catalogues for delivery in late summer/autumn ready for potting up. Add them to your spring containers as they come into flower – they will grow happily in a cold greenhouse or porch.

RANUNCULUS AT A GLANCE

A half-hardy annual grown for its large, double, buttercup-like flowers which appear in spring. Frost hardy to –5°C (23°F).

JAN	grow 🌱	**RECOMMENDED VARIETIES**
FEB	grow 🌱	**Ranunculus hybrids:**
MAR	flowering 🌸	'Bloomingdale Mixture'
APR	flowering 🌸	
MAY	flowering 🌸	
JUN	/	
JULY	/	
AUG	sow ✏️	
SEPT	sow/transplant ✏️	
OCT	sow/grow ✏️	
NOV	grow 🌱	
DEC	grow 🌱	

CONDITIONS

Aspect Give as much sun as possible, and move containers into shelter during stormy or very frosty weather to stop damage to the flowers.

Site Use a multipurpose compost for potting up and potting on, and for filling containers if you are creating an 'instant' display as the plants come into flower from early spring.

GROWING METHOD

Sowing Sow seed August–October in 9cm (3½in) pots of peat-based compost, just covering the seeds. Stand outdoors in shade and keep moist – if they get too hot the seeds will not come up. When seedlings appear, bring them into full light and transplant when large enough into 10cm (4in) pots. Grow outdoors until frosts start, then move under protection at night and out during the day. A cool porch is useful. In winter keep plants dry under cover.

Feeding Feeding is not usually required.

Problems No special problems.

FLOWERING

Season Late winter and throughout spring.

Cutting Cut when the buds are just unfurling.

AFTER FLOWERING

General Plants will survive most winters in a sheltered spot and can be planted out in borders.

RESEDA
Mignonette

MIGNONETTE FLOWERS *individually are insignificant, but the strong sweet fragrance is striking and well worth the effort of sowing.*

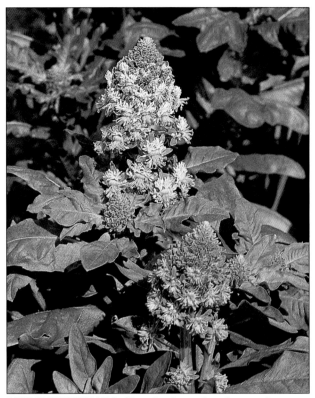

THE FLOWERHEADS *of* Reseda odorata *branch out as they develop. Sow along path edges so the fragrance can be enjoyed.*

FEATURES

Mignonette has greenish, pink, red, yellow, or coppery flowers and grows to 30cm (12in). It is not particularly striking but is grown mainly for its strong, fruity fragrance – grow it near doors, windows, in patio pots, and near sitting areas to appreciate the qualities of this easily grown hardy annual. It makes a good addition to cottage-style borders.

RESEDA AT A GLANCE

An easily grown hardy annual grown for its highly fragrant spikes of summer flowers. Frost hardy to –15C (5°F).

Month	Activity	Recommended Varieties
JAN	/	
FEB	/	*Reseda odorata:*
MAR	sow	'Crown Mixture'
APR	sow/thin out	
MAY	thin out	'Machet'
JUN	flowering	'Sweet Scented'
JULY	flowering	
AUG	flowering	
SEPT	flowers/sow	
OCT	sow	
NOV	/	
DEC	/	

CONDITIONS

Aspect   Needs full sun.
Site   Needs well-drained soil – dig in organic matter and add lime to acid soils.

GROWING METHOD

Sowing   Seed is sown directly into the ground in short drills 1cm (½in) deep, 15cm (6in) apart. Thin seedlings to 15cm (6in) apart. Sowing can take place in March/April or September/October. Autumn-sown plants need protecting with cloches during cold spells, and should not be thinned until spring. For pots, sow a pinch of seeds in each unit of a cell tray and thin to 2–3 seedlings, grow on and plant up when ready – reseda does not like root disturbance.

Feeding   Extra feeding is not usually necessary
Problems   Free of troubles.

FLOWERING

Season   Flowers appear from late spring on autumn-sown plants, later on spring-sown.
Cutting   Cut when just a few flowers are opening. Dried flowers retain their fragrance.

AFTER FLOWERING

General   Pull plants up when they are past their best, but leave a few to produce seeds and self-sow.

RICINUS
Castor oil plant

THE VARIETY 'IMPALA' is an excellent choice is you want bold, dark leaves for a dramatic show, growing 1.2m (4ft) tall.

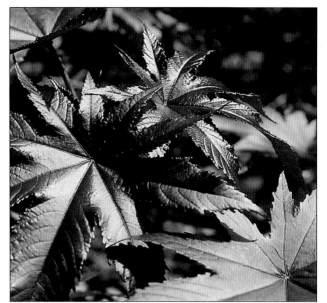

BY MIDSUMMER the leaves of ricinus will have formed a dense canopy when grown in beds and planted 60–90cm (2–3ft) apart.

FEATURES

A striking and memorable plant grown for its large, lobed, exotic-looking leaves, which are used for bedding, borders and large tubs and containers. The often brightly-coloured summer flowers are followed by spiny seed clusters. By nature an evergreen shrub, ricinus is fast growing and plants are raised fresh from seed each year – in long hot summers they can reach 1.8m (6ft) by 1m (3ft) tall and wide. Annual flowering climbers like thunbergia or ipomoea will climb its stems, their bright orange/blue flowers contrasting with the often deeply coloured ricinus foliage. All parts of the plant are poisonous, especially the seeds. Treat as a half-hardy annual and scrap plants at the end of the summer.

RICINUS AT A GLANCE

A half-hardy annual with large, exotic leaves in a range of colours, and prized as bold bedder. Frost hardy to 0°C (32°F).

JAN	/	
FEB	/	
MAR	sow	
APR	pot on	
MAY	harden/plant	
JUN	leaves	
JULY	leaves	
AUG	leaves	
SEPT	leaves	
OCT	/	
NOV	/	
DEC	/	

RECOMMENDED VARIETIES

Ricinus communis:
  'Carmencita'
  'Carmencita Pink'
  'Impala'
  'Gibbsonii'
  'Red Spire'
  'Zanzibarensis'

CONDITIONS

Aspect Must have full sun. In northern areas choose a sheltered, south-facing spot.

Site Soil should be well-drained with plenty of rotted compost or manure dug in. Use loam-based or multipurpose potting compost in containers. In windy spots, stake plants.

GROWING METHOD

Sowing Soak the hard seeds overnight in warm water, then sow individually in 9cm (3½in) diameter pots of soil-based compost, 5cm (2in) deep in March, and keep at 21°C (70°F). Seedlings appear within three weeks. Pot on into 12.5cm (5in) diameter pots when 15cm (6in) tall. In beds plant 1–1.8m (3–6ft) apart after the last frosts.

Feeding Apply liquid feed weekly from early summer, or mix slow-release fertiliser with the potting compost before planting.

Problems Red spider mite attacks leaves. Wetting the leaves thoroughly every day can help, or use a spray containing bifenthrin.

FLOWERING

Season The large leaves keep coming all summer long and are joined later by clusters of flowers which rise up above them.

Cutting Leaves are useful for flower arranging, but avoid getting the sap on skin.

AFTER FLOWERING

General Plants are usually killed by the first frosts of autumn. Ripe seeds can be saved for sowing again the following spring.

RUDBECKIA
Coneflower

RUDBECKIA 'RUSTIC DWARFS' is one of the best seed-raised foms. It produces a range of flower colours, yellow through to red, with dark firey centres or cones. Rudbeckia is also known as black-eyed Susan.

FEATURES

Rudbeckia or coneflower is one of the easiest and most versatile of all annuals. Try tiny 'Toto' at just 20cm (8in) in patio containers, or, where space allows, 'Indian Summer' at 90cm (3ft). There are intermediate varieties in many shades, and some have an unusual and striking green centre or 'cone'. Half-hardy.

CONDITIONS

Aspect	Rudbeckias need full sun to succeed.
Site	Soil must be well-drained but have rotted

RUDBECKIA AT A GLANCE

Grown for its large, showy flowers, rudbeckia grows well in bedding/containers and is half-hardy. Frost hardy to –15°C (5°F).

JAN	/	**RECOMMENDED VARIETIES**
FEB	sow	*Rudbeckia hirta:*
MAR	sow/transplant	**Tall varieties**
APR	grow on	'Goldilocks'
MAY	harden off/plant	'Indian Summer'
JUN	flowering	'Marmalade'
JULY	flowering	'Rustic Dwarfs'
AUG	flowering	**Short varieties**
SEPT	flowering	'Becky Mixed'
OCT	flowering	'Sonora'
NOV	/	'Toto'
DEC	/	**Green cone/centre**
		'Irish Eyes'

compost or manure worked in before planting out. For container growing use multipurpose compost with slow-release fertiliser mixed in.

GROWING METHOD

Sowing	Sow February/March in pots of multipurpose compost and keep at 18°C (64°F). Seedlings appear in 1–2 weeks and are fast growing, soon ready for transplanting into cell trays or 9cm (3½in) pots. Pot larger varieties on into 12.5cm (5in) pots when roots fill the pots, and grow outdoors from mid-May, covering with garden fleece at night if frosty. Plant 15–60cm (6–24in) apart after the last frosts.
Feeding	Rudbeckias are strong growers and need little extra feeding in the soil, but give container plants a fortnightly liquid feed unless fertiliser granules are mixed with the compost first.
Problems	Slugs can attack after planting so protect with slug pellets or a barrier of sharp grit.

FLOWERING

Season	Summer is the peak period for flowering and regular removal of faded heads should ensure some colour right up to the first autumn frosts.
Cutting	Good for cutting because of its strong stems. 'Sonora' is especially good, and 'Indian Summer' has flowers up to 20cm (8in) across.

AFTER FLOWERING

General	Pull plants up and use for compost when they have been knocked down by frosts.

SALPIGLOSSIS
Salpiglossis

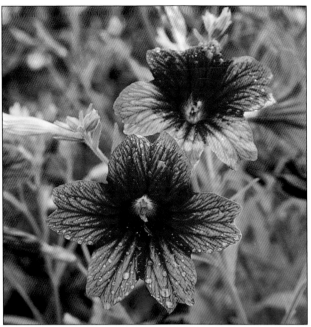

PETAL VEINING in salpiglossis is intricate and gives rise to the common name of painted tongue. Many different colours are available.

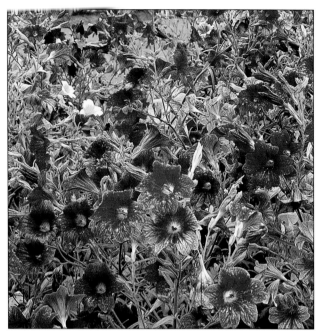

THE EXOTIC LOOK can be had by growing mixed salpiglossis in large bold drifts. Choose a variety like 'Casino' at just 45cm (18in).

FEATURES

Salpiglossis blooms are trumpet-shaped and come in a range of colours, all with patterned veins. They must have shelter and warmth to do well, so for guaranteed success use them in containers on sunny patios or in south-facing beds protected from the wind. Choose mixed colours or try dark brown 'Chocolate Pot', striking 'Kew Blue' or even the blue/yellow mix 'Chili Blue'. Half-hardy, growing up to 60cm (2ft). Available as young plants.

CONDITIONS

Aspect   Must be in full sun and protected from wind.

SALPIGLOSSIS AT A GLANCE

Half-hardy annual grown for its exotic flowers but needing a sheltered spot in the garden to do well. Frost hardy to 0ºC (32ºF).

JAN	/	
FEB	sow	
MAR	transplant/sow	
APR	grow on	
MAY	harden off/plant	
JUN	flowering	
JULY	flowering	
AUG	flowering	
SEPT	flowering	
OCT	/	
NOV	/	
DEC	/	

RECOMMENDED VARIETIES

Salpiglossis sinuata:
'Batik'
'Bolero'
'Carnival'
'Casino'
'Chili Blue'
'Chocolate Pot'/
'Chocolate Royale'
'Festival Mixed'
'Flamenco Mixed'
'Kew Blue'
'Triumph Mixed'

Site   Drainage must be good or plants will rot – prepare soil by digging in plenty of rotted manure or compost well before planting. Use multipurpose compost in containers and make sure there is a 5cm (2in) layer of gravel in the base to guarantee good drainage. Support plants with twigs or short canes as they get taller and begin to flower.

GROWING METHOD

Sowing   Sow in a 9cm (3½in) pot in February/March and just cover the fine seed. Keep at a temperature of 24ºC (75ºF) in a light place, and when seedlings are large enough transplant to cell trays or 9cm (3½in) pots. Grow on and then harden off in late May before planting after frosts in early June. Plants are quite brittle so handle carefully.

Feeding   Little additional feeding should be needed for plants in bedding displays, but containers can be liquid fed every two weeks if slow-release fertiliser is not used, otherwise just water well.

Problems   The flowers are very prone to bruising and damage by wind and heavy rain, so pick off casualties after unsettled spells to avoid an attack by grey mould which can cause rotting.

FLOWERING

Season   Flowers appear throughout the summer.
Cutting   Weak stemmed as a cut flower.

AFTER FLOWERING

General   Pull up after autumn frosts and compost.

SALVIA
Scarlet sage

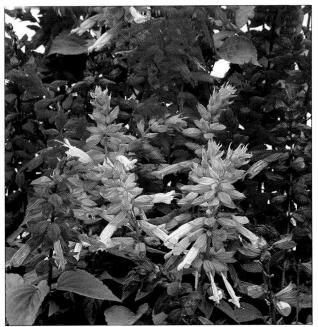

IF BRIGHT RED hurts your eyes, try one of the newer mixed salvia varieties containing more subtle shades of mauve, pink and salmon.

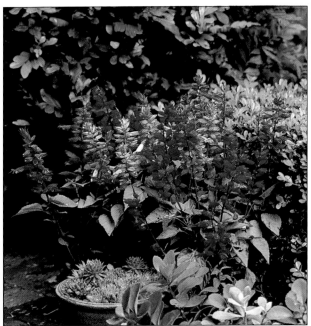

TO APPRECIATE SALVIAS to the full, grow them in wide, low pans on the patio and keep fed and watered throughout the summer.

FEATURES

Salvia splendens or scarlet sage is used in bold groups in bedding and is also a useful container plant. Most varieties grow to 30cm (1ft) with similar spread, but giants like 'Rambo' with red flowers reach 60cm (2ft). Flowers are long and tubular, in spikes, and colours other than the typical vibrant red include pink, mauve, salmon, pastel shades and even bicolours such as 'Salsa Bicolour Mixed' with white tipped blooms. Choose single colours or mixtures. Grown as a half-hardy annual but is in fact a perennial plant. Several varieties are usually available as young plants by mail order.

SALVIA AT A GLANCE

A half-hardy annual grown for its often bright and brash flowers which are useful for bedding and pots. Frost hardy to 0°C (32°F).

		RECOMMENDED VARIETIES
JAN	/	*Salvia splendens:*
FEB	sow	'Blaze of Fire'
MAR	sow/transplant	'Firecracker'
APR	grow on	'Orange Zest'
MAY	harden off/plant	'Phoenix Mixed'
JUN	flowering	'Phoenix Purple'
JULY	flowering	'Rambo'
AUG	flowering	'Red Arrow'
SEPT	flowering	'Scarlet King'
OCT	/	'Scarlet O'Hara'
NOV	/	'Sizzler Burgundy'
DEC	/	'Sizzler Mixed'

CONDITIONS

Aspect Plant salvias in a warm spot in full sun.
Site Tolerates a wide range of soils but drainage must be very good or plants may rot. Mix in well-rotted compost or manure before planting and use multipurpose compost for filling patio pots and windowboxes. Make sure plastic containers have drainage holes, and drill some if necessary, then put in 5cm (2in) of gravel.

GROWING METHOD

Sowing February/March is the time to sow salvias, using 9cm (3½in) pots of multipurpose compost. Lightly cover seeds and keep in a bright spot such as a windowsill at 18°C (64°F); expect seedlings in 2–3 weeks. Transplant into cell trays or 10cm (4in) pots, grow on, harden off in late May before planting 15–30cm (6–12in) apart.
Feeding Liquid feed plants in beds monthly. Mix slow-release fertiliser with compost at planting.
Problems Heavy wet soils can cause root rots, and slugs and snails will eat leaves of young plants in damp and wet spells. Use slug pellets.

FLOWERING

Season Cut faded spikes right back and plants will often produce a succession of flowers right into the late summer months.
Cutting Not suitable.

AFTER FLOWERING

General Dig out when over and compost.

SCABIOSA

Sweet scabious

FOR A COTTAGE GARDEN feel make sure you include pink scabious heads with other plants such as this white candytuft.

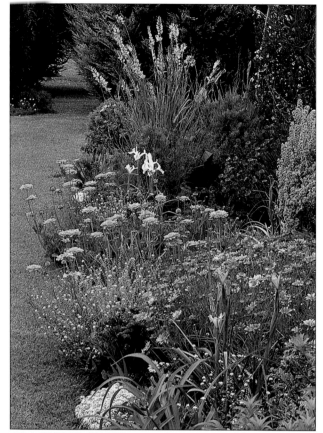

AS A BORDER FILLER sweet scabious is very useful and can be sown in any gaps during March and April for flowers from June.

FEATURES

Also known as pincushion flower, varieties of *Scabiosa atropurpurea* are easily grown hardy annuals. The rounded flowerheads come in shades of blue, mauve, purple, pink, white or crimson. Growing to 30–50cm (12–20in) with tall, wire-like stems, scabious is best used for growing in big patches and for use as a filler in between other plants in a mixed or cottage-garden style border. A related variety, 'Paper Moon', is grown for its spherical heads of dry bracts which follow the flowers.

SCABIOSA AT A GLANCE

An easily-grown hardy annual with rounded flowerheads that are useful in borders and for cutting. Frost hardy to -15°C (5°F).

JAN	/	
FEB	/	
MAR	sow	
APR	sow/thin out	
MAY	thin out	
JUN	flowers/thin out	
JULY	flowering	
AUG	flowering	
SEPT	flowering	
OCT	/	
NOV	/	
DEC	/	

RECOMMENDED VARIETIES

Scabiosa atropurpurea:
'Ace of Spades'
'Border Hybrids'
'Dobies Giant Hybrids'
'Double Mixed'
'Dwarf Double Mixed'
'Tall Double'

Scabiosa stellata:
'Paper Moon'/'Ping Pong'/'Drum Stick'

CONDITIONS

Aspect
Site
Prefers full sun and protection from wind. Well-drained soil is best – prepare ground by digging in organic matter well in advance.

GROWING METHOD

Sowing
Sow outdoors March/April where plants are to flower, in short drills 1cm (½in) deep. Thin plants to 15–30cm (6–12in) apart by early summer, and keep weed free.

Feeding
Extra feeding in summer is not needed.

Problems
No particular problems.

FLOWERING

Season
Flowers appear from mid- to late summer.

Cutting
Excellent and long-lasting cut flower.

AFTER FLOWERING

General
Pull plants up when they are over.

SCHIZANTHUS

Poor man's orchid

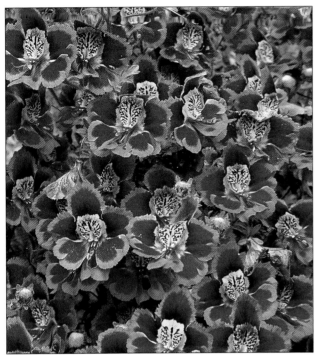

THE EXOTIC APPEAL of schizanthus earns it the common name of poor man's orchid. Each flower has a network of darker veining.

THE FINELY DIVIDED leaves are the perfect foil for the large heads of flowers. Varieties like 'Pierrot' are distinctly dome-shaped.

FEATURES

Also known as butterfly flower, schizanthus is stunning when used in bedding or in large pots and troughs. It has fern-like foliage and brilliantly coloured, trumpet-shaped flowers in rich tones of pink, purple, magenta, pastels or white. The flower throats are intricately patterned. Only the dwarf varieties reaching 20–30cm (8–12in) are worth growing outdoors, and they must have shelter from strong winds and the hot midday sun. Schizanthus is a half-hardy annual and very sensitive to even slight frost.

SCHIZANTHUS AT A GLANCE

A half-hardy annual grown in containers on patios or in south-facing borders for summer flowers. Frost hardy to 0°C (32°F).

JAN	/	
FEB	/	
MAR	sow	
APR	transplant	
MAY	harden off	
JUN	plant/flowers	
JULY	flowering	
AUG	flowering	
SEPT	flowering	
OCT	/	
NOV	/	
DEC	/	

RECOMMENDED VARIETIES

Schizanthus pinnatus:
  'Angel Wings Mixed'
  'Disco'
  'My Lovely'
  'Pierrot'
  'Star Parade'

CONDITIONS

Aspect   Must be sheltered and have full sun.
Site   Well-drained soil that has been enriched before planting with rotted manure or compost produces strong plants. Peat- or coir-based potting compost guarantees good results when containers are used.

GROWING METHOD

Sowing   Seeds are sown in March at 16°C (61°F) in small pots of peat- or coir-based seed compost, and seedlings appear after 1–2 weeks. Transplant to cell trays or 9cm (3½in) pots, grow through spring and plant after hardening off, in early June. Space plants 15–30cm (6–12in) apart. Pinch out growing tips when 10cm (4in) high to make bushy plants.
Feeding   Liquid feed monthly, and water containers regularly – if slow-release fertiliser was added to the compost extra feeding is not necessary.
Problems   No special problems.

FLOWERING

Season   Flowers reach a peak in mid- to late summer and keep coming if faded stems are removed.
Cutting   Not usually used as a cut flower.

AFTER FLOWERING

General   The soft leafy plants soon break down when put on the compost heap.

SENECIO
Dusty miller

A WHITE WOOLLY LAYER covering the otherwise green leaves gives Senecio cineraria *its attractive silvery-grey appearance.*

OVERWINTERED PLANTS will keep on growing the following season, get larger and also produce heads of bright yellow flowers.

FEATURES

Grown for its attractive silver-grey foliage, *Senecio cineraria* is often found listed under 'cineraria' in seed catalogues. Use in bedding schemes and as a foliage container plant. Plants grow up to 30cm (12in) tall and wide in summer, but if left outdoors over winter can be twice that if the yellow flowerheads are allowed to develop. Usually grown as a half-hardy annual, senecio is naturally an evergreen, eventually developing a tough woody base.

SENECIO AT A GLANCE

Prized for its silver-grey leaves and grown as a foliage bedding plant and for using in containers. Frost hardy to –5°C (23°F).

JAN	/	
FEB	sow	RECOMMENDED VARIETIES
MAR	sow	*Senecio cineraria:*
APR	transplant	**Fine, divided leaves**
MAY	harden off/plant	'Dwarf Silver'
JUN	leaves	'Silver Dust'
JULY	leaves	
AUG	leaves	**Rounded leaves**
SEPT	leaves	'Cirrus'
OCT	leaves	
NOV	/	
DEC	/	

CONDITIONS

Aspect   Must have full sun.
Site   Well-drained soil is needed, but plants do well in light, sandy soils, especially in seaside gardens. Use multipurpose compost in pots.

GROWING METHOD

Sowing   Start plants in February/March at 20°C (68°F), by sowing seed in a small pot of compost and just covering. Expect seedlings after 1–2 weeks and keep in good light. Keep compost slightly on the dry side to avoid 'damping off'. Transplant to cell trays or 9cm (3½in) pots, grow on, then harden off at the end of April and plant in May, 30cm (12in) apart.

Feeding   Planted containers need liquid feed every two weeks, and regular watering. Plants stand dry spells outside but water them if they wilt.

Problems   If seedlings collapse, give a light watering with a copper-based fungicide.

FLOWERING

Season   The silvery leaves are attractive all summer.
Cutting   Foliage can be used in arrangements.

AFTER FLOWERING

General   Pull up and compost in autumn. In many areas plants will survive the winter if left and produce bigger clumps of leaves and flowers.

SOLENOSTEMON

Coleus or flame nettle

'BLACK DRAGON' is a modern variety of coleus with black-edged, pinkish-red leaves, and is useful for specific colour themes.

LEAF COLOUR is apparent from an early age with solenostemon, making it possible to group the different colours when planting.

FEATURES

Look under 'coleus' in seed catalogues for a wide range of varieties of this striking foliage plant. A half-hardy annual, solenostemon is a valuable bedding and container plant with large multicoloured leaves that add a certain 'tropical' and eccentric element to summer gardens. As well as mixtures, dark-leaved varieties like 'Black Dragon' can be put to use in colour-themed displays. Size range is 20–45cm (8–18in) depending on variety, and it is important to remove all flowerheads as they appear or the plant will stop producing leaves. Varieties are available as young plants.

CONDITIONS

Aspect   Flame nettles need full sun to really thrive and also need shelter from persistent winds.

Site   Well-drained soil that has had plenty of rotted

manure or compost mixed in before planting produces strong plants with good colour. Where they are grown in patio containers use multipurpose compost with slow-release fertiliser granules added at planting time.

GROWING METHOD

Sowing   March is the time to sow seed, in 9cm (3½in) pots of multipurpose compost, just scattering the seed on the surface – don't cover. Keep at 24°C (75°F) where they get bright light. Seedlings grow slowly but when they are large enough, transplant to 9cm (3½in) pots or large cell trays. Pinch out the growing tip when plants are 7.5cm (3in) tall to encourage bushy growth and the maximum number of leaves. Harden off in late May and plant after frosts, 15–30cm (6–12in) apart.

Feeding   Liquid feeding every two weeks during summer maintains vigorous leaf growth. If slow-release fertiliser has been used, feed only monthly with half-strength liquid feed.

Problems   Slugs and snails attack young plants, so protect with slug pellets or a barrier of sharp grit around each plant.

FLOWERING

Season   All flowers should be removed as soon as they appear to encourage maximum leaf growth. Plants generally stay colourful until frosts.

Cutting   Not suitable.

AFTER FLOWERING

General   Favourite plants can be lifted and potted up in autumn, and kept dry over winter in a frost-free greenhouse or cool room. Take cuttings from these plants in spring.

SOLENOSTEMON AT A GLANCE

A half-hardy annual grown for its brightly-coloured leaves which are used in bedding and for patio pots. Frost hardy to 0°C (32°F).

		RECOMMENDED VARIETIES
JAN	/	*Solenostemon scutellarioides:*
FEB	/	'Black Dragon'
MAR	sow	'Camelot Mixed'
APR	transplant	'Dragon Sunset &
MAY	harden off/plant	Volcano, Mixed'
JUN	leaves	'Fairway'
JULY	leaves	'Flame Dancers'
AUG	leaves	'Magic Lace'
SEPT	leaves	'Salmon Lace'
OCT	/	'Top Crown'
NOV	/	'Wizard Mixed'
DEC	/	

TAGETES
Marigold

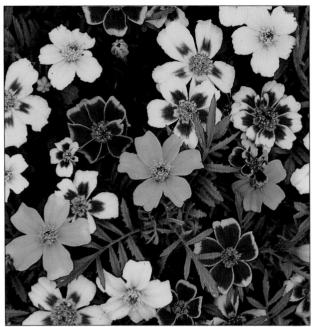

THESE SINGLE-FLOWERED French marigolds are much daintier than their loud cousins with larger double flowers.

SINGLE FLOWER COLOURS are useful in colour-themed displays and this double-flowered French marigold would go well with blues.

FEATURES

The marigold 'family' is made up of African and French types, and tagetes. All are easily grown half-hardy annuals and their flowers are among some of the loudest available – bright oranges, reds, yellows and bronzes that set borders and containers alight. Plant size varies from 15cm (6in) dwarfs to 90cm (3ft) giants, and there are unusual flower colours such as 'Vanilla' and even bright stripey-petalled varieties such as 'Mr Majestic'. Use them for bold bedding or as reliable patio container plants. Flowers can be single, semi or fully double and up to 7.5cm (3in) across. Many varieties are also available as young plants.

TAGETES AT A GLANCE

A half-hardy annual grown for its bright flowers which are ideal for bedding and patio pots/troughs. Frost hardy to 0°C (32°F).

		RECOMMENDED VARIETIES
JAN	/	**African marigolds**
FEB	sow 🌱	'Inca Mixed'
MAR	sow 🌱	'Shaggy Maggy'
APR	sow/transplant 🌱	'Vanilla'
MAY	harden off/plant 🌱	**French marigolds**
JUN	flowering ✿	'Boy O'Boy Mixed'
JULY	flowering ✿	'Mischief Mixed'
AUG	flowering ✿	'Mr Majestic'
SEPT	flowering ✿	*Tagetes tenuifolia:*
OCT	/	'Lemon Gem'
NOV	/	'Red Gem'
DEC	/	

CONDITIONS

Aspect Must have a sunny position.
Site Marigolds are not too fussy about soils, but mixing in rotted compost before planting helps keep soil moist. For container growing use multipurpose compost with slow-release fertiliser granules mixed well in. Tall varieties of African marigold need shelter from wind.

GROWING METHOD

Sowing All marigolds can be sown February–April, but a May sowing on a windowsill will also be successful as they are fast growers and soon catch up. Just cover the large seeds with compost and keep at 21°C (70°F). Seedlings will appear in a week and can be transplanted to cell trays. Grow on, harden off in late May and plant after frosts. Nip off any flower buds that appear before and two weeks after planting.
Feeding Fortnightly liquid feeding keeps plants in beds going strong. Keep containers well watered.
Problems Slugs and snails can strip plants overnight so protect with slug pellets in wet/warm spells.

FLOWERING

Season Early sowings produce earlier flowers and vice-versa. Late sowings provide handy colour in late summer and if grown in pots, plants can be used to revive flagging summer containers.
Cutting African marigolds are useful for cutting.

AFTER FLOWERING

General Pull plants up when finished and compost.

THUNBERGIA
Black-eyed Susan

BLACK-EYED SUSAN is one of the brightest and showiest of all the annual climbers, and readily entwines the stems of other plants. It hates having its roots disturbed so sow seeds straight into small pots, and pot 2–3 plants on together when necessary. Plant out after frosts.

FEATURES

The flowers of thunbergia can be orange, yellow or white, and sometimes the black eye is missing altogether. Grow as a half-hardy annual for indoors and out. Outdoors, grow up wigwams of 1.5m (5ft) canes, either in borders, or large tubs for a moveable display of colour. In hanging baskets thunbergia soon entwines the chains, making an effective camouflage. In patio tubs train plants up through other tall annuals like ricinus and sunflowers, or plant them around the base of outdoor plants in early summer. In colder areas grow plants in the conservatory or porch to guarantee a good show of flowers. Seed pods tend to set very easily which reduces the ability of the plant to keep flowering, so nip these off regularly.

THUNBERGIA AT A GLANCE

A half-hardy annual climber flowering in summer for patio containers, baskets and bedding. Frost hardy to 0°C (32°F).

JAN	/	RECOMMENDED VARIETIES
FEB	/	
MAR	sow	*Thunbergia alata:*
APR	pot on/grow on	'Susie Mixed'
MAY	harden/plant out	
JUN	flowers	
JULY	flowers	
AUG	flowers	
SEPT	flowers	
OCT	/	
NOV	/	
DEC	/	

CONDITIONS

Aspect A south-facing spot in full sun is essential. In conservatories direct hot sun should be avoided or the leaves may be scorched.

Site In containers use multipurpose compost with slow-release fertiliser added. Well-drained, moisture retentive soil, with rotted manure or compost is needed outdoors.

GROWING METHOD

Sowing Soak seeds overnight then sow three to a 9cm (3½in) diameter pot in March. Germinate at 18°C (64°F). Germination is erratic and seedlings may take a month to emerge. A small wigwam of canes will support the shoots. Grow several plants on in large pots during May, then harden off and plant after the last frosts. They dislike root disturbance.

Feeding Liquid feed once a week in summer.

Problems Red spider mite attacks leaves. Wet the leaves daily or use a spray containing pirimiphos-methyl. Indoors use the predator phytoseiulus. Whitefly will feed on the leaves and cause sticky 'honeydew'. Use a spray containing permethrin or the natural encarsia indoors.

FLOWERING

Season Flowers appear all summer and the flowering period is extended when plants are grown under some form of protection.

Cutting Not suitable.

AFTER FLOWERING

General Nip off faded flowers. Remove outdoor plants after frosts and add to the compost heap.

TITHONIA
Mexican sunflower

THE DAHLIA-LIKE FLOWERS of tithonia have an 'exotic' feel to them and each one can be up to 7.5cm (3in) across, on strong stems.

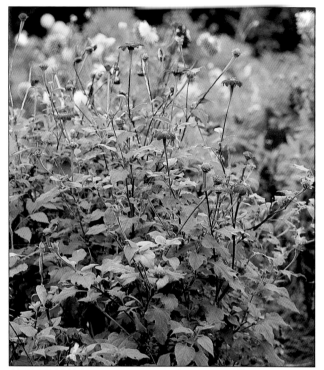

THE HEART-SHAPED LEAVES of Mexican sunflower are an added bonus, and each flower also has a distinct swollen 'neck'.

FEATURES

Tithonia, as its common name suggests, comes from warmer areas, so does well here when there is plenty of sun. Grow as a half-hardy annual. 'Fiesta del Sol' is just 30cm (1ft) tall, while 'Torch' can reach 1.2m (4ft). Flowers are large, exotic-looking and dahlia-like, red-orange, and have a distinct swollen 'neck'.

CONDITIONS

Aspect Must have full sun or plants will suffer.

TITHONIA AT A GLANCE

A half-hardy annual grown for its large orange flowers held on strong stems. Use in bedding and pots. Frost hardy to 0°C (32°F).

JAN	/	
FEB	sow ✍	
MAR	sow ✍	
APR	sow/transplant ✍	
MAY	harden off/plant ✍	
JUN	flowering ✿	
JULY	flowering ✿	
AUG	flowering ✿	
SEPT	flowering ✿	
OCT	/	
NOV	/	
DEC	/	

RECOMMENDED VARIETIES

Tithonia rotundifolia:

Tall varieties
  'Goldfinger'
  'Torch'

Short varieties
  'Fiesta del Sol'

Site Not fussy about soil, but needs good drainage. Plant in a fairly sheltered spot away from cold driving winds. Tithonia has a tendency to go pale and yellow when growing conditions are poor. Grow plants in containers if the soil is heavy, using multipurpose compost.

GROWING METHOD

Sowing Sow seeds February to April in 9cm (3½in) pots of multipurpose compost, just covering them, and germinate at 18°C (64°F) in a warm place or heated propagator. Transplant to individual 9cm (3½in) pots or large cell trays and grow on. Harden off for 2–3 weeks and plant in early summer when the soil warms up. If seedlings or young plants turn yellow they are being kept too cold. Can also be sown outdoors in early June where plants are to flower.

Feeding Feed container-grown plants twice a month with liquid feed.

Problems Slugs may attack the leaves after early summer rains so protect with slug pellets.

FLOWERING

Season Flowers appear from midsummer and later sowings continue to give colour into autumn.

Cutting Suitable for use as a cut flower.

AFTER FLOWERING

General Pull up after flowering. May self-seed.

TORENIA
Wishbone flower

WISHBONE FLOWER *gets its common name from the dark markings found on the lower lip of the flowers of some varieties.*

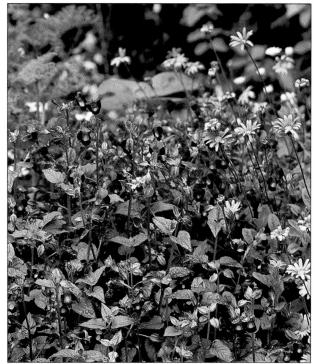

SHELTER IS ESSENTIAL *for success with torenia, which can also be potted up and grown-on as a flowering plant for indoors.*

FEATURES

Wishbone flower needs to be in the 'front row' of a summer bedding scheme, or used around the edge of pots and troughs. The variety 'Susie Wong' has bright yellow flowers with black throats, and a spreading habit making it ideal for baskets. Half-hardy annuals, torenias grow no more than 30cm (1ft) in height.

CONDITIONS

Aspect   Choose a sheltered spot with sun.

TORENIA AT A GLANCE

A low growing half-hardy annual grown for its colourful lipped flowers, for edging in beds and pots. Frost hardy to 0°C (32°F).

JAN	/	RECOMMENDED VARIETIES
FEB	/	
MAR	sow	*Torenia fournieri:*
APR	sow/transplant	'Clown Mixed'
MAY	grow/harden off	'Susie Wong'
JUN	plant/flowers	
JULY	flowering	
AUG	flowering	
SEPT	flowering	
OCT	/	
NOV	/	
DEC	/	

Site   Dig in rotted manure or compost a few weeks ahead of planting out, or use multipurpose compost for container growing. Soil and compost used must be free draining. Avoid planting where winds are persistent.

GROWING METHOD

Sowing   Sow the very small seeds in pots or trays in March/April, barely cover and keep at 18°C (64°F) in a well-lit place. When large enough the seedlings can be transplanted to cell trays and grown on until late May, then hardened off and planted well after the last frosts, 15cm (6in) apart, or in groups in patio pots. Plant five plants to a 40cm (16in) diameter hanging basket, four around the sides and one in the centre. 'Susie Wong' will creep in and out of other plants.

Feeding   Feed regularly every 2–3 weeks with a balanced liquid plant food.

Problems   Trouble free.

FLOWERING

Season   Throughout summer.
Cutting   Not used as a cut flower.

AFTER FLOWERING

General   Pull or dig out the plants once flowering has stopped. They will sometimes self-seed, and they will then produce seedlings in the following year.

TROPAEOLUM

Nasturtium

'MOONLIGHT' is a climbing variety of nasturtium reaching 1.8m (6ft) with soft yellow flowers against light green leaves.

FOR DOUBLE VALUE grow 'Alaska Mixed' with light green leaves speckled with creamy-white, plus red and yellow flowers.

FEATURES

With big seeds and quick growth, tropaeolum, better known as nasturtium, is one of the easiest of all hardy annuals to grow. Plants just 23cm (9in) tall are perfect for bedding and patio planters, while others will scramble up thought a dull hedge. The colour range is huge, and single and mixed colours are available. For pretty leaves too, grow 'Alaska Mixed' which is speckled with white.

TROPAEOLUM AT A GLANCE

A hardy annual grown for its colourful flowers and often variegated leaves. For beds and containers. Frost hardy to 0°C (32°F).

JAN	/	
FEB	sow	
MAR	sow	
APR	transplant	
MAY	transplant	
JUN	flowering	
JULY	flowering	
AUG	flowering	
SEPT	flowering	
OCT	/	
NOV	/	
DEC	/	

RECOMMENDED VARIETIES

Tropaeolum majus:
Tall climbers
  'Climbing Mixed'
  'Jewel of Africa'
Short, mixed colours
  'Alaska Mixed'
  'Gleam Mixed'
  'Tip Top Mixed'
Single colours
  'Empress of India'
  'Gleaming Mahogany'
  'Moonlight'

CONDITIONS

Aspect   Needs full sun.
Site   Poor, thin soil gives excellent results when grown under hedges or in bedding displays.

GROWING METHOD

Sowing   Simply push the large seeds 2.5–5cm (1–2in) into the soil in April, in groups of 3–5 where plants are to flower. Fleshy seedlings appear 2–3 weeks later and they can all be left to develop and form a large clump. If needed for containers, sow three seeds to a 9cm (3½in) pot at the same time and keep warm until seedlings appear, then keep outdoors.

Feeding   Feeding encourages leaves at the expense of flowers, although if other plants are growing in a container or basket, some extra feeding is unavoidable. Don't feed plants growing in soil.

Problems   Aphids and caterpillars feed under the leaves, so check regularly and squash if seen.

FLOWERING

Season   Flowering is all summer long.
Cutting   Not used cut, but flowers and the peppery leaves can be used raw in summer salads.

AFTER FLOWERING

General   Pull up and compost. Self-seeds very easily.

VERBENA

Verbena

SOFTER PASTEL SHADES can be found in modern varieties of verbena – these are just a few flowers of the variety 'Romance Pastels'.

'PEACHES & CREAM' has a unique colour that makes it a real winner, at 20cm (8in), for patio containers and hanging baskets.

FEATURES

Most verbenas grow 15–30cm (6–12in) tall and are prized for their heads of bright flowers. Mixtures or single shades like 'Peaches & Cream' are used for planting containers or for bedding. Raise from seed – although this is tricky – or grow them from mail order plants. Most trailing verbenas are not seed raised but bought as ready-grown plants from garden centres and mail order catalogues in spring.

VERBENA AT A GLANCE

A half-hardy annual used in bedding and containers. Masses of bright flowers appear during summer. Frost hardy to 0°C (32°F).

JAN	/	
FEB	/	
MAR	sow	
APR	transplant	
MAY	grow/harden off	
JUN	flowering	
JULY	flowering	
AUG	flowering	
SEPT	flowering	
OCT	/	
NOV	/	
DEC	/	

RECOMMENDED VARIETIES

Verbena hybrida:

Mixed colours
'Crown Jewels'
'Novalis Mixed'
'Raspberry Crush'
'Romance Pastels'
Single colours
'Adonis Blue'
'Apple Blossom'
'Peaches & Cream'
Spreading/trailing
'Misty'

CONDITIONS

Aspect   Needs full sun for best results.
Site   Use multipurpose compost in containers, and mix rotted compost with soil outdoors.

GROWING METHOD

Sowing   To succeed with verbena seed, sow on the surface of peat-based seed compost in March and cover the seeds with a thin layer of fine vermiculite. Water and keep at 21°C (70°F). Seedlings appear 2–3 weeks later, and should be kept slightly on the dry side. When large enough, transplant seedlings to cell trays or individual 7.5cm (3in) pots, and grow on. Plant after hardening off in late spring/early summer.
Feeding   Feed monthly with balanced liquid feed.
Problems   Powdery mildew can attack leaves – use a spray containing sulphur at the first signs.

FLOWERING

Season   Flowers appear all summer.
Cutting   Not used for cutting.

AFTER FLOWERING

General   Pull up when finished and use for compost.

VIOLA CORNUTA
Viola

DIMINUTIVE 'Bambini' violas are guaranteed to steal your heart with their inquisitive whiskery faces.

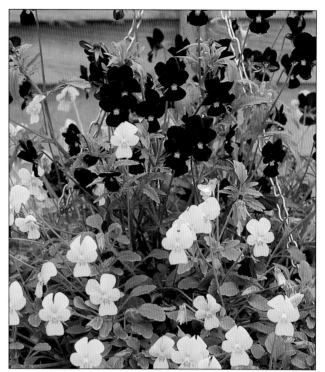

FOR A TOUCH OF DRAMA try combining the moody 'Blackjack' with a clear yellow variety in a hanging basket.

FEATURES

Violas are smaller than pansies but they are no less prolific, and what they lack in size they make up for in sheer character. Most are varieties of *Viola cornuta*, and all are quite hardy, being sown in spring or summer. Grow single colours, mixtures like 'Bambini', or trailing yellow 'Sunbeam' for hanging baskets. Violas grow to around 15cm (6in), making bushy little plants for bedding or containers. Try planting them in cottage style wicker baskets. Available as young plants.

VIOLA AT A GLANCE

A hardy annual grown for its pretty little pansy flowers which appear on branching plants. Frost hardy to −15°C (5°F).

		RECOMMENDED VARIETIES
JAN	/	**Viola hybrids:**
FEB	sow	'Bambini Mixed'
MAR	sow	'Blackjack'
APR	sow/flower	'Blue Moon'
MAY	sow/flower	'Cuty'
JUN	sow/flower	'Juliette Mixed'
JULY	sow/flower	'Midnight Runner'
AUG	grow on/flowers	'Princess Mixed'
SEPT	grow on/flowers	'Sorbet Yesterday, Today & Tomorrow'
OCT	plant	'Sunbeam'
NOV	/	
DEC	/	

CONDITIONS

Aspect Grows well in sun or dappled, light shade.
Site Soil does not need to be over prepared, but must be well-drained. For container growing use multipurpose compost.

GROWING METHOD

Sowing Sow from February under cover for flowers the same summer, or outside May–July for flowers the following spring. Either way, sow in a 9cm (3½in) pot of multipurpose compost and barely cover seeds. In early spring keep at 15°C (60°F) and transplant seedlings when large enough to cell trays, grow, harden off and plant in late May. When summer sowing, stand the pot outside in shade to germinate then treat seedlings the same, planting out in October where you want the plants to flower.
Feeding Extra feeding is not usually necessary.
Problems Use slug pellets if the leaves are attacked.

FLOWERING

Season Spring-sown plants flower during summer, summer-sown the following spring/summer.
Cutting The delicate cut stems of 'Queen Charlotte' are sometimes used for making scented posies.

AFTER FLOWERING

General Plants often carry on as short-lived perennials, and also self-seed freely.

VIOLA TRICOLOR
Wild pansy

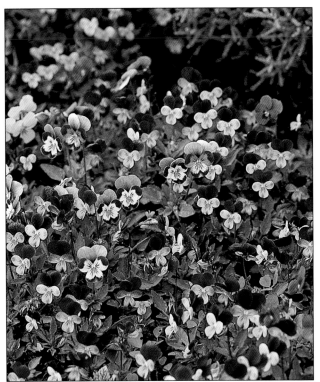

EACH FLOWER of wild pansy is like a tiny whiskered 'face' and individual plants all vary from each other very slightly.

ONE PLANT left in the ground to mature through the summer will shed hundreds of seeds which will germinate the next spring.

FEATURES

Viola tricolor is the wild pansy, also known commonly as heartsease or Johnny-jump-up. It is usually grown as a hardy annual but can also be treated as a biennial. Much daintier than its relatives the pansies, these plants are at home in cottage-style beds and as pot edging. A few single coloured varieties are available, such as the unusual 'Bowles' Black', having black flowers with a small central yellow 'eye'.

VIOLA AT A GLANCE

A hardy annual grown for its pretty little pansy flowers which appear on branching plants. Frost hardy to –15°C (5°F).

		RECOMMENDED VARIETIES
JAN	/	
FEB	sow	*Viola tricolor*
MAR	sow	**Single colours:**
APR	sow/flower	**Blue**
MAY	sow/flower	'Prince Henry'
JUN	sow/flower	**Yellow**
JULY	sow/flower	'Prince John'
AUG	grow on/flowers	
SEPT	grow on/flowers	
OCT	plant	
NOV	/	
DEC	/	

CONDITIONS

Aspect Grows well sun or dappled, light shade.
Site Soil does not need to be over prepared, but must be well-drained. Multipurpose compost is best for growing *Viola tricolor* in containers.

GROWING METHOD

Sowing Sow from February under cover for flowers the same summer, or outside May–July for flowers the following spring. Either way, sow in a 9cm (3½in) pot of multipurpose compost and barely cover seeds. In early spring keep at 15°C (60°F) and transplant seedlings when large enough to cell trays, grow, harden off and plant in late May. When summer sowing, stand the pot outside in shade to germinate, treat seedlings the same, and plant in October.

Feeding Extra feeding is not usually necessary.
Problems Use slug pellets if the leaves are attacked.

FLOWERING

Season Spring-sown plants flower during summer, summer-sown the following spring/summer.
Cutting Not suitable for cutting.

AFTER FLOWERING

General Pull plants up and compost, or leave a few to shed seeds. They will sometimes grow as perennials and last for several years.

VIOLA WITTROCKIANA
Pansy

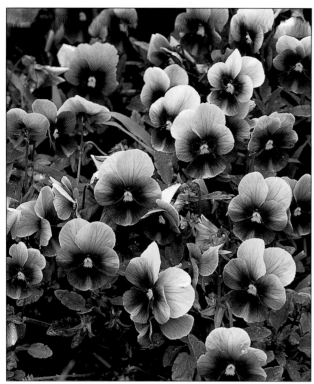

PANSY FLOWERS have 'faces' that tend to face the sun, especially in early spring. Use them in patio pots with bulbs like tulips.

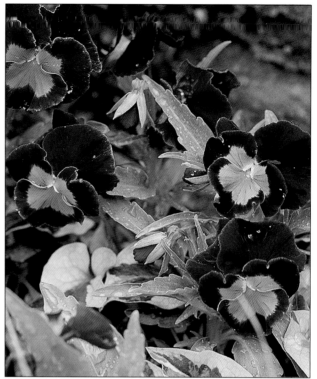

'JOLLY JOKER' is a unique and prolific variety of summer-flowering pansy with orange and rich royal purple two-tone flowers.

FEATURES

Pansies are hardy and will flower almost all year round. There are two groups, summer flowering, and autumn/winter flowering. None grow more than 20cm (8in) tall. Flowers are like large flat 'faces' up to 7.5cm (3in) across. Colours vary enormously from single, pastel shades to striking bicolours, and are available in mixtures or as single colours. Many varieties are available as young plants by mail order. Most are varieties of *Viola wittrockiana*.

VIOLA AT A GLANCE

Hardy and grown either as an annual or a biennial for flowers in summer and autumn/winter. Frost hardy to –15°C (5°F).

		RECOMMENDED VARIETIES
JAN	/	*Viola wittrockiana:*
FEB	sow	**Summer flowers**
MAR	sow	'Antique Shades'
APR	sow/flower	'Padparadja'
MAY	sow/flower	'Romeo & Juliet'
JUN	sow/flower	'Watercolours'
JULY	sow/flower	**Autumn/winter flowers**
AUG	grow on/flowers	'Homefires'
SEPT	grow on/flowers	'Ultima Pastel Mixed'
OCT	plant	'Universal Mixed'
NOV	/	'Velour Mixed'
DEC	/	

CONDITIONS

Aspect	Autumn/winter pansies need full sun. Summer flowering varieties like dappled shade.
Site	Add plenty of manure to the soil. Winter pansies need excellent drainage. Use multipurpose compost for containers.

GROWING METHOD

Sowing	Sow from February under cover for flowers the same summer, or outside May–July for flowers the following spring. Either way, sow in a 9cm (3½in) pot of multipurpose compost and barely cover seeds. In early spring keep at 15°C (60°F) and transplant seedlings when large enough to cell trays, grow, harden off and plant in late May. When summer sowing, stand the pot outside in shade to germinate then treat seedlings the same, planting out in October where you want the plants to flower.
Feeding	Liquid feed summer plants fortnightly.
Problems	Spray with permethrin if aphids attack.

FLOWERING

Season	Spring-sown plants flower in summer, autumn-sown from October onwards.
Cutting	Pansies last a few days in water.

AFTER FLOWERING

General	Pull up and compost when finished.

ZINNIA
Zinnia

ZINNIA FLOWERS *tend to come as doubles but plants sometimes appear that are single like this. Zinnias are good bee plants.*

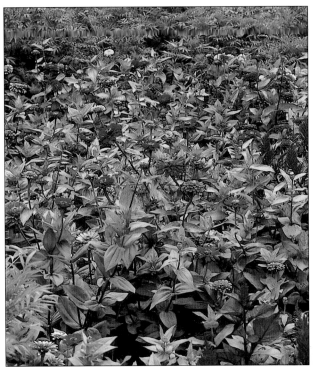

IF PINCHED WHEN YOUNG *zinnias make bushy, branching plants that fill gaps in mixed borders quickly. Take dead flowers off.*

FEATURES

There is a zinnia for every garden. Dwarf varieties at 15cm (6in) tall are suited to beds and containers, while 'Dahlia-Flowered Mixed' has big heads on stems 60cm (2ft) high, and is useful for mixed borders. Modern varieties have fully double flowers, and some like 'Zebra Mixed' are stripey. 'Starbright Mixed' is an unusual variety with masses of small orange and gold flowers. Red, yellow, pink, scarlet, orange, lavender, purple, white and even green are typical flower colours. Half-hardy annual.

ZINNIA AT A GLANCE

A half-hardy annual grown for its bright flowers in a wide range of colours, for bedding and cutting. Frost hardy to 0°C (32°F).

		RECOMMENDED VARIETIES
JAN	/	
FEB	/	**Zinnia hybrids:**
MAR	/	**Tall varieties**
APR	/	'Allsorts'
MAY	sow	'Dahlia-Flowered Mixed'
JUN	thin out	'Zebra Mixed'
JULY	flowering	**Short varieties**
AUG	flowering	'Belvedere'
SEPT	flowering	'Fairyland'
OCT	flowering	'Persian Carpet Mixed'
NOV	/	'Starbright Mixed'
DEC	/	'Thumbelina'

CONDITIONS

Aspect
Site
Zinnias enjoy heat and need sun and shelter. Must have well-drained soil, previously improved with rotted organic matter. For containers use multipurpose compost.

GROWING METHOD

Sowing
Although half-hardy, zinnias grow best when sown direct where they are to flower, in short drills 1cm (½in) deep. Do this is in May and cover seedlings with a piece of garden fleece on frosty nights. Thin out seedlings so the young plants are eventually 15–60cm (6–24in) apart, depending on their final size. To grow dwarf varieties in containers sow 2–3 seeds to a 7.5cm (3in) pot at the same time, leave just the strongest, grow on, and plant when ready, not disturbing the roots.

Feeding
Extra feeding is usually not necessary.

Problems
Powdery mildew can be a problem, so avoid planting too close – sulphur sprays can help. Stem rots cause plants to collapse suddenly.

FLOWERING

Season
Cutting
Flowers appear from midsummer onwards. Very good cut flower. 'Envy Double' is a striking plant with double green flowers.

AFTER FLOWERING

General
Pull up in autumn and compost.

GROWING CLEMATIS

Swagging walls, fences and pergolas or scrambling over trees and shrubs, clematis is the queen of climbers. It ascends by wrapping leaf stalks around a support and blooms strikingly for most of the year.

FEATURES

Starry or flared bell flowers, in a kaleidoscope of dashing hues, flourish on new or one-year-old shoots. Many, such as *C. tangutica* are followed by spheres of feathery seed heads, which look dramatic when sparkling with frost.

There are species and hybrids to suit every situation and most are frost hardy. In tiny gardens or on patios or terraces, you can grow smaller varieties so that they cascade over the side. Although most shed their leaves, a small group of sculptural evergreens have a special charm.

There are six fascinating groups:

Early-flowering species (Group 1)
Choice spring varieties include blue *C. alpina* 'Pamela Jackman', *C. macropetala* 'Markham's Pink' and white *C. montana* f. *grandiflora*.

Early-flowering hybrids (Group 2)
Resulting from a cross between two or more species and cheering early summer, double-flowered, silver-mauve 'Belle of Woking' and purple-blue 'The President' will glorify a west-facing wall or fence.

Late-flowering species (Group 3)
Clouds of tiny, fragrant, starry white blooms billowing from *C. flammula* and flared tulip-like red blooms peeping from *C. texensis* 'Princes of Wales', make July to October special.

Late-flowering hybrids (Group 3)
Rich purple 'Jackmanii' and any of plants of the *C. viticella* clan, such as white and green 'Alba Luxurians', flourish from July to September.

Evergreens (Group 1)
Skeined with scented pink-budded, white-flowered blooms in spring, leathery scimitar-leaved 'Apple Blossom' enjoys a warm, sunny aspect. In winter, reddish-spotted, cream- and fern-leaved *C. cirrhosa* 'Freckles' prefers in a sheltered spot.

Herbaceous varieties (Group 3)
A small non-climbing group of clematis that complements border perennials. An enchanting combination is the deep blue and hyacinth-flowered *C. heracleifolia* 'Wyevale,' which grows to 90cm (3ft) and the scented, white- and bronze-leaved *C. recta* 'Purpurea', which grows to 60–120cm (2–4ft). Both flower from late summer to autumn.

LEFT: Many people grow clematis because of their attractive and often scented flowers: they come in a wide variety of different colours, shapes and sizes. They also have long-flowering periods so, if you select the varieties carefully, you can have year-round blooms.

CONDITIONS

Aspect Site
There are species and varieties to suit every spot. Soil should be free-draining and fortified with well-rotted organic matter. Ideally, you should grow plants where the roots are shaded but the stems can climb into bright sunlight.

GROWING METHOD

Planting
Take out a generous hole 45cm (18in) across and 37cm (15in) deep, and fork old manure or rotted garden compost into the base. Fill in with a mix of fertile top soil and add two very well worked-in gloved handfuls of bone meal. Tap the plant from its pot, tease out coiled roots at the base and set the root ball 15cm (6in) deeper than it was in its pot to encourage a multi-stemmed branching system to form. Water in copiously. Finish by mulching with old manure or pulverised bark to keep roots cool. Fan-train shoots over trellis or plastic-coated wires spaced 1ft apart.

Feeding
Clematis are voracious feeders, so top dress them with 113g per square metre (4oz per square yard) of blood, fish and bone meal in spring, mid and late summer. Water it in.

Pruning
Group 1 (early-flowering species and evergreens): Don't cut them back unless they outgrow their allotted space. Shorten flowered shoots when blooms fade to just above a joint.
Group 2 (early-flowering hybrids): Cut out dead shoots in February. Shorten stems when blooms fade to encourage a second flush of blossom in late summer. Dead-head regularly.
Group 3 (late-flowering hybrids, species and herbaceous varieties): Shorten all stems to fat buds 30cm (12in) from the base in February or March.

Problems
Slugs and snails rasp bark and devour new buds and shoots. Control with blue slug pellets. Wilt Disease causes shoots to collapse suddenly and die back to ground level. Thankfully, new stems appear from the base. There are no effective fungicides, so instead cut back affected shoots. Plant deeply so that if stems die back to soil level, underground buds are triggered into growth and replace them.

FLOWERING

Season
By selecting varieties carefully, you can have blossom from late winter to late autumn.

Cutting
Although blooms last for only for a few days, they look captivating floating in a shallow bowl of water. Gather seed heads when fluffy, spray them with hair lacquer to stop seeds from loosening and add them to dried winter displays.

AFTER FLOWERING

Requirements
Nourish spring and summer performers with fertiliser over root area when blooms fade. Water in. Feed summer to autumn bloomers with bone meal in October or November.

NELLY MOSER

MONTANA 'TETRAROSE'

'Nelly Moser', which blooms twice (in May and again in September), flaunts 17–22cm (7–9in) carmine-striped, pale mauve-pink blooms. It colours well if trained against an east-, north- or west-facing wall or fence, but objects to direct sunlight, which causes its magnificent flowers to fade. Growing only to around 3m (10ft), it is ideal for clothing an arch or a trellis around a patio.

It flowers on shoots made the previous year, so remove dead or weak stems in late June and tie in the strongest new growth to flower the following season. Devise a riveting focus by planting it next to lavender-blue 'Lasurstern', which is similar in height and should be treated in the same way.

Transforming May and June with a foam of large, 7–10cm (3–4in), lilac-rose flowers amid bronzy-green foliage, Clematis montana 'Tetrarose' grows to 6m (20ft) on a large wall, fence or sizeable pergola.

Though happy facing north, east, south or west, it is sensible to capitalise on its hardiness by planting it to cloak a cold, shaded wall or fence seared by icy winds. Alternatively, set it to climb and drape a conifer or umbrella over an old apple tree. No pruning is necessary. If it outgrows its allotted space, trim it when flowers fade in early summer.

NELLY MOSER AT A GLANCE

Flowers well when positioned against an east-, west- or north-facing wall or fence. Fully hardy to frost hardy.

JAN	rest	NOV	rest
FEB	rest	DEC	rest
MAR	planting		
APR	feeding, mulching	OTHER EARLY-FLOWERING FORMS:	
MAY	flowering		
JUN	flowering	'Royalty'	
JULY	pruning, propagation	'Proteus'	
AUG	tie in shoots	'Guernsey Cream'	
SEPT	flowering		
OCT	planting		

MONTANA AT A GLANCE

This variety is especially good for covering a north-facing wall. Fully hardy to frost hardy.

JAN	rest	OCT	planting
FEB	rest	NOV	rest
MAR	planting, feeding	DEC	rest
APR	planting, mulching	OTHER MONTANA FORMS:	
MAY	flowering		
JUN	flowering	'Elizabeth'	
JULY	pruning	'Alexander'	
AUG	propagation, feeding	'Pink Perfection'	
SEPT	planting		

SILVER MOON

LIBERATION

'Silver Moon' is a large-flowered variety that will enliven a dull north-facing wall or fence, but will be equally happy elsewhere. Cloaked with pearly-pink blooms, which will grow to 12–17cm (5–7in) across, on stems up to 2.4–3m (8–10ft) high, it brightens May, June and August. It is suitable, too, for planting in a large patio pot from which blossom-clad shoots will spill appealingly. Create a feature that all will admire by combining it with a contrasting-hued climbing rose, such as 'Royal Gold', scarlet 'Sympathie', yellow and red 'Night Light' or rose-pink 'Parade'. No pruning is necessary unless it outgrows its allotted space. Then, in a mild spell in February or early March, shorten all stems to within a pair of fat buds, 30–45cm (12–18in) from the ground.

Introduced in 1995 to commemorate the Channel Islands' 50th year of freedom from oppression by occupying forces, 'Liberation' is a joy. Flaunting deep pinkish-red blooms with cerise-barred petals, up to 15cm (6in) in diameter, on robust stems up to 3m (10ft), it flourishes in late spring and early summer and again in early autumn. It needs tempering with white-flowered plants because of its vibrant colours. Ideally, twin it with Solanum jasminoides 'Album', a scrambler whose clusters of starry flowers stud shoots from July to October. It performs on one-year-old stems, so no regular pruning is required – merely shorten dead or weak growth to stocky buds from February to early March. Prune again, cutting back flowered stems by half their length in midsummer in order to trigger new shoots and a dazzling bonus of autumn blossom.

SILVER MOON AT A GLANCE

Thrives when grown against a west-facing wall. Fully hardy to frost hardy.

JAN	rest	NOV	rest
FEB	pruning	DEC	rest
MAR	planting, feeding		
APR	planting, mulching		
MAY	flowering		
JUN	flowering		
JULY	propagation		
AUG	flowering, feeding		
SEPT	planting		
OCT	planting		

LIBERATION AT A GLANCE

Flourishes against an east or west-facing wall. Fully hardy to frost hardy.

JAN	rest	NOV	rest
FEB	rest	DEC	rest
MAR	planting, feeding		
APR	planting, mulching		
MAY	flowering		
JUN	flowering		
JULY	propagation		
AUG	feeding		
SEPT	planting		
OCT	planting		

GROWING
PERENNIALS

Many of the loveliest and best-loved flowering plants are perennials. Like annuals, perennials provide a colourful display, but they have the advantage that they don't need to be changed at least twice a year. Perennials are easy-care plants which have a major place in low maintenance gardens.

Perennials remain alive for a number of years, unlike annuals which usually last only one season, and biennials which grow and flower through a second season or year. Perennials form a variable group in terms of their size and foliage, flower shape, style and colour. In fact, there is a perennial to suit almost every climate, aspect and soil, and some can even be grown in containers. Perennials can also be planted among shrubs, to form a background for bulbs or annuals, or in their own separate areas. Perennial borders make lively, exciting features.

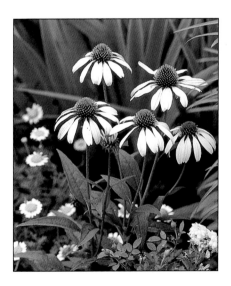

ABOVE: *The white form of the purple coneflower showing its attractive, recurved petals.*

LEFT: *A tender, bright pink argyranthemum, and scabious, in the foreground add perennial interest to this colourful, mixed border featuring soft hues offset by green.*

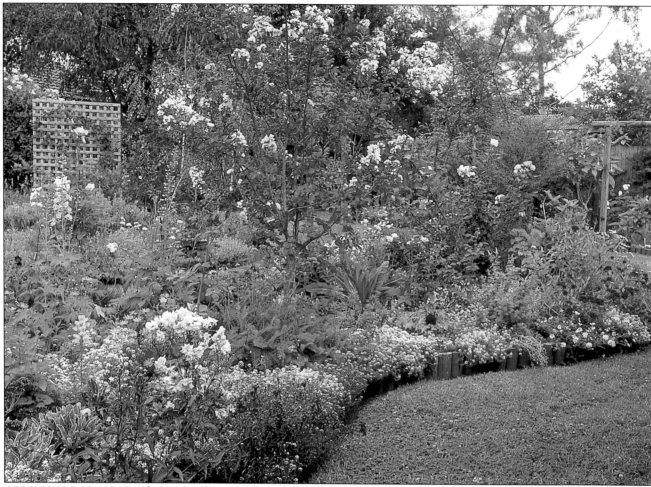

PERENNIALS COMBINE with annuals to form a free-flowing, rich, colourful border, a highlight of mid-summer in this gorgeous cottage garden. A pink shrub rose is flanked by two varieties of aster, while deep blue delphiniums add scale and height at the back.

EVERGREEN OR HERBACEOUS?

Some perennials are evergreen but many are herbaceous. Most herbaceous perennials grow rapidly during spring and summer to flower during the summer and autumn. After flowering they gradually die back to the crown or fleshy roots, and they remain dormant during cold winters. Since most of the hardy herbaceous perennials come from climates with very severe, cold winters they die down naturally in the autumn. In warmer areas, where they do not become completely dormant and some growth continues year round, the plants do not live as long. However, it is simple to renew these perennials as division is easy, and most increase rapidly. In time, a few can even become invasive.

PLANTING PERENNIALS

Soil preparation

Because perennials are long-term plants and because they are close planted, good soil preparation is essential. Although some perennials, such as astilbes and hostas, enjoy damp soil, many prefer well-drained conditions. If you are planting any of the latter group, check your drainage before planting. Dig some holes in the bed, fill them with water and see how long

PERENNIALS FOR SUN AND SHADE

SUNNY BORDERS

- Agapanthus
- Delphinium
- Diascia
- Eryngium
- Gypsophila
- Helenium
- Hemerocallis
- Miscanthus
- Oenothera
- Papaver
- Sedum
- Stachys

SHADY BORDERS

- *Alchemilla mollis*
- Aquilegia
- Bergenia
- Candelabra primula
- Digitalis
- Epimedium
- *Gunnera manicata*
- Helleborus
- Hosta
- Polygonatum
- Primula
- Pulmonaria
- Rodgersia (dappled)

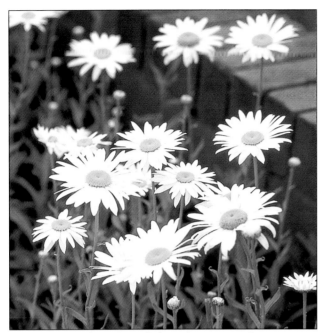

PURE WHITE shasta daisies light up the summer garden, putting on a strong display from early summer to early autumn.

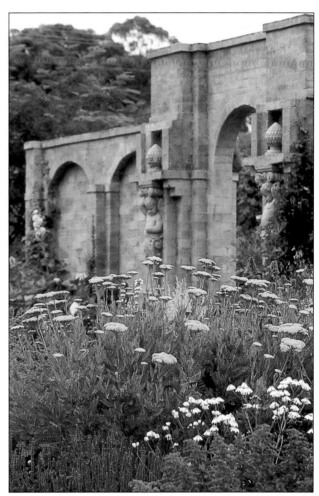

A HIGH STONE WALL marks the boundary of this meadow garden filled with golden fern-leaf yarrow, daisies and purple loosestrife.

it takes to drain away. If there is still water in the holes 12 hours later, you will need to improve the drainage by installing a system of sub-soil drains.

If the soil is very heavy clay, which remains wet but not waterlogged for a long time, you should dig in some gypsum, about 300g per sq m (10.5oz per sq yd). Digging in large quantities of decayed manure or compost a few weeks before planting will also improve clay soils, and it is a must in sandy soils that have poor moisture and nutrient retention.

Thorough weeding of the area is essential, too, as it is difficult to remove weeds in densely planted beds. Remove the weeds you can see, dig or fork over the area again, water and wait for the next lot of weeds to emerge. You may need to repeat this step if the area has been neglected for any length of time. Hand weeding or spraying with glyphosate should eliminate most weeds, but you will need to be persistent to control oxalis, bindweed and ground elder. This sounds like a lot of work when you are eager to plant out your garden, but it will be worth the wait and the effort in the long run.

Planting perennials from containers

Garden centres and nurseries will stock some perennials, especially when they are in flower. These can be planted in the garden like any other container-grown plant. When the plant is removed from its pot, loosen the rootball a little so that the roots can extend into the surrounding soil. It is essential that the planting hole is about twice the width of the container and approximately the same depth. The soil level around the plant should be exactly the same as it was in the container. Give a thorough soaking after planting. Also apply a deep mulch to the soil around the plant.

Planting bare-rooted perennials

There are also nurseries that specialise in perennials. These nurseries usually advertise in popular gardening magazines, have detailed catalogues with thorough plant descriptions, and sell by mail-order. Plants are delivered during their dormant season, which for the majority is from late autumn

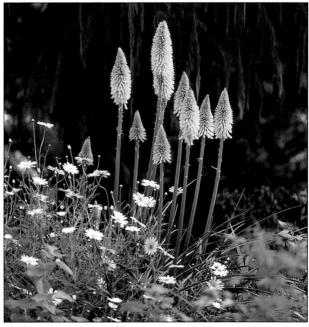

THESE GOLDEN-YELLOW, green-tipped spikes of a red hot poker cultivar provide a strong focus in this pastel border.

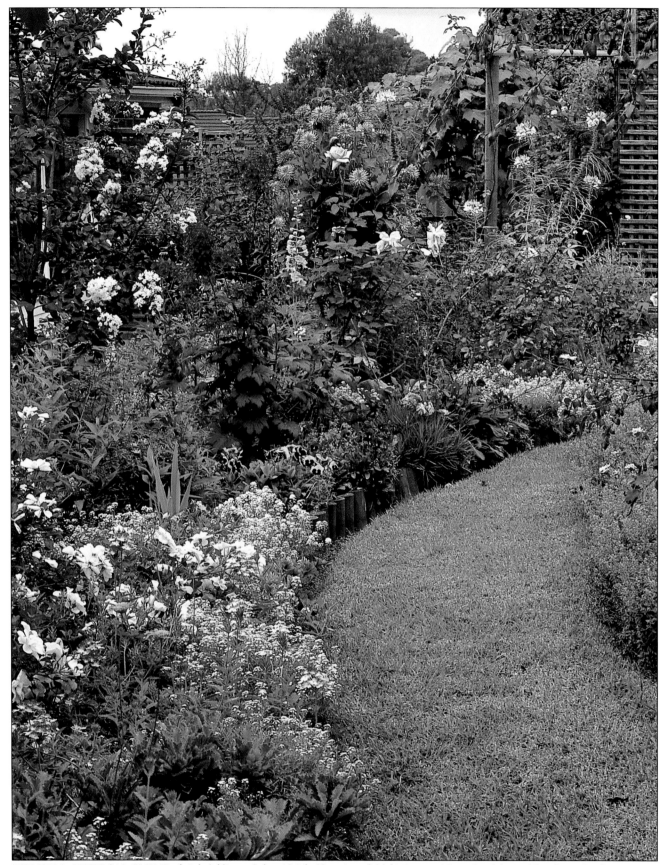

THE TALL, VERTICAL CLUMP of pink dahlias and the midnight blue spires of delphinium provide a colourful mix. They form a bright imaginative backdrop for the rich mix of annuals and perennials edging this beautiful garden bed, clearly illustrating the versatility of perennials.

through the winter. Plants are mailed, bare-rooted, or in small pots, having been carefully packed and labelled. On arrival, they should be planted at once. However, if the ground is frozen, or you are not ready to plant them, either unpack and water them (if necessary), and store in a bright, cool, frost-free place, or 'heel in' as a temporary measure. To do this, dig a trench large enough to contain the plant roots in a sheltered part of the garden. Finally, lay the plants on their sides, cover the roots with soil, and lightly water them.

When planting bare-rooted plants, again make sure the hole is at least twice the width of the rootball, and deep enough to take the roots without kinking them. If some roots are very long, trim them cleanly with secateurs. Hold the plant in the hole in one hand and fill the hole, poking soil between the roots. Sometimes you can make a slight mound in the centre of the hole so that the roots can be spread out over it, keeping the crown high. Make sure the crown of the plant is not buried: if necessary, lift the plant and push more soil in around the roots.

Water thoroughly immediately after planting if the soil is dry, but until the plants have developed plenty of shoot growth they will not require too much watering. The area around the plants should be mulched. If the soil has been well prepared, feeding at this time is not necessary but you may give a very light sprinkling of general fertiliser if you wish.

CARE OF PERENNIALS

Perennial plantings in areas that have been well prepared need little maintenance. You must deadhead through the flowering season to prolong blooming, and cut back or tidy up after flowering. Established perennials will only need watering in prolonged dry spells, and feeding in spring as growth commences. When they become too crowded they are divided between autumn and late winter, or early spring. This may be only necessary every three or four years. For details, see plant entries in the A-Z section.

Watering
Never give perennials a light watering because it will encourage surface rooting at the expense of a deep, root system. The plants need big, strong roots to sustain several years of growth, and benefit most from being given a deep, regular watering. On sandy soils choose such perennials as sedum, oenothera and dianthus that tolerate dry conditions. A deep mulch around the plants will help conserve moisture, as will adding quantities of organic matter to the soil as the mulch breaks down.

Feeding
Perennials should not need a lot of feeding. Apply an all-purpose plant food as growth begins; if the soil has been well prepared this should be enough for the whole growing season. If your soil is very poor though, you may like to use a slow-release granular fertiliser to feed plants through the growing season, or to apply a second helping of plant food as the flower buds start to appear. A mulch of decayed manure or compost around the plants serves two functions. It improves the soil condition, and also supplies small amounts of nutrients to the plants.

Keep the entire area free of weeds until the plants cover the ground. This will ensure that any fertiliser you apply will feed your perennials and not any unwanted weeds. Avoid high nitrogen fertilisers as they tend to promote leaf growth at the expense of flowers. Rose food is ideal.

THE PENSTEMONS AND SALVIAS in the foreground make a gorgeous foil for the stiff, upright growth of Russell lupins.

Cutting flowers and deadheading
A number of perennials make very good cut flowers, and many are grown for the cut flower trade. The various daisies, chrysanthemums, Russell lupins, delphiniums, pinks and Peruvian lilies are just a few of the perennials that are commercially grown. Regularly picking the flowers will help to ensure a long succession of bloom, If the flowers are not removed they will mature, most setting seed so that the flowering cycle will finish abruptly as the plant decides its reproductive work is over. If you do not want to take cut flowers, remember to deadhead regularly.

Exceptions to this rule are plants such as cardoon and globe thistle that have decorative seedheads. Some gardeners prefer to leave them on the plant. Many remain attractive even when dry, and they can add interest to the garden in late autumn and winter, especially when covered in frost or snow.

AFTER FLOWERING

After the flowering season is over, perennials can be cut back almost to the ground. If you live in an area prone to heavy frosts, some of the more tender perennials will then need to have the crown of the plant covered. A thick layer of straw, or autumn leaves, held in place by a few sticks in windy sites, will protect them from winter damage.

Alternatively, you could leave some stems sticking out of the ground to create extra, interesting shapes over winter. Grasses are especially invaluable. They are at their best when covered with frost or snow, or when helping to cast a web of shadows from the low winter sun. The birds also benefit from the seedheads.

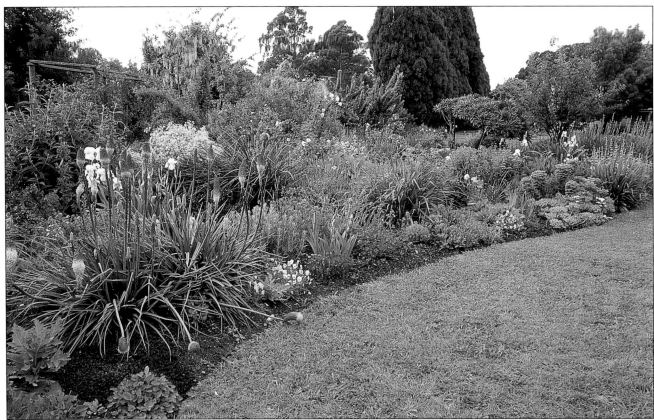

THE BRIGHT, HOT COLOURS of orange and yellow feature in this very effective planting, which shows up so impressively against the cool green of the lawn. The large clump of red hot pokers and a generous drift of deep apricot-orange geum are especially notable.

INCREASING YOUR STOCK OF PERENNIALS

Division

Clumps of perennials are divided either when they become congested, or when you want to plant sections elsewhere in the garden. In general, most perennials need dividing about every three or four years, possibly longer. Division is done after flowering or while the plants are dormant.

If you want some pieces to plant elsewhere you can sever a section with a knife, or put a spade through the clump, and lift away what you want. This might lose some of the peripheral pieces but the process is quick and simple. Otherwise, dig up the whole clump, shake off the excess soil and pull the clump apart or cut it into sections. Replant the sections immediately, trimming off very long roots. Remember that the outer growths are the youngest, to be saved, and that the centre of the plant may have died, in which case it can be discarded. You may need to divide very large, heavy clumps by pushing two garden forks, back to back, into the centre to prise it apart. A sharp spade may also be used but this needs a lot of force and will, of course, result in the loss of some sections of plant. This may not be of any consequence with vigorous perennials.

If you are unable to replant at once or have pieces to give away, wrap them in damp newspaper or hessian and keep in a shaded, sheltered spot, giving time to decide where to plant them. 'Heeling in', as described on the previous page, is another way to store plants temporarily, and they are less likely to dry out. They can, of course, be potted up in a good quality potting mix.

Taking cuttings

Many perennial plants can be grown from cuttings and a number, including geraniums and diascias, are among the easiest plants to strike. Others that will grow readily from cuttings include penstemons and sedums.

Make a mix of two or three parts of coarse sand and one of peat, or peat substitute compost. Put the prepared mix in clean pots, preferably no larger than 10cm (4in) across. A pot of this size will take a good number of cuttings which will not be forced to sit in a large amount of soil that remains wet when watered, taking too long to dry out, consequently rotting the roots.

Take tip cuttings of unflowered shoots, no more than 5–10cm (2–4in) long. Cut, do not tear, pieces from the parent plant. Take the cuttings early in the morning, placing the pieces in a clean plastic bag, and quickly put in a cool, shady place. Trim the cuttings by removing the lower leaves, allowing just a very few to remain on top. Cleanly cut the base of the cutting below a node (leaf junction). Another aid to rooting is to 'wound' the cutting by carefully scraping about 1cm (3/8in) of the outer bark or stem cover at the base of the stem. Hormone rooting powders can also be used but are not usually necessary with most perennials.

Use a clean stick or pencil to make a hole in the compost. Put the cutting in the hole and carefully firm the surrounding mix. Once all your cuttings are in the pot you can water them thoroughly and put the pot in a warm, sheltered place out of direct sun. In warm months geraniums and daisies may be well rooted after three weeks, but many plants can take a considerable time. Check regularly to see if the cuttings need water but do not keep them wet or, as explained they will rot.

DIVIDING A CLUMP

Step 1: Use a garden fork to lift the whole perennial clump from the soil.

Step 2: Separate matted clumps by inserting two garden forks, back to back, firmly into the clump.

Step 3: First press the fork handles together, and then force them apart to split the clump in two. Repeat until the clumps are the size you want.

Step 4: Use secateurs to cut off dead, rotten or damaged roots. The clumps are now ready for replanting.

STRIKING A CUTTING

Step 1: Take a cutting just below a leaf node or joint. Use a sharp knife or secateurs so that the cutting is not bruised. Trim it if necessary.

Step 2: Make a hole in the compost with your finger and insert the cutting into it. Firm the soil gently around it. If you are placing more than one cutting in the pot, plant them around the edge, giving them plenty of space.

Step 3: Water the cuttings in well, but take care not to dislodge them. Make sure the water is draining away well as the cuttings will rot if the soil remains wet.

Step 4: To make a humid atmosphere and keep the soil and cuttings moist, make a frame of sticks or wire tall enough to cover the cuttings. Place a polythene bag over the frame, and stand the pot out of direct sunlight.

A ROMANTIC GARDEN PATH is bordered by old-fashioned favourites, including perennial daisies and scented pinks.

Taking root cuttings

A number of plants, including perennials such as sea lavender, romneya and perennial phlox, can be grown from root cuttings. As the plant will be disturbed when the cuttings are taken, this task is best done in winter.

• Remove the soil from around the base of the plant until you reach the roots. Trace them back until they are 3–5mm ($\frac{1}{8}$–$\frac{3}{16}$in) thick, and cut off some cleanly with a sharp knife or secateurs. Immediately place them in a plastic bag so they do not dry out.

• Wash the soil from the roots and cut them into 2.5–5cm (1–2in) lengths. If you intend to plant them vertically you will need to know which way is up; cut all the tops straight across and the bottoms at an angle.

• Place the cuttings vertically in a container, or lay them in horizontally and cover with about 5mm ($\frac{3}{16}$in) of John Innes No.1. Water thoroughly and check regularly to see whether further watering is needed.

• Once good shoots have appeared, your new plants can be potted up individually into small pots or planted into the ground. It is important to keep the cuttings moist, but if you saturate the compost the roots will rot.

WHAT CAN GO WRONG?

Perennials can be attacked by a number of insect pests and diseases, and problems that occur on specific plants will be discussed in the individual plant entries. Slugs and snails are among the worst pests for herbaceous perennials since they can destroy newly emerging growth as it appears in spring. If each successive burst of leaves is destroyed, the plant will eventually give up. You must search for and destroy these pests, perhaps picking them off by hand, or using bait or beer traps.

Overwatering or poorly drained heavy soils can also damage or kill perennials, especially if they are too wet during their dormant period when there is no foliage to transpire moisture from the plant. Waterlogged soils also provide ideal conditions for the growth and spread of various soil-borne, root-rotting fungi. A few plants, such as astilbe and hosta, actually enjoy damp or boggy ground, but most enjoy conditions with good drainage.

Yellow leaves

• Plants may have been overwatered or they may be too dry. You are actually more likely to overwater a perennial in a pot than in a border. They may also need feeding if this has not been done for some time. Try a light application of fertiliser; in warm weather there should be an improvement within two to three weeks. Towards the end of the growing season you can expect to see some leaf yellowing as they finish their useful life. Do not worry if a few leaves, especially down towards the ground, become brown or yellow during the active spring period.

Curled or distorted leaves

• Keep a regular check against aphids. They can be a terrible problem. They are small, sap-sucking insects that may be black, brown, green or clear. They cluster thickly on the new growth of plants, sucking out the sap. This may cause curling or distortion of leaves, and flowers may fail to open if the sap has been sucked from the buds or they, too,

A HEALTHY display of violets.

may be distorted. Close inspection usually reveals these tiny insects; they can be squashed and wiped off the stems, hosed off or sprayed with insecticidal soap or pyrethrum-based sprays. Aphids need to be controlled as they also transmit virus diseases from plant to plant.

Silvery mottling on foliage

• Silver markings or discolouration of foliage may be the first sign of thrip attack. These tiny insects attack plant tissue and suck the sap. Unlike most sap-sucking insects they attack the top, not the under leaf. There are several different types that cause plant damage. They are readily recognisable, usually having black bodies and wings edged with hairs. Apart from the physical damage, some thrips are also responsible for transmitting virus diseases from plant to plant. Since many thrips use weeds as hosts it is important to keep them out of your beds and borders. If thrips are causing damage, make sure that the plants are not stressed through lack of water. When spraying, use an appropriate contact or systemic insecticide.

Curled and browned flowers

• Check plants for thrips because they can attack pale-coloured flowers. For their control, see 'Silvery mottling on foliage'.

TAKING ROOT CUTTINGS

Step 1: To take root cuttings from most perennials, trace the roots back and cut out a section some 3–5mm (⅛–³⁄₁₆in) thick.

Step 2: Wash any soil from the roots and cut them into sections 2.5–5cm (1–2in) long. Mark the top of each so you know which way up to plant them.

Step 3: Place the root cuttings vertically in a container, making sure that they are the right way up. Water them in thoroughly.

Alternatively, if plants have thin roots, take cuttings in the same way but lay them horizontally and cover with a thin layer of compost.

Holes in leaves or on leaf edges

- If your plants have chewed edges or large areas of leaf missing, check for snails. They are the most likely culprits. Pick the snails off and destroy them, or use a bait if you do not have a pet.
- If there is no sign of snails, start looking for caterpillars. Chewing insects such as caterpillars can do a great deal of damage in quite a short time because they can be such voracious feeders. They can be well camouflaged, lying along leaf margins or hiding under leaves. Try first to find and destroy them, but if the damage continues, dust the plants with derris.

Mottled leaves

- Leaf mottling may be the result of mite damage. Mites are not true insects, having eight legs like other members of the arachnid family. Mites are sap suckers, and foliage attacked by mites appears mottled and discoloured. With the aid of a magnifying glass the tiny creatures and their clear circular eggs can sometimes be seen on the underside of leaves. If severe mite attacks go unnoticed initially, there may be fine webbing on the underside of foliage too. Sometimes with light attacks hosing under the leaves every two to three days is enough to reduce their population to an acceptable, non-

damaging level. Mites are much worse in warm, dry weather or on plants that may be sheltered by the overhanging eaves of a house. Make sure that plants are well watered and well nourished. If mite numbers do reach unacceptable levels, clearly getting out of hand, you may need to spray with an appropriate insecticide. Many general, broad spectrum insecticides are useless against mites.

Grey/white powder on leaves

- This is probably caused by the common fungal disease, powdery mildew. In humid areas this disease is a constant problem. For plants that are very susceptible to powdery mildew, much work is being done to breed plant-resistant varieties. Meanwhile, it may be necessary to spray with a fungicide such as carbendazim or copper oxychloride or, alternatively, you can dust the plants with sulphur. If you have any

A VIBRANT show of argyranthemums.

kind of problem with powdery mildew, avoid watering the plants late in the day so that you do not increase the humidity around them overnight.

Black or dark spots on leaves

- There are many strains of fungal leaf spots that can attack a wide range of plants. If only a few leaves are affected, remove and destroy them. Avoid watering late in the day and, where possible, avoid splashing the foliage which will spread the fungal spores. Many fungal leaf spots respond well to simple fungicides such as copper oxychloride, but there are other effective fungicides available to the home gardener.

Yellow spots on top of leaves

- Yellow spots on the upper side of leaves that have blisters, or pustules on the underside, are likely to be some form of rust. There is an enormous number of rust strains, and they can attack a wide range of plants and perennials, including chrysanthemums. It is a good idea to remove the worst affected leaves immediately, and to avoid overhead watering which quickly splashes the spores around, increasing contamination. Copper oxychloride will control some rusts, though you may find you need to use a more specific fungicide.

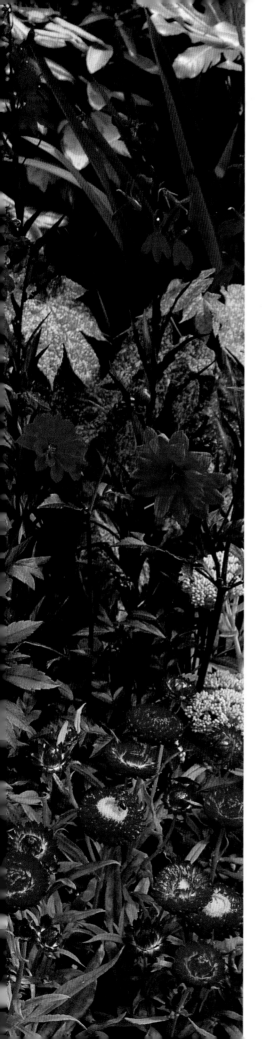

PLANNING A PERENNIAL GARDEN

Many perennials have a long flowering period, and well-planned beds of perennials can display a succession of flowers over many months. This does, however, take a good deal of planning and probably some trial and error.

If you are planting a large area, it's best to design it on paper first so that you can place the tallest plants at the back or in the centre of the bed, also giving you time to devise your colour scheme. You can experiment by using a variety of plants, all with flowers in one colour or shades of one colour, or you may opt for a planting of bright contrasts. Whatever scheme you choose, allow for plenty of plants to create a full, rich scene. A well-planted perennial border or garden is close planted so that every bit of soil is covered, providing foliage and floral interest throughout the season.

ABOVE: These rich purple spikes belong to the spectacular Salvia 'Ostfriesland', a cultivar of Salvia nemorosa.

LEFT: True perennials such as purple Liatris spicata, and the yellow daisies of Coreopsis verticillata, mix well with annual red strawflowers and Dahlia 'Bishop of Llandaff '.

THE LUSH GREEN SCENE, composed of hostas, candelabra primulas, and other shade-tolerant perennials, in a fern-filled woodland garden on the mild west coast of Scotland. Such a scene can easily be reduced and modified for the borders in a shady city garden.

USING PERENNIALS

Perennials are among the most versatile of plants, and the vast majority of gardeners use them in conjunction with permanent plantings of shrubs, annuals and bulbs. They are plants that require far less work and maintenance than annuals while still giving a great deal of seasonal colour and interest. In fact many low-growing perennials, such as penstemon, lamb's ears, pinks and bergenia, make excellent border plantings, while taller growers, such as phlox and *Acanthus mollis*, can be planted among shrubs. Long-flowering plants, such as achillea and corydalis, can be used to give colour between seasonal annual displays. They also give interest to a garden bed where bulbs have finished flowering, and are in the process of dying down.

PERENNIAL BORDERS

Traditionally, perennials have often been close planted in a border. To get an idea of how a well-grown perennial border should look, visit the great gardens like Sissinghurst in Kent, and Arley Hall in Cheshire. Gardeners have been refining the art of perennial borders for a very long time, and both first-time and experienced gardeners will find plenty of new, imaginative ideas in these schemes. Specialist nurseries often have special exhibit beds where you can also see how well various perennials combine.

FORMAL GARDENS

It is difficult for a perennial garden to look really formal, but many of the best perennial schemes have been informally planted within a formal framework. Some are enclosed within walls, while many are contained within low, formally trimmed hedges. The garden beds are laid out in strict geometric style, resembling an ornate piece of embroidery when viewed from above, their angular shapes defined by tightly pruned hedges, often of box or lavender. Sometimes the garden beds are also defined by close-mown paths of grass.

Probably the closest one can get to a formal perennial scheme is by creating a mirror-planting effect. Each part of the design mirrors the next, and the sections are divided by paths of grass, brick, gravel or stone. For a mirror planting to be successful, the whole of the area must be in full sun, otherwise there is absolutely no chance of growth rates and flowering times being the same, or as near as one can get to that given you are dealing with living plant material.

PLANT ARRANGEMENT

Perennials come in many shapes and sizes, which is a great advantage when planning a garden. If your perennial garden is to be sited against a fence or wall you might decide to place the tallest growers at the back. This both forms a backbone and gives you the space to stand back and fully appreciate them. So, for example, the long tall spears of delphiniums generally stand behind their lower-growing neighbours. If you are designing an island bed, the tall plants are traditionally placed right in the centre for a formal effect, or slightly off-centre so it does not look quite so inflexibly schematic. Smaller plants radiate out, down towards the front of the border, giving a graduated, tiered effect. But such arrangements are not strictly necessary. You might prefer, instead, to give a more informal look by gently mixing heights, creating undulations. When doing this the most important point to remember is that no plant should be hidden by its neighbour, or cast in total shade, and that all should be visible from some vantage point so that you can appreciate their colour and shape.

A number of plants, such as mulleins and red hot pokers, give very strong vertical accents which contrast well with lower, more variably shaped plants. And striking foliage plants, such as cardoon and *Melianthus major*, are grown more for their strong structural shape than for their flowers. (Note that the latter is rather tender for the first two years, but once it has a shrubby base can be left outside all-year round in milder areas, provided it is given some frost protection.) These big plants must be sited carefully and probably not used to excess. A contrast in leaf colour, shape and texture will also add considerable interest to the perennial garden. If you have the luxury of being able to create a very large or long perennial border, you will need to think about repeating some of the shapes and colours to tie the planting together. The other great advantage of growing perennials is that you can move them around when they are dormant, or semi-dormant, if you are not totally satisfied with their appearance or performance. They let you modify the design.

Everyone would love to have a garden that was in full flower for months at a time. Planning to ensure a succession of blooms over many months is the hard part of designing a garden. Even if you consult the best reference books by the best writers, reliable local nurseries and experienced friends, you will find that plants behave differently in different situations; in the end what counts is personal experience. Prior research is essential, providing vital guidance, and it is worth walking around your neighbourhood to see exactly which plants are being grown successfully.

USING COLOUR

Colour is, of course, a most important consideration. If you are making a large perennial garden it is a good idea to put your planting suggestions on paper, even using coloured pencils or paints to help you see how the colours work together. You do not need to be an artist as rough shapes or blobs of colour will do. You would not want or expect to have all the plants in flower at the one time, but you need to think about overlapping flowering times.

If you want a cool looking garden you could restrict yourself to white, blue, cream or pale pink flowers, with some silver foliage plants as accents. Red, yellow and orange flowering plants will give you a hot and vibrant look. Sometimes the addition of an area of very strong colour lifts the garden out of the ordinary. Some very famous long perennial borders cover a wide colour range, starting with very soft pastel colours, ending with strong, hot colours. Another idea is to position clumps of the same plant at intervals along a border as the repetition adds to the effect of the design. Even if you have only a small space to work with, you will find the repetition gives more form to the garden.

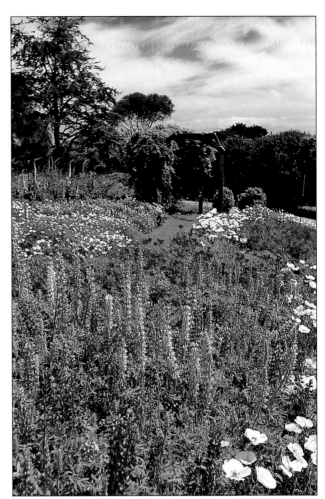

BLUE LUPINS and white poppies provide a cool contrast with the bright reds and yellows in the extensive borders behind.

PERENNIALS FOR ALL SEASONS

At every season of the year there is some perennial plant in flower. Winter brings the delicate and subtle beauty of the winter or Lenten rose (*Helleborus* spp.), and also bergenia in mild areas. Spring brings a succession of flowers in both mild and cold districts. Columbines, armeria, Solomon's seal, candelabra primula, geum, pinks and heuchera are just a few of the lovely spring-flowering perennials. Summer brings bergamot, achillea, platycodon, and rudbeckias, some of which flower well into autumn. Autumn perennials include chrysanthemums, favoured for their garden display and cut flowers, while red hot pokers, sedum and asters provide colour and interest at a time when annuals are either being pulled out or planted for the next season. These autumn-flowering perennials, along with some autumn-flowering bulbs such as colchicums and nerines, will carry your garden beautifully into winter.

Perennials also generally combine well with spring bulbs. While the perennials are still dormant, or are just beginning to put on new growth, the bulbs flower providing a combination of foliage and blooms. Then, when the bulbs have finished performing and the foliage is beginning to look tatty and start dying, the perennials begin to take over, becoming the dominant garden feature.

ACANTHUS MOLLIS
Bear's breeches

LITTLE FLOWERS *in purple and white open along tall spikes above the foliage.*

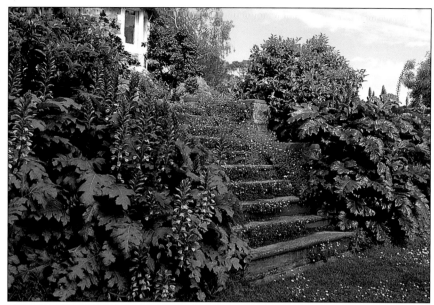

THE BEAR'S BREECHES *in this Scottish garden are thriving in the open. The masses of handsome foliage suit a large garden where you can stand back and see the plants in perspective.*

FEATURES

HERBACEOUS

Also known as bear's breeches, this handsome foliage plant grows from 70cm–1m (28-39in) high, and can make a clump close to 1m (39in) wide. The dark glossy leaves provided the inspiration and model for the decoration on Corinthian columns. This striking feature plant is at its best when mass planted, though one generous clump can be extremely effective in quite a small area. It enjoys full sun, but also tolerates shade. The stiff flower spikes of purple and white flowers appear among the foliage from spring into summer. It can be quite a vigorous grower although it dies back after flowering. It can multiply quickly once established, but is rarely troublesome.

ACANTHUS AT A GLANCE

A. mollis is a vigorous Mediterranean perennial liking dry, stoney ground. Hardy to –15°C (5°F), with bold shapely foliage.

JAN	/	**RECOMMENDED VARIETIES**
FEB	sow	*Acanthus mollis* 'Fielding Gold'
MAR	divide	
APR	transplant	*A.m.* 'Hollard's Gold'
MAY	flowering	*A.m.* Latifolius Group
JUN	flowering	
JULY	/	**COMPANION PLANTS**
AUG	/	*Bergenia* x 'Ballawley'
SEPT	/	Forsythia
OCT	divide	Gypsophila
NOV	/	*Syringa vulgaris*
DEC	/	

CONDITIONS

Aspect   It flowers best in full sun, but also grows in light shade.

Site   Needs well-drained soil that contains plenty of organic matter to aid water retention. Give plants a deep layer of mulch with compost in the spring, and then a second application if necessary in mid-summer.

GROWING METHOD

Propagation   Grows from seed sown in spring, or divide clumps in the spring or autumn. Plant new divisions 30–40cm (12–16in) apart. Young plants must be given ample water in dry weather during spring and summer. After flowering cut back on the watering.

Feeding   Apply a complete plant food as growth starts during the spring.

Problems   Since slugs and snails can cause a lot of damage to young growth, badly disfiguring it, take precautions. No other problems are known.

FLOWERING

Season   The tall spikes of purple and white flowers appear in late spring and summer.

Cutting   It is possible to use this as a cut flower; the dried spikes make good indoor decoration.

AFTER FLOWERING

Requirements   Protect young plants with straw overwinter. Cut off the flowering stems once faded.

ACHILLEA
Yarrow

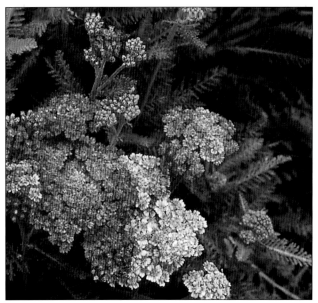

LONG-FLOWERING and not as invasive as the species, the new hybrid achilleas will give great pleasure for months.

ACHILLEA IS ALSO KNOWN as soldier's woundwort, nosebleed and sanguinary, which reflects its value in herbal medicine.

FEATURES

HERBACEOUS

Yarrow are vigorous perennials offering heights from 5cm–1.2m (2in–4ft). The species has flattish heads of white flowers and feathery foliage, but cultivars have flowers in a lovely range of shades, including yellow, pink, apricot and crimson. Flowers are long lasting. Yarrow is quick and easy to establish, and may need to be controlled, however the runners are quite easy to pull out. Some of the cultivars are less invasive than the species.
A. filipendulina has flat heads of bright yellow flowers lasting all summer. Selected forms have deep or pale yellow blooms. Best planted in large drifts, yarrow is ideal for the back of borders or among annuals.

ACHILLEA AT A GLANCE

Mainly deciduous perennials grown for their attractive, daisy-like summer and autumn flowers. Hardy to –15°C (5°F).

		RECOMMENDED VARIETIES
JAN	/	*Achillea* 'Coronation Gold'
FEB	sow	*Achillea filipendulina*
MAR	sow	'Cloth of Gold'
APR	transplant	*A. f.* 'Gold Plate'
MAY	divide	*A.* x *lewisii* "King Edward'
JUN	flowering	*A. millefolium*
JULY	flowering	'Cerise Queen'
AUG	flowering	*A. m.* 'Lilac Beauty'
SEPT	flowering	*A. m.* 'White Queen'
OCT	/	*A.* 'Moonshine'
NOV	/	*A. tomentosa*
DEC	/	

CONDITIONS

Aspect   Needs full sun for the best results, but will tolerate some shade for part of the day.
Site   Any well-drained soil is suitable.

GROWING METHOD

Propagation   Grows easily if established clumps are lifted and divided in the spring. Plant the vigorous new divisions 20–30cm (8–12in) apart, and discard the old. New, young plants need regular watering in prolonged, dry spells, but once established achillea is remarkably drought tolerant, and needs only an occasional deep drink.
Feeding   Apply a complete plant food as growth commences in spring.
Problems   No specific pest or disease problems are known to attack achillea.

FLOWERING

Season   The long flowering period lasts throughout summer into early autumn. Regular removal of the spent, fading flower stems will significantly prolong blooming.
Cutting   The flowers are good for cutting because they have a reasonably long vase life. Take handfuls of cut flowers for the vase as soon as the heads are fully open. Also excellent for drying.

AFTER FLOWERING

Requirements   Cut off any spent flower stalks that remain on the plant in late autumn.

AGAPANTHUS
African blue lily

THE BLUE AND WHITE flowering heads of agapanthus are composed of numerous flowers. They make a striking feature.

THIS DENSE PLANTING of agapanthus needs little attention and rewards the gardener with its wonderful summer flowers.

FEATURES

SUMMER AUTUMN WINTER SPRING

HERBACEOUS

Agapanthus has dark green, strap-shaped leaves that grow to about 50cm (20in) long. It produces rounded heads of blue or white flowers on top of stems 1m (39in) or more high, but even without the flowers it makes a great foliage accent. It is hardy in the south and west, but in colder regions needs winter protection. The Headbourne hybrids are particularly hardy. It can be grown in containers, and looks excellent in eye-catching tubs. Several attractive dwarf forms have foliage that rarely exceed 20cm (8in).

CONDITIONS

Aspect   Tolerates some shade, but the flowering will be poor. Full sun is ideal.

AGAPANTHUS AT A GLANCE

A vigorous perennial, forming bold, eye-catching flowering clumps, from southern Africa. Many hardy to –5°C (23°F).

		RECOMMENDED VARIETIES
JAN	/	
FEB	sow	*Agapanthus africanus*
MAR	sow	A. a. 'Albus'
APR	divide	A. *caulescens*
MAY	transplant	'Lilliput'
JUN	/	'Loch Hope'
JULY	flowering	'Peter Pan'
AUG	flowering	A. *praecox* 'Variegatus'
SEPT	flowering	
OCT	/	
NOV	/	
DEC	/	

Site   Grows in almost any soil, but well-drained ground with organic matter is perfect. In colder gardens, grow by a south-facing wall.

GROWING METHOD

Propagation   Divide clumps in the spring, ensuring that each division has a crown and a decent batch of healthy roots. The latter can be shortened and some outer leaves removed if necessary. Plant about 25cm (10in) apart. Also grows from seed sown in the spring. Needs regular watering to establish, but once settled it can cope with long, dry periods. However, for the best growth and flowering, do not let new young plants dry out.

Feeding   Apply complete plant food in the early spring. Potted plants will perform better with an application of slow-release granules, or a monthly liquid feed, carefully following the manufacturer's recommended rate.

Problems   There are no particular problems, but clumps will harbour groups of snails. Pick off.

FLOWERING

Season   Blooms appear in mid- to late summer, depending on the conditions.

Cutting   Agapanthus can be used as a cut flower if the stems are plunged into boiling water for 15 seconds immediately after cutting.

AFTER FLOWERING

Requirements   No pruning needed other than cutting off spent flower stems and dead leaves. Protect crowns over winter with a thick mulch of straw or dry leaves.

ALCHEMILLA MOLLIS
Lady's mantle

LONG USED as a folk medicine to help heal wounds and gynaecological problems, lady's mantle is today usually grown for its decorative value, and ability to self-seed. The pure lime-green flowers brighten the garden, making a marvellous contrast against the wide, lobed leaves.

FEATURES

HERBACEOUS

This is a quick-growing herbaceous perennial mostly used as a border plant to edge paths and beds. An abundant self-seeder, it is good for suppressing weeds, filling any free spaces, often popping up in cracks in paving. Growing anywhere between 20–40cm (8–16in) high, one plant may spread to 28–40cm (11–16in). The rounded, slightly hairy leaves overlap one another, and the plant produces trusses of bright lime-green flowers through summer. It provides a lovely contrast with other, stronger colours. The leaves tend to trap raindrops or dew, adding to the effect.

ALCHEMILLA AT A GLANCE

A. mollis is a hardy perennial grown for its prolific self-seeding, and attractive lime-green foliage. Hardy to –15°C (5°F).

		COMPANION PLANTS
JAN	/	
FEB	sow	Delphinium
MAR	sow	Dicentra
APR	transplant	Eremurus
MAY	transplant	Eucomis
JUN	flowering	Euonymus
JULY	flowering	Geranium
AUG	flowering	Gladiolus
SEPT	flowering	Lupin
OCT	divide	Rose
NOV	/	
DEC	/	

CONDITIONS

Aspect   Thrives in full sun, though it tolerates a degree of light shade.

Site   Needs well-drained soil that has a high organic content.

GROWING METHOD

Propagation   Self-sown seedlings can be easily transplanted to other positions. Clumps can be divided in the spring or autumn with the divisions spaced 20–25cm (8–10in) apart. Newly planted specimens may need watering, but mature plants tolerate dry periods. Justifiably known as a great survivor and spreader.

Feeding   Apply a complete plant food as the new growth begins.

Problems   No specific problems are known.

FLOWERING

Season   Masses of lime-green flowers appear from late spring through summer.

Cutting   A great favourite with flower arrangements.

AFTER FLOWERING

Requirements   If you do not want plants to self-seed, trim spent flowers as soon as they fade. Once flowering has finished and growth begins to die down, the plants can be cut back hard with shears, or even a trimmer if you want to be ruthless.

ALSTROEMERIA
Peruvian Lily

ALSO KNOWN AS THE LILY of the Incas, the Peruvian lily can be placed in a mixed perennial border as here, or planted between shrubs. Bold groupings are best. Gardeners can choose from a colourful range of species and cultivars, but may be unable to obtain some of the varieties sold by florists.

FEATURES

HERBACEOUS

The Peruvian lily is grown commercially on a large scale as the flowers are long lasting when cut. In the garden it is a herbaceous perennial with flower spikes growing mostly 30–60cm (12–24in) high, although there are dwarf forms and very tall ones. The flowers are beautifully marked with streaks and spots of colour, contrasting with a wide range of base colours of cream, yellow, orange, pink and red. If conditions suit, these plants spread by means of fleshy rhizomes (roots) to form large clumps. Also excellent when grown in pots.

ALSTROEMERIA AT A GLANCE

A hardy perennial surviving –10°C (14°F). Grown for their excellent showy flowers, many make unbeatable cut flowers.

		RECOMMENDED VARIETIES
JAN	/	*Alstroemeria ligtu* hybrids
FEB	/	'Orange Gem'
MAR	/	'Orange Glory'
APR	sow	'Princess Mira' (and all
MAY	/	'Princess' varieties)
JUN	transplant	'Solent Crest'
JULY	flowering	
AUG	flowering	
SEPT	flowering	
OCT	divide	
NOV	/	
DEC	/	

CONDITIONS

Aspect   Needs full sun and shelter to thrive, especially in colder areas. Also requires shelter from strong wind. Makes an excellent potted, greenhouse plant.

Site   Must have very free-draining soil containing plenty of decayed organic matter.

GROWING METHOD

Propagation   Many grow readily from seed sown in spring, but division of established clumps is easiest; spring is generally considered the best time. Bare-root plants can be hard to establish; pot-grown plants, available in the summer, are better. Plant roots 5cm (2in) deep and about 15cm (6in) apart. In a prolonged dry period, water bedded plants regularly in spring and summer, but restrict watering after flowering.

Feeding   Apply slow-release granular fertiliser in spring.

Problems   No specific problems are known.

FLOWERING

Season   Most species and their cultivars flower from spring into summer, some into autumn.

Cutting   This is a first-class cut flower.

AFTER FLOWERING

Requirements   Cut off spent flower stems at ground level. Protect crowns with straw in cold winters.

ANEMONE X HYBRIDA
Windflower (Anemone x hybrida, syn. A. hupehensis var. japonica)

ELEGANT SIMPLICITY is the best way to describe the form of the Japanese anemone with its white, yellow and green colour scheme.

RELIABLE IN BLOOM year after year, the Japanese anemone is an attractive garden addition, softening stiff, geometric schemes.

FEATURES

HERBACEOUS

Also known as the Japanese windflower, this herbaceous perennial is one of the great joys of the autumn garden. The leaves are three-lobed, somewhat maple-like, and the single or double flowers are carried on stems up to 1m (39in) high. Flowers may be single or double-coloured white, pale or deep pink. Once established, they spread into large clumps quite rapidly, travelling by underground stems, and also self-seeding. Some consider them invasive but plants can be easily dug out, and a mass planting in full bloom is a real delight. Grow where they can remain undisturbed for some years. Site at the back of a shady bed or in dappled sunlight under trees.

ANEMONE AT A GLANCE

A. x hybrida is a free-flowering, quick spreading herbaceous perennial with lovely, pale pink flowers. Hardy to –15°C (5°F).

		RECOMMENDED VARIETIES
JAN	/	*Anemone x hybrida*
FEB	/	'Honorine Jobert'
MAR	divide	*A. x h.* 'Konigin Charlotte'
APR	transplant	*A. x h.* 'Luise Uhink'
MAY	/	*A. x h.* 'Margarete'
JUN	/	*A. x h.* 'Pamina'
JULY	/	*A. x h.* 'Richard Ahrends'
AUG	flowering	
SEPT	flowering	
OCT	sow	
NOV	/	
DEC	/	

CONDITIONS

Aspect   Prefers shade or semi-shade with shelter from strong winds.

Site   Grows best in well-drained soil that contains plenty of organic matter.

GROWING METHOD

Propagation   Increase from root cuttings in winter, or divide established clumps in early spring, ensuring that each division has a decent set of roots. This vigorous plant can sometimes be tricky to divide and transplant. Replant the new, vigorous younger growths from the outside of the clump, generally about 30cm (12in) apart. New young plants need ample watering in prolonged dry spells during the growing season.

Feeding   Fertilising is not essential, but a complete plant food can be applied in the spring.

Problems   No specific problems are known.

FLOWERING

Season   Flowers appear prolifically from late summer through the autumn months.

Cutting   Though they seem perfect for cut flower displays, the flowers do not last that well.

AFTER FLOWERING

Requirements   Cut back spent flower stems to ground level once they begin to fade, and cut the plant right back to the ground in late autumn.

AQUILEGIA
Columbine

WIDELY CONTRASTING COLOURS successfully combine in the flowers of this modern, long-spurred hybrid columbine.

AN OPEN WOODLAND SETTING is ideal for columbines, letting them freely self-seed forming, bold, distinctive groups.

FEATURES

HERBACEOUS

These old-fashioned favourites, also called granny's bonnets, give a fine display in the garden and make decorative cut flowers. The foliage is often blue-green, and the flowers come in single colours – white, pink, crimson, yellow and blue – and combinations of pastel and brighter shades. There are also excellent black and whites ('Magpie'). The older forms have short-spurred flowers that resemble old-fashioned bonnets, especially 'Nora Barlow', a good double which is a mix of red, pink and green. Modern hybrids are long spurred, and available in many single colours and bicolours. Plants may be 40–70cm (16–28in) high. Columbines are not long lived but are easily seed grown. Ideal for the dappled garden, grow them under deciduous trees and in borders.

AQUILEGIA AT A GLANCE

A clump-forming perennial, happy in semi-shade, perfect for the cottage garden where it freely self-seeds. Hardy to −15°C (5°F).

Jan	/	**RECOMMENDED VARIETIES**
Feb	/	
Mar	sow	*Aquilegia bertolonii*
Apr	transplant	*A. canadensis*
May	flowering	*A. flabellata*
Jun	flowering	*A. f.* var. *pumila*
July	/	*A. f.* var. *f. alba*
Aug	/	'Henson Harebell'
Sept	divide	'Magpie'
Oct	sow	Music series
Nov	/	*A. vulgaris* 'Nora Barlow'
Dec	/	

CONDITIONS

Aspect Prefers semi-shade, and thrives in woodland gardens, but full sun is not a problem.
Site Needs well-drained soil that contains plenty of organic matter.

GROWING METHOD

Propagation Clumps are actually quite hard to divide, but it can be done, autumn being the best time. Columbine also grows from seed sown in early spring, or in the autumn. Self-sown plants are hardy, but note that they may not always be true to type. Space plants about 30cm (12in) apart. New young plants must not be allowed to dry out in prolonged dry spells in the spring and summer months. Keep a careful watch.
Feeding Apply complete plant food in the spring as the new growth begins to emerge.
Problems No particular pest or disease problems are known for this plant.

FLOWERING

Season There is a long flowering period from mid-spring to mid-summer.
Cutting Flower stems can be cut for the vase, and they make an attractive display, but the garden show lasts considerably longer.

AFTER FLOWERING

Requirements Spent flower stems can either be removed or left on the plants enabling the seeds to mature. Cut back the old growth to ground level as it dies off.

ARMERIA MARITIMA
Sea thrift

EACH FLOWERHEAD resembles a tiny posy, which is why thrift makes a fine cut flower, alone or in a composition with other flowers.

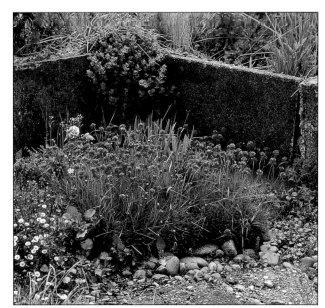

POOR STONY GROUND, which resembles thrift's natural habitat, provides ideal conditions for growing this plant.

FEATURES

EVERGREEN

Also known as sea thrift, this evergreen perennial grows in little grassy mounds 5–12.5cm (2–5in) high. It occurs naturally in northern Europe and around the Mediterranean, often in very exposed situations, including cliff tops. The rounded flowerheads are carried above the foliage on stems 15–30cm (6–12in) high. Flowers vary in colour in the species and may be white, pink or almost red, and there are a number of named cultivars available. Thrift can be used as a groundcover or edging plant, or can be planted in rockeries, on dry walls, or in poor soil where few other plants will survive. It also makes a good container plant.

ARMERIA AT A GLANCE

A. maritima is an attractive evergreen, clump-forming perennial which colonises inhospitable areas. Hardy to –18°C (0°F).

		RECOMMENDED VARIETIES
JAN	/	
FEB	/	*Armeria maritima* 'Alba'
MAR	division	*A. m.* 'Corsica'
APR	/	*A. m.* 'Launcheana'
MAY	transplant	*A. m.* 'Ruby Glow'
JUN	flowering	*A. m.* 'Splendens'
JULY	flowering	*A. m.* 'Vindictive'
AUG	flowering	
SEPT	/	
OCT	/	
NOV	/	
DEC	/	

CONDITIONS

Aspect Needs full sun all day. Thrift tolerates dry, windy conditions and salt spray, and is an excellent choice for coastal gardens.

Site Grows in any kind of soil so long as it is very well drained. Adding sharp sand will improve the drainage.

GROWING METHOD

Propagation Divide established clumps in the spring and replant about 15–20cm (6–8in) apart. The species can be grown from seed sown in the spring, or from semi-ripe cuttings taken in the summer

Feeding Give a light dressing of complete fertiliser in early spring.

Problems Thrift has a tendency to rot if soils are in any way too heavy, poorly drained or overwatered. In humid weather and in sheltered positions it may also be susceptible to the fungal disease which is called rust. Use a fungicide to attack the problem.

FLOWERING

Season Thrift has a long flowering period through spring and summer, provided the plants are deadheaded regularly.

Cutting Makes a good cut flower.

AFTER FLOWERING

Requirements Regularly remove spent flower stems to give a prolonged flowering period.

ASTER
Michaelmas daisy

RICH MAUVE flowers virtually obscuring the foliage on a mature plant.

THE ATTRACTIVE Aster ericoides, which has produced many excellent cultivars.

ONE OF the best of the reds is the low growing 'Winston Churchill'.

FEATURES

HERBACEOUS

There is a wide variety of asters, and all of them flower in late summer and autumn. The most commonly grown is *A. novi-belgii*, which has a range of cultivars from dwarf forms 25cm (10in) high to tall varieties reaching 1m (39in). Flowers are blue, violet, pink, red or white, and all are good for cutting. *A. ericoides* has very small leaves and produces stems of white flowers up to 1m (39in) high. *A. x frikartii* grows about 76cm (30in) high and has violet-blue flowers. These plants are all extremely easy to grow and tolerate a wide range of conditions. They multiply readily. Taller varieties need staking.

ASTER AT A GLANCE

Hardy perennials creating large clumps, giving strong autumn colour in most situations. Hardy to –15°C (5°F).

JAN	/	
FEB	sow	
MAR	sow	
APR	divide	
MAY	transplant	
JUN	/	
JULY	flowering	
AUG	flowering	
SEPT	flowering	
OCT	divide	
NOV	/	
DEC	/	

RECOMMENDED VARIETIES

Aster alpinus
A. amellus 'Framfieldii'
A. a. 'Jacqueline Genebrier'
'Coombe Fishacre'
A. ericoides 'Golden Spray'
A. x frikartii 'Monch'
A. novae-angliae
A. novi-belgii 'Audrey'

CONDITIONS

Aspect   Grows best in full sun. Tolerates light shade, but blooming may not be so prolific and growth will be less compact.

Site   Add well-rotted organic matter to the soil. Feed and water well to counter disease.

GROWING METHOD

Propagation   Divide clumps in late winter. These plants are prolific growers and one plant will multiply itself tenfold in a season. Replant divisions 20cm (8in) apart. The best results are from regular watering during the spring and summer, especially in long, dry periods.

Feeding   Apply complete plant food in early spring.

Problems   Powdery mildew can be a major problem, especially with varieties of *A. novi-belgii*. Mildew resistant varieties include *A. x frikartii* and varieties of *A. amellus*.

FLOWERING

Season   The long flowering display lasts from late summer into autumn.

Cutting   Cut flowers last very well if given a frequent change of water.

AFTER FLOWERING

Requirements Cut off spent flower stems close to ground level after blooming. Plants will gradually die back, but should not need more close attention until new growth appears next spring.

ASTILBE HYBRIDS
Astilbe

SOFT AND FEATHERY, the pale pink plumes on this astilbe will provide a long display of bright flowers and fern-like foliage.

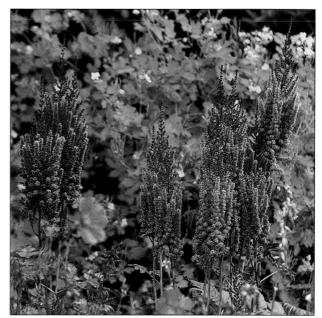

UPRIGHT SIDE BRANCHES are an unusual feature of this deep pink astilbe cultivar. They give an eye-catching, stiff appearance.

FEATURES

HERBACEOUS

These perennial hybrids revel in moist soil and light shade, although they can be grown in an open, sunny position if well watered. The shiny, compound leaves are quite attractive, with astilbe also bearing tall plumes of soft flowers 50cm (20in) or more high, in shades of pink, red, mauve or white. They look best when mass planted, and are ideal for surrounding ponds, or naturalising in a wild garden. They can be used as cut flowers, but they are probably best left in the garden where their big, theatrical effect can be enjoyed for much longer. They can quickly flag in a heat wave; water at the first sign of wilting.

ASTILBE AT A GLANCE

A rhizomatous perennial that enjoys damp soil. Striking, tall flowerheads can reach 1.2m (4ft) high. Hardy to −15°C (5°F).

		RECOMMENDED VARIETIES
JAN	/	*Astilbe* x *arendsii*
FEB	sow	'Brautschleier'
MAR	divide	*A.* x *a.*'Bronce Elegans'
APR	transplant	*A.* x *a.*'Fanal'
MAY	flowering	*A.* x *a.* 'Irrlicht'
JUN	flowering	*A.* x *a* 'Snowdrift'
JULY	flowering	*A.* x *crispa* 'Perkeo'
AUG	flowering	'Rheinland'
SEPT	flowering	*A. simplicifolia*
OCT	/	'Sprite'
NOV	divide	
DEC	/	

CONDITIONS

Aspect These are versatile plants, performing equally well in bright sun and dappled shade.

Site The ideal soil is rich in organic matter and retains plenty of moisture. Regular, heavy applications of mulch are essential.

GROWING METHOD

Propagation Divide clumps in late autumn, ensuring that each division has a crown and a decent set of roots. Plant at 20–25cm (8–10in) spacings. New young plants need plenty of water in prolonged dry spells in the spring and summer months. Do not let them dry out.

Feeding Apply a general fertiliser as growth starts in the spring, and repeat 6–8 weeks later.

Problems No specific problems are known.

FLOWERING

Season Flowers from late spring through the summer. The flower display is longer lasting in a cooler summer.

Cutting Flowers can be cut for indoor decoration.

AFTER FLOWERING

Requirements Spent flowerheads will turn a pleasant rich brown colour, and are quite attractive through the winter months. They add considerable interest to the garden. Do not cut back spent flower stems to ground level until the following spring.

ASTRANTIA MAJOR
Masterwort

ASTRANTIA MAJOR 'HADSPEN BLOOD' is a striking, vibrant red, more of an eye-catcher than the species which is much whiter. Both can be used to link and soften more permanent shrubby features, or as part of a free-flowing, flowery display for late spring and early summer.

FEATURES

HERBACEOUS

Also known as masterwort, *Astrantia major* is a 'must' for the cottage garden. A clump-forming perennial producing delightful sprays of green or pink, sometimes reddish flowers, surrounded by green-veined white bracts. A native of central Europe, it grows about 60cm (24in) high, forming clumps 45cm (18in) wide. Flowering in early and mid-summer, it can be left to colonise areas of dappled shade, though it also enjoys full sun. There are some excellent cultivars including the new 'Hadspen Blood', a striking blood red, 'Shaggy' with long bracts, and 'Sunningdale Variegated' with pale pink bracts and yellow/cream leaves. Best in large clumps.

ASTRANTIA AT A GLANCE

A. major is a clump-forming perennial grown for its abundant, attractive flowers. Excellent cultivars. Hardy to −18°C (0°F).

		RECOMMENDED VARIETIES
JAN	/	*Astrantia major alba*
FEB	/	*A. m.* 'Claret'
MAR	divide	*A. m.* 'Hadspen Blood'
APR	divide	*A. m. involucrata* 'Shaggy'
MAY	transplant	*A. m. rosea*
JUN	flowering	*A. m. rubra*
JULY	flowering	*A. m.* 'Sunningdale
AUG	sowing	Variegated'
SEPT	/	
OCT	/	
NOV	/	
DEC	/	

CONDITIONS

Aspect   Thrives in either dappled shade, or in a more open sunny position.

Soil   Likes compost-rich, moist, fertile soil, though it will also tolerate drier conditions. Woodland gardens and streamsides are ideal.

GROWING METHOD

Propagation   Can either be grown from seed sown in late summer, once ripe, or by spring division. Plant out at least 45cm (18in) apart, or closer for an immediate covering. Do not let young plants begin to dry out in a prolonged dry spring or summer spell. The variants do not require such moist conditions, and will tolerate drier soil.

Feeding   Lay a mulch around the plants in spring. This has two advantages – it enriches the soil and also prevents moisture loss.

Problems   Slugs can be a major problem, attacking the stems and foliage. Pick off when seen. Powdery mildew can also strike; spray against attacks.

FLOWERING

Season   The one flowering spell is in early and mid-summer.

Cutting   Makes good cut flowers, which can be used to soften a stiff, structural arrangement, or as part of a more flowery display.

AFTER FLOWERING

Requirements Cut down the spent flower stems, and tidy up the foliage.

AURINIA SAXATILIS

Golden dust

A SHARP, ATTRACTIVE CONTRAST with the bright yellow flowers of golden dust, against clusters of green, spoon-shape foliage.

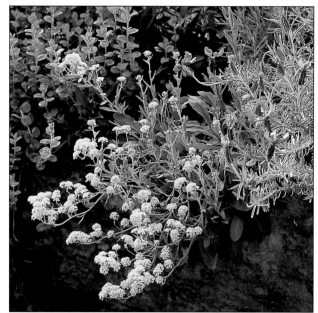

YELLOW AND BLUE always make a lively colour combination, as this wonderful planting of golden dust and Italian lavender proves.

FEATURES

EVERGREEN

This is a little, rounded, evergreen perennial that can grow from 10–30cm (4–12in) high, forming a mound up to 40–50cm (16–20in) across. In the species the flowers are a clear yellow, but the various cultivars produce flowers in white, cream, lemon or rich gold. Since its natural habitat is rocky, mountainous country it is ideal for a rock garden, for dry, sloping ground, or for edging garden beds provided the drainage is excellent. It is also ideally suited to troughs and the edges of large pots perhaps containing a shrub. Although golden dust is a perennial, some gardeners grow it as part of an annual spring display.

AURINIA AT A GLANCE

A. saxatilis is an evergreen, hardy perennial forming decent clumps topped by yellow flowers. Hardy to –18°C (0°F).

JAN	/	
FEB	/	**RECOMMENDED VARIETIES**
MAR	transplant	*Aurinia saxatilis* 'Citrina'
APR	/	*A. s.* 'Compacta'
MAY	flowering	*A. s.* 'Dudley Nevill'
JUN	flowering	*A. s.* 'Goldkugel'
JULY	/	*A. s.* 'Silver Queen'
AUG	/	
SEPT	/	**COMPANION PLANTS**
OCT	sow	*Aurinia corymbosa*
NOV	/	Aubrieta
DEC	/	

CONDITIONS

Aspect	Needs an open position in full sun.
Site	Soil must contain plenty of chalk, sand or grit, and be free draining but not rich.

GROWING METHOD

Propagation	Grows readily from seed sown in the autumn. Cultivars can be grown from tip cuttings taken in late spring and early summer. Space the plants about 10cm (4in) apart, giving them plenty of growing room. Aurinia is sold among the alpines at garden centres.
Feeding	Small amounts only of complete plant food may be given in early spring as a boost, but feeding is not essential.
Problems	No specific problems are known besides poor drainage. Overwatering pot-grown specimens can quickly rot and kill the plants.

FLOWERING

Season	Flowers appear from mid- to late spring, the flowers completely covering the plant and hiding the foliage.
Cutting	The flowers are not suitable for picking.

AFTER FLOWERING

Requirements	It is probably easiest to shear radically over the whole plant with clippers, unless you are waiting for the seed to ripen. Shearing the plants also helps to keep a compact, neatly rounded shape.

BERGENIA
Elephant's ears

THE WELL-DEFINED, SOLID SHAPE of bergenias makes them ideal edging plants, as this neat row beside a path demonstrates. Bergenias have other advantages, too, in that they flower in the shade and from late winter on, both features that are not common among perennials.

FEATURES

EVERGREEN

An excellent evergreen, groundcover plant, also known as elephant's ears because of the large, rounded leaves about 20–30cm (8–12in) long. They are often leathery and glossy, generally green, many turning reddish in the autumn. The flowers are held on short stems, from mid-spring to early summer, some, such as 'Morgenrote', repeat flowering in cool conditions. The colour range is invariably shades of pink, with some white forms. Bergenia is not a fussy plant, and enjoys a wide range of conditions from bright sun to shade, from moist to dry ground. Long living and easy to propagate, it can colonise areas beneath trees, edge paths, or front a border.

BERGENIA AT A GLANCE

A versatile evergreen with large, ornamental foliage, that thrives in a range of conditions. Hardy to –18°C (0°F).

		RECOMMENDED VARIETIES
JAN	/	
FEB	flowering	*Bergenia* 'Abendglut'
MAR	flowering	B. 'Baby Doll'
APR	flowering	B. 'Bressingham Salmon'
MAY	flowering	B. 'Bressingham White'
JUN	/	B. *cordifolia* 'Purpurea'
JULY	/	B. 'Morgenrote'
AUG	/	B. *purpurescens*
SEPT	/	B. 'Silberlicht'
OCT	divide	
NOV	divide	
DEC	/	

CONDITIONS

Aspect Grows in either full sun or shady areas, but avoid extremes of the latter.

Site Likes well composted, moist soil with good drainage, but it will also tolerate much poorer conditions which brings out a richer winter leaf colour. Provide a late autumn mulch.

GROWING METHOD

Propagation Grows from seed sown in spring, producing hybrids, or divide in the spring or autumn every five years or so, to rejuvenate a declining plant. Plant up to 60cm (24in) apart, depending on the variety, or closer for immediate coverage.

Feeding Feed generously in early spring with a complete plant food, especially on poorer ground, and give a generous layer of mulch later in the autumn.

Problems Slugs and snails can be a major problem to the new young foliage, ruining its shapely appearance. Pick off, or treat with chemicals. Spray with a fungicide if leaf spot occurs.

FLOWERING

Season The flowers appear from late winter or early spring, depending on variety, for a few weeks.

Cutting Though the flowers are useful in cut flower arrangements, the foliage, especially when red in winter, makes a particularly attractive foil.

AFTER FLOWERING

Requirements Remove the spent flower stems and foliage.

CAMPANULA
Bellflower

CAMPANULA PERSICIFOLIA ALBA makes a valuable addition to a white border, flowering prolifically in early and mid-summer.

CAMPANULAS ARE THE MAINSTAY of the cottage or woodland garden, freely spreading, adding plenty of colour and charm.

FEATURES

HERBACEOUS

Also known as the bellflower, campanula contains about 300 species of annuals, biennials and perennials. Generally easy to grow in either full sun or dappled shade, on walls, banks and in borders, it has a wide range of flowers from the tubular to saucer-shaped. They also vary considerably in height from the low, 8cm (3in) high spreaders, like *C. betulifolia,* to the 1.5m (5ft) high *C. lactiflora.* The former are excellent at the front of a border, the latter need staking at the back. There are many excellent forms, *C. glomerata* 'Superba' is a vigorous grower, reaching 60 x 60cm (24 x 24in), while C. 'Burghaltii' produces pale lavender tubular bells around the same time.

CAMPANULA AT A GLANCE

A near 300-strong genus, thriving in a wide variety of conditions, grown for their abundant flowers. Hardy to −15°C (5°F).

		RECOMMENDED VARIETIES
JAN	/	
FEB	/	*Campanula arvatica*
MAR	sow	*C. carpatica*
APR	transplant	*C. garganica*
MAY	flowering	*C. latiloba*
JUN	flowering	*C. medium*
JULY	flowering	*C. persicifolia*
AUG	flowering	*C. thyrsoides*
SEPT	flowering	*C. trachelium*
OCT	divide	
NOV	/	
DEC	/	

CONDITIONS

Aspect Campanula thrive in both sunny gardens and those with dappled shade.

Site There are three broad types of campanula requiring different conditions: well-drained, fertile soil for border plants; moist, fast-draining ground for the rock garden species; and a gritty scree bed for the alpines that dislike being wet over winter.

GROWING METHOD

Propagation Grow the species from seed in spring in a cold frame, or from cuttings, and sow alpines in a frame in autumn. Varieties must be propagated by spring cuttings, or spring or autumn division if they are to come true to the parent.

Feeding Apply a complete plant food in spring, especially on poorer soils, or plenty of dug-in, organic material.

Problems Slugs and snails are the major problem, and if not kept under control they can ruin a border display. In some areas *C. persicifolia* is prone to rust.

FLOWERING

Season The long-lasting flowers appear from midwinter to spring.

Cutting Makes an excellent display of cut flowers, especially the taller plants.

AFTER FLOWERING

Requirements Cut back to the ground in late autumn.

CENTRANTHUS RUBER
Red valerian

TRUSSES *of rich crimson and softer pink valerian provide months of bright colour in the garden, rivalling the display of annuals.*

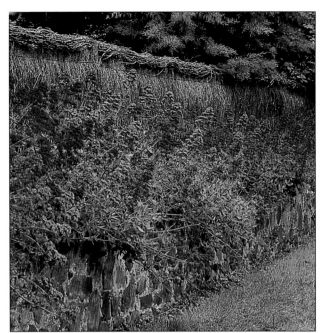

RED VALERIAN *flourishing in the conditions that suit it best – the fence provides shelter, and the raised bed warmth and good drainage.*

FEATURES

SUMMER AUTUMN WINTER SPRING

HERBACEOUS

This evergreen perennial is very easy to grow, but it often exceeds its allotted space by self-seeding (seedlings are easy to pull out). It has a long flowering period and can survive in poor, dry soil. It generally reaches 40cm (16in) high, but in good soil tops 70cm (28in). Flowers are a deep pink to red and there is a white form too. Ideal for a low-maintenance garden, it is often planted in mixed borders for its long display. It is also grown in large rockeries or on dry, fast-draining slopes. Self-sown plants can be found in almost no soil on rocky outcrops, and thrive in chalky ground.

CENTRANTHUS AT A GLANCE

C. ruber is a hardy, herbaceous perennial, a favourite in cottage gardens, with tall, red summer flowers. Hardy to −12ºC (10ºF).

		COMPANION PLANTS
JAN	/	
FEB	sow	*Argyranthemum foeniculaceum*
MAR	sow	*A. frutescens*
APR	transplant	Cytisus
MAY	transplant	*Geranium robertianum*
JUN	flowering	*Hedera colchica* 'Dentata Variegata'
JULY	flowering	*Helleborus orientalis*
AUG	flowering	Stipa
SEPT	flowering	Yucca
OCT	/	
NOV	/	
DEC	/	

CONDITIONS

Aspect   Likes full sun all day.
Soil   Needs very well-drained soil, but it need not be particularly rich.

GROWING METHOD

Propagation   Grows readily from tip cuttings taken in late spring and summer, or from seed sown in the spring. Space the plants 20cm (8in) apart.
Feeding   Fertiliser is generally not necessary, but you may give a little complete plant food in spring, as new growth begins. Needs regular water to establish, after which plants are extremely drought tolerant.
Problems   No specific problems are known.

FLOWERING

Season   The very long flowering period extends from spring until early autumn, especially if plants are cut back after each flowering flush to encourage plenty of new buds.
Cutting   Does not make a good cut flower.

AFTER FLOWERING

Requirements No attention is needed beyond removing the spent flower stems. This has a double advantage: it keeps the plant looking neat, and prevents abundant self-seeding.

CHRYSANTHEMUM HYBRIDS
Dendranthema

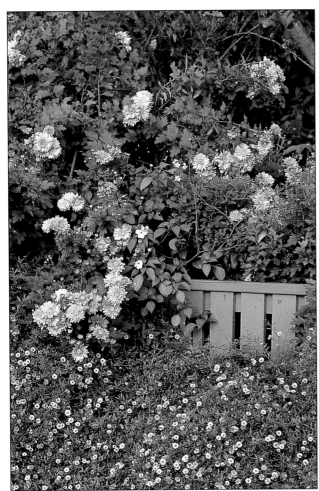

CASCADING OVER the fence onto the massed erigeron below, this wonderful garden chrysanthemum gives a prolific display.

THE QUILLED PETALS are characteristic of this open 'spider' style of chrysanthemum, as is the shading of colour.

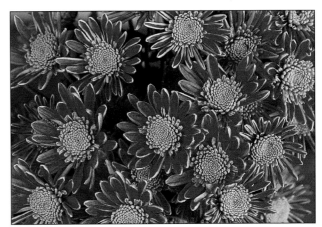

HYBRID CHRYSANTHEMUMS are justifiably highly popular in the cut flower trade, and are available for most of the year.

FEATURES

SUMMER AUTUMN WINTER SPRING

HERBACEOUS

Chrysanthemums probably originated in China, but were introduced into Japan a very long time ago. A big favourite in garden and florists' displays, they are the highlight of the late summer and autumn border. They are also widely used as a long-lasting cut flower. Chrysanthemums have been renamed and moved to the genus *Dendranthema*, though the name has yet to catch on. Four kinds to look out for include: the Korean (e.g. 'Yellow Starlet'), which give a long flowering performance but dislike excessive winter wet (store inside in severe conditions); the thigh-high, dwarf, bushy pompons ('Mei Kyo') with a sea of rounded flowers; the clump-forming rubellums (named hybrids of *C. rubellum*) which are hardiest, have a woody base, but again dislike extreme damp; and the sprays ('Pennine') which are grown both for the border and cutting.

Colour The colour range is wide, covering white, cream, yellow, many shades of pink and lilac, burgundy, pale apricot and deep mahogany.

Types There are many forms of chrysanthemums, and they have been classified by specialist societies and nurseries according to floral type. Some of the types are decorative, anemone centred, spider, pompon, single, exhibition, and Korean spray. There is virtually a shape for every taste.

Staking Many of the taller varieties need staking, which needs to be carefully thought out if the display is to avoid looking too structured. One reliable, traditional method is to insert bamboo canes at intervals around and through the planting, and thread twine from cane to cane in a criss-cross fashion, perhaps 50–60cm (20–24in) above the ground.

CONDITIONS

Aspect Grows best in full sun with protection from strong winds.

Site Needs well-drained soil that has been heavily enriched with organic matter before planting. Plants should also be mulched with decayed compost or manure.

THIS UNUSUAL chrysanthemum has the central petals incurved like those of the Korean spray, while the outer ones are widespread.

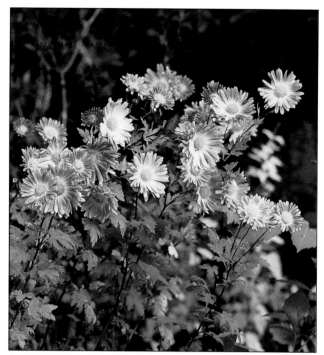

THE RUSSET COLOURS of these flowers seem appropriate to their autumn flowering season, when the leaves are turning.

GROWING METHOD

Propagation In spring lift and divide the new suckering growth so that each new plant has its own roots and shoots. Cuttings of the new growth can be taken. Space plants 40cm (16in) apart.

Feeding Once the plants are well established you can fertilise them every four to six weeks with a soluble liquid fertiliser.

Problems • You can spot chrysanthemum leaf miners by the wavy white or brown lines in the foliage. Furthermore, hold up the leaf to the light and you might see the pupa or grub. Control by immediately removing the affected leaves and crushing the grubs, or better still by regular spraying with a systemic insecticide.

• Chrysanthemum eelworm is evident by browning, drying leaves. Immediately destroy all infected plants. There is no available remedy.

• A number of fungal diseases can attack these plants, including leaf spot, powdery mildew, rust and white rust. Avoid overhead watering or watering late in the day, and ensure that residue from previous plantings is cleared away. You may need to spray with a registered fungicide. White rust is a particularly serious disease, and affected plants are probably best removed and destroyed.

• Watch for aphids clustering on new growth. Pick them off by hand, wash them off, or use an insecticidal spray.

FLOWERING

Season Flowering time is mid- to late autumn. The exciting new race of Yoder or cushion chrysanthemums from America are dwarf, hardy, free-flowering (starting in late summer), and perfect for the front of the border. Those to look out for include 'Lynn', 'Robin', and 'Radiant Lynn'.

Cutting Cut flowers will last two to three weeks with frequent water changes, as long as the foliage is removed from the parts of the stems that are under water.

AFTER FLOWERING

Requirements Once flowering has finished, cut off plants 12.5–15cm (5–6in) above the ground.

CHRYSANTHEMUM AT A GLANCE

Chrysanthemums are the colourful mainstay of the the end-of-season border. The hardy forms will tolerate –15°C (5°F).

		RECOMMENDED VARIETIES
JAN	/	
FEB	sow	'Anna Marie'
MAR	sow	'Bronze Elegance'
APR	divide	'Cappa'
MAY	transplant	'Faust'
JUN	/	'Lord Butler'
JULY	/	'Mrs Jessie Cooper'
AUG	flowering	'Poppet'
SEPT	flowering	'Salmon Fairie'
OCT	/	
NOV	/	
DEC	/	

CONVALLARIA
Lily-of-the-valley

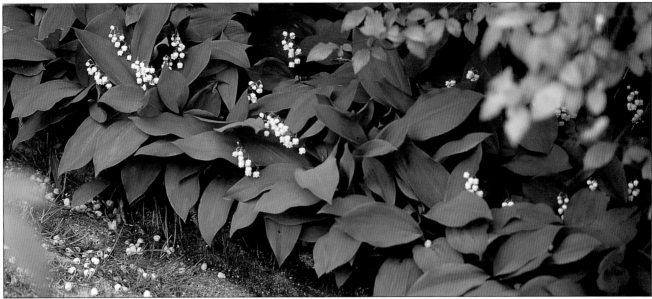

LILY-OF-THE-VALLEY makes a vivid display because of the strong contrast between the shapely, oval leaves, and the small, bright white flowers. It can be left to naturalise in woodland conditions, or allowed to spread through a shady border. Though invasive, it is quite easily controlled.

FEATURES

HERBACEOUS

Lily-of-the-valley is a one species (sometimes considered three) genus, featuring the bell-shaped, fragrant *Convallaria majalis*. A native of Europe, it grows in woods and meadows, and produces 20cm (8in) tall stems of nodding white flowers shortly after the foliage has unfurled. Given the right conditions, namely a cool, moist area, it can spread extremely quickly by means of underground shoots, but it is easily controlled. There are several attractive forms, 'Albostriata' having cream striped foliage, and 'Fortin's Giant' flowers up to 15mm (½in) across. Lily-of-the-valley is essential in a woodland area, or in a damp shady spot where little else of note will grow.

CONVALLARIA AT A GLANCE

Basically a one-species genus with wonderful, waxy, scented spring flowers. Hardy to −15°C (5°F). Good cultivars available.

Month	Activity		Companion Plants
Jan	/		
Feb	/		Bergenia
Mar	/		*Euphorbia robbiae*
Apr	transplant	🌱	Galanthus
May	flowering	🌿	Primula
Jun	/		Pulmonaria
July	/		Rodgersia
Aug	sow		
Sept	division	🌿	
Oct	division	🌿	
Nov	/		
Dec	/		

CONDITIONS

Aspect Shade is essential.

Site The soil must be damp, rich and leafy. For an impressive, vigorous display, apply a thick mulch of leaf mould around the clumps of plants every autumn.

GROWING METHOD

Propagation When the seed is ripe remove the fleshy covering, and raise in a cold frame. Alternatively, divide the rhizomes in the autumn. A 15cm (6in) piece will provide approximately six new plants. The success rate is generally high. Make sure that young plants are not allowed to dry out. Mulch them to guarantee against moisture loss.

Feeding Every other year apply a scattering of complete fertiliser in the spring.

Problems *Botrytis* can be a problem, but is rarely anything to worry about.

FLOWERING

Season One brief display in late spring.

Cutting Lily-of-the-valley makes excellent cut flowers, providing a striking spring display, while emitting a gentle sweet scent. They can also be lifted and grown indoors in a pot to flower the following spring. When finished, replace in the garden.

AFTER FLOWERING

Requirements Remove the spent flower stems, but leave the foliage intact to provide the energy for next year's display.

COREOPSIS
Coreopsis

COREOPSIS ARE wonderful plants which can quickly colonise a space, say between shrubs, producing striking, bright yellow flowers.

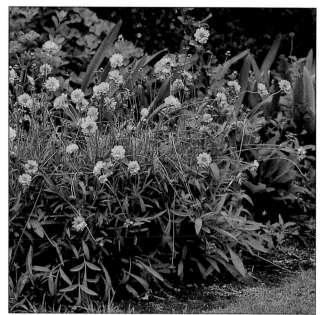

THIS DOUBLE-FLOWERED FORM of golden coreopsis provides many weeks of marvellous colour throughout the summer.

FEATURES

HERBACEOUS

Perennial coreopsis carries a profusion of bright yellow daisy-like flowers over a long period, generally through summer into the autumn, though some do flower in spring. Regular deadheading will ensure a long display. *C. lanceolata*, known as calliopsis, has become naturalised in many parts of the world. The strong-growing *C. grandiflora* may grow 60–90cm (24–36in) high, with *C. verticillata* about 20cm (8in) shorter. There are several species worth trying, some with dwarf form or flowers displaying a dark eye. The foliage is variable, too. The plants are easy to grow. Plant in bold clumps in a mixed border.

COREOPSIS AT A GLANCE

A genus with well over 100 species that make a big contribution to the summer and early autumn display. Hardy to –15° (5°C).

		RECOMMENDED VARIETIES
JAN	/	*Coreopsis auriculata*
FEB	/	'Schnittgold'
MAR	/	*C.* 'Goldfink'
APR	sow	*C. grandiflora* 'Early Sunrise'
MAY	divide	*C. g.* 'Mayfield Giant'
JUN	flowering	'Sunray'
JULY	flowering	*C. verticillata*
AUG	flowering	*C. v.* 'Grandiflora'
SEPT	flowering	*C. v.* 'Zagreb'
OCT	/	
NOV	/	
DEC	/	

CONDITIONS

Aspect   Prefers an open, sunny position right through the day, with little shade.

Site   Performs best in well-drained soil enriched with organic matter, but it will grow in poor soils too. Over-rich soil may produce a profusion of foliage with poor flowering.

GROWING METHOD

Propagation   Grows most easily from divisions of existing clumps lifted in the spring. Space new plants at about 30cm (12in) intervals. Species can be grown from seed sown in mid-spring. Since cultivars of *C. grandiflora* can be ephemeral, sow seed for continuity.

Feeding   Apply complete plant food as growth begins in the spring. However, no further feeding should be needed.

Problems   No pest or disease problems are known.

FLOWERING

Season   The long flowering period extends through summer and autumn. *C.* 'Early Sunrise', *C. lanceolata*, and 'Sunray' flower in their first year from an early sowing.

Cutting   Flowers can be cut for indoor decoration.

AFTER FLOWERING

Requirements   Cut off spent flower stems and tidy up the foliage as it dies back. In mild, frost-free winters coreopsis may not totally die back.

CORYDALIS
Corydalis

THE FOLIAGE and flowers of Corydalis ochroleuca *are dainty and highly decorative. Looks good in walls and ornamental pots.*

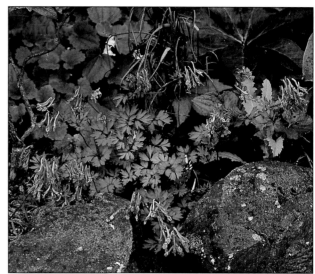

THE BLUE SPECIES and forms of corydalis are highly prized. This is Corydalis flexuosa *with long, upcurving spurs on its flowers.*

FEATURES

HERBACEOUS

Pretty, fern-like foliage and tubular, spurred flowers are characteristic of the 300 or so species of corydalis. Only a small number of species are actually grown in cultivation, and they mainly flower in shades of yellow or blue, but there are some in pink or crimson. Some of the brilliant blues make a distinctive feature, and a recent cultivar with electric blue flowers, known as *C. flexuosa* 'China Blue', is now widely available. It mixes well with *C. solida* 'George Baker', salmon-pink, and *C. ochroleuca*, white. Heights vary from 15–60cm (6–24in). Many corydalis are excellent rock garden plants, while others are suitable for mixed borders or planting under deciduous trees. Many varieties may be available only from specialist nurseries growing alpine plants.

CORYDALIS AT A GLANCE

A large group of annuals, biennials, and perennials, growing in a wide range of moist and dry conditions. Hardy to –15°C (5°F).

JAN	/	
FEB	/	RECOMMENDED VARIETIES
MAR	/	*Corydalis cashmeriana*
APR	divide	*C. cava*
MAY	transplant	*C. cheilanthifolia*
JUN	flowering	*C. elata*
JULY	flowering	*C.lutea*
AUG	flowering	*C.sempervirens*
SEPT	divide	*C. solida*
OCT	sow	*C. s.* 'Beth Evans'
NOV	/	*C. s.* f. *transsylvanica*
DEC	/	*C. s.* f. 'George Baker'

CONDITIONS

Aspect The preferred aspect varies with the species. Some tolerate an open, sunny position, while others need degrees of dappled sunlight. Species grown in 'hot spots' should be given plenty of shade.

Site Needs very well-drained soil that is able to retain some moisture in summer.

GROWING METHOD

Propagation Grows from seed sown as soon as it is ripe, in the autumn. The seed is ripe when the small elongated capsules, which form after the flowers have fallen, turn brown and dry. Some species can be divided, while others produce tubers from which offsets can be taken. Plant at approximate 10–15cm (4–6in) intervals. New young plants need regular watering in prolonged, dry weather during the spring and summer months.

Feeding Apply a sprinkling of slow-release fertiliser as growth commences in the spring.

Problems There are no specific pest or disease problems.

FLOWERING

Season Most species flower in spring, or from spring into summer. *C. flexuosa* dies down in the summer.

Cutting The flowers are unsuitable for cutting.

AFTER FLOWERING

Requirements Remove spent flower stems unless you are waiting for seed to set. Tidy up the foliage as it dies back.

CYNARA CARDUNCULUS
Cardoon

CARDOON LOOKS rather like a Scotch thistle. Its purple flowers can be left to dry, and then used for a striking indoor arrangement.

THE SILVERY LEAVES of cardoon are distinctive, large and shapely, and a big clump provides a geometric, sculptural feature.

FEATURES

HERBACEOUS

A close relative of the globe artichoke, the cardoon is generally grown for its arching, 1m (39in) long, silver-grey foliage. Growing up to 2m (78in) high and almost 2m (78in) wide, it is a terrific accent plant for the back of a border, or it can be combined with low-growing green plants in an open position. Both the colour and form stand out against most other plants. The purple, thistle-like flowers develop in summer, and the dried heads left on the plant make a decorative autumn feature. Cardoon is edible, being grown for the tasty, fleshy base of each leaf. It is difficult to place in a small garden since you need room to stand back and appreciate its startling form.

CYNARA AT A GLANCE

C. cardunculus is a clump-forming perennial grown for its long, striking foliage and purple flowers. Hardy to −18°C (0°F).

		COMPANION PLANTS
JAN	/	
FEB	/	Brugmansia
MAR	sow	Centranthus
APR	divide	Echinops
MAY	transplant	Geranium
JUN	flowering	Miscanthus
JULY	flowering	Rose
AUG	flowering	Salvia
SEPT	flowering	Yucca
OCT	/	
NOV	/	
DEC	/	

CONDITIONS

Aspect   Needs full sun all day for best results. Also needs shelter from strong, leaf-tearing winds.
Soil   Needs rich, well-drained soil. Before planting, dig in large amounts of manure or compost.

GROWING METHOD

Propagation   Propagate in late spring, or grow from seed. Position plants at least 1.2m (4ft) apart. Seed-grown plants are variable in quality, and do not normally reach maturity in their first year. During the growing season regular, deep watering is essential for new, young plants in prolonged, dry spells.
Feeding   Apply a complete plant food as growth commences in the spring, and repeat mid-summer. When cardoon is grown as a vegetable it is given a weekly liquid feed.
Problems   Beware of the sharp points on the flowerheads.

FLOWERING

Season   The purple, thistle-like flowers appear during summer on stems 2–3m (6½–10ft) high.
Cutting   If the flowers are allowed to dry on the plant, they can be cut and used as part of a big, bold indoor decoration.

AFTER FLOWERING

Requirements   Once the flowers have lost their decorative value, cut off the whole stem low down. As the plant starts to die off and look tatty, cut it back just above the ground.

DELPHINIUM
Delphinium

DOZENS OF individual flowers make up the striking spires of the delphinium. Blue shades, from pale to purple, predominate.

THESE STAKED DELPHINIUMS, growing in the shelter of a house, should remain stately and upright through the flowering season.

FEATURES

HERBACEOUS

Tall, handsome and stately, delphiniums make an outstanding feature in perennial borders. Growing from 1–2m 39–78in) high, the long-lasting spires of blooms originally came in a rich blue only, but now offer shades of pink, lavender, white and red. Delphiniums should be mass planted at the back of a border for the best effect, but they can also be placed as accent plants at intervals across a border. They mix well with climbers like clematis. Tall-growing varieties may need staking unless they are in a very sheltered spot. Colours can be mixed, but the best effect comes from massing plants of the same colour.

DELPHINIUM AT A GLANCE

A hardy annual, biennial and perennial it is grown for its strik-ing, vertical spires, thick with flowers. Hardy to –15°C (5°F).

JAN	/	
FEB	sow	
MAR	sow	
APR	transplant	
MAY	transplant	
JUN	flowering	
JULY	flowering	
AUG	flowering	
SEPT	/	
OCT	divide	
NOV	/	
DEC	/	

RECOMMENDED VARIETIES

Delphinium 'Bruce'
'Cassius'
'Emily Hawkins'
'Lord Butler'
'Our Deb'
'Rosemary Brock'
'Sandpiper'
'Sungleam'
'Walton Gemstone'

CONDITIONS

Aspect Needs full sun and shelter from strong winds, and staking if not well sheltered.

Soil Needs well-drained soil enriched with copious amounts of decayed manure or compost before planting. Water regularly and mulch.

GROWING METHOD

Propagation Divide established clumps in the autumn, ensuring each division has a crown and its own roots. Space about 30cm (12in) apart. Grows from seed sown in spring, but the results are variable. Take 8cm (3in) basal cuttings in mid-spring.

Feeding Apply complete plant food once growth begins in the spring, and each month until flowering.

Problems Watch for aphids on new growth, and hose off or spray with pyrethrum or insecticidal soap. In humid conditions a bad attack of powdery mildew may need to be tackled by spraying with a fungicide. Beware slugs.

FLOWERING

Season Blooms for a long season through early and late summer.

Cutting Flowers make a good display, and can be dried.

AFTER FLOWERING

Requirements Remove the flower stems when the main blooms fade and small spikes may flower in late summer and early autumn.

DIANTHUS CARYOPHYLLUS
Wild carnation

FRINGED PINK FLOWERS and silver-grey buds and stems make this a classic.

UPWARD-ANGLED CANES are one way of making sure that top-heavy blooms do not tumble onto a path. The other, more discrete method is to employ a series of small twiggy sticks.

FEATURES

SUMMER AUTUMN WINTER SPRING
EVERGREEN

Carnations are very popular both as cut flowers and as a garden subject. Flowers are carried singly or in groups on stems 30–50cm (12–20in) high, although florists' carnations may be taller. *Dianthus caryophyllus* from the Mediterranean, a woody perennial with elegant stiff stems, bears richly scented, purple-pink flowers which grow taller than the average, reaching 80cm (32in) under perfect conditions. It has given rise to several excellent series. The Floristan Series comes in a wide colour range, and makes good cut flowers, the Knight Series is shorter and bushier, and includes yellow, white and orange, and the Lilliput Series, shorter still at 20cm (8in), includes a rich scarlet.

DIANTHUS AT A GLANCE

D. caryophyllus is a colourful woody perennial, part of the large dianthus family of over 300 species. Hardy to –15°C (5°F).

		COMPANION PLANTS
JAN	/	
FEB	/	Campanula
MAR	sow	Cistus
APR	/	Crepis
MAY	transplant	Eryngium
JUN	flowering	Helianthemum
JULY	flowering	Portulaca
AUG	flowering	Sedum
SEPT	/	Tulip
OCT	/	
NOV	/	
DEC	sow	

CONDITIONS

Aspect   Needs full sun all day. Protect from very strong winds.

Soil   Needs very well-drained soil with plenty of additional, well-decayed organic matter. Unless the soil is alkaline, apply a light dressing of lime before each planting.

GROWING METHOD

Propagation   Grows easily from cuttings taken at almost any time. Use leafy side shoots and strip off all but the top leaves. Roots form in 3–5 weeks. Space newly rooted plants 20cm (8in) apart. Water regularly to establish, then occasionally in dry weather. Carnations tolerate dry conditions well.

Feeding   Little fertiliser is needed if the soil contains plenty of organic matter, but you may give a complete feed twice – in spring and again in mid-summer.

Problems   Carnation rust, a fungal disease, is common in warm, humid conditions. Greyish spots appear on leaves or stems, and the foliage may curl and yellow. Take prompt action by immediately spraying with a fungicide. Squash caterpillars when seen.

FLOWERING

Season   The crop of flowers appears in summer, but it can be forced for other times. Remove any excess buds to produce good-sized, main blooms.

Cutting   An excellent cut flower. Recut stems between nodes (joints) to aid water uptake.

DIANTHUS CULTIVARS
Pinks

DIANTHUS CULTIVARS make reliable, popular edging plants with bright colours and, in many cases, a rich, pervasive scent.

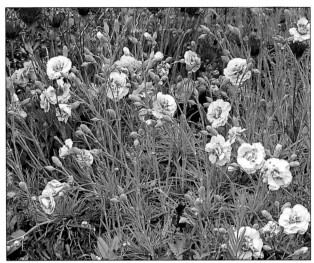

ONE OF THE BEST pinks for the garden, or as a cut flower, 'Doris' is vigorous, long flowering and sweetly scented. A 'must'.

FEATURES

EVERGREEN

Pinks are crosses of *D. caryophyllus* (wild carnation) and *D. plumarius* (cottage pink). Allwood Brothers nursery in West Sussex has bred an enormous range of cultivars that are free flowering given the right conditions. The grey-green foliage grows in a tufted mat and flowering stems are 10–30cm (4–12in) high. Most flowers are heavily scented and may be single or bicoloured, some with a clear margin of contrasting colour. Most are white, pink, red, deep crimson or salmon, with cultivars ideally suited for the rock garden.

CONDITIONS

Aspect   Needs full sun all day, and protection from strong winds.
Site   Needs very free-draining soil, enriched with

additional decayed organic matter, well ahead of planting. Use a soil-testing kit to determine whether your soil is acid – if so, add quantities of lime according to the manufacturer's instructions. Beware of exceeding the recommended rate, it will simply do more harm than good.

GROWING METHOD

Propagation   Grows easily from cuttings taken in late summer and autumn. Start fresh plants every three or four years to keep vigorous compact growth. Space the plant approximately 15–30cm (6–12in) apart, depending on variety. Water until the plants are well established.
Feeding   Apply complete plant food in early spring, as active spring growth begins.
Problems   Aphids and slugs are the two major problems. The former can be tackled by a regular spraying programme with, for example, malathion. The latter can be spotted late at night or early in the morning. Either treat chemically, or pick off by hand and drown.

FLOWERING

Season   Some pinks flower during spring only, others have a long flowering period from spring to early autumn.
Cutting   Pinks make excellent cut flowers, providing indoor decoration and scent.

AFTER FLOWERING

Requirements   Cut off any spent flower stems to the ground as they fade. No other pruning action is necessary.

DIANTHUS AT A GLANCE

The cultivars include perennials in a wide colour range, many richly scented. Generally hardy to –15°C (5°F).

JAN	/	
FEB	/	
MAR	sow	
APR	transplant	
MAY	transplant	
JUN	flowering	
JULY	flowering	
AUG	flowering	
SEPT	/	
OCT	sow	
NOV	/	
DEC	/	

RECOMMENDED VARIETIES

Dianthus alpinus
'Bovey Belle'
'Devon Glow'
D. deltoides
'La Bourboule'
'Monica Wyatt'
'Sam Barlow'
'Whitehill'
'Widecombe Fair'

DIASCIA
Twinspur

ONE OF THE MOST USEFUL garden plants, twinspur flowers right through the season, from spring to autumn. And being 30cm (12in) high, it makes the perfect front-of-border filler, tolerating a sunny position, and one with a degree of shade. Despite a short lifespan, it is easily propagated.

FEATURES

EVERGREEN

Twinspur has an extremely long flowering season, lasting from spring until the first frosts. Though there is a large number of forms available, ranging from 'Lilac Mist' to 'Salmon Supreme', the colour range is quite limited, essentially being shades of pink. Diascia requires moist, rich soil, but over-feeding will result in fewer flowers. The height ranges from 15–30cm (6–12in), which means the taller plants can be given free reign to burst through their neighbours, adding to the display. 'Salmon Supreme' is an attractive low-spreader, being 15cm (6in) high. *D. vigilis* is twice as tall, hardier, and even more free flowering.

DIASCIA AT A GLANCE

A near 50-strong genus of annuals and perennials, with a pink colour and a long flowering season. Hardy to –5°C (23°F).

JAN	/	
FEB	sow	
MAR	divide	
APR	transplant	
MAY	flowering	
JUN	flowering	
JULY	flowering	
AUG	flowering	
SEPT	flowering	
OCT	/	
NOV	/	
DEC	/	

RECOMMENDED VARIETIES

Diascia barberae 'Ruby Field'
D. 'Dark Eyes'
D. 'Hector's Hardy'
D. integerrima
D. 'Lilac Mist'
D. 'Rupert Lambert'
D. vigilis

CONDITIONS

Aspect Enjoys full sun; though it tolerates some shade it will not flower as long or as prolifically.
Soil Moisture-retentive, well-drained ground.

GROWING METHOD

Propagation This is essential since diascias are short-lived, but propagation is easily managed. Success rates are high by all methods, though cuttings are particularly easy. Either sow seed when ripe, or the following spring, take cuttings during the growing season, or divide in spring. Since young plants might die in severe winters, keep indoor cuttings as possible replacements.
Feeding Mulch well in the spring to enrich the soil.
Problems Slugs and snails are the main enemies. Pick them off or use a chemical treatment.

FLOWERING

Season An unusually long season from spring, beyond the end of summer to the first frosts.
Cutting Diascias cut well, and though they do not last particularly long in water, replacements are quickly available fom the parent plant.

AFTER FLOWERING

Requirements Cut ruthlessly to the ground after flowering to promote a second flush of flowers.

DICENTRA SPECTABILIS
Bleeding heart

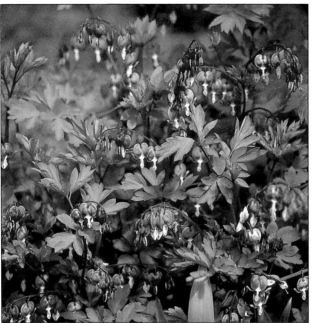

THE ARCHING STEMS of this bleeding heart carry masses of bright pink, heart-shaped flowers resembling tiny lockets.

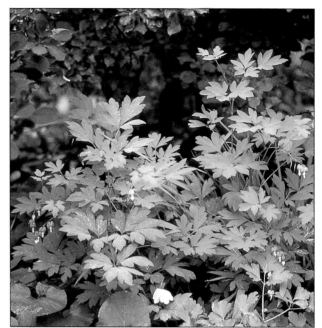

THE BLEEDING HEART is well worth growing for its foliage alone as the delicate, fern-like leaves are very decorative.

FEATURES

SUMMER AUTUMN WINTER SPRING

HERBACEOUS

With fern-like foliage and curving stems bearing pretty pink and white, heart-shape flowers, bleeding heart is an all-time favourite perennial. It appeals to children and adults alike. There is a cultivar, 'Alba', which has pure white flowers. Another species less commonly grown is *D. formosa*, which has very ferny foliage, but its flowers are not so completely heart-shaped. Bleeding heart can be grown in a mixed border or in the filtered shade of trees. Plants may reach 40–60cm (16–24in) high in good conditions, and form a clump 50cm (20in) or so wide.

DICENTRA AT A GLANCE

D. spectabilis is a clump-forming perennial, with arching stems and decorative deep pink flowers. Hardy to –18°C (0°F).

Month	Activity		Recommended Varieties
JAN	/		
FEB	/		*D.* 'Adrian Bloom'
MAR	sow		'Bountiful'
APR	transplant		*D. cucularia*
MAY	transplant		*D. f. alba*
JUN	flowering		'Langtrees'
JULY	flowering		'Ruby Slippers'
AUG	/		*D. macrantha*
SEPT	/		*D. spectabilis*
OCT	division		*D. s.* 'Alba'
NOV	sow		'Stuart Boothman'
DEC	/		

CONDITIONS

Aspect Grows best in filtered sunlight. Strong, hot, drying winds make it shrivel up. A sheltered position protects against late frosts.

Site Needs well-drained soil rich in organic matter. Dig in copious quantities of decayed manure or compost several weeks before planting.

GROWING METHOD

Propagation Divide large established clumps in the autumn, and plant divisions 25–30cm (10–12in) apart. Also grows from seed sown in the spring or autumn. Needs regular, deep watering during dry periods in spring and summer.

Feeding Apply a sprinkling of a complete plant food whenever growth begins in the spring.

Problems There are no specific pest or disease problems known for this plant.

FLOWERING

Season Blooms for several weeks during late spring and early summer.

Cutting Flowers are not suitable for cutting.

AFTER FLOWERING

Requirements Cut out spent flower stems. As the foliage yellows and dies off, cut it off just above the ground.

DIGITALIS
Foxglove

A SUPERB DISPLAY of Digitalis grandiflora, *the yellow foxglove, which sends up 1m (39in) high spires. It is an excellent choice for gaps towards the back of the border, though you may well have to weed out some seedlings that spread beyond the main clump.*

FEATURES

HERBACEOUS

Foxgloves are essentials for the cottage garden, self-seeding in unexpected places, with their tall spires of often richly coloured flowers. They grow in most soils and situations, from the shady to sunny, and dryish to damp, though performance is variable at these extremes. They also make a large group of biennials and perennials ranging in height from 60cm–2m (24in–6½ft). The common foxglove *(D. purpurea)* can be grown as a perennial, but its lifespan is short, the biennial generally being the preferred option. The colour range includes red, yellow, white and pink with the early summer Fox Hybrids. *D. grandiflora* has the largest flowers.

DIGITALIS AT A GLANCE

Foxgloves are grown for their tall spires of attractive, tubular flowers, generally in soft hues. Hardy to –15°C (5°F).

		RECOMMENDED VARIETIES
JAN	/	
FEB	/	*Digitalis ferruginea*
MAR	sow	*D. grandiflora*
APR	transplant	*D. lanata*
MAY	transplant	*D. parviflora*
JUN	flowering	*D. purpurea*
JULY	flowering	*D. p.* Excelsior Group
AUG	/	
SEPT	/	
OCT	/	
NOV	/	
DEC	/	

CONDITIONS

Aspect　Dappled shade for part of the day is ideal, but it is not absolutely essential. Foxgloves are undemanding plants, and will grow in a wide range of gardens.

Site　The soil conditions can vary, but humus-rich ground gives the best results.

GROWING METHOD

Propagation　Sow seed of new varieties in containers, in a cold frame, in late spring. Space seedlings up to 45cm (18in) apart. If you already have some plants it is not necessary since the foxglove is a prolific self-seeder. Dig up a new plant and transplant to where it is required. Water in well, and do not let it dry out.

Feeding　Provide a complete feed in the spring. In particularly dry soil provide a protective spring mulch.

Problems　Leaf spot and powdery mildew can strike, spraying being the best treatment.

FLOWERING

Season　Flowers appear in early and mid-summer.

Cutting　While they make good cut flowers, handle with extreme caution. The foliage can irritate the skin, and all parts are poisonous.

AFTER FLOWERING

Requirements　Leave just a few stems to seed where the foxgloves look good, mixing well with other plants, otherwise deadhead to avoid masses of invasive seedlings.

ECHINACEA PURPUREA
Purple coneflower

BOLDER THAN many perennials, coneflowers are sometimes slow to appear in spring but they are definitely well worth the wait.

THIS FINE STAND of bright purple coneflowers adds a striking touch to this scheme. The flowers fade as they age, but petals don't fall.

FEATURES

HERBACEOUS

Native to the prairie states of the United States, the coneflower is a hardy, drought-resistant plant. Its dark, cone-shape centre is surrounded by rich pink ray petals, and there are cultivars available in shades of pink-purple and white. They make excellent cut flowers. Coneflowers often grow over 1m (39in) high, and are a great addition to a perennial border because they bloom over a long period from mid-summer into autumn, when many other plants have finished. Ideally Echinacea should be mass planted to get the best effect. Excellent varieties include *E. purpurea* Bressingham Hybrids, 'Magnus', and 'White Swan'.

ECHINACEA AT A GLANCE

E. purpurea is an attractive, daisy-like perennial with purple flowers, ideal for naturalising or borders. Hardy to −15°C (5°F).

		COMPANION PLANTS
JAN	/	
FEB	sow	Allium
MAR	sow	Delphinium
APR	transplant	Geranium
MAY	transplant	Gladiolus
JUN	/	Iris
JULY	flowering	Lavandula
AUG	flowering	Rosemary
SEPT	flowering	Yucca
OCT	divide	Delphinium
NOV	/	Rose
DEC	/	

CONDITIONS

Aspect Prefers full sun all day. Although it is tolerant of windy conditions, the blooms will have a better appearance if the plants are sheltered from strong winds.

Site Needs well-drained, rich soil. Poor or sandy soils can be improved by digging in large quantities of compost or manure before planting.

GROWING METHOD

Propagation Divide existing clumps in early spring or autumn, and replant divisions 20–25cm (8–10in) apart. It can be grown from seed sown in early spring, which may produce colour variations. Needs regular water to establish in prolonged dry spells, but occasional deep soakings in dry weather are enough, as it tolerates dry conditions well.

Feeding Apply complete plant food in early spring and again in mid-summer.

Problems No specific problems are known.

FLOWERING

Season There is a long flowering period from late summer into autumn.

Cutting Cut flowers for the vase when fully open, but before the petals separate out.

AFTER FLOWERING

Requirements Remove spent flower stems. The whole plant can be cut back to ground level in winter.

ECHINOPS
Globe thistle

THESE METALLIC BLUE globe thistles form an elegant picture against a stone wall.

EARLY MORNING LIGHT accentuates the rounded, slightly spiky heads of these globe thistle flowers, planted here in a bold drift in a country garden.

FEATURES

SUMMER AUTUMN WINTER SPRING

HERBACEOUS

This is a very distinctive looking plant that makes a good accent in a mixed planting. Taller species need to be placed at the back of a border, but others can be planted in bold groups through the bed. Most have foliage that is stiff, prickly and finely divided, with silvery stems growing from 30cm–2m (12in–6½ft). Some of the species have foliage that is covered with fine white hairs on the underside. The flowerheads are usually white or metallic blue, and are highly prized for their decorative value when cut and dried. The most commonly grown is *E. ritro* and its cultivars, some of which have deep blue flowers. *E. sphaerocephalus* has pale grey to silvery flowers.

ECHINOPS AT A GLANCE

A group of annuals, biennials and perennials grown for their geometric shapes and blue flowers. Hardy to –5/10°C (23°/5°F).

JAN	divide	
FEB	divide	
MAR	sow	
APR	/	
MAY	transplant	
JUN	/	
JULY	flowering	
AUG	flowering	
SEPT	flowering	
OCT	divide	
NOV	divide	

RECOMMENDED VARIETIES

Echinops bannaticus 'Blue Globe'

E. b. 'Taplow Blue'

E. ritro ruthenicus

E. r. Veitch's Blue'

COMPANION PLANTS

Buddleja

Kniphofia

Perovskia

CONDITIONS

Aspect Prefers full sun all day.
Site Soil must be very well drained but need not be rich. The globe thistle can be grown in poor, gravel-like or sandy soils.

GROWING METHOD

Propagation It can either be grown from seed, from division of existing clumps, or from root cuttings. All propagation is done from autumn to winter. Plant out about 40cm (16in) apart. Water regularly to establish. Although drought tolerant, this plant benefits from occasional deep watering during prolonged dry spring and summer periods.
Feeding Apply a complete plant food or poultry manure in early spring.
Problems There are no known pest or disease problems, but plants will rot on sticky clay or poorly drained soil.

FLOWERING

Season Each species or variety will flower for approximately two months.
Cutting Flowerheads required for drying should be cut before the blooms are fully open.

AFTER FLOWERING

Requirements Cut off any remaining spent flowerheads unless you want the seed to ripen. As the plant dies down, clean away dead foliage wearing gloves to protect against the foliage.

EPIMEDIUM
Barrenwort / Bishop's mitre

NEW GROWTH on the bishop's mitre bears attractive bronze or pink shadings, but the older foliage is plain green.

A DENSE CARPET of bishop's mitre makes a wonderful groundcover under a grove of shapely Japanese maples.

FEATURES

HERBACEOUS

EVERGREEN

This low-growing perennial is grown more for its attractive foliage than its flowers, although the flowers are quite attractive. The shape resembles a bishop's mitre, giving rise to its common name. Many species have small, starry flowers in white, cream or yellow, although there are pale and rose-pink varieties too. This is a woodland plant which makes a good groundcover or filler for shady parts of the garden. Some die down completely in winter, while others remain evergreen. Plants are rarely more than 30cm (12in) tall. Combine it with plants such as Solomon's seal, primrose or lenten rose, which enjoy similar woodland-type conditions.

EPIMEDIUM AT A GLANCE

An evergreen, deciduous perennial making excellent groundcover in shady situations. Small flowers. Hardy to –15°C (5°F).

		RECOMMENDED VARIETIES
JAN	/	*Epimedium cantabrigiense*
FEB	sow	*E. grandiflorum*
MAR	/	*E. g.* 'Nanum'
APR	transplant	*E. g.* "Rose Queen'
MAY	flowering	*E. perralderianum*
JUN	/	*E. pinnatum colchicum*
JULY	/	*E.* x *rubrum*
AUG	/	*E.* x *versicolor* 'Sulphureum'
SEPT	sow	
OCT	divide	
NOV	/	
DEC	/	

CONDITIONS

Aspect   Needs dappled shade with protection from strong winds.

Site   Needs well-drained soil heavily enriched with organic matter. Regular mulching is beneficial to retain moisture.

GROWING METHOD

Propagation   Clumps can be divided in the autumn although with some varieties this is not easy. Pull apart or cut away sections of plant, keeping both roots and a bud or shoot on each piece. Plant 15–20cm (6–8in) apart. Some species seed readily. Keep young plants well watered until well established.

Feeding   Apply a slow-release fertiliser in the spring.

Problems   Snails may attack soft new growth as it appears, so take precautions.

FLOWERING

Season   The small flowers appear in spring along with the leaves. But shear off the foliage of all varieties in winter even when green (except *E. perralderianum)*, to prevent the flowers being hidden. Fresh leaves will quickly follow.

Cutting   Flowers can be cut for the vase and last quite well in water.

AFTER FLOWERING

Requirements   Spent flower stems can be clipped off. Old, dead foliage should be tidied up and removed by the end of autumn.

ERYNGIUM
Sea holly

AN OUTSTANDING PLANT for the Mediterranean garden is Eryngium maritimum. *It has strong architectural features with a stiff, branching habit, and mid- to late summer flowers. It can be grown in the border, or better still in a gravel bed to highlight the shape.*

FEATURES

HERBACEOUS

EVERGREEN

Sea holly is a 230-species strong genus, with annuals, biennials and perennials. Though they are related to cow parsley they bear no resemblance, being grown for their marvellous, attractive, spikey appearance, blue flowers (though some are white or green), and ability to thrive in poor, rocky, sunny ground. Heights can vary considerably from *E. alpinum,* 70cm (28in) tall, which as its name suggests grows in the Alps, to *E. eburneum* from South America which can reach 1.5m (5ft), and *E. pandanifolium* which is much taller at 3m (10ft). One of the most attractive is the Moroccan *E. variifolium* which has rounded, white-veined foliage setting off the pale blue

flowers. It is also more manageable at 35cm (14in) high – good for the front of a border.

CONDITIONS

Aspect   Grow in full sun, well out of the shade.
Site   There are two types of sea holly, with different growing needs. Most prefer fast-draining, fertile ground (e.g. *E. alpinum* and *E. bourgatii),* and some (e.g. *E. eburneum)* poor stoney ground, out of the winter wet.

GROWING METHOD

Propagation   Sow the seed when ripe; alternatively take root cuttings in late winter, or divide in the spring.
Feeding   Only for the first kind of sea holly which benefits from a spring feed, and some well-rotted manure. Good drainage is important.
Problems   Slugs and snails are the main problem when sea holly is grown in the border, damaging the new young leaves. Promptly remove when seen, or use a chemical treatment.

FLOWERING

Season   The earliest sea hollies begin flowering in early summer, while others last from mid- to early or mid-autumn in dry weather.
Cutting   Sea holly makes an invaluable cut flower. They also make exceptional dried arrangements, combining with other architectural plants and softer, flowery ones.

AFTER FLOWERING

Requirements   Cut back the spent flowering stems to the ground.

ERYNGIUM AT A GLANCE

Annuals, and deciduous/evergreen perennials grown for their shape. Hardiness varies from –10°C (13°F) to –18°C (0°F).

		RECOMMENDED VARIETIES
JAN	/	
FEB	sow	*Eryngium alpinum*
MAR	division	*E. a.* 'Blue Star'
APR	transplant	*E. bourgatii*
MAY	transplant	*E. b.* 'Oxford Blue'
JUN	flowering	*E. giganteum*
JULY	flowering	*E. x oliverianum*
AUG	flowering	*E. x tripartitum*
SEPT	flowering	
OCT	sow	
NOV	/	
DEC	/	

EUPHORBIA
Spurge

THE HIGHLY VERSATILE spurge tolerates a wide range of conditions. One of its chief attractions is its striking bracts.

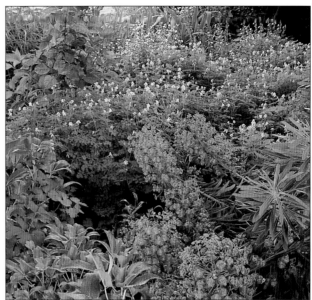

A MIXED BORDER showing the value of propagating your own euphorbia. Strong shapes, flowing clumps, it even thrives in the shade.

FEATURES

HERBACEOUS

EVERGREEN

A large group of important shrubs, annuals, biennials, perennials and subshrubs, ranging from tree-like succulents to structural clumps for the border. The latter spurges, evergreen and deciduous, grow in a wide range of conditions, from shade to sun, and tend to be quite sturdy, many leaning at 45° if not standing upright. Many of the evergreens actually benefit from being cut back to produce vigorous new spring growth. For example *E. characias* yields stems covered in small, stiff, outward pointing leaves and yellow-green flowers. A big clump makes a bold, striking feature. *E. griffithii* 'Fireglow', deciduous, is about half as high and produces early summer orange-red terminal bracts. It spreads to form a large colony. And *E. schillingii*, a recent find in Nepal by plant hunter Tony Schilling, flowers in late summer and has yellow bracts.

CONDITIONS

Aspect	Depending on your choice of plant, spurges like full sun or light shade.
Soil	This too can vary from light, fast-draining soil to damp, moist ground, rich with leaf mould.

GROWING METHOD

Propagation	Sow the seed when ripe, or the following spring. Alternatively divide perennials in the spring, or take spring cuttings.
Feeding	Spurges requiring rich soil can be given a scattering of complete plant food and mulched in spring. Spurges requiring fast-draining ground need only be fed.
Problems	Aphids can be a problem in a bad year; spray at the first sign of an attack.

FLOWERING

Season	Flowers appear in spring or summer.
Cutting	While the stem structure of most spurges makes them theoretically good as cut-flowers, note that the milky sap can badly irritate the skin; if any part of the plant is ingested, severe discomfort results. Wear gloves and goggles.

AFTER FLOWERING

Requirements	Cut back the brownish or lacklustre stems in the autumn to promote fresh new growth.

EUPHORBIA AT A GLANCE

A genus of some 2,000 species. The border kind tend to be grown for their structure. Frost tender to hardy −18°C (0°F).

		RECOMMENDED VARIETIES
JAN	/	
FEB	/	*Euphorbia amygdaloides* var. *robbiae*
MAR	divide	
APR	transplant	E. characias
MAY	flowering	E. characias wulfenii
JUN	flowering	E. griffithii 'Dixter'
JULY	flowering	E. myrsinites
AUG	flowering	E. palustris
SEPT	flowering	E. polychroma
OCT	sow	
NOV	/	
DEC	/	

GERANIUM
Cranesbill

THE FOLIAGE *on this clump-forming, North American* Geranium macrorrhizum *is as attractive as the lovely pink white or pink flowers. The leaves are scented and quickly form a dense carpet.*

GERANIUM PRATENSE *with its deep violet flowers that bloom over a long period.*

FEATURES

HERBACEOUS

EVERGREEN

There are a great many perennial species of the true, hardy geranium, and many are reliable, long-flowering plants. Most cranesbill geraniums (not to be confused with tender, pot-plant pelargoniums) are easy to grow, and are ideal in perennial borders, as edging plants, or as an infill between shrubs. Some species self-sow freely but unwanted seedlings are easily removed. Cranesbills range from about 15cm–1m (6-39in) tall. Most have attractive, deeply divided leaves, and the flowers cover a range of shades, mostly in violet, blue, pink, rose and cerise. Species worth seeking out include *G. endressii* and its cultivars, especially 'Wargrave Pink', *G. pratense*, *G. psilostemon*, *G. himalayense* and *G. sanguineum*. A variety of *G. sanguineum*, 'Lancastriense', is a dwarf-growing type that can be used as groundcover.

GERANIUM AT A GLANCE

A genus of some 300 annuals, biennials, and perennials grown for their big flowering clumps. Most hardy to –15°C (5°F).

		RECOMMENDED VARIETIES
JAN	/	
FEB	sow	*Geranium himalayense*
MAR	sow	'Gravetye'
APR	divide	'Johnson's Blue'
MAY	transplant	*G.* x *oxonianum* 'Wargrave Pink'
JUN	flowering	*G. palmatum*
JULY	flowering	*G. pratense* 'Mrs Kendall Clark'
AUG	flowering	*G. psilostemon*
SEPT	flowering	
OCT	sow	
NOV	/	
DEC	/	

CONDITIONS

Aspect Most like sun; others prefer shade.

Site Needs open, well-drained soil, but it need not be rich. Very acid ground should be limed before planting; use a soil-testing kit to ascertain the quantity required.

GROWING METHOD

Propagation Most cranesbills are easily grown from seed sown in the autumn, but note that the results will be variable. They can also be grown from cuttings taken in the growing season. Established clumps can be lifted and divided in the spring. The exact spacing depends on the variety, but it is usually within the range of 20–40cm (8–16in). Established plants tolerate dry conditions and rarely need watering, except in prolonged droughts.

Feeding Apply a little complete plant food as growth starts in the spring.

Problems No specific pest or disease problems are known for these plants.

FLOWERING

Season Cranesbills flower through the spring, into late summer.

Cutting Flowers do not cut well.

AFTER FLOWERING

Requirements Remove spent flower stems unless you want the plants to seed. Some pruning may be needed through the growing season if growth becomes much too rampant. Prune to maintain shape.

GEUM CHILOENSE
Avens

THE BRIGHT RED double geum 'Mrs J Bradshaw', a justifiably popular perennial.

LIKE MOST PERENNIALS, geums look best when planted together in large numbers. Here a mass of deep red flowers looks wonderful against a background of green foliage.

FEATURES

HERBACEOUS

Although there are many species of geum, the two most commonly grown are cultivars. 'Lady Stratheden' has double yellow flowers, and 'Mrs J Bradshaw' bright scarlet double flowers. Flowers appear on stems 30–50cm (12–20in) high that emerge from large rosettes of slightly hairy, lobed compound leaves. Foliage is generally evergreen, but may be herbaceous in some areas. Geums can be planted as accent plants, preferably in groups, in the wild garden or near the front of a mixed border. While flowers are not very suitable for cutting, they give a long, vibrant display in the garden if they are regularly deadheaded.

GEUM AT A GLANCE

Brightly coloured perennial, essential for the spring border, with plenty of attractive cultivars. All hardy to –18°C (0°F).

JAN	/	RECOMMENDED VARIETIES
FEB	sow	'Borisii'
MAR	divide	'Fire Opal'
APR	transplant	'Lady Stratheden'
MAY	flowering	*G. montanum*
JUN	flowering	'Mrs J Bradshaw'
JULY	/	*G. rivale*
AUG	/	*G. urbanum*
SEPT	/	
OCT	divide	
NOV	/	
DEC	/	

CONDITIONS

Aspect   Prefers full sun, but it can also be grown successfully in dappled shade.

Site   Needs well-drained soil. Plants will benefit from the addition of plenty of decayed manure or compost before planting.

GROWING METHOD

Propagation   Clumps can be divided in the spring or autumn. Cut back foliage to reduce moisture loss while divisions re-establish. Also grows from seed sown in spring, but plants may not be true to type. Plant about 25–30cm (10–12in) apart. Since most popular varieties tend to be short lived, propagate often for a regular supply.

Feeding   Apply complete plant food in early spring and again in mid-summer.

Problems   No particular problems are known.

FLOWERING

Season   There is a long flowering display through late spring and mid-summer. Young vigorous plants will keep going to the autumn.

Cutting   Regular cutting (or deadheading) is essential to prolong the display.

AFTER FLOWERING

Requirements   None, apart from the removal of spent flower stems and any dead foliage which may accumulate under the rosette.

GUNNERA MANICATA
Gunnera

THE HUGE, theatrical, eye-catching leaves of Gunnera manicata.

*DAMP GROUND at the bottom of this steep bank allows the clump of gunnera to thrive in its favourite conditions. The lovely pink-flowering shrub beside it is a hawthorn (*Crataegus *species).*

FEATURES

HERBACEOUS

This is not a plant for small gardens. Growing to 2.5m (8½ft) high, clumps grow 3–4m (10–13ft) wide. The huge rhubarb-like leaves can be well over 1m (42in) in diameter, and are supported by long, stout, hairy stems. This is a magnificent feature plant from Africa, Australasia, and S. America. It needs a damp or wet garden area, beside a pond or stream, or to the edge of a lawn. In summer it produces a dramatic tall spike of greenish flowers, often completely concealed by the foliage, but this plant is grown for the impact of its giant, architectural foliage. It is herbaceous, dying right back to the ground in winter. This is not a difficult plant to grow in the right conditions, but it must be carefully sited. It needs space to grow, and gardeners need space to stand back and admire it.

GUNNERA AT A GLANCE

One of the largest, most spectacular perennials, producing huge, often lobed, leaves. Spectacular flower spike. Hardy to –10° (5°F).

JAN	/	
FEB	/	
MAR	/	
APR	transplant	
MAY	transplant	
JUN	/	
JULY	flowering	
AUG	/	
SEPT	sow	
OCT	/	
NOV	/	
DEC	/	

RECOMMENDED VARIETIES

Gunnera arenaria
G. flavida (groundcover)
G. hamiltonii
G. magellanica (groundcover)
G. manicata
G. prorepens
G. tinctoria

CONDITIONS

Aspect Grows both in semi-shade and sun in cool, damp areas.
Site Likes a rich, moist soil. Dig plenty of organic matter into the ground before planting, and mulch crowns heavily with decayed compost or manure for protection.

GROWING METHOD

Propagation Divide small clumps in the spring, replanting them no less than 2m (6½ft) apart. Cuttings can be taken from new growth, too. Pot them up and nurture them until they are well rooted. Plants can be raised from seed, but this is slow and difficult. Keep moist throughout spring and summer.
Feeding Apply pelleted poultry manure as new growth commences in the early spring to give a boost. Add a fresh mulch of rotted manure at the same time.
Problems No specific pest or disease problems are known for gunnera.

FLOWERING

Season Heavy spikes of greenish flowers are produced in early summer.
Fruits The inflorescence is followed by fleshy red-green fruits, which can be ornamental.

AFTER FLOWERING

Requirements As the weather becomes cold in the autumn and leaves begin to brown, cut off the foliage and cover the crown of the plant with a thick layer of straw. Use a large leaf as a hat to keep it dry.

GYPSOPHILA PANICULATA
Baby's breath

THE WONDERFUL, MASSED DISPLAY OF Gypsophila paniculata 'Pink Star' in full bloom. The rippling, airy mound of flowers justifiably led to its common name, baby's breath. It makes a stunning sight in its native habitats, spreading across the sandy steppes of the Far East and eastern Europe.

FEATURES

HERBACEOUS

Baby's breath is an eye-catching border perennial that grows to 1.2m (4ft) high, and produces a summer flower display that looks like a puffy aerial cloud. The flowers appear in mid- and late summer, and are white on the species, though there are gently coloured cultivars. 'Compacta Plena' is soft pink, 'Flamingo' is lilac-pink, and 'Rosenschleier' pale pink. The latter is also quite short, at 30cm (1ft) high, and is worth repeat planting in a long border. 'Bristol Fairy' has the advantage of large white flowers, 1.5cm (½in) across, but it is not as vigorous as the rest and is relatively short lived, needing to be propagated every few years. *G. paniculata* mixes well with contrasting, vertical plants.

CONDITIONS

Aspect	Full sun is required for it to thrive.
Site	Free-draining soil is essential since the plant's native habitat is sandy steppes and stony sites in eastern Europe, central Asia and China.

GROWING METHOD

Propagation	Sow seed in a cold frame in spring, or in pots in a gently heated greenhouse in winter. Species can be propagated by root cuttings, again in late winter. Though adult plants tolerate some dryness, the young plants must not be allowed to dry out. Water regularly in the growing season. Plant out in its final position since it dislikes disturbance.
Feeding	A scattering of complete plant food in the spring.
Problems	Generally problem free.

FLOWERING

Season	The one flowering period is mid- and late summer; an unmissable sight.
Cutting	Makes excellent cut flowers, the light sprays of white to pink flowers considerably add to any arrangement, formal or flowery.

AFTER FLOWERING

Requirements	Cut back to ground level in the autumn.

GYPSOPHILA AT A GLANCE

A striking, tallish herbaceous perennial giving an impactful, flowery mid-summer display. Hardy to −18° (0°F).

		COMPANION PLANTS
JAN	/	*Agapanthus africanus*
FEB	/	*Geranium himalayense*
MAR	sow	*Iris* 'Magic Man'
APR	transplant	*Osteospermum* 'Whirligig'
MAY	/	*Salvia cacaliifolia*
JUN	/	*Silene coeli-rosa*
JULY	flowering	*Solanum crispum*
AUG	flowering	
SEPT	/	
OCT	/	
NOV	/	
DEC	/	

HELENIUM AUTUMNALE
Sneezeweed

STILL ONE OF THE BEST and most popular cultivars of sneeze-weed, 'Moerheim Beauty' has been a favourite since the 1930s.

ORANGE AND TAWNY COLOURS are a feature of sneezeweed, a reliable perennial that brightens the autumn garden.

FEATURES

HERBACEOUS

As its Latin name suggests, this herbaceous perennial flowers from late summer to mid-autumn. The straight species has bright golden, daisy-like flowers with dark centres, but many of the most popular cultivars have flowers in rich tones of orange-red or copper-red. 'Butterpat', 'Moerheim Beauty' and 'Waldtraut' are among the most popular varieties. Sneezeweed can grow 1–1.5m (39–60in) or more high, eventually forming large clumps over 50cm (20in) across. Flowers cut well, but the plant is probably more valuable for its contribution to the autumn garden. Place at the back of a perennial border or among shrubs. Easy to grow.

HELENIUM AT A GLANCE

A group of annuals, biennials and perennials. Grown for their prolific, bright flowering display. Hardy to –15°C (5°F).

		RECOMMENDED VARIETIES
JAN	/	
FEB	sow	'Butterpat'
MAR	sow	'Chipperfield Orange'
APR	transplant	'Crimson Beauty'
MAY	transplant	'Moerheim Beauty'
JUN	/	'Rotgold'
JULY	flowering	'The Bishop'
AUG	flowering	
SEPT	flowering	
OCT	/	
NOV	/	
DEC	/	

CONDITIONS

Aspect Needs to be grown in full sun right through the day. Avoid shade.

Site Needs a moisture-retentive soil heavily enriched with organic matter. It will not thrive in dry soil. Mulch around clumps to help keep soil moist.

GROWING METHOD

Propagation Established clumps can be lifted and divided about every three years. Discard the oldest central sections and replant the divisions about 30cm (12in) apart in spring or autumn. Give new young plants a regular watering right through the growing season.

Feeding Apply complete plant food as new growth commences in spring.

Problems Sneezeweed is generally free from problems, although slugs and snails can damage newly emerging growth in damp weather.

FLOWERING

Season The flowering season starts in mid-summer and continues into the autumn.

Cutting Flowers cut well for indoor decoration.

AFTER FLOWERING

Requirements Spent flower stems should be removed. As the plant dies down, cut off and remove dead foliage. It can be chopped and left on the ground as a mulch. With flowers blooming into the autumn, the foliage remains in good condition until attacked by frost.

HELLEBORUS
Lenten rose

PRETTY SHADINGS of colour are shown on the Lenten rose. Seedlings often produce unexpected colours, which can be maintained if the plants are then propagated by division.

NATIVE to Corsica and Sardinia, this is the green-flowered Helleborus argutifolius.

FEATURES

EVERGREEN

Various species of hellebores are known as the Christmas or Lenten rose because of their flowering times – mid-winter or early spring. *H. niger*, which has pure white flowers with green centres, can be tricky to grow to perfection; *H. argutifolius (syn. H. corsicus)* and *H. orientalis* are more resilient. *H. argutifolius* has lovely lime-green flowers and spiny-toothed leaf margins, while *H. orientalis* is more variable and may have white, green, pink or mottled flowers. Cultivars include a deep crimson variety. These perennials are mostly evergreen and are best planted under deciduous trees where they can remain undisturbed. Some are fairly short lived, but they tend to self-seed freely so that numbers readily increase, creating an impressive sight.

HELLEBORUS AT A GLANCE

A free-spreading, attractively flowering perennial in a wide range of colours. Excellent in woodland. Hardy to –5/15°C (23/°5F).

		RECOMMENDED VARIETIES
JAN	flowering	*Helleborus argutifolius* (syn.
FEB	flowering	*H. corsicus)*
MAR	flowering	*H. foetidus*
APR	divide	*H. lividus*
MAY	transplant	*H. niger*
JUN	/	*H. x nigercors*
JULY	/	*H. orientalis* Cultivars
AUG	/	*H. x sternii* Blackthorn
SEPT	/	Group
OCT	/	*H. viridis*
NOV	/	
DEC	/	

CONDITIONS

Aspect   Prefers dappled sunlight under trees, or in other partially shaded spots.

Site   Soil must be well enriched with organic matter, and able to retain moisture. Excellent in winter containers.

GROWING METHOD

Propagation   Divide clumps in the spring or summer, straight after flowering, replanting the divisions about 20–30cm (8–12in) apart. Seed can be sown when ripe, but seedlings will take about three years to flower. Seedlings often produce interesting shades. Recently planted hellebores need plenty of water in prolonged, dry spells in spring and summer.

Feeding   Apply a little complete plant food in the spring. Mulch each spring with manure or compost to aid moisture retention.

Problems   Leaf blotch can disfigure and weaken plants. Spray with a fungicide. Beware aphids, particularly after flowering. Slugs attack the flowers and foliage.

FLOWERING

Season   From mid-winter to early spring.

Cutting   Lenten roses provide attractive cut flowers at the time of year when supply is rather short.

AFTER FLOWERING

Requirements   Prune off the dead flower stems and any dead leaves. Do not disturb.

HEMEROCALLIS
Daylily

MAHOGANY RED is one of the many strong colours available in the huge range of daylily cultivars now available from specialist growers.

THE MASS PLANTING of this creamy yellow daylily increases its impact. Blooms will appear one after the other for many weeks.

FEATURES

HERBACEOUS

EVERGREEN

Easily grown in a wide range of conditions, the daylily is a trouble-free plant with single or double flowers. As its name suggests, individual flowers last only one day, but they are produced over a long period. They come in a wide range of colours, the main ones being shades of yellow, orange, red, magenta and purple. There is an enormous number of exciting, attractive hybrids available from specialist growers. The clumps of grassy foliage may be from 25cm–1m (10–39in) high; some are evergreen while others die down in winter.

While straight species are not as readily available as the hybrids, they are important in hybridising new varieties and several species are worth seeking out. They include *H. altissima* from China, which has pale yellow fragrant flowers on stems 1.5m (5ft) or so high, and *H. lilio-asphodelus*, which has pale yellow fragrant flowers above leaves 55cm (22in) high.

Categories Daylilies have been divided into five categories which list them according to flower type. The divisions are circular, double, spider-shaped, star-shaped and triangular. Most are single; hot weather can produce extra petals and stamens.

Dwarf forms The number of dwarf forms available is steadily increasing and they may be better suited to today's smaller gardens. Those with a reliable reflowering habit can also be successfully grown in pots. Use a good quality potting mix and crowd three plants into a 20cm (8in) pot for good effect. 'Little Grapette', 'Little Gypsy Vagabond', 'Penny's Worth', and 'Stella d'Oro' are good ones to try, all growing about 30 x 45cm (12 x 18in).

Uses Mass plantings of dwarf or tall forms create the best effect. Daylilies are not plants that should be dotted about in the garden. Use large numbers of either the one variety or use varieties of similar colour; it is clearly preferable to planting a mixture of types or colours. In a mixed border they give a very pleasing effect as the foliage is very full.

'BURNING DAYLIGHT', one of the top daylilies, blooms prolifically in sun or semi-shade.

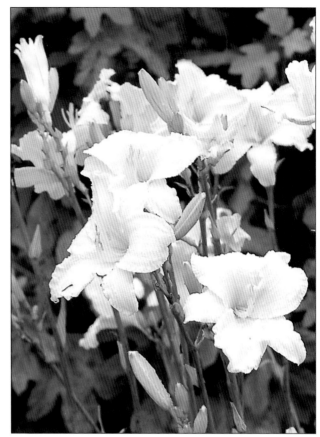

MANY OF the finest daylily cultivars are in creamy yellow or orange tones, not surprisingly as these are the colours of many of the species.

CONDITIONS

Aspect Grows best in full sun but tolerates semi-shade. Can be mass planted on banks or sloping ground as the roots are very efficient soil binders.

Site Grows in any type of soil, wet or dry, but to get maximum growth from the newer hybrids the soil should be enriched with manure or compost before planting.

HEMEROCALLIS AT A GLANCE

A genus of semi-, evergreen, and herbaceous perennials; 30,000 cultivars that give a long summer show. Hardy to –15°C (5°F).

			RECOMMENDED VARIETIES
JAN	/		'Burning Daylight'
FEB	sow	🌱	'Cartwheels'
MAR	sow	🌱	'Golden Chimes'
APR	transplant		'Neyron Rose'
MAY	transplant		'Pink Damask'
JUN	flowering		'Red Precious'
JULY	flowering		'Stafford'
AUG	flowering		'Whichford'
SEPT	flowering		'Zara'
OCT	divide		
NOV	/		
DEC	/		

GROWING METHOD

Propagation Divide established clumps in spring or autumn. Cut back foliage before or straight after division. Spacing may be from 15–30cm (6–12in), depending on variety. New plants need regular watering to establish. Once established, plants are very drought tolerant, but better sized blooms can be expected if deep waterings are given every week or two.

Feeding Grows without supplementary fertiliser, but an application of complete plant food in early spring encourages stronger, more vigorous growth.

Problems Daylilies growing in very soggy ground tend to survive quite well but produce few flowers. Otherwise no problems.

FLOWERING

Season Depending on variety, plants may be in bloom any time from late spring until autumn. Most flowers only last one day.

Cutting Single flowers can be cut for the vase. Attractive and well worth using.

AFTER FLOWERING

Requirements Cut off any spent flower stems. Herbaceous types that die down in the autumn can have their foliage cut back too.

HEUCHERA SANGUINEA
Coral flower

DAINTY LITTLE PINK FLOWERS are massed above the attractive foliage, making the North American coral flower an excellent choice for the front of a border or a garden bed. Here they are planted to provide an excellent foil for the abundant blooms of white roses behind.

FEATURES

EVERGREEN

This perennial forms a low rosette of lobed leaves which make a neat plant for edging, or mass planting at the front of the border. The foliage is evergreen. Established plantings produce a striking display of blooms. The flower stems, which stand above the foliage, are from 30–45cm (12–18in) high. The species has red flowers, cultivars are available with pink, white or deeper crimson blooms. Note the superb foliage varieties ('Palace Purple' – chocolate coloured, 'Pewter Moon' – grey, and 'Snow Storm' – white flecked). New American ones include 'Pewter Veil'.

HEUCHERA AT A GLANCE

H. sanguinea is a red-flowering, summer perennial forming low, wide clumps, 15 x 30cm (6 x 12in). Hardy to –15°C (5°F).

		RECOMMENDED PLANTS
JAN	/	
FEB	sow	*Heuchera americana*
MAR	sow	'Chocolate Ruffles'
APR	divide	*H. cylindrica*
MAY	transplant	'Green Ivory'
JUN	flowering	'Helen Dillon'
JULY	flowering	'Persian Carpet'
AUG	flowering	'Pewter Moon'
SEPT	/	'Rachel'
OCT	divide	'Red Spangles'
NOV	/	'Scintillation'
DEC	/	

CONDITIONS

Aspect   Prefers full sun but tolerates light shade.
Site   Needs very well-drained, open-textured soil. Permanently wet soil will kill this plant.

GROWING METHOD

Propagation   Clumps can be divided in the spring or in the autumn, but do ensure that each division has its own set of healthy roots. It can also be grown from seed sown in the spring; cuttings will also root quite freely. Plant at approximately 20–25cm (8–10in) intervals for a good effect.
Feeding   Apply a complete plant food when growth commences in the spring.
Problems   Vine weevil grubs may devour roots and stems. Destroy the infected clump, and use severed shoots as cuttings.

FLOWERING

Season   It flowers well through most of the summer, with a few spikes hanging on until the early autumn.
Cutting   Flowers do not last well as cut blooms.

AFTER FLOWERING

Requirements   Promptly remove any spent flower stems once they begin to look tatty and untidy. Apart from the removal of any dead leaves, this is all that is necessary.

HOSTA
Plantain lily

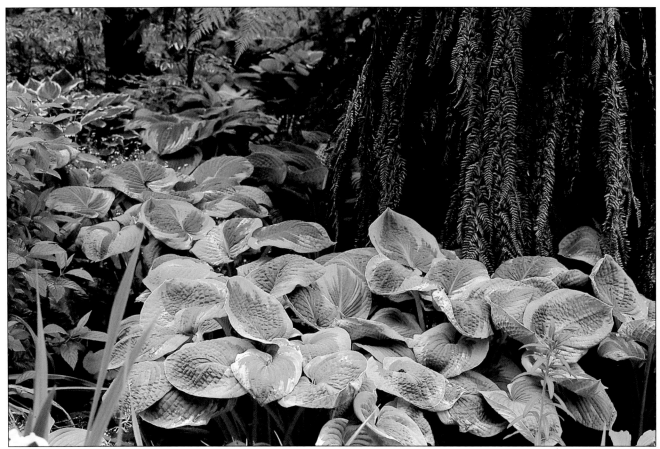

LEAVES PATTERNED VARIOUSLY in lime-green and blue make this Hosta 'Frances Williams' an outstanding garden feature. Here it lights up a dull area under a tree, the little available light being reflected outwards by the lime-green. In shady areas where few flowers bloom, it is a real bonus.

FEATURES

HERBACEOUS

Also known as the plantain lily, this herbaceous perennial is grown for its attractive, decorative foliage. It is long lived, and foliage may be tiny or up to 45cm (18in) wide and 90cm (36in) high. There are hundreds of cultivars with leaves that may be light or dark green, chartreuse or yellow, grey-green or blue. Many are variegated. Leaf texture also varies: it can be smooth or shiny, matt or powdery, puckered or corrugated. Hostas are excellent at forming big, bold clumps that keep down the weeds, but until they emerge in late spring some weeding will be necessary; they also benefit from heavy mulching. Hostas look best mass planted near water features, or when allowed to multiply in shady areas under trees.

Variegations
Cultivars with cream, white or yellow variegations will brighten a shady part of the garden, and as long as the tree or shrub canopy is high enough to let sufficient light reach the hostas, they will maintain their variegation. Likewise plants with sharp chartreuse or acid-lime coloured foliage can be used to give a lift to shady areas. Types can be mixed to create a wealth of different effects.

Flowers
The bell-shape flowers, mostly in mauve shades, appear in summer, being held high above the foliage. Some species such as *H. plantaginea* and its cultivar 'Grandiflora' produce pure white, lightly fragrant flowers. However, few plant hostas just for the flowers; the leaves alone are good enough.

HOSTA AT A GLANCE

A mainly clump-forming perennial from the Far East. Grow in pots or the garden for the foliage. Hardy to –18°C (0°F).

JAN	/	RECOMMENDED VARIETIES
FEB	/	'Aureomarginata'
MAR	sow	'Blue Angel'
APR	divide	'Francee'
MAY	transplant	'Frances Williams'
JUN	flowering	'Golden Tiara'
JULY	flowering	'Love Pat'
AUG	divide	*H. lancifolia*
SEPT	flowering	'Shade Fanfare'
OCT	/	'Wide Brim'
NOV	/	
DEC	/	

PURE WHITE FLOWERS appear on some species of hosta such as Hosta plantaginea *and some of its cultivars.*

STRONGLY PUCKERED LEAVES in a bluish colour and white flowers are characteristic of Hosta sieboldiana *'Elegans'.*

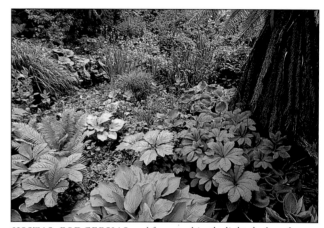

HOSTAS, RODGERSIAS and ferns revel in the light shade and constant damp soil prevalent in woodlands.

Companions Since hostas do not come into leaf early in spring, the early-flowering bulbs, such as snowdrops and snowflakes, or early perennials, such as corydalis, can be planted among them. They make a bright, successful show.

CONDITIONS

Aspect Most hostas grow in full sun if well watered. They thrive in shade or dappled light. Blue-leaved forms can be the hardest of all to place because they turn green with either too much sun, or too heavy shade. Yellow or gold forms are best with direct sun in the early morning, or late in the afternoon.

Site Needs rich, moisture-retentive soil. Large amounts of decayed manure or compost should be dug into the ground well before planting. Mulch plants after planting. Superb in tubs, getting bigger and better each year.

GROWING METHOD

Propagation Divide the fleshy underground rhizomes in early spring. Most hostas are best divided every four to five years. Plant the dwarf cultivars 15cm (6in) apart, the larger ones at intervals of 90cm (36in). Several species can be raised from seed, though they may not be true to type.

Feeding Apply pelleted poultry manure in the spring.

Problems Slugs and snails can be a major problem. Pick off snails, and avoid watering in the evening. Place slug pellets or sharp sand around the leaves.

FLOWERING

Season Flowers are produced in the summer. The colour range varies from white to purple.

Cutting Hosta provides cut flowers; the foliage is also attractive.

AFTER FLOWERING

Requirements Cut off any spent flower stems in spring. Continue watering the plants until the foliage begins to die down, and then tidy up the clumps which can look rather unsightly. Mulch the area with supplies of compost or manure. Some hostas (*sieboldiana*) produce good autumn tints. The seedheads can be left on for winter decoration.

KNIPHOFIA
Red hot poker

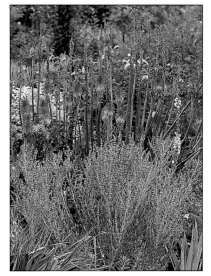

FLAME COLOURED *pokers and soft pur-ple perovskia both tolerate dry conditions.*

THE COLOURS *in this generous planting of red hot pokers reflect both the yellow achillea behind and the red plants in the foreground. The abundant grassy foliage provides a valuable contrast.*

FEATURES

EVERGREEN

These evergreen perennials, also known as torch lilies, make great feature plants with their bright flower spikes in cream, orange, red, yellow and many shadings of these colours. Flower stems stand high above the grassy foliage, which may be anywhere from 60cm–2m (24in–6½ft) high. Even out of flower the distinctive foliage makes red hot poker a good accent plant. Since clumps should remain undisturbed for many years, plant in their final position.

CONDITIONS

Aspect Needs full sun all day. A valuable plant because it tolerates a wide range of exposed windy or coastal areas.

KNIPHOFIA AT A GLANCE

A genus of some 70 species of evergreen and deciduous perenni-als, grown for their flowering spires. Hardy to –15°C (5°F).

JAN	/	
FEB	/	**RECOMMENDED VARIETIES**
MAR	sow	'Bees Sunset'
APR	divide	'Brimstone'
MAY	transplant	'Buttercup'
JUN	flowering	*K. caulescens*
JULY	flowering	'Little Maid'
AUG	flowering	'Royal Standard'
SEPT	flowering	'Samuel's Sensation'
OCT	flowering	'Sunningdale Yellow'
NOV	/	*K. triangularis*
DEC	/	

Site Needs well-drained soil. Although it tolerates poorer soils, especially sandy ones, you will get better results if the soil is enriched with manure or compost.

GROWING METHOD

Propagation Well-established clumps can be divided in late spring. Foliage on new divisions must be reduced by half to allow successful root regrowth to take place. The smaller-growing forms can be planted at 50cm (20in) spacings, but the large growers may need up to 76cm (30in) or more. Needs regular watering to establish in prolonged dry spells, after which it is very drought tolerant.

Feeding Grows without supplementary fertiliser, but complete plant food applied in the spring should noticeably increase the quantity and quality of the flowers.

Problems No specific problems are known.

FLOWERING

Season Flowering times can vary slightly with species and cultivar. Generally, red hot pokers flower in late summer and early autumn.

Cutting The flowers last well when cut if the stems are scalded for approximately 10 seconds. They make an invaluable tall, stiff background for a display of smaller, flowery cuttings.

AFTER FLOWERING

Requirements Spent flower stalks should be promptly cut off. Any dead leaves should be pulled away to give the clump a clean look. Protect the crown with straw or leaves in cold areas.

LEUCANTHEMUM
Shasta daisy

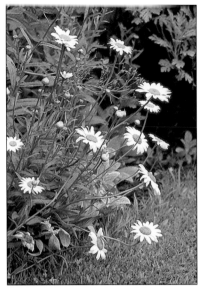

LONG-STEMMED shasta daisies are an ideal component of flower arrangements.

A CONTINUOUS PLANTING of shasta daisies fills this awkward narrow space between a path and a low brick wall. The cheerful white flowers appear throughout the summer.

FEATURES

HERBACEOUS

Leucanthemum x *superbum* (Shasta daisy) looks wonderful when planted in a mixed border where the large white flowers mix with more brightly coloured flowers. Despite being easy to grow and multiplying rapidly, the daisies do not become a menace. Flower stalks can grow 60–90cm (24–36in) high, while the dark green leaves are only 10–15cm (4–6in) high. Shasta daisies make striking cut flowers, livening up any arrangement. There are a number of named cultivars, some such as 'Esther Read', 'Wirral Supreme' and 'Cobham Gold' with double flowers. (Despite its name, the flowers on 'Cobham Gold' are cream, not gold.) 'Everest' is probably the largest of the single cultivars, though it is rarely available.

LEUCANTHEMUM AT A GLANCE

L. x *superbum* is a vigorous, clump-forming perennial with many attractive cultivars mainly in white. Hardy to –5°C (5°F).

JAN	/	
FEB	/	
MAR	divide	
APR	transplant	
MAY	transplant	
JUN	flowering	
JULY	flowering	
AUG	flowering	
SEPT	flowering	
OCT	divide	
NOV	/	
DEC	/	

RECOMMENDED VARIETIES

Leucanthemum x *superbum*
'Aglaia'
'Alaska'
'Bishopstone'
'Cobham Gold'
'Horace Read'
'Phyllis Smith'
'Snowcap'

CONDITIONS

Aspect   Prefers full sun all day and wind protection.
Site   The soil should be well drained, and improved by the addition of decayed compost or manure.

GROWING METHOD

Propagation   Divide the clumps in early spring or late summer, replanting only the younger, vigorous, outer growths, each with its own set of roots and shoots. Plant the divisions approximately 25cm (10in) apart. Cuttings of young, short shoots can also be taken in early spring.
Feeding   Apply complete plant food as growth begins in spring. Liquid fertiliser applied in late spring should help produce better blooms.
Problems   The main problems are aphids, slugs, earwigs, and chrysanthemum eelworm. The first can be tackled with a proprietary spray, and the second and third by traps (saucers filled with beer, and inverted flower pots filled with straw placed on bamboo canes). In the case of eelworm, evident from browning–blackening, drying foliage from the base up, the whole plant must be destroyed.

FLOWERING

Season   Flowering is all summer long.
Cutting   Cut flowers regularly for indoor decoration, which will also prolong the garden display.

AFTER FLOWERING

Requirements Cut back spent flower stems to the ground.

LIGULARIA
Ligularia

A MARVELLOUS ligularia display. Spikes of bright yellow, eye-catching flowers. No matter what size your border, there is a suitable ligularia. They vary from the medium to tall, at 1.8m (6ft). Big groupings invariably succeed much better than a few individual flowers.

FEATURES

HERBACEOUS

Ligularia, with its bright yellow daisies, has four key advantages. It mainly flowers in mid- and late summer, tolerates dappled shade making it invaluable for the border, and often has interesting, well-displayed foliage. It can be shaped like a kidney, a five-pointed star, or be oval, held on tallish stems. The fourth advantage is that these are tall plants, adding height to schemes, being from 90cm–1.8m (36in–6ft) tall. They can be used in small groups to punctuate arrangements of smaller plants, or form an impressive massed display. The flowers are yellow or orange. *L. dentata* 'Othello' has purple-tinged leaves with a red underside and 'Desdemona' has brownish-green leaves, similarly coloured beneath. With room for only one, 'The Rocket' offers height, yellow flowers, black stems, and interesting, big toothed foliage.

CONDITIONS

Aspect   Tolerates full sun and some light shade. Also requires shelter from cutting winds.
Site   The soil must be moist – ligularias grow well beside ponds and streams – for a big performance. If the soil begins to dry out to any degree the plants quickly show signs of distress by wilting.

GROWING METHOD

Propagation   Increase the species by sowing seed or division in the spring or autumn. Cultivars can only be raised by division. Make sure that the emerging new growth is well-watered, and never allowed to dry out. Set out from 60cm–1.2m (24in–4ft) apart.
Feeding   Border plants need plenty of well-rotted manure or compost, and a deep mulch to guard against moisture loss.
Problems   Slugs and snails can be a major problem, especially as the leaves emerge. Pick off or treat chemically.

FLOWERING

Season   Generally from late summer into autumn, but some flower in mid-summer, and *L. stenocephala* in early summer.
Cutting It is not advisable to strip the plants of their impressive flowering stems, especially when you only have room for a few plants.

AFTER FLOWERING

Requirements Cut back to the ground.

LIGULARIA AT A GLANCE

A genus of 150 species of perennials grown for their tall flower spikes and large, architectural foliage. Hardy to –18°C (0°F).

Month	Activity	Recommended Varieties
Jan	/	
Feb	sow	*Ligularia dentata*
Mar	sow	*L. d.* 'Desdemona'
Apr	transplant	*L. d.* 'Othello'
May	transplant	'Gregynog Gold'
Jun	/	*L. przewalskii*
July	flowering	'The Rocket'
Aug	flowering	*L. wilsoniana*
Sept	/	
Oct	divide	
Nov	/	
Dec	/	

LOBELIA CARDINALIS
Cardinal flower

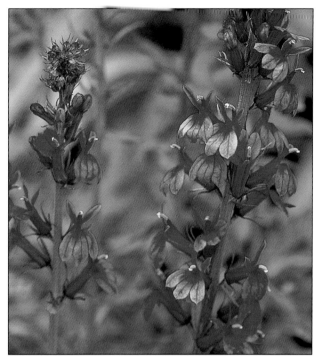

THIS LOBELIA is also known as cardinal flower, an apt description as the tall spikes of flowers are the same scarlet as a cardinal's robes.

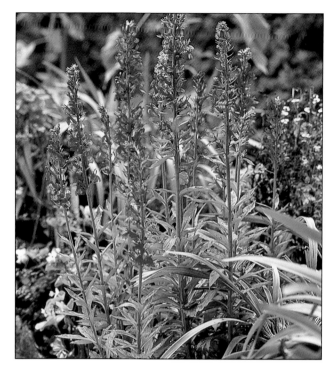

IN ITS NATURAL HABITAT in North America this lobelia grows on wet meadows and river banks. It thrives on plenty of moisture.

FEATURES

HERBACEOUS

Lobelia to most people is a small edging plant with bright blue flowers. There are, however, about 400 species of lobelia, many of them perennials. This herbaceous species with bright scarlet flowers is also known as the cardinal flower and grows to about 90cm (36in) tall. With its dark green leaves and bright flowers it really stands out and it is sometimes used as a feature plant. It can also be used in a mixed border or mass planted among shrubs as long as the ground retains plenty of moisture.

LOBELIA AT A GLANCE

L. cardinalis is a clump-forming, short-lived perennial, grown for its striking, vivid red flowers. Hardy to –15°C (5°F).

		RECOMMENDED VARIETIES
JAN	/	
FEB	/	*Lobelia* 'Cherry Ripe'
MAR	sow	'Dark Crusader'
APR	divide	'Kompliment Scharlach'
MAY	transplant	'Queen Victoria'
JUN	/	*L. siphilitica*
JULY	flowering	*L. tupa*
AUG	flowering	
SEPT	flowering	
OCT	/	
NOV	/	
DEC	/	

CONDITIONS

Aspect Grows in full sun or semi-shade.
Site Needs rich and moisture-retentive soil as these plants are not tolerant of drought. A streamside setting is ideal.

GROWING METHOD

Propagation Plants are usually divided every two or three years, in spring. Plant the divisions about 30cm (12in) apart. Lobelia must be kept moist and well watered while it is in active growth, especially during prolonged dry spells in the spring and summer.
Feeding Apply a complete plant food, and a mulch of compost or manure in the spring.
Problems Slugs and snails will attack the flower spikes. Put down slug pellets or beer traps.

FLOWERING

Season There is a long flowering period through the summer and autumn period when the brilliant scarlet blooms appear.
Cutting Flowers are not suitable for cutting.

AFTER FLOWERING

Requirements Cut off spent flower stems. The dark-leaved hybrids ('Cherry Ripe') are not fully hardy and need a thick, protective winter mulch.

LUPINUS POLYPHYLLUS
Lupin

RUSSELL LUPINS are noteworthy for their rich colours, including this pinky-red.

LUPINS ARE traditional favourites for perennial borders, where they provide vertical interest. Here they are growing among oriental poppies, campion and grey-leaved germander.

FEATURES

HERBACEOUS

This herbaceous perennial lupin is generally known as the Russell lupin, named after the hybridiser who began developing many fine strains of this plant early this century. It produces tall, densely-packed spires of blooms in a myriad of colours. Growing well over 1m (42in) high, these are plants for a massed display. They flower in early to mid-summer and can look unsightly after flowering; placed at the back of a border the problem is solved. Although they can be cut for indoor use they give much more value in the garden, with several spikes per plant. The only irritation is that plants can be short lived, and should therefore be divided regularly.

LUPINUS AT A GLANCE

L. polyphyllus is an attractive, summer-flowering perennial with striking vertical spires of purple flowers. Hardy to –15°C (5°F).

		RECOMMENDED VARIETIES
JAN	/	
FEB	/	Band of Noble Series
MAR	sow	'Esmerelder'
APR	transplant	'Helen Sharman'
MAY	transplant	'Kayleigh Ann Savage'
JUN	flowering	'Olive Tolley'
JULY	flowering	'Pope John Paul'
AUG	/	'The Page'
SEPT	/	'The Chatelaine'
OCT	sow	
NOV	/	
DEC	/	

CONDITIONS

Aspect Grows in full sun or semi-shade, but it does need wind protection.

Site Soil need not be rich, moderate fertility will suffice, but it must be well drained. Light, slightly sandy, acidic soil is ideal.

GROWING METHOD

Propagation Division of these plants may be difficult. Many strains come true from seed, which should be soaked in warm water before planting in the spring or autumn. Cuttings can be taken from new shoots emerging from the crown in early spring. Set plants approximately 30–40cm (12–16in) apart. Give ample water to young plants to help them establish.

Feeding Needs little fertiliser as lupins fix nitrogen in nodules on their roots. High potash fertiliser may be applied as buds begin to form.

Problems Powdery mildew may be a problem in humid conditions; if necessary spray with a fungicide. Control lupin aphids with an appropriate spray. Virus may cause stunting and discoloration. Destroy affected plants.

FLOWERING

Season Early and mid-summer.

Cutting Flowers may be cut for the vase.

AFTER FLOWERING

Requirements Cut off spent flower stems before they manage to set seed. This will encourage smaller spikes to follow.

LYCHNIS CORONARIA
Rose campion

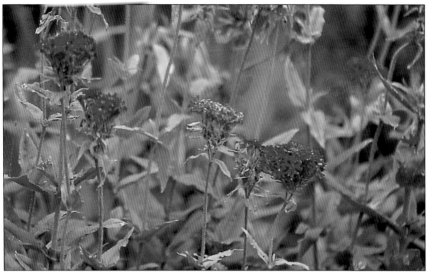

THE DISTINCTIVE ARRANGEMENT of petals on Lychnis chalcedonica *has given rise to its common name, Maltese cross. The bright red flowers show up well against white or blue flowers.*

TRUE CAMPION, Lychnis coronaria, *has abundant, bright cerise flowers.*

FEATURES

HERBACEOUS

Rosettes of soft, silver-grey foliage make *Lychnis coronaria* a very useful plant in the garden, and they contrast with the deep cerise or magenta flowers that appear on stems 30–40cm (12–16in) high. There is also a white flowered form. Easily grown in a sunny, well-drained spot, rose campion tends to be short lived, but it self-seeds prolifically providing a fresh supply. It can be grown as a border plant or as part of a mixed perennial display. *L. flos-jovis* is another species where silvery foliage effectively combines with purple-red blooms. Another popular species of lychnis is the Maltese cross, *L. chalcedonica*, which has mid-green leaves and produces a rounded head of bright scarlet flowers. Pink and white forms, and a double, 'Flore Plena', are also available.

LYCHNIS AT A GLANCE

L. coronaria is a flowery, short-lived purple-red perennial that gives a prolific late summer display. Hardy to –15°C (5°F).

		RECOMMENDED VARIETIES
JAN	/	*Lychnis alpina*
FEB	/	*L. chalcedonica*
MAR	sow	*L. coronaria* Alba Group
APR	division	*L. c.* Atrosanguinea Group
MAY	transplant	*L. flos-cuculi*
JUN	/	*L. viscaria* subsp. 'Splendens
JULY	flowering	Plena'
AUG	flowering	*L. yunnanensis*
SEPT	flowering	
OCT	sow	
NOV	/	
DEC	/	

CONDITIONS

Aspect Grows best in full sun, but it tolerates shade for part of the day.
Site Needs very well-drained soil, but the soil need not be especially rich.

GROWING METHOD

Propagation Tends to self-seed. These plants may show variation from the parent plant. Divide clumps in spring, discard the oldest, lack-lustre sections, and space the new vigorous ones about 20cm (8in) apart. There are some lovely strains to be raised from seed, with mixtures of white, deep violet, carmine, and rose-pink flowers, and a pastel eye.
Feeding Needs little fertiliser. A little complete plant food may be given in early spring.
Problems No pest or disease problems are known, but overwatering or prolonged summer rain in heavy ground may cause rotting.

FLOWERING

Season Flowers in mid- to late summer, but the wait is well worth it with a big showy display that maintains interest in the border at a time when many other plants are flagging.
Cutting Flowers are unsuitable for cutting.

AFTER FLOWERING

Requirements If you do not want plants to self-seed, dead-head with vigilance as the flowers fade. This should also prolong blooming. Completely spent stems should be cut off as low to the ground as possible.

LYSIMACHIA PUNCTATA
Loosestrife

A STRONG, MASSED DISPLAY of loosestrife. Individually unremarkable, a clump makes a splendid feature beside a pond or stream.

FEATURES

EVERGREEN

HERBACEOUS

Loosestrife, which is widely naturalised in Europe and north-east North America, has stalks of bright yellow flowers in summer. It thrives in damp, boggy ground and can easily become invasive. The flowering stems reach 90cm (3ft) high, bearing slightly coarse foliage. Other species offer white flowers on stiff, blue-green stems *(L. ephemerum)*, while *L. nummularia* 'Aurea' is a complete contrast. It grows 5cm (2in) high, but spreads indefinitely with evergreen, bright yellow leaves and summer flowers in a matching colour. With room for only one, try *L. clethroides* which has attractive white flowers (90 x 60cm (36 x 24in)). The new variegated form *L. p.* 'Alexander' is a great success.

LYSIMACHIA AT A GLANCE

L. punctata is an erect, herbaceous perennial grown for its yellow flowers and ability to colonise damp areas. Hardy to −18°C (0°F).

JAN	/	
FEB	/	
MAR	/	
APR	divide	
MAY	/	**RECOMMENDED VARIETIES**
JUN	flowering	*Lysimachia atropurpurea*
JULY	flowering	*L. ciliata*
AUG	flowering	*L. clethroides*
SEPT	/	*L. minoricensis*
OCT	divide	*L. nummularia* 'Aurea'
NOV	/	*L. thyrsiflora*
DEC	/	*L. vulgaris*

CONDITIONS

Aspect   Loosestrife tolerates both full sun and light, dappled shade, but growing in the former gives by far the best results.

Site   Moist ground is essential. Add plenty of organic matter to border plants, and mulch well to guard against moisture loss.

GROWING METHOD

Propagation   Seed can be difficult. The most reliable method is by spring or autumn division.

Feeding   Humus-rich ground produces the best display. Fork plenty of well-rotted manure and compost around the plants in the spring.

Problems   Colonies of slugs and snails can be a major problem, attacking and disfiguring the new, emerging foliage. Either pick off by hand or treat chemically. Plants grown in areas cut by strong winds may need to be staked.

FLOWERING

Season   Flowers appear in summer, timing depending on your chosen variety.

Cutting   They make unremarkable cut flowers, given the enormous competition in summer, but are nonetheless very useful when bulking out large displays with their flowering spires.

AFTER FLOWERING

Requirements   Cut back the old, spent flowering stems down to the ground.

MACLEAYA CORDATA
Plume poppy

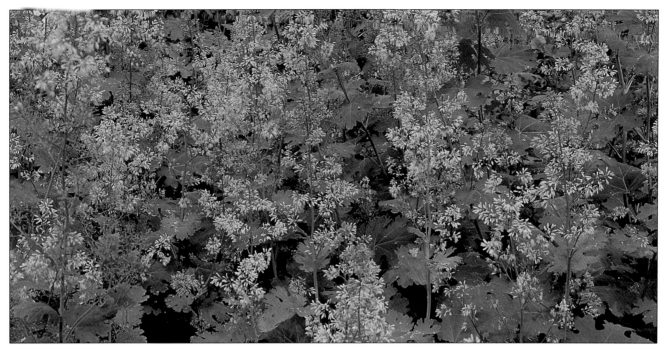

THE PLUME POPPY starts inauspiciously, but quickly puts out tall, white summer flowers making it an indispensable feature. It is a key ingredient for the back of the border, where its lobed, olive-green foliage makes a lovely background for smaller plants. The plume poppy does not need staking.

FEATURES

HERBACEOUS

The plume poppy is an essential plant for the back of the border, tall, graceful and showy. Growing 2.5m (8ft) high, it sports long, thin stems with mid- and late summer panicles of pale white flowers. 'Flamingo' has pinkish flowers. The large, lobed foliage is equally attractive. With more room in the border *M. microcarpa* can be grown. It is slightly invasive and has pink flowers, while 'Kelway's Coral Plume' produces coral-pink flowers opening from pure pink buds. The plume poppy's natural habitat is Chinese and Japanese meadows where it makes large impressive colonies, spreading quickly through the damp soil by underground rhizomes, flowering all summer long.

MACLEAYA AT A GLANCE

M. cordata is a rhizomatous perennial with grey-green foliage, grown for its tall flower spikes. Hardy to −18°C (0°F).

			COMPANION PLANTS
JAN	/		
FEB	/		Clematis
MAR	/		Gypsophila
APR	division		Hibiscus
MAY	/		Miscanthus
JUN	/		Lobelia
JULY	flowering		Osteospermum
AUG	flowering		Rose
SEPT	/		Salvia
OCT	division		
NOV	/		
DEC	/		

CONDITIONS

Aspect Macleaya likes full sun and light shade, though the former produces a longer, better display. Avoid dark areas. Also avoid open windy sites; shelter is required.

Site Light, well-drained soil is ideal.

GROWING METHOD

Propagation The quickest, easiest results are either by making spring or autumn divisions, or by separating lengths of rhizome when the plant is dormant. Make sure each has its own root system. Water new plants well, and space out at 90cm (3ft) intervals.

Feeding Provide moderate applications of compost and well-rotted manure in the spring as a mulch.

Problems Colonies of slugs can be a severe problem, badly attacking the new, vigorous growth. Either pick off by hand or treat accordingly with chemicals.

FLOWERING

Season Flowers appear in mid- and late summer on long, thin stems producing an airy display.

Cutting Macleaya make very attractive cut flowers, requiring a regular change of water, their airy panicles adding considerably to both formal and flowery arrangements.

AFTER FLOWERING

Requirements Cut back old growth to the ground.

MECONOPSIS
Himalayan blue poppy

NO OTHER blue flower has quite the same startlingly clear colour as the amazing blue poppy, a true delight whenever it can be grown.

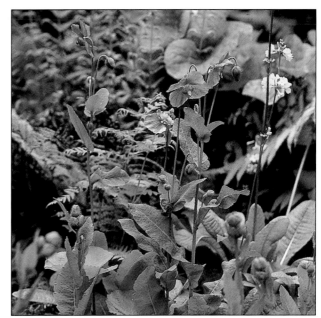

WOODLAND CONDITIONS where the soil never really dries out are essential for the Himalayan or Tibetan blue poppy.

FEATURES

HERBACEOUS

Meconopsis betonicifolia is the beautiful blue poppy everyone loves. There is probably no other plant that produces such an intense sky-blue flower. Its natural habitat is very high altitude alpine meadows in China. Plants do not flower the first year, and they die down in winter, growing and blooming the second year. If meconopsis is prevented from blooming the first time it sets buds, it is more likely to become perennial. Growing to almost 2m (6½ft) in its native habitat, in cultivation it is more likely to be 50–70cm (20–28in) high. Looks best when grown as part of a massed display, or threaded through a border.

MECONOPSIS AT A GLANCE

M. betonicifolia is a deciduous perennial, making a strong show, with blue or white, early summer flowers. Hardy to –18° (0°F).

JAN	/	RECOMMENDED VARIETIES
FEB	/	
MAR	sow	*Meconopsis cambrica*
APR	transplant	*M. betonicifolia*
MAY	transplant	*M. grandis*
JUN	flowering	*M. napaulensis*
JULY	flowering	*M. quintuplinervia*
AUG	flowering	*M. x sheldonii*
SEPT	flowering	*M. x s. 'Slieve Donard'*
OCT	sow	*M. superba*
NOV	/	
DEC	/	

CONDITIONS

Aspect Needs partial, dappled shade; also provide some protection from strong, cutting, drying winds.

Site Needs a well-drained soil that is rich in organic matter. In colder regions it grows best in acid soil.

GROWING METHOD

Propagation Grows from fresh ripe seed sown in the autumn, or in spring. Give winter seedlings frost protection in a greenhouse, but beware of damping off, and plant out in late spring or early summer. Initially water well. Do not waterlog or the crowns will rot.

Feeding Apply a little general fertiliser in the spring.

Problems Overwet soil, especially during winter, will rot the crown. Downy mildew may be a problem in some seasons. Spray plants with a fungicide at the first sign of an attack.

FLOWERING

Season Abundant flowers begin appearing at the start of summer.

Cutting While they make extremely good cut flowers, they do not last that long.

AFTER FLOWERING

Requirements Remove spent flower stems unless you are waiting for seed to ripen. Once growth dies down, cut it off at ground level.

MELIANTHUS MAJOR
Honey bush

NECTAR RICH, these dark red flowers are very attractive to insects. The foliage too, is unusual, with its distinctive colour and form.

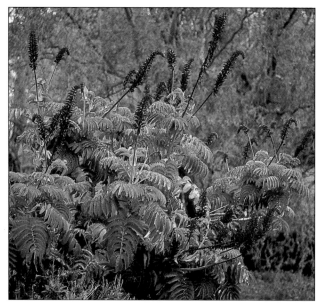

THE BLUE-GREEN FOLIAGE of honey flower is a feature in itself. Only in a largish garden will you appreciate the full effect.

FEATURES

EVERGREEN

This very striking evergreen plant with its unusual blue-green foliage really stands out. It is grown as a feature in a mixed border or as a focal point in an annual or perennial display. In a large garden it could be repeat planted to tie together various arrangements. Honey bush can grow to 2m (6ft) in height, and it spreads by suckers, forming a large clump if left undivided. The dark mahogany-red flowers contain copious quantities of nectar, attractive to bees. Although native to South Africa, and initially tender here, after two years the base becomes woody and it can survive outside if given good frost protection in mild areas. It can also be grown in a large pot.

MELIANTHUS AT A GLANCE

M. major is a tender, southern African plant with wonderful, architectural foliage. It is damaged below 5°C (41°F).

		COMPANION PLANTS
JAN	/	
FEB	/	Canna
MAR	sow	Choisya
APR	divide	*Hosta* 'Krossa Regal'
MAY	transplant	Philadelphus
JUN	flowering	Pinus
JULY	flowering	Pseudopanax
AUG	flowering	Salvia
SEPT	/	
OCT	/	
NOV	/	
DEC	/	

CONDITIONS

Aspect   Needs full sun all day (i.e. a south-facing wall).
Site   Soil must be well drained but it need not be specially rich, in fact over-rich soils will produce good foliage effects but poor flowering. However, the outstanding architectural foliage is the main reason for growing this striking plant.

GROWING METHOD

Propagation   Grows from seed sown in spring or from division of suckers on an existing plant, also in spring. Plant at least 1m (39in) apart. For best growth give deep watering every week or two in hot, dry spells during the growing season. It will, however, tolerate drought well.
Feeding   Apply a complete plant food in spring.
Problems   Red spider mites may strike. Use an appropriate insecticide.

FLOWERING

Season   Dark crimson flowers may appear in late summer or earlier on long stems that survived the winter.
Cutting   Flowers are probably best left on the plant as they do not smell particularly pleasant.

AFTER FLOWERING

Requirements   Cut off the spent flower stems unless you are waiting for seed to set and ripen. Protect the base and roots with straw or bracken against frost. The older and woodier the plant, the better its chance of survival.

MONARDA DIDYMA
Bergamot

THE HOT-PINK FLOWERS on this bergamot are easy to place in the garden. They combine well with blue or white schemes.

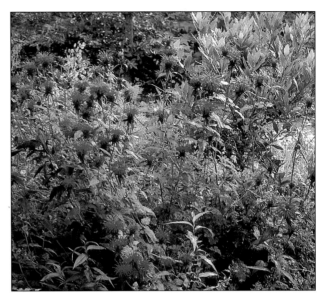

FOR COLOUR over a long period, this brilliant red variety of bergamot, 'Cambridge Scarlet', is hard to beat. It requires little care.

FEATURES

HERBACEOUS

This is an aromatic herbaceous perennial which is also known as bee balm and Oswego tea. The name bee balm refers to its nectar-rich flowers, which are very attractive to bees, and Oswego tea to its use by the Oswego Indians and early colonists of North America as a tea substitute. Growing about 90cm (36in) high, bergamot flowers from mid- to late summer. The heads of tubular flowers are red, pink, white or purple with some outstanding named cultivars, including 'Cambridge Scarlet' and 'Croftway Pink'. It is easy to grow. Being a member of the mint family its roots spread vigorously, but it makes a lively addition to a mixed planting for its bright scarlet or pink flowers.

MONARDA AT A GLANCE

M. didyma is a clump-forming perennial with lance-shape leaves, and bright late summer flowers. Hardy to –18°C (0°F).

JAN	/	
FEB	sow	
MAR	sow	
APR	transplant	
MAY	transplant	
JUN	/	
JULY	flowering	
AUG	flowering	
SEPT	/	
OCT	sow	
NOV	/	
DEC	/	

RECOMMENDED VARIETIES

'Aquarius'
'Beauty of Cobham'
'Cambridge Scarlet'
'Croftway Pink'
'Fishes'
'Mahogany'
'Prarienacht'
'Sagittarius'
'Scorpion'

CONDITIONS

Aspect   Grows in either full sun or semi-shade, but flowering will be best in the open.

Site   Needs well-drained soil that is made moisture retentive by the addition of large amounts of decayed organic matter.

GROWING METHOD

Propagation   Lift and divide clumps in spring before new growth begins. Replant the young, vigorous outer growths 20–30cm (8–12in) apart. Plants usually need dividing every two or three years. Bergamot may be also be grown from seed sown either in the early spring or autumn, but this does not come true to type. Needs regular, deep watering through prolonged dry spells in the heat of summer.

Feeds   If the soil is well supplied with humus, but a little fertiliser is needed. Apply some complete plant food in the spring.

Problems   Since snails love to eat the new growth as it appears, take precautions. Mildew can be a problem at times. You may need a fungicide spray or it might become severe. Remove all dead and diseased leaves.

FLOWERING

Season   Flowers in mid- and late summer.

Cutting   Makes a decent cut flower. Use the scented leaves in a pot-pourri.

AFTER FLOWERING

Requirements   Prune off spent flower stems. Cut plants back to ground level once growth begins to die off.

OENOTHERA
Evening primrose

THOUGH EVENING PRIMROSE is thought of as yellow, the flowers of Oenothera speciosa *'Rosea' are pink and white, with yellow.*

O. SPECIOSA 'ROSEA' *is doubly attractive because it grows 30cm (12in) high, mixes well with argyranthemum, and forms large clumps.*

FEATURES

SUMMER AUTUMN WINTER SPRING

HERBACEOUS

Evening primrose is an essential plant for formal and cottage-style gardens. While each flower (white, yellow or pink, depending on variety) opens and fades fast, barely lasting 24 hours, there is an abundance of new buds developing through summer and early autumn. The plant has two extra advantages. Often fragrant, and often tall, it can make an eye-catching addition to the border. *O. biennis,* the traditional favourite is actually an annual or biennial. *O. fruticosa,* a biennial or perennial, has two fine forms, 'Fyrverkeri' ('Fireworks') which has red buds opening to yellow flowers and purple-tinged leaves, and subsp. *glauca,* with yellow flowers and purple leaves.

CONDITIONS

Aspect   Grow in an open, sunny position.
Site   Moderately rich soil will suffice, though evening primrose can self-seed and appear in even the stoniest ground.

GROWING METHOD

Propagation   Sow seed or divide in early spring, or take cuttings of non-flowering shoots. Keep in a frost-free place in winter, plant out in spring.
Feeding   Not necessary, though moderate quantities of manure will suffice in especially poor soil.
Problems   Slugs tend to be the main problem, attacking tender new growth. Pick off or treat with chemicals. The sturdy kinds of evening primrose are free-standing, but others (*O. macrocarpa*) may require support.

FLOWERING

Season   Lasts from late spring to late summer, with flowers tending to open in early evening when they release their scent.
Cutting   Short-lived but attractive flowers.

AFTER FLOWERING

Requirements   Collect seed when ripe, if required, and then cut spent stems to the ground.

OENOTHERA AT A GLANCE

A genus of mainly annuals and biennials, with excellent perennials. Scented and yellow flowering they are hardy to –15°C (5°F).

JAN	/	
FEB	sow	
MAR	divide	
APR	transplant	
MAY	flowering	
JUN	flowering	
JULY	flowering	
AUG	flowering	
SEPT	/	
OCT	/	
NOV	/	
DEC	/	

RECOMMENDED VARIETIES

Oenothera biennis
O. fruticosa
O. f. 'Fyrverkeri'
O. f. subsp. *glauca*
O. macrocarpa
O. speciosa 'Rosea'
O. stricta 'Sulphurea'

PAEONIA
Paeony species and cultivars

GLORIOUS COLOUR *and perfume combine in this extensive planting of peony cultivars to produce a spectacular result.*

THIS HALF-OPENED *peony flower gives a hint of delights to come, with a touch of white against the bright pink.*

FLUTED PETALS *give extra interest to this single white peony. The large mass of central stamens adds a touch of colour.*

FEATURES

HERBACEOUS

Beautiful to look at and fragrant too, peonies are among the aristocrats of the plant world, and although there are only 33 wild species, there are many hundreds of cultivars. Peonies were prized by the Chinese for many hundreds of years, and by the early 18th century they had developed the garden peonies from which the forms of *P. lactiflora* (often referred to as Chinese peonies) are generally descended. Peonies were first introduced into Europe at the end of the 18th century. Peonies are divided into two groups: the tree peonies, which are shrubby and derived from *P. suffruticosa*, and the herbaceous peonies, of which the cultivars of *P. lactiflora* are most commonly grown. Although the name 'tree peony' is used this is an exaggeration, they rarely grow more than 2m (6½ft) high. Herbaceous peonies grow about 1m (39in) high and wide. Plants are long lived.

Flowers Flowers may be single or double and come in every shade of pink, red, purple, white and cream, many with a delicious light perfume. Some flowers have a large central boss of golden stamens, and some have fringed or crimped edges on the petals. Among the categories of flowers recognised are: small, 5–10cm (2–4in) across; medium, 10–15cm, (4–6in); large, 15–20cm (6–8in); and very large, over 20cm (8in). Tree peonies are generally 5–30cm (2–12in). Other categories have been developed in the United States where a great deal of hybridising is practised.

CONDITIONS

Aspect Needs full sun or semi-shade with protection from strong winds.

Site Soil must be well drained, but heavily enriched with manure or compost. Dig it over deeply to allow the free spread of the roots.

THE ATTRACTIVE FOLIAGE greatly adds to the value of peonies and often emerges with lovely rich red and bronze tints.

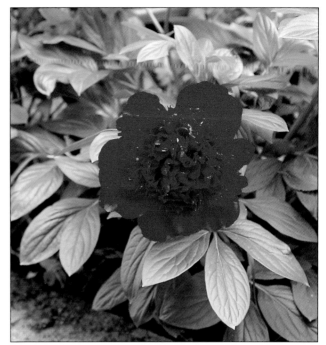

THE VERY POPULAR double cultivar 'Rubra Plena' is a rich crimson anemone-centred peony that looks very like a camellia.

GROWING METHOD

Propagation Divide plants in the spring or autumn, taking care not to break the brittle roots. Each division must have roots and dormant growth buds. Crowns should be replanted 2.5cm (1in) below the surface, and spaced about 50cm (20in) apart. Plants can be raised from seed but they will take four to five years to reach flowering size, and only the species will be true to type. Peony seeds generally need two periods of chilling with a warm period between, and care should be taken not to disturb the seeds during this time. Most seeds germinate the second spring after sowing.

Feeding Apply a general fertiliser in early spring. At the same time mulch but avoid the crown.

PAEONIA AT A GLANCE

A genus of over 30 species of clump-forming perennials and sub-shrubs, often with highly scented flowers. Hardy to −15°C (5°F).

JAN	/	
FEB	/	
MAR	/	
APR	divide	
MAY	transplant	
JUN	flowering	
JULY	/	
AUG	/	
SEPT	/	
OCT	sow	
NOV	sow	
DEC	sow	

RECOMMENDED VARIETIES

P. cambessedesii
'Defender'
P. lactiflora 'Bowl of Beauty'
P. l. 'Festiva Maxima'
P. l. 'Sarah Bernhardt'
P. mlokosewitschii
P. obovata

Problems Botrytis or grey mould is the main problem with peonies. It can cause rotting of stems and leaf bases. Destroy affected foliage, improve drainage and air circulation, and spray with a fungicide. Replace the top layer of soil carefully around the plants.

FLOWERING

Season The flowering period is invariably early summer. Some peonies bloom for only a short time, but the flowers on other types are much longer lasting.

Cutting Cut flowers for indoor use just as the blooms are opening. Peonies are excellent cut flowers, which will last longer if kept in a cool part of the house and given frequent water changes.

AFTER FLOWERING

Requirements Remove spent flower stems but allow the foliage to die down naturally before trimming it back. Some varieties produce lovely autumn colour. Do not to cut down the flowering stems of varieties such as *P. mlokosewitschii* that produce handsome berries.

HINT

Disturbance Peonies may flower poorly, if at all, the first year after planting, but this should improve year by year. Generally speaking, peonies are best left undisturbed; even 50-year-old clumps can be seen flowering profusely. You may be wiser to increase your stock by buying young container-grown plants than split a precious specimen.

PAPAVER ORIENTALE
Oriental poppy

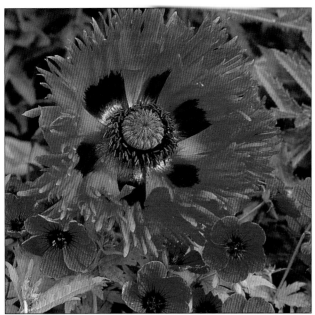

THIS FRINGED red flower indicates the wide range of colours within P. orientale. *No border should be without one.*

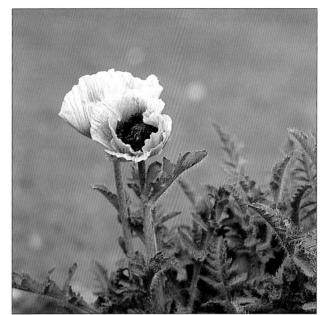

THE STRIKING SHAPE of Papaver orientale. *Note the straight, slightly furry stem with, here, pink flowers and a black basal mark.*

FEATURES

HERBACEOUS

The oriental poppy is a clump-forming perennial with a variety of different forms, and colours ranging from soft hues to sharp red. They all bear the hallmarks of the species, *P. orientalis,* from north-east Turkey and Iran, which has a large cupped bowl of a flower with paper thin petals. Growing up to 90cm (36in) tall, with a similar spread, they self-seed freely, creating attractive colonies. They look the part in both wild, or natural gardens, and large mixed borders. 'Black and White' is a striking contrast of white petals and a black mark at its base. 'Cedric Morris' is soft pink with a black base.'Indian Chief' is reddish-brown.

PAPAVER AT A GLANCE

P. orientalis is a perennial with 30cm (12in) long leaves, and big, cupped flowers in a range of colours. Hardy to –18°C (0°F).

		RECOMMENDED VARIETIES
JAN	/	*Papaver orientale* 'Allegro'
FEB	/	P. o. 'Beauty of Livermere'
MAR	/	P. o. 'Black and White'
APR	division	P. o. Goliath Group
MAY	flowering	P. o. 'Mrs Perry'
JUN	flowering	P. o. 'Patty's Plum'
JULY	flowering	P. o. 'Perry's White'
AUG	/	P. o. 'Picotee'
SEPT	/	P. o. 'Turkish Delight'
OCT	sow	
NOV	/	
DEC	/	

CONDITIONS

Aspect   Provide full sun, the conditions it receives in its natural habitat.

Site   Rich soil and good drainage bring out the best in these plants.

GROWING METHOD

Propagation   Since they self-seed freely, propagation may not be necessary. Slicing off sections of root in late autumn or early winter will provide abundant new plants. The success rate is invariably high. Alternatively, divide clumps in the spring, or sow seed in pots in the autumn in a cold frame. Plant out the following spring, 23cm (9in) apart.

Feeding   Add plenty of rich, friable compost in spring to add fertility to poor soils, also improving the drainage which needs to be quite good.

Problems   Fungal wilt and downy mildew can be problems; spray at the first sign.

FLOWERING

Season   The flowers appear from late spring to mid-summer.

Cutting   Poppies do not make good cut flowers.

AFTER FLOWERING

Requirements   When the flowers have died down, severely cut back the foliage to the ground. This will produce a second showing of attractive summer leaves.

PENSTEMON
Beard tongue

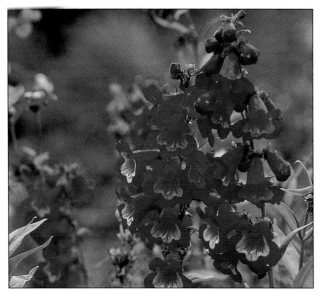

MANY MONTHS of fine bloom can be expected from this fine red cultivar, well into autumn, if it is regularly deadheaded.

A GENEROUS PLANTING of these attractive white cultivars makes a perfect surround for this small ornamental fountain.

FEATURES

EVERGREEN

This very large group of perennials consists of 250 species and countless cultivars, all originating in a wide variety of habitats in the southern and western United States. Their tubular or funnel-shaped flowers come in a range of shades of pink, red, purple, lavender, blue and white, some with a contrasting throat. There is a large range of cultivars in many of these shades. Collections can also be bought as young rooted cuttings. Penstemons have a long flowering period through summer to mid-autumn, especially if the spent blooms are regularly cut, but many plants can be short-lived. Take cuttings regularly. The various species and hybrids grow anything from 10cm–60cm (4–24in) high.

PENSTEMON AT A GLANCE

A large genus of perennials grown for their late-season flower display. Hardiness varies from the frost tender to –15ºC (5ºF).

		RECOMMENDED VARIETIES
JAN	/	
FEB	sow	'Alice Hindley'
MAR	sow	'Beech Park'
APR	transplant	'Chester Scarlet'
MAY	transplant	'Evelyn'
JUN	flowering	'Garnet'
JULY	flowering	'Margery Fish'
AUG	flowering	'Osprey'
SEPT	flowering	'Pennington Gem'
OCT	flowering	'Rubicundus'
NOV	/	
DEC	/	

CONDITIONS

Aspect Grows best in full sun with some protection from strong, cutting winds. Since most varieties are not fully hardy, warmth and shelter are essential.

Site Needs very open, and well-drained soil.

GROWING METHOD

Propagation They grow well from cuttings taken mid-summer, then overwintered in a greenhouse frame. A wide range of penstemons can also be grown from seed which is widely available. They need a cold period before germination; sow in the autumn or refrigerate the seed for three weeks before sowing in the spring.

Feeding Apply a general fertiliser as new growth commences in the spring.

Problems No specific pest or disease problems, but root rot may occur on sticky clay soil.

FLOWERING

Season Most have a fairly long flowering period from summer to mid-autumn. However, many can only be seen as true perennials in milder parts of the country, being killed by winter frosts; raise new stock to replace any losses. 'Garnet' is the hardiest.

Cutting This is not a satisfactory cut flower.

AFTER FLOWERING

Requirements Either cut entirely to the ground, or leave some stems as frost protection. Protect clumps with a mulch of straw or bracken.

PHLOX PANICULATA
Perennial phlox

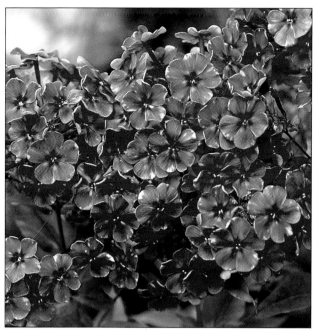

THE ATTRACTIVE, individual flowers on the heads of perennial phlox last right through the season, making it essential in any border.

A GREAT STANDBY for the summer garden, perennial phlox fills the whole of the back of this border with two shades of pink.

FEATURES

HERBACEOUS

Easy to grow and producing a summer-long display of flowers, perennial phlox has a place in any perennial collection. Plants may grow from 40–90cm (16–36in) high, and the clumps spread rapidly; space new plantings 30cm (12in) apart. The large heads of flowers, some with a contrasting eye, come in shades of red, pink, orange, mauve, purple and white. This plant looks best mass planted, either in solid blocks of one colour or in mixed colours. Also note the highly popular, new variegated cultivars. With mixed plantings ensure that the taller forms do not obscure the shorter ones.

PHLOX AT A GLANCE

P. paniculata is an erect, herbaceous perennial with scented flowers, and many excellent cultivars. Hardy to –15°C (5°F).

JAN	/	
FEB	sow	
MAR	sow	
APR	transplant	
MAY	transplant	
JUN		
JULY	flowering	
AUG	flowering	
SEPT	flowering	
OCT	divide	
NOV	/	
DEC	/	

RECOMMENDED VARIETIES

Phlox paniculata 'Alba Grandiflora'
P. p. 'Blue Ice'
P. p. 'Bumble's Delight'
P. p. 'Eventide'
P. p. 'Le Mahdi'
P. p. 'Prince of Orange'
P. p. 'Prospero'
P. p. 'White Admiral'

CONDITIONS

Aspect Prefers full sun with some protection from strong wind.
Site Needs a well-drained soil enriched with organic matter.

GROWING METHOD

Propagation Divide clumps in the autumn every three or four years, making sure that each division has a crown and a decent set of roots. Replant only the younger, vigorous outer growths, discarding the rest. Plants propagated from root cuttings will be free of eelworm.
Feeding Apply a complete plant food in spring and mulch well with rotted manure or compost, but do not cover the crowns.
Problems Powdery mildew can be a problem. Spray with a fungicide. Phlox eelworm causes leaves to shrivel, and shrubs distort. Plants must be destroyed.

FLOWERING

Season From summer into early autumn.
Cutting It makes a good cut flower.

AFTER FLOWERING

Requirements Remove spent flower stems as they fade. In late autumn cut off any remaining growth. Give the plants a thorough tidy up for the winter.

PHYSOSTEGIA VIRGINIANA
Obedient plant

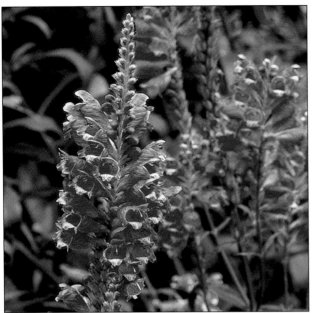

THE SHORT SPIKES of flowers are attached to the obedient plant by a joint so that they can be rearranged as you please.

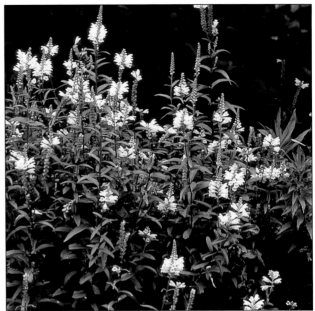

OBEDIENT PLANT looks best in large plantings and it is well worth devoting garden space to it as the flowers last for several months.

FEATURES

HERBACEOUS

This is an easy-care, fast-growing perennial. Since it spreads by stolons (runners) and seed, large clumps can develop in one season. Excess plants are quite easily removed. The dark green leaves are only 10–15cm (4–6in) high, but flowering stems bring the height up to 1.2m (4ft). The flowers in the species are pinky mauve, but there are cultivars with flowers in various shades of pink, red and white. It looks best planted in large drifts in a border, or among shrubs. The common name refers to the fact that flowers remain fixed the way they are turned. It is also sometimes known as false dragon's head.

PHYSOSTEGIA AT A GLANCE

P. virginiana is a spreading, tall perennial with purple or lilac-tinged flowers lasting into autumn. Hardy to 0°C (32°F).

JAN	/	RECOMMENDED VARIETIES
FEB	/	*Physostegia virginiana* 'Alba'
MAR	divide	*P. v.* 'Crown of Snow'
APR	transplant	*P. v.* 'Red Beauty'
MAY	transplant	*P. v.* 'Summer Snow'
JUN	/	*P. v.* 'Vivid'
JULY	flowering	*P. v.* subsp. *speciosa*
AUG	flowering	'Bouquet Rose'
SEPT	flowering	
OCT	sow	
NOV	/	
DEC	/	

CONDITIONS

Aspect   Grows well in both full sun and semi-shade. However, some form of protection from strong winds is desirable. The taller varieties may need staking.

Site   Tolerates a wide range of soils, but the best results are when grown in well-drained soil, rich in organic matter.

GROWING METHOD

Propagation   Divide old clumps in spring, planting new divisions in groups for the best effect. The oldest sections can be discarded. Because of its vigorous habit you need to divide every couple of years. Tolerates dry periods well, but you must water young plants regularly until they are established.

Feeding   Apply a complete plant food in spring. Mulch with decayed organic matter at the same time.

Problems   No specific problems are known.

FLOWERING

Season   Flowers appear from mid- to late summer into the autumn.

Cutting   Frequent cutting of blooms should produce a second flush of flowers. Scald cut stems to prolong their vase life.

AFTER FLOWERING

Requirements   Remove spent flower stems and tidy up growth as it dies down.

PLATYCODON
Balloon flower

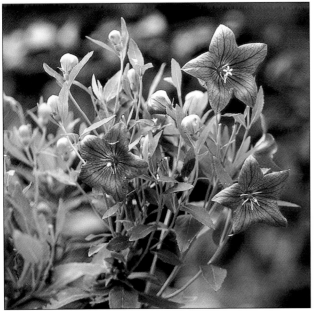

THE BUDS *of platycodon swell into a balloon-shape, hence the common name, then pop open revealing these beautiful flowers.*

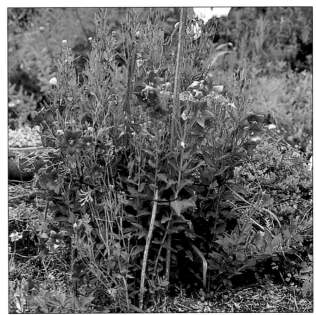

THIS WELL-ESTABLISHED CLUMP *of balloon flower is supported by stakes guaranteeing height as well as colour.*

FEATURES

HERBACEOUS

Also known as Chinese bellflower, this herbaceous perennial grows around 50cm (20in) high, slightly taller in perfect conditions. It has a shortish flowering period in late summer, and the open, bell-shape flowers come in a range of blue shades, but also in white and pale pink. Flowers last well when cut. There are several named cultivars available, including double and semi-double ones. Since clumps are compact and spread slowly, they are best planted where they can remain undisturbed for some years. The new growth appears in late spring; mark its position to avoid hauling it out as a weed.

PLATYCODON AT A GLANCE

P. grandiflorus is a one-specie genus grown for its beautiful purple-blue flowers. Several fine cultivars. Hardy to −15°C (5°F).

		COMPANION PLANTS
JAN	/	
FEB	/	Aster
MAR	sow	Clematis
APR	divide	Dahlia
MAY	transplant	Fuchsia
JUN	/	Osteospermum
JULY	/	Phygelius
AUG	flowering	*Rhodochiton atrosanguineus*
SEPT	flowering	Rose
OCT	/	
NOV	/	
DEC	/	

CONDITIONS

Aspect   Grows in sun or dappled sunlight.
Site   Grows best in a well-drained soil enriched with plenty of organic matter.

GROWING METHOD

Propagation   Seed is the best means of propagation; sow in the spring. Young shoots can be taken as cuttings, and the double forms must be grown from cuttings. Also, clumps can be lifted and divided in the spring; replant the divisions about 20–25cm (8–10in) apart. Give newly bedded plants a regular watering during prolonged dry spells in the spring and summer.

Feeding   Apply a complete plant food when the new growth begins to appear in the spring.

Problems   Slugs can be a major problem devouring new growth. Either pick off by hand or treat chemically.

FLOWERING

Season   A relatively short display, which is more than compensated for by the nature of the exquisite flowers.

Cutting   Flowers can be cut for the vase.

AFTER FLOWERING

Requirements   Cut right back to the ground all spent flower stems, and then the whole plant as the growth dies off.

POLYGONATUM
Solomon's seal

A HORIZONTAL STEM of pretty white Solomon's seal flowers is suspended above a groundcover of lungwort and dead nettle.

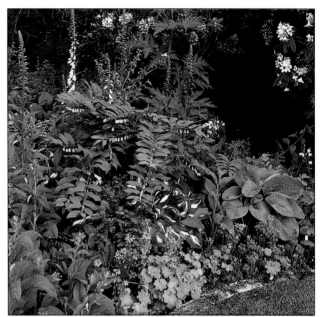

SOLOMON'S SEAL grows tall in the dappled shade of this garden, where it is teamed with hostas, lady's mantle and foxgloves.

FEATURES

HERBACEOUS

This lovely herbaceous perennial is ideal for naturalising in the dappled shade of a garden. The plant has a graceful, arching habit with stems 60–90 cm (24–36in) long. The finely veined foliage tends to stand up on the stem, while the tubular white bell flowers hang down. It grows from a creeping rhizome and will spread to form a colony of plants given the right conditions. If space is no problem, plant several to start your display, letting them form large colonies. A number of other species are grown, some, such as *P. odoratum*, with scented flowers. 'Flore Pleno' has double flowers. There are two variegated, eye-catching forms.

POLYGONATUM AT A GLANCE

P. x *hybridum* (*multiflorum*) is a rhizomatous perennial with green-tipped white flowers; black fruit. Hardy to −18°C° (0°F).

		RECOMMENDED VARIETIES
JAN	/	
FEB	/	*P. biflorum*
MAR	divide	*P. falcatum*
APR	transplant	*P. f.* 'Variegatum'
MAY	flowering	*P. hookeri*
JUN	/	*P. odoratum* 'Flore Pleno'
JULY	/	*P. verticillatum*
AUG	/	
SEPT	/	
OCT	sow	
NOV	/	
DEC	/	

CONDITIONS

Aspect Needs a sheltered spot in part or full shade.
Site The soil should drain well but be heavily enriched with organic matter to retain some moisture at all times. The plants benefit from an early spring mulch.

GROWING METHOD

Propagation Established clumps can be divided in early spring, new divisions being spaced 20–25cm (8–10in) apart. This plant is best left undisturbed for several years if possible. Young plants need to be watered regularly during the growing season; do not let them dry out.
Feeding Apply complete plant food as new growth commences in spring.
Problems Plants can be severely devastated by attacks of sawfly larvae, which reduce them to skeletons. Either treat with a spray, or pick off the caterpillars.

FLOWERING

Season Flowers appear in late spring.
Cutting Flowers can be cut for indoor decoration. They last fairly well and make a good display.

AFTER FLOWERING

Requirements Do not cut down the flower stems or you will end up weakening the plant, and consequently losing the attractive, yellow autumn tints.

POTENTILLA
Cinquefoil

A SMART RED AND WHITE MIX of cinquefoil with annual heartsease, or Viola tricolor, *growing through it.*

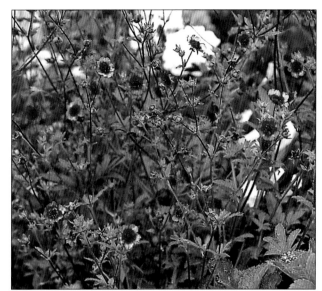

DESPITE THE SMALL FLOWERS, these bright little plants are difficult to overlook in any perennial garden.

FEATURES

HERBACEOUS

There are over 500 species of cinquefoil, including annuals, perennials and small shrubs. All have the characteristic five-lobed leaf, and the single or double flowers may be white or in shades of yellow, red or pink. Cinquefoil belongs to the rose family, and the foliage can be attractive even when plants are not in flower. They may be from 5–50cm (2–20in) or more high. The short types make good edging plants, while the taller ones can be used successfully in a mixed planting. Since flower stems tend to flop over they may need light support. Many red cinquefoils are hybrids of *P. atrosanguinea,* while some yellows derive from *P. argyrophylla* and *P. recta.* Some cinquefoils tend to self-seed.

POTENTILLA AT A GLANCE

A 500-species genus, mainly of herbaceous perennials and shrubs. An excellent colour range. Hardy to −18°C (0°F).

JAN	/	
FEB	/	RECOMMENDED VARIETIES
MAR	sow	*Potentilla cuneata*
APR	transplant	'Gibson's Scarlet'
MAY	transplant	*P. megalantha*
JUN	flowering	*P. nepalensis* 'Miss
JULY	flowering	Willmott'
AUG	flowering	'William Rollison'
SEPT	flowering	
OCT	sow	
NOV	/	
DEC	/	

CONDITIONS

Aspect While it needs full sun it will also tolerate some dappled shade.

Site Needs well-drained soil enriched with some organic matter.

GROWING METHOD

Propagation Species and single-flowered varieties grow from both seed and cuttings. Sow the seed in early to mid-spring. The hybrid doubles must be grown from divisions taken during the spring or autumn, or you can use spring cuttings. The plant spacing depends on ultimate size, and may be anywhere from 15–40cm (6–16in).

Feeding Apply a complete plant food as new growth commences in the spring.

Problems Since these plants can easily flower themselves to death, propagate regularly to ensure you always have a good supply.

FLOWERING

Season Flowers may begin in late spring in warm spells, but the main flowering period is during the summer months. Give the plant a light trim in early spring to force plenty of new growth and buds.

Cutting Flowers do not last well when cut.

AFTER FLOWERING

Requirements Cut off spent flower stems at ground level, and tidy up the plants as the growth dies off. In milder areas the foliage may hang on.

PRIMULA VULGARIS
Primrose

A CARPET OF PALE YELLOW PRIMROSES is one of the finest ways of announcing the arrival of spring in the garden. Given a cool, sheltered spot they will thrive and multiply year by year, even if they receive remarkably little attention.

FEATURES

HERBACEOUS

This is the true primrose of European woodlands. The species generally has soft, pale yellow flowers tucked in among the leaves on very short stalks, though occasionally white or pale pink forms are found. Cultivars come in a huge range of colours with single or double flowers, some on short stalks, others on quite tall ones. Primroses look their best mass planted under deciduous trees, or in drifts at the front of a lightly shaded bed or border. They can also be grown well in pots. Plants grow from about 10–15cm (4–6in) high, with flowering stems about the same height.

PRIMULA AT A GLANCE

P. vulgaris is an evergreen or semi-evergreen with scented, spring, generally pale yellow flowers. Hardy to –15°C (5°F).

JAN	/	**RECOMMENDED VARIETIES**
FEB	sow	'Ken Dearman'
MAR	flowering	'Miss Indigo'
APR	flowering	*Primula vulgaris* 'Lilacina
MAY	flowering	Plena'
JUN	/	*P. v.* subsp. *sibthorpii*
JULY	/	'Wanda'
AUG	/	
SEPT	sow	
OCT	divide	
NOV	/	
DEC	/	

CONDITIONS

Aspect Prefers to grow in semi-shade, and must have protection from the summer sun.

Site Grows best in a medium to heavy moisture-retentive soil, heavily enriched with organic matter. Mulch around the plants in spring.

GROWING METHOD

Propagation Lift and divide the crowns after flowering, in late autumn, and replant about 10–15cm (4–6in) apart. Sow your own seed when ripe (from late spring to early autumn); sow bought seed in early spring. Do not let young plants dry out.

Feeding Little fertiliser is needed if the soil is well enriched with plenty of humus, but a little general fertiliser in early spring gives an extra boost.

Problems Generally trouble free.

FLOWERING

Season Flowering usually lasts for several weeks during the spring. Deadheading prolongs the blooming. Massed displays look best.

Cutting Makes a fine posy, mixed with a range of more, early spring miniatures.

AFTER FLOWERING

Requirements In suitable conditions plants may self-seed. Remove dead leaves around the plant base.

PRIMULA SPECIES
Candelabra primulas

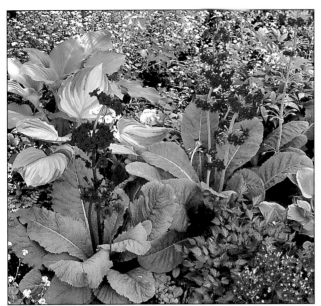

PRIMULA PULVERULENTA *happily combine here with hostas, both enjoying the damp conditions of a bog garden.*

THE CHARACTERISTIC TIERS *of flowers are well displayed in this healthy clump of white perennial primulas.*

FEATURES

HERBACEOUS

EVERGREEN

Candelabra primulas, which produce their flowers in distinct whorls or tiers up the stems, form one group among the several hundred species of primula. Most are herbaceous, but *P. helodoxa*, which has clear yellow flowers, is evergreen. Other species in this group include *P. aurantiaca*, *P. bulleyana*, *P. japonica* and *P. pulverulenta*. Flowers may be white, or in shades of yellow, orange, pink, red and purple. Plant heights vary from 30cm–1m (24–39in). These are plants that need to be placed in big groups for maximum impact. They need damp soil, being often planted around ponds and water features. Given the right conditions these plants will give a great show every year.

PRIMULA AT A GLANCE

Candelabra primulas are deciduous or semi-evergreen, flower on tall stems, and brighten up damp areas. Hardy to -15ºC (5ºF).

		RECOMMENDED VARIETIES
JAN	/	
FEB	sow	*Primula beesiana*
MAR	sow	*P. bulleyana*
APR	flowering	'Inverewe'
MAY	flowering	*P. japonica*
JUN	/	Pagoda Hybrids
JULY	/	*P. japonica*
AUG	/	*P. pulverulenta*
SEPT	sow	
OCT	divide	
NOV	/	
DEC	/	

CONDITIONS

Aspect Thrives in dappled shade.
Site Needs deep, moisture-retentive soil that is heavily enriched with organic matter, but it clearly dislikes being waterlogged over the winter months.

GROWING METHOD

Propagation Lift and divide the crowns after flowering, in late autumn, and replant about 10–15cm (4–6in) apart. Sow your own seed when ripe (from late spring to early autumn); sow bought seed in early spring. Do not let young plants dry out.
Feeding Little fertiliser is needed if the soil is well enriched with plenty of humus, but a scattering of general fertiliser in early spring gives an extra boost.
Problems Generally trouble free.

FLOWERING

Season This charming, essential garden primula flowers during the spring.
Cutting Flowers probably last a few days in the vase, and they add considerable charm to any arrangement, but the massed garden display will be the more rewarding.

AFTER FLOWERING

Requirements Spent flower stems can be cut off, unless you are waiting for seed to set. In good conditions many of the species will self-seed.

PULMONARIA
Lungwort

FLOWERING PULMONARIA are an essential feature of the spring garden.

THE SPOTTED FOLIAGE of lungwort makes a dense and attractive groundcover under trees. It is a reliable grower as long as it gets regular water in the spring and summer.

FEATURES

HERBACEOUS

EVERGREEN

Lungwort is well suited to planting under trees, between shrubs or at the front of a shady border. The abundant flowers appear before the leaves have fully developed, and are mostly in shades of blue, pink, and white. The foliage is very handsome, often silver spotted, and if sheared over after flowering produces a second, fresh mound of leaves. The whole plant is rarely more than 25–30cm (10–12in) high, and when established is very decorative, even out of flower. The plant gets its common name from the similarity between a spotted leaf and a diseased lung.

PULMONARIA AT A GLANCE

A genus of 14 species of deciduous and evergreen perennials. A flowering spreader for damp shade. Hardy to –18°C (0°F).

		RECOMMENDED VARIETIES
JAN	/	*Pulmonaria angustifolia*
FEB	/	*P. a.* 'Munstead Blue'
MAR	flowering	*P. longifolia* 'Bertram
APR	flowering	Anderson'
MAY	flowering	*P. officinalis* Cambridge
JUN	divide	Blue Group
JULY	/	*P. o.* 'Sissinghurst White'
AUG	/	*P. rubra*
SEPT	/	*P. saccharata* Argentea Group
OCT	divide	
NOV	/	
DEC	/	

CONDITIONS

Aspect   Grows best in light shade, or in borders that are shady during the hottest part of the day. The leaves quickly wilt under a hot sun.

Site   The soil should be heavily enriched with decayed organic matter, but it also needs to drain quite well.

GROWING METHOD

Propagation   Grows from ripe seed, or by division of clumps either after flowering or in the autumn. Replant divisions about 15cm (6in) apart. Better still, let plants freely hybridise. Young and established plants need moist soil during the growing season.

Feeding   Apply a little complete fertiliser in early spring and mulch well.

Problems   No specific problems are known.

FLOWERING

Season   Lungworts flower in the spring.

Cutting   Flowers last quite well in a vase.

AFTER FLOWERING

Requirements   Spent flowers can be cut off if you do not want seeding to occur. After the flowers have finished the foliage can be cut back to produce new fresh growth for the summer. Otherwise, little attention is required until the autumn, when the foliage can be tidied up as it fades.

PULSATILLA VULGARIS
Pasque flower

FOLK MEDICINE makes use of the pasque flower, but it should be treated with caution as it can be fatal if used incorrectly.

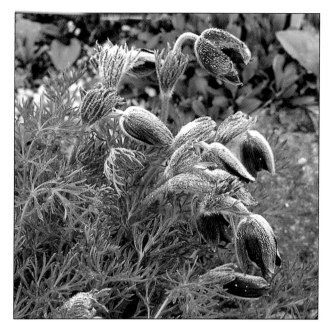

LIGHT FROST here coats buds of the pasque flower, showing up the silky hairs. They will be more obvious on the seedheads.

FEATURES

HERBACEOUS

The soft purple flowers appear before the leaves on this small, spring-flowering perennial. The whole plant is covered with silky hairs, giving it a delicate appearance that belies its hardy nature. After the petals have fallen, a decorative seedhead forms. The finely divided leaves grow from 10–15cm (4–6in) long, while the flowers may be on stems from 10–30cm (4–12in) high. Pasque flower should be planted in groups or drifts to get the best effect. There are now pink, white and red forms available. Since the leaves and flowers may cause skin irritation, wear gloves when handling if you have sensitive skin.

PULSATILLA AT A GLANCE

P. vulgaris is an attractive, clump-forming perennial with bell-like, silky flowers in shades of purple. Hardy to –18°C (0°F).

		Recommended Varieties
Jan	/	
Feb	/	*Pulsatilla alpina* subsp.
Mar	/	*apiifolia*
Apr	flowering	*P. halleri*
May	flowering	*P. halleri* subsp. *slavica*
Jun	flowering	*P. vernalis*
July	sow	*P. vulgaris*
Aug	sow	*P. v.* 'Eva Constance'
Sept	/	*P. v.* var. *rubra*
Oct	divide	
Nov	/	
Dec	/	

CONDITIONS

Aspect   Prefers full sun but tolerates some semi-shade.
Site   Needs very well-drained, gritty soil, rich in organic matter. They thrive on lime.

GROWING METHOD

Propagation   Divide existing clumps after the foliage has died down, and then replant the divisions about 15–20cm (6–8in) apart. Named varieties must be divided, but the species can also be grown from seed sown as soon as it is ripe in July. Overwinter the seedlings in a greenhouse or frame. Pot up when the new leaves begin to show in the spring.
Feeding   Apply a little general fertiliser as growth commences in the spring.
Problems   No specific pest or disease problems are known for this plant.

FLOWERING

Season   Flowers appear in the spring and early summer, generally before the leaves. They last well and the display is prolonged by the pretty, silky seedheads.
Cutting   Flowers are unsuitable for cutting, but the seedheads add to an attractive display.

AFTER FLOWERING

Requirements   Plants should be left alone until the seedheads have faded or fallen. Cut off spent stems, and as the plant dies trim off the foliage.

ROMNEYA COULTERI
Californian tree poppy

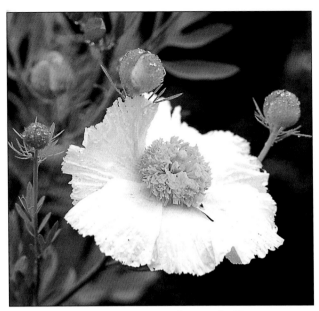

CRIMPED WHITE PETALS *around a mass of golden stamens, making the matilija poppy as effective in close-up as in a group.*

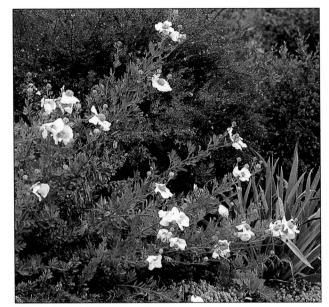

THE BLUE-GREEN FOLIAGE *and splendid white flowers of the matilija poppy make an eye-catching display in the garden.*

FEATURES

EVERGREEN

Also known as the matilija poppy, this lovely perennial is not always easy to accommodate. It is native to the canyons and dry riverbeds in parts of California where there is generally rain only in winter, and where summers are hot and dry. When conditions are suitable this plant can spread via underground roots. The large, white, summer flowers have beautiful crinkled petals that look like silk. Plants grow from 1–2m (3–6½ft) high, and the blue-green foliage is deeply cut and attractive. Place these perennials in groups among shrubs or mixed perennials. Most plants available are likely to be hybrids of the straight species and *R. coulteri* var. *trichocalyx*.

ROMNEYA AT A GLANCE

R. coulteri is a deciduous sub-shrub with grey-green leaves and highly attractive white summer flowers. Hardy to −18°C (0°F).

		COMPANION PLANTS
JAN	/	
FEB	/	Ceanothus
MAR	sow	Clematis
APR	division	Delphinium
MAY	transplant	Helenium
JUN	flowering	Hemerocallis
JULY	flowering	Pelargonium
AUG	flowering	Pennisetum
SEPT	/	Philadelphus
OCT	/	
NOV	/	
DEC	/	

CONDITIONS

Aspect Needs bright, full sun all day.
Site Needs well-drained, preferably sandy or gravelly loam; avoid thick, heavy, wet clay. They can be tricky and slow to establish, but thereafter thrive given the right conditions.

GROWING METHOD

Propagation Grows from seed sown in the spring, but it is easiest propagated from root cuttings or suckers growing away from the main plant in spring. Wait until plants are very well established before attempting to disturb the roots – something they do not react well to. Space plants approximately 40cm (16in) apart. Water regularly in the spring when the foliage is growing and buds are appearing; thereafter water occasionally in prolonged, dry spells.
Feeding Give a little complete plant food in early spring.
Problems Poor drainage can kill Californian tree poppies. Can become invasive.

FLOWERING

Season Right through the summer.
Cutting Like all poppies they make lovely cut flowers. Scald or burn the stems before arranging.

AFTER FLOWERING

Requirements Cut off spent flowers. As the plant flowers on new growth it is best to cut it down to the ground in winter. Protect the crown with straw or bracken in cold areas.

RUDBECKIA
Coneflower

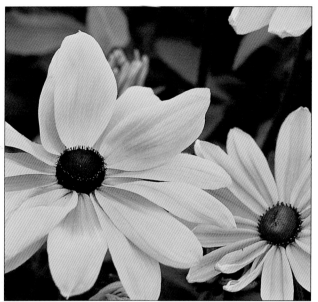

THE DAISY-LIKE flower shape of the coneflower, a bright colour, and a central dark marking. It looks best in a bold group display.

A VALUABLE, forceful, late summer display from a mass planting of coneflowers, especially useful when many borders are starting to fade.

FEATURES

HERBACEOUS

The coneflower rewards a bright, sunny position with a bold display of daisy-like flowers. The genus consists of annuals, biennials and perennials, with some traditional garden favourites. *R. fulgida,* black-eyed Susan, grows 90 x 45cm (36 x 18in), producing yellow-orange flowers at the end of summer, into the autumn. 'Goldsturm' has bigger flowers but only grows two-thirds as tall. For a powerful, vigorous display at the back of the border, try *R. lacinata.* It has thin wiry stems, lemon-yellow flowers, and puts on a mid-summer to mid-autumn display that can reach 2.4m (8ft) high, while its spread is relatively contained, just 1m (3ft).

RUDBECKIA AT A GLANCE

A near 20-species genus with annuals, biennials and perennials, often with striking, yellowish flowers. Hardy to –18°C (0°F).

JAN	/	
FEB	/	
MAR	sow	
APR	divide	
MAY	transplant	
JUN	/	
JULY	flowering	
AUG	flowering	
SEPT	flowering	
OCT	flowering	
NOV	divide	
DEC	/	

RECOMMENDED VARIETIES

'Goldquelle'
'Herbstonne'
Rudbeckia fulgida var. *deamii*
R. f. var. *sullivantii*
 'Goldsturm'
R. laciniata
R. maxima

CONDITIONS

Aspect A bright, open sunny position is essential. Avoid shady areas. The plant's natural habitat is North American meadows and big, open woods.

Site Do not plant in over-dry, Mediterranean-type gardens. The soil must remain heavy, on the damp side. In the wild *R. fulgida* grows in marshy valleys.

GROWING METHOD

Propagation Either divide in the spring or autumn, or sow seeds in spring in a cold frame. Do not let the new young plants dry out.

Feeding Fertility must be quite high. Dig in large quantities of well-rotted manure and compost to poor soil.

Problems Slugs can be a major problem. Keep watch, and pick them off by hand or treat chemically. A potentially good flowering display can be quickly ruined if they take control.

FLOWERING

Season A long flowering season from the summer to late autumn.

Cutting Rudbeckia make good cut flowers, adding height and colour to any arrangement. They are especially useful having a dark coloured central disc (black, brown or green) in the centre of the flower.

AFTER FLOWERING

Requirements Cut back to the ground, though some stems can be left to provide interesting shapes over winter, especially when frosted.

SALVIA
Sage

SALVIA X SYLVESTRIS 'MAINACHT' ('MAY NIGHT') is a wonderful, clumpy perennial that sends up spires of rich blue flowers. It can be guaranteed to soften even the most rigid landscaped garden, flowering in early and mid-summer. 'Blauhugel' ('Blue Mound') is very similar.

FEATURES

HERBACEOUS

EVERGREEN

Salvias are a huge plant group of over 700 species, comprising shrubs, herbaceous perennials and annuals. Most people associate salvias with red or purple flowers but there are also species with cream, yellow, white, blue or pink flowers. Many have highly aromatic foliage with scents ranging from the delicious to the outright unpleasant: the foliage of pineapple sage, *S. elegans* (syn. *S. rutilans*) has a delicious perfume while the bog sage (*S. uliginosa*) smells rather unpleasant. Most salvias are extremely easy to grow and once established need little attention beyond occasional deep watering in hot weather and some cutting back after flowering. The tall salvias are ideal for the back of the border or for fillers between shrubs. There are many others of varying heights that are suitable as edging plants or for planting among annuals, bulbs and other perennials. *Salvia* x *sylvestris* 'Mainacht" ('May Night'), shown above, is an exceptionally good border perennial, but if it is unavailable there are plenty of fine alternatives, including 'Rose Queen'. Common sage, *S. officinalis*, is a highly popular salvia. It has grey, rather wrinkly foliage and flowers that are usually pale violet. The one problem is that in the right conditions it spreads like a weed. Coming from the Mediterranean it demands sharp drainage and dislikes a soaking wet summer.

Others For spring–summer flowers in a range of colours, from cream to lilac and blue, try *S. sclarea*. It is perfectly hardy, and grows up to 90cm (3ft) high. *S. bulleyana* is equally easy, and grows about 40–90cm (16in–3ft) high. It has yellow flowers with a brownish lower lip appearing from the middle to the end of summer, and is also fully hardy, coming from western China. For an early summer–autumn flower show, use *S. forsskaolii* from the Black Sea coast. It grows 90cm (3ft) high, and bears white flowers with lips in violet, and faint yellow. Alternatively try *S.* x *superba*. It has violet flowers from mid-summer to autumn, and reaches the same height. For mild areas where you can grow half-hardy plants, there are plenty more salvias including *S. microphylla*, and the bog sage, *S. uliginosa*. The former has rich green leaves and magenta flowers at the end of summer–early autumn. Bog sage has bright blue flowers with a touch of white, and blooms from late summer to autumn. Both reach 90cm (3ft) high.

CONDITIONS

Aspect Provide full sun, perhaps in a scree bed, and, in the case of half-hardy plants, a place against a south-facing wall.

Site Any well-drained soil is suitable. Mulching with decayed manure in early spring improves the soil condition.

SALVIA SCLAREA *VAR.* TURKESTANICA *can be grown as a perennial or biennial. It produces wonderful pink stems of pinky-white flowers, and is perfectly hardy.*

THE ELECTRIC BLUE Salvia transsylvanica contrasting with a Star Gazer lily.

GROWING METHOD

Propagation Salvias grow from seed that has been sown in the spring, or from cuttings which have been taken in late summer through to the autumn. Many species can also be propagated from rooted divisions of an established clump. Simply lift such a clump and you will find numerous pieces with both roots and shoots. The divisions are best taken in the spring months. Set each division approximately 25cm (10in) apart. Needs regular watering to establish. Once established, plants can be drought tolerant.

Feeding A complete plant food or pelleted poultry manure can be applied in the spring, in poor soil, as the new growth commences. However, note that too much fertiliser will be counter-productive, merely resulting in all foliage and very few flowers.

Problems The worst problems tend to occur when you provide a certain species with the wrong conditions. Carefully check the notes invariably supplied with plants when buying from a garden centre, or specialist nursery. As a general rule, avoid damp ground and any shady areas.

FLOWERING

Season Many salvias have a very long flowering period, extending into the autumn before being cut down by the frosts.

Cutting None of the salvias mentioned makes a particularly good cut flower, but their long, dependable flowering season does make them a great asset in any part of the garden.

AFTER FLOWERING

Requirements Borderline, half-hardy species will need plenty of protection in cold areas over winter. Provide a thick, protective layer of straw or bracken, held in place with sticks. As a precaution against any losses, keep a stock of new, young plants. The tender salvias must be kept indoors in winter, in a frost-free place. Plants can be tip pruned after each flowering flush to promote further blooming. In late autumn plants can be cut back just above ground level. If you do not want to lift and divide a clump you can wait until new growth starts in the spring, and simply divide any growth that is becoming too crowded. A number of perennial salvias are extremely vigorous, but they can be kept in control by pulling out the new plants or running roots when they are getting invasive.

SALVIA AT A GLANCE

A large genus with fine perennials. The colour range is mainly blue. Hardy plants to –18°C (0°F); half-hardy –5°C (23°F).

		RECOMMENDED VARIETIES
JAN	/	
FEB	/	*Salvia argentea*
MAR	sow	*S. bulleyana*
APR	divide	*S. forsskaolii*
MAY	transplant	*S. involucrata* (half-hardy)
JUN	flowering	*S. microphylla* (half-hardy)
JULY	flowering	*S. patens* (half-hardy)
AUG	flowering	*S. sclarea*
SEPT	flowering	*S. x superba*
OCT	flowering	*S. uliginosa* (half-hardy)
NOV	/	
DEC	/	

SCABIOSA
Scabious

SCABIOSA CAUCASICA 'CLIVE GREAVES' is a wonderful lavender-blue, looking especially impressive when planted in clusters.

SCABIOUS ARE VERSATILE PLANTS. They make a wonderful addition to most gardens, whether schematic or cottagey.

FEATURES

HERBACEOUS

Scabious is a vital ingredient of cottage-style, flowery gardens, rock gardens and mixed borders. From hot, dry, stoney sites, mainly in the Mediterranean, it provides pale hues in blue, pink, yellow or white. The flowers are held above long, thin stems, many attracting bees and butterflies. Heights generally range from 30–90cm (12–36in). There are plenty of interesting choices, and top of the list are the dwarf forms 'Butterfly Blue' and 'Pink Mist', both relatively new, and proving extremely popular. On the plus side they flower for six months; the down side is they are short lived. Take cuttings to maintain the display.

SCABIOSA AT A GLANCE

A genus of annuals, biennials and perennials, providing abundant soft colours. Good for romantic displays. Hardy to –18°C (0°F).

		RECOMMENDED VARIETIES
JAN	/	
FEB	/	*Scabiosa caucasica*
MAR	sow	'Clive Greaves'
APR	divide	*S. c.* 'Miss Willmott'
MAY	transplant	'Chile Black'
JUN	flowering	*S. columbaria* var. *ochroleuca*
JULY	flowering	*S. lucida*
AUG	flowering	'Pink Mist'
SEPT	flowering	
OCT	sow	
NOV	/	
DEC	/	

CONDITIONS

Aspect   Full sun is essential.
Site   Dryish, free-draining soil is important so that the roots are not plunged in soaking wet ground over the winter months. The soil must also veer from the neutral towards the slightly alkaline.

GROWING METHOD

Propagation   Scabious is not long-living, and begins to lose its vigour and impact after three years. It is therefore vital to replenish the garden with either spring divisions, or to sow fresh, ripe seed in pots in a cold frame to maintain a good supply.
Feeding   Do not over-feed the soil which will be counter-productive, producing leaf growth at the expense of flowers. Very poor soils, though, might need some additions of compost in the early spring.
Problems   Spray at the first sign of powdery mildew.

FLOWERING

Season   The flowers appear right through the summer, in some cases not until mid-summer, often into early autumn.
Cutting   Scabious make excellent sprays of cut flowers, and are indispensable for indoor arrangements, either adding to flowery schemes or softening more rigid, structural ones.

AFTER FLOWERING

Requirements   Cut all spent stems down to the ground.

SEDUM SPECTABILE
Ice plant

DENSE FLOWERHEADS of Sedum spectabile *'Brilliant' provide a rich source of nectar, attracting butterflies and other insects.*

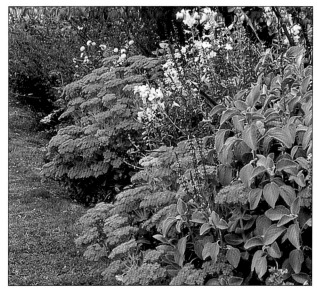

BILLOWING HEADS of sedum add colour to the autumn garden. Here they edge a mixed border, with white beard tongue behind.

FEATURES

HERBACEOUS

One of over 600 species of succulent sedums, this is unusual because it is frequently used in perennial plantings where many succulents look out of place. It has fleshy, soft green leaves on stems that can reach 60cm (24in) high. Similar varieties are available with purple and variegated leaves. Since the new growth appears at the base of older stems, dividing plants is easy. The large heads of flowers are a soft mauve-pink in the species, but there are cultivars with colours ranging from bright hot pinks to rosy red, and the brick red of 'Herbstfreude' ('Autumn Joy'). The plants flower from late summer into autumn. This is an easy-care plant that accepts a wide range of conditions.

SEDUM AT A GLANCE

S. spectabile is a clump-forming, late season perennial with pink flowers. Many excellent forms. Hardy to –15°C (5°F).

		RECOMMENDED VARIETIES
JAN	/	
FEB	/	*Sedum alboroseum*
MAR	/	'Mediovariegatum'
APR	divide	*S. cauticola*
MAY	/	'Herbstfreude' ('Autumn
JUN	/	Joy')
JULY	/	'Ruby Glow'
AUG	flowering	*S. spectabile* 'Brilliant'
SEPT	flowering	*S. telephium maximum*
OCT	divide	'Atropurpureum'
NOV	sow	
DEC	/	

CONDITIONS

Aspect Prefers full sun, but tolerates some light shade for part of the day.

Site While it can grow in a sandy, well-drained soil, it will tolerate a heavier soil which gives it an advantage over other sedums.

GROWING METHOD

Propagation Clumps of plants are easily pulled, or sliced, apart with a spade in the spring or late autumn. The divisions are best replanted at approximately 15–20cm (6–8in) intervals. Division gives very high success rates. It is also possible to propagate sedum by striking from stem cuttings. Water regularly to establish new young plants.

Feeding Slow-release fertiliser can be applied in the spring, as new growth commences. Avoid overfeeding because this may result in plenty of sappy leaf growth at the expense of a display of flowers.

Problems Plants in containers may rot at the base if overwatered. Vine weevil grubs may also devour both bases and roots with devastating effect.

FLOWERING

Season The late, highly rewarding display occurs at the end of summer, running through autumn.

Cutting A long-lasting cut flower.

AFTER FLOWERING

Requirements Leave the skeletal flowerheads over winter to provide attractive, burnished tints.

SISYRINCHIUM
Sisyrinchrium

SISYRINCHIUM IDAHOENSE 'ALBUM' *is a clump-forming white flower that at 12cm (5in) high is ideal for edging borders.*

SISYRINCHIUM MACROCARPON *is 75cm (30in) tall, has eye-catching vertical foliage, and gentle yellow flowers in early summer.*

FEATURES

EVERGREEN

This is a star plant for the border, with spires of pale yellow flowers over summer, 90cm (36in) high, and iris-like, strap-shape foliage. The only problem is that it can self-seed too much for the liking of some, though with vigilance the seedlings are easily removed. The genus also offers blue, mauve and white flowers. *S. idahoense* is a lovely violet-blue, with a yellow throat, growing 30cm (12in) high, while *S. graminoides* is slightly taller at 20in (50cm), with a deeper blue flower, though it does self-seed more prolifically. For a dwarfish, low-growing white try 'Pole Star', good for the rock garden where it can best be seen and appreciated. It grows just 2.5 x 6cm (1 x 2⅜in), and is perfectly hardy.

SISYRINCHIUM AT A GLANCE

S. striatum is an evergreen perennial with spires of pale yellow flowers, and long, stiff, pointed leaves. Hardy to –15°C (5°F).

		RECOMMENDED VARIETIES
JAN	/	*Sisyrinchium angustifolium*
FEB	/	'Biscutella'
MAR	sow	'Californian Skies'
APR	transplant	*S. californicum*
MAY	/	'E. K. Balls'
JUN	flowering	*S. idahoense*
JULY	flowering	*S. macrocarpon*
AUG	/	'Quaint and Queer'
SEPT	divide	*S. striatum* 'Aunt May'
OCT	/	
NOV	/	
DEC	/	

CONDITIONS

Aspect Full sun is required, well away from the shade.
Site Relatively poor soil is quite adequate, but free-draining ground is essential. Do not let the plants stand out in damp, wet soil over the winter months.

GROWING METHOD

Propagation Divide in late summer to guarantee a supply of vigorous plants since mature ones become quite lack-lustre after three years. Alternatively, sow seed in the spring. To prevent any established plants from self-seeding, cut off the flowers the moment they begin to fade.
Feeding Some enriching with well-rotted manure or compost will provide a boost to poor areas of ground. High levels of fertility, however, are not necessary.
Problems Generally trouble free.

FLOWERING

Season Flowers in early and mid-summer.
Cutting They make unusual, striking cut flowers, adding smart verticals to any arrangement, forming the basic structure. Use both flowering stems and foliage.

AFTER FLOWERING

Requirements Cut back the flowering stems to the ground, either promptly to prevent large-scale self-seeding, or later to increase numbers, especially when established plants are past their best.

SOLIDAGO
Golden rod

THE HIGHLY DISTINCTIVE sight of golden rod. A bright spray of yellow flowers, and the long, thin, dark green leaves.

A PERFECT EXAMPLE OF HOW an invasive plant, such as golden rod, can be reigned in and controlled by hard landscaping.

FEATURES

HERBACEOUS

Golden rod forms large colonies of sometimes quite tall yellow plants, reaching 1.8m (6ft) high. The small flowers in themselves are nothing special, but they appear in such profusion that they actually make quite an impact. There are plenty of varieties to choose from. The key differences are more to do with height than colour. 'Crown of Rays' grows 60cm (24in) high, and as its name suggests has bright yellow flowers. 'Goldenmosa' is almost as bright and grows slightly taller, and also has yellow-green foliage. But if you need a golden rod for the back of the border, especially one where the soil is quite poor, the best choice is 'Golden Wings'. It can reach 1.8m (6ft) high,

topping smaller plants with its late summer and early autumn show. The best choice of golden rod for growing at the front of the border is the 20cm (8in) high 'Queenie' or *S. virgaurea minuta*.

CONDITIONS

Aspect Grow in full sun in the border. Avoid borders that are in the shade.

Site Free-draining soil, preferably quite sandy or gritty, is ideal.

GROWING METHOD

Propagation Golden rod self-seeds but to be sure of getting new plants that are true to type, spring or autumn division invariably give successful results.

Feeding High soil fertility is not in any way essential. Very poor ground can be improved, though, in the spring by digging in some quantities of well-rotted manure.

Problems Powdery mildew can strike quite severely; treat with a fungicide at the first sight of an attack, repeat sprayings being necessary to control major outbreaks.

FLOWERING

Season Generally mid- to late summer, though sometimes slightly before and after.

Cutting Not the best cut flowers, there are better alternatives, but they effectively bulk up any arrangement.

AFTER FLOWERING

Requirements Cut back spent flower stems.

SOLIDAGO AT A GLANCE

Varieties of golden rod create mainly big, bold, clumps of bright yellow flowers. Can be invasive. Hardy to −18°C (0°F).

		RECOMMENDED VARIETIES
JAN	/	
FEB	/	*Solidago cutleri*
MAR	/	*S. flexicaulis* 'Variegata'
APR	divide	'Golden Baby'
MAY	transplant	'Goldenmosa'
JUN	/	'Queenie'
JULY	flowering	*S. virgaurea minuta*
AUG	flowering	
SEPT	/	
OCT	/	
NOV	/	
DEC	/	

STACHYS BYZANTINA
Lamb's ears

SINCE LAMB'S EARS, or lamb's tails, needs good drainage, grow it in an attractive container if your soil is relentlessly heavy and damp.

MORE TRADITIONAL is this planting, where lamb's ears edge a garden bed. The plants will multiply rapidly given the right situation.

FEATURES

HERBACEOUS

Lamb's ears is a low-growing, evergreen perennial most often used as an edging plant. It could also be used to edge rose beds, but wherever it is planted it must have excellent drainage and full exposure to the sun. The leaves are densely covered with hairs, giving them a white, or pale grey, woolly appearance, hence its common name. It does produce pink-purple flowers on spikes that stand above the foliage, but they are not especially attractive; it is grown for its foliage, not the flowers (*S. macrantha* 'Robusta, and *S. officinalis* are the exception). 'Cotton Boll' has woolly flowers good for dried flower arrangements if they are cut when fully open. Plants grow 15–20cm (6–8in) high, but spread a good distance.

STACHYS AT A GLANCE

S. byzantina is a valuable garden plant, noted for its front-of-the-border colour and soft, silky foliage. Hardy to –18°C (0°F).

		Recommended Varieties
Jan	/	
Feb	/	*S. coccinea*
Mar	sow	*Stachys byzantina* 'Big Ears'
Apr	divide	*S. b.* 'Cotton Boll'
May	transplant	*S. b.* 'Primrose Heron'
Jun	flowering	*S. macrantha*
July	flowering	*S. m.* 'Robusta'
Aug	flowering	*S. officinalis*
Sept	flowering	
Oct	divide	
Nov	/	
Dec	/	

CONDITIONS

Aspect   Full sun is essential all day for the plants to thrive and perform well.

Site   Needs very fast draining soil. It grows well in poor, sandy or gravelly soil. Avoid thick, wet heavy clay at all costs.

GROWING METHOD

Propagation   Grows readily from cuttings that are taken in the spring or autumn. The new divisions must be planted out about 20cm (8in) apart. Water new plants regularly. Once they are established, they need only be watered very occasionally.

Feeding   Grows without supplementary fertiliser, but a little complete plant food can be applied in the early spring.

Problems   There are no specific problems but container plants will quickly fail if they are overwatered, and border plants rot if they are waterlogged.

FLOWERING

Season   Flowers are produced in the summer, sometimes into autumn, but the tactile grey foliage is by far the chief attraction.

Cutting   Use the foliage in an arrangement; the flower spikes can be cut and dried for later use.

AFTER FLOWERING

Requirements Cut spent flower stems right at the base. Trailing growth can be shortened back at any time, but plants may need to be cut back hard in the early spring.

STOKESIA LAEVIS
Stokes' aster

THE FLOWERING HEADS of Stokes' aster are quite complex, made up of many 'petals' (more properly bracts or ray florets).

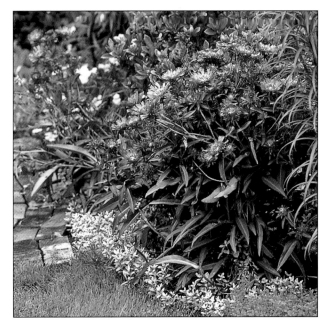

IT IS HARD to understand why the pretty Stokes' aster should go out of fashion but it is certainly grown less often than before.

FEATURES

HERBACEOUS

Stokes' aster is an easy to grow plant that provides great decorative value throughout its long flowering period from mid-summer to early autumn. It makes excellent cut flowers, too. Flower stems 30–50cm (12–20in) high rise from a cluster of dark green basal leaves. Although this plant is completely herbaceous in cold areas, the basal growth remains evergreen in mild winters. Flowers are reminiscent of large cornflowers or asters, and come in shades of blue, white and mauve. This plant can look outstanding in mass plantings but is equally at home in a mixed border, or when grown in wooden tubs or pots.

STOKESIA AT A GLANCE

S. laevis is an evergreen, perennial, sprawling plant with large, purple, flat, late summer flowers. Hardy to −15°C (5°F).

		Companion Plants
Jan	/	
Feb	sow	Aster
Mar	divide	Box
Apr	transplant	Dahlia
May	transplant	Fuchsia
Jun	/	Miscanthus
July	/	Penstemon
Aug	flowering	Potentilla
Sept	flowering	Stipa
Oct	flowering	
Nov	divide	
Dec	/	

CONDITIONS

Aspect   While it prefers full sun, it just about tolerates dappled shade. Provide a shelter to protect from strong winds.

Site   Needs well-drained soil enriched with compost or manure.

GROWING METHOD

Propagation   Divide established clumps in spring or autumn, replanting divisions about 25cm (10in) apart. The plant can also be grown from root cuttings taken in early spring, and from autumn seed. Tolerates dry periods, but looks best if given an occasional deep watering in prolonged, dry spells. Provide young plants with twiggy support.

Feeding   Apply some complete plant food in the spring.

Problems   Poorly drained, heavy soils induce root or crown rot, which kills plants.

FLOWERING

Season   The long flowering period is from late summer into the autumn.

Cutting   Cut flowers regularly for the vase. This both gives a good ornamental display and prolongs the garden show, inducing plenty of new flower buds.

AFTER FLOWERING

Requirements   Prune all spent flower stems. As the growth dies back, promptly clear away all the dead foliage.

THALICTRUM
Meadow rue

THE FLUFFY PINK FLOWERS of meadow rue do not last long, but the pretty foliage persists well until the autumn.

FINER FOLIAGE, smaller starry flowers and very full growth are features of the related Thalictrum delavayi *and its cultivars.*

FEATURES

HERBACEOUS

Thalictrum aquilegiifolium is easy and quick to grow, a herbaceous perennial reaching about 1m (42in) high. The rather fern-like, blue-green foliage is attractively lobed, and the flowers are mauve-pink in dense, fluffy heads. While the floral display does not last long, the foliage adds months of charm. Meadow rue can be planted in mixed borders or in light shade under trees. There are a number of cultivars, including a white form and one with violet blooms. Also try *T. delavayi* (syn. *T. dipterocarpum*) and its cultivars 'Album' and 'Hewitt's Double'. This has finer foliage and the pink-mauve flowers are star shaped.

THALICTRUM AT A GLANCE

T. aquilegiifolium is a clump-forming, rhizomatous perennial with lovely sprays of purple flowers. Hardy to –18°C (5°F).

JAN	/	
FEB	/	
MAR	divide	
APR	transplant	
MAY	/	
JUN	flowering	
JULY	flowering	
AUG	/	
SEPT	/	
OCT	sow	
NOV	/	
DEC	/	

RECOMMENDED VARIETIES

Thalictrum aquilegiifolium var. *album*
T. a. 'Thundercloud'
T. delavayi
T. flavum subsp. *glaucum*
T. kiusianum
T. minus
T. rochebruneanum

CONDITIONS

Aspect Grow in either light shade, or in a border with morning sun followed by plenty of afternoon shade.

Soil Likes well-drained soil that has been enriched with organic matter.

GROWING METHOD

Propagation Grows from seed sown in the spring or autumn, or by divisions of a clump made in spring. Plant the new divisions about 25–30cm (10–12in) apart. Do not let the young plants dry out, giving regular, deep watering through a dry spring and summer.

Feeding As growth begins in the spring apply complete plant food, and mulch around the plants with well-decayed manure or compost.

Problems No specific pest or disease problems are known to attack this plant. Generally trouble free. Note that growth begins late in spring, so avoid damaging new growth while weeding.

FLOWERING

Season Flowers appear during early summer, depending on the temperatures.

Cutting Both the foliage and flowers can be cut for the vase.

AFTER FLOWERING

Requirements Cut off any spent flower stems unless you want to save seed. When the plants die down in the autumn, cut off the foliage at ground level.

TIARELLA
Foam flower

THE FOAM FLOWER produces both a fine early summer flower display, and often burnt-red coloured autumn foliage.

GIVEN A FREE RUN, Tiarella polyphylla produces a large, spreading clump with wonderful spires of white flowers.

FEATURES

HERBACEOUS

Tiarella trifoliata is a North American clump-forming rhizomatous perennial, making excellent groundcover in light shade. From late spring to mid-summer it produces light airy sprays of white flowers, on 30cm (12in) long panicles, held above the foliage. A more invasive plant is *T. cordifolia,* foam flower, from east North America where it grows in mountainside woods, forming extensive colonies, remorselessly spreading by underground stolons. *T. wherryi,* also from North America, is more compact and less invasive – the better choice for a smaller, shady area. Its natural habitat is shady ravines and rocky woods. The white flowers are tinged pink. 'Bronze Beauty' is a popular choice, benefiting from contrasting white flowers and bronze-red foliage.

CONDITIONS

Aspect   Thrives in both dappled and darkish shade, which is its natural habitat.

Site   It tolerates a wide range of soils, but naturally prefers rich, fertile ground, damp but definitely not boggy.

GROWING METHOD

Propagation   Division is the simplest method, though ripe seed can also be sown. Sow in pots in the autumn in a cold frame, and keep young plants well watered. Do not let them dry out.

Feeding   The ground needs to be quite rich. Fork in leafmould and compost in the early spring, and again in the autumn, between plants.

Problems   Slugs can strike but given the situation, out of the way in the shade, and the plant's vigour, it is rarely a major problem. Treat with slug pellets if matters get out of hand.

HARVESTING

Season   A profusion of white flowers appear from late spring to mid-summer.

Cutting   There are better choices for airy white sprays in the summer, but nonetheless they make decent cut flowers.

AFTER FLOWERING

Requirements Cut back to the ground.

TIARELLA AT A GLANCE

T. trifoliata is a North American, white perennial, ideal for spreading quickly through shady sites. Hardy to -15°C (5°F).

		RECOMMENDED VARIETIES
JAN	/	
FEB	/	*Tiarella cordifolia*
MAR	sow	'Elizabeth Oliver'
APR	divide	*T. polyphylla*
MAY	flowering	*T. p.* pink
JUN	flowering	*T. wherryi*
JULY	flowering	*T. w.* 'Bronze Beauty'
AUG	/	
SEPT	sow	
OCT	/	
NOV	/	
DEC	/	

TRADESCANTIA
Tradescantia / spiderwort

SPIDERWORT FLOWERS look like small purple irises but each lasts only a day. The surrounding buds are waiting their turn to open.

DENSE PLANTINGS of spiderwort produce plenty of flowers that thrive in filtered sunlight, ideal for a mixed or herbaceous border.

FEATURES

HERBACEOUS

This North American herbaceous perennial is a spreading plant with tapering, strap-like leaves and showy, triangular flowers in rich purple, rose-pink or white. The flowers generally last only one day but they appear in succession over a long period. There are several named cultivars available. Spiderwort grows from 30–60cm (12–24in) high, and is multi-stemmed. It is easy to grow in the right conditions and can make a tall groundcover in filtered sunlight under trees. In a mild winter it may not die down completely.

TRADESCANTIA AT A GLANCE

T. virginiana is a purple, repeat flowerer in a genus of largely tender indoor plants. Ideal for the border. Hardy to −15°C (5°F).

		RECOMMENDED VARIETIES
JAN	/	
FEB	/	*Tradescantia* x *andersoniana*
MAR	divide	'Bilberry Ice'
APR	/	*T.* x *a.* 'Isis'
MAY	/	*T.* x *a.* 'Osprey'
JUN	flowering	*T.* x *a.* 'Purple Dome'
JULY	flowering	*T.* x *a.* 'Red Cloud'
AUG	flowering	*T.* x *a.* 'Zwanenburg Blue'
SEPT	flowering	
OCT	divide	
NOV	divide	
DEC	/	

CONDITIONS

Aspect   It requires full sun or partial shade.
Site   It grows best in soil that is well drained, but is also heavily enriched with plenty of decayed, organic matter.

GROWING METHOD

Propagation   Clumps can be lifted and divided in the spring and autumn. The species can be grown from seed sown in autumn. It is occasionally self-sown. New plantings should be approximately 30–45cm (12–18in) apart, depending on how rapidly you need cover. Needs regular watering during a prolonged, dry growing period.
Feeding   Apply a complete plant food, as growth starts in the spring.
Problems   No specific problems are known.

FLOWERING

Season   The long succession of flowers starts in early summer and continues through to mid-autumn.
Cutting   The buds continue to open when cut.

AFTER FLOWERING

Requirements Growth starts to yellow and die back after flowering. Clean away dead foliage, and tidy up for the winter.

TRILLIUM
Wake robin

THE WAKE ROBIN *is the perfect plant for a moist shady area, whether it be light or deep shade. The plants are quickly identified by having three leaves, three calyces and three petals.*

FEATURES

SUMMER AUTUMN WINTER SPRING

HERBACEOUS

Trilliums are deciduous perennials which make excellent groundcover in partial or full shade, with spring and early summer flowers. The colour range includes white, maroon, pink, yellow, bronze-green, and red-purple. *T. grandiflorum,* the North American wake robin, has 7.5cm (3in) long white flowers and veined petals. It is long-lived and easy to grow, requiring little attention. *T. sessile* 'Rubrum' has claret petals and attractively mottled foliage. Several clones bear this name and there is little to choose between them. At the front of a shady, slightly acidic border try *T. rivale.* It grows 12cm (6in) high and wide, has pointed ovate petals, white or pale pink, with purple speckling towards the base. *T. luteum* has

scented yellowish flowers and mottled, pale and dark leaves. It grows 40cm (16in) high, spreading by almost the same amount.

CONDITIONS

Aspect Mottled or deep shade is required. Avoid open areas with full sun.

Site The soil should be the acid side of neutral, though in fact some trilliums will tolerate low levels of alkalinity.

GROWING METHOD

Propagation Preferably divide the rhizomes when dormant, ensuring each section has one strong growing point. Note that they are slow to establish, though. It is quite possible to sow ripe, late summer seed in a cold frame, but the 5–7 years to flower is prohibitively long.

Feeding The soil needs to be rich with plenty of well-rotted leafmould and compost, being damp and free draining. Where necessary provide a thick mulch every spring and autumn.

Problems Both slugs and snails feed on the tender new foliage. Pick off by hand when this becomes a problem, or use a chemical treatment.

FLOWERING

Season The flowers appear in spring and summer.

Cutting They make attractive cut flowers, especially *T. grandiflorum* with its near diamond-shape white flowers.

AFTER FLOWERING

Requirements Cut spent stems to the ground.

TRILLIUM AT A GLANCE

A 30-species strong genus with rhizomatous perennials, excellent for flowering ground cover in shade. Hardy to –15°C (5°F).

		RECOMMENDED VARIETIES
JAN	/	
FEB	/	*Trillium cernuum*
MAR	/	*T. chloropetalum*
APR	transplant	*T. cuneatum*
MAY	flowering	*T. erectum*
JUN	flowering	*T. grandiflorum*
JULY	/	*T. g. flore-pleno*
AUG	/	*T. luteum*
SEPT	sow	*T. rivale*
OCT	divide	*T. viride*
NOV	/	
DEC	/	

VERBASCUM
Mullein

MULLEINS ARE FAMED for their striking shape and their bright flowers, but as seen here they can blend with the gentlest design.

MULLEINS HAVE few equals as accent plants as they are tough and adaptable, capable of tolerating many climates and conditions.

FEATURES

EVERGREEN

HERBACEOUS

Not all mulleins are reliably perennial, some being best treated as biennials and replaced after two years. However, most are easy to raise. They are grown for their large rosettes of foliage, often silver or grey, from which emerges a tall, striking spike of flowers up to 1.8m (6ft) high. They make eye-catching accent plants in any sunny part of the garden. The various species and their cultivars have flowers in a range of colours, including white and gentler shades of yellow, pink and purple. The common mullein, *V. thapsus*, also known as Aaron's rod, freely self-seeds. Mullein has a long folk history, first as a candle, then as a medical treatment.

VERBASCUM AT A GLANCE

A 360-species genus, famed for its dramatic, coloured spires in summer. Heights 30cm–1.8m (12in–6ft). Hardy to –15°C (5°F).

		RECOMMENDED VARIETIES
JAN	/	
FEB	/	*Verbascum bombyciferum*
MAR	/	*V. chaixii* 'Album'
APR	sow	*V. c.* 'Cotswold Beauty'
MAY	transplant	*V. c.* 'Gainsborough'
JUN	flowering	*V. dumulosum*
JULY	flowering	'Golden Wings'
AUG	flowering	'Helen Johnson'
SEPT	sow	'Letitia'
OCT	/	*V. phoeniceum*
NOV	/	
DEC	/	

CONDITIONS

Aspect Grows best in full sun all day.
Site Grows in any kind of well-drained soil, even poor and alkaline ones.

GROWING METHOD

Propagation Grows from seed sown as soon as it is ripe, or from root cuttings taken in late autumn or winter. The seed forms on the spike after the flowers have fallen, and is ripe when it has changed colour, becoming brown or black. Sow in pots in a cold frame in either the spring or autumn. Plants of the larger mullein species need to be planted out approximately 1m (39in) apart.

Feeding Apply a complete plant food in early spring, as new growth commences.

Problems No specific problems are known.

FLOWERING

Season Mullein flowers right through the summer, but its amazing spire of a stem remains a big architectural feature long after the flowers have finished.

Cutting A nipped off section of the flowering spire considerably adds to a formal, architectural display.

AFTER FLOWERING

Requirements Cut off the spent flower spike unless you want seed to set.

VIOLA ODORATA
English violet

DESPITE the range of cultivars available, the violet species is still a big favourite.

VIOLETS PROVIDE great groundcover under deciduous trees or in other shaded, sheltered spots. They do, however, need decent levels of sun to put on a good flowering display.

FEATURES

EVERGREEN

Violets have been in cultivation since ancient times, and were highly valued by the ancient Greeks. In Victorian times an enormous number of varieties was grown, including a wide range of the double Parma violets. The violet's sweet fragrance and elegant flowers make them big favourites with gardeners and florists alike. The plants have a creeping habit, spreading up to 30cm (12in), and are rarely more than 15–20cm (6–8in) high. There are cultivars with single or double flowers in purple, pink, white or bicolours, but the deep purple is probably the best loved. There are other violet species to grow in the garden, from the summer-flowering V. *cornuta,* fine under hybrid tea roses, to the spring/summer V. *sororia,* and its form 'Freckles'.

VIOLA AT A GLANCE

V. odorata is a rhizomatous, semi-evergreen perennial with blue or white flowers. Good self-seeder. Hardy to –18°C (0°F).

		RECOMMENDED VARIETIES
JAN	/	
FEB	/	*Viola cornuta*
MAR	flowering	V. *c.* Alba Group
APR	flowering	V. *c.* Lilacina Group
MAY	flowering	V. *c.* 'Minor'
JUN	/	V. *odorata* 'Alba'
JULY	/	V. *o.* 'Rosea'
AUG	/	V. *sororia* 'Freckles'
SEPT	divide	V. *s.* 'Priceana'
OCT	/	
NOV	/	
DEC	/	

CONDITIONS

Aspect   It needs either shade, or light dappled sunlight.

Site   It needs well-drained, moisture-retentive soil, heavily enriched with organic matter for the best results.

GROWING METHOD

Propagation   Clumps can be lifted and divided, or runners can be dug up and replanted every couple of years, in the the spring or autumn. Set out at 20cm (8in) spacings, with the plant crowns kept just above soil level. Violets self-seed, too. Keep young plants well watered during the first growing season.

Feeding   Apply complete plant food in spring after flowering ceases.

Problems   Slugs and snails can be a major nuisance, devouring tasty new growth. Pick off by hand, or treat chemically.

FLOWERING

Season   Violets flower from late winter into early spring.

Cutting   Scalding the stems of cut violets before arranging them will certainly increase their vase life.

AFTER FLOWERING

Requirements No special treatment is needed, but excess runners can be removed during the growing season if they are invasive. This has the added benefit of channelling vigour back to the main crown.

GROWING ROSES

A favourite of many, roses, with their single, semi-double or fully double flowers, and their bicoloured, multicoloured, striped or 'hand-painted' blooms, are often richly scented and deck bushy stems.

FEATURES

Plant roses to colour beds, borders, patio pots, hanging baskets and rock gardens. Position them so that they form a canopy over pergolas, obelisks, arches, trees, walls and fences.

There are seven distinct groups of roses:

Large-flowered roses (hybrid tea)
These form shapely double blooms on long stems and are good for cutting. They are usually grown as bushes to 90cm (3ft) high. Choice varieties are peachy-pink 'Scent-Sation', golden-yellow 'Lions International' and white 'Polar Star'.

Cluster-flowered roses (floribunda)
Sumptuous heads adorn stems from 60–90cm (2–3ft). Plant tangerine-orange 'Razzle Dazzle', sparkling yellow 'Charter 700' and scarlet 'Invincible' to fringe a path or drive.

English roses
These combine the scent and cupped- or rosette-shaped flower of an old-fashioned rose with the colour range and repeat-flowering qualities of a cluster-flowered variety. Forming plants from 90–180cm (3–6ft), newcomers include warm-pink 'Anne Boleyn', yellow 'Blythe Spirit' and scarlet 'Falstaff.'

Miniature and patio
Small cluster-flowered roses that reach 37–60cm (15–24in) – they flower all summer and spill from patio pots. Look out for peachy-apricot 'Sweet Dream' and vermilion 'Top Marks'.

Shrub roses
Some varieties treat us to a succession of flowers, others to a billowing surge of bloom in mid-summer. Outstanding varieties include repeat-flowering, creamy white 'Sally Holmes' and single pink and white 'Ballerina'.

Carpeters
Also known as ground-cover roses, which spread and suppress weeds, the famed County Series yields a spectacular display of blossom. Riveting varieties include single, scarlet and golden-centred 'Hampshire' and semi-double, bright yellow 'Gwent'.

Climbers and ramblers
Thrusting skywards to cloak walls and trees with a welter of blossom, climbers, such as honey-coloured 'Penny Lane', delight us with a succession of blooms. Ramblers (including cream 'Bobbie James') usually flower once in midsummer.

LEFT: The shape of rose flowers vary considerably, from high and split-centred, globular, open cup-shaped and quatered to flat, rosette and pompon. Most are grafted onto rootstocks in order to charge them with vigour.

CONDITIONS

Aspect	Roses need bright sunlight to excel. Some, such as 'Canary Bird' and 'Flower Carpet' also flower magnificently in light shade.
Site	Though a few kinds thrive in light sandy or stony soils, most benefit from humus-rich loam. Drainage must be good.

GROWING METHOD

Planting	Garden-centre plants can be planted throughout the year, provided the soil is 'open'. Mail-order plants are delivered bare rooted and dispatched from November to March.
Feeding	Sprinkle a high-potash and magnesium rich granular fertiliser over the root area in April and prick it into the surface. Follow with a 7cm (3in) mulch. Repeat feeding in June.
Dead heading	Nip off faded blooms at the 'knuckle' to channel energy into new flowering shoots.
Propagation	Take 22cm (9in) cuttings of ramblers, climbers, miniatures and vigorous cluster-flowered varieties from the fully mature middle part of a pencil-thick side shoot in September. Remove all but two leaves at the top. Make a horizontal cut below the bottom bud and a sloping cut above the top bud. Nip off thorns. Insert cuttings 15cm (6in) deep in a straight-backed trench lined with sharp sand. Firm soil around them. Roots will form within eight weeks.
Pruning	Prune with secateurs from March to early April. *Large-flowered and cluster-flowered bushes and standards:* Shorten main stems by half their height, cutting to a bud. Reduce side shoots to two buds. *Miniature and shrub roses:* Shorten dead and broken stems to live wood. *Climbers:* Cut back flowered shoots to within 7cm (3in) of the main stem. *Ramblers:* Prune in September. Remove flowered shoots at ground level and replace with current-year stems.
Problems	Control black spot, mildew and rust disease, together with greenfly and other sap-sucking insects, by spraying with a pesticide containing pirimicarb, bupirimate and triforine. Wearing gloves, remove the suckers, which are more thorny, with paler green leaves than varietal shoots. Twist them from the stock.

FLOWERING

Season	Flowers grow from mid-spring to late autumn.
Cutting	Gather when dew fresh and plunge them up to their necks in water. Make a pin-prick hole beneath the bloom so air is expelled when water rises up the stem.

AFTER FLOWERING

Requirements	*Large and cluster-flowered bushes:* Reduce extra long stems by half their height in November to minimise wind rock in winter.

SCEPTERED ISLE

GRAHAM THOMAS

Raised by David Austin Roses, 'Sceptred Isle' is an English Rose whose cupped and perfumed soft pink blooms grow freely above the foliage on stems of up to 90cm (3ft). Blooming continuously from early summer to mid-autumn, it needs full sun to form a stocky bush. Dead-head regularly.

Create an arresting feature by inter-planting it with silver- and fern-leaved Artemisia 'Powis Castle'. Grown as a standard, it rewards with you with a large head of blossom, which makes a stunning focal point in a bed or border.

A glorious English Rose, 'Graham Thomas' (named after the famed rosarian and writer) sports unusually rich golden yellow flowers. This colour is missing from old-fashioned roses from which the variety was born. Forming a rounded bush to 1.2m (4ft) high and across, its branches form an elegant arch. Interestingly, it can also be trained as a climber up to 1.8–2.4m (6–8ft). If you plant it to cover a wall, set the root system at least 37cm (15in) from the brickwork to avoid moisture being sucked from the root area. Fan-train shoots as low as possible to trigger an abundance of blossom.

SCEPTERED ISLE AT A GLANCE

Must have full sunlight in order to thrive and bloom freely.
Fully hardy to frost hardy.

JAN	rest	OCT	light pruning
FEB	rest	NOV	planting
MAR	planting, pruning	DEC	rest
APR	feeding		
MAY	mulching		OTHER ENGLISH ROSES:
JUN	flowering		
JULY	flowering, deadheading		'The Countryman'
			'Port Meirion'
AUG	flowering, deadheading		'Barbara Austin'
			'Dr Herbert Gray'
SEPT	flowering, deadheading		'Gertrude Jeckyll'

GRAHAM THOMAS AT A GLANCE

Flowers best when grown in full sunlight. Fully hardy
to frost hardy.

JAN	rest	SEPT	flowering, deadheading
FEB	rest	OCT	light pruning
MAR	planting, pruning	NOV	planting
APR	feeding	DEC	rest
MAY	mulching		
JUN	flowering, deadheading		
JULY	flowering, feeding		
AUG	flowering, deadheading		

FELICIA

FLOWER CARPET

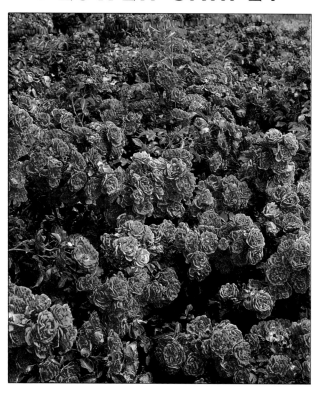

Felicia is a prized hybrid musk – the family bears large trusses of bloom in early summer and intermittently later. Yielding aromatic silver-pink blooms amid dark green leaves on sturdy shoots up to 1.5m (5ft) long, it is a very healthy plant that seldom suffers from pests and diseases.

If there is room, encourage it to flower bounteously by pegging down shoots so they radiate from the centre of the bush. Alternatively, position 'Felicia' to cover a trellis-clad sunny wall or fence.

Spreading enthusiastically to 1.2m (4ft), 'Flower Carpet', which grows up to 60cm (2ft) high, treats us to an almost non-stop parade of huge trusses of semi-double bright pink flowers from June to November. Unlike many varieties, it flowers as well in light shade as it does in full sun. Its shining, glossy leaves appear to be fully resistant to black spot, mildew and rust.

It is even more alluring when trained as a standard. It is such a profuse performer that flower-bowed branches are liable to snap, so support them with strings tied to a cane fastened to the main stem.

FELICIA MOON AT A GLANCE

Performs best when grown in full sunlight. Fully hardy to frost hardy.

JAN	rest	SEPT	flowering, deadheading
FEB	rest		
MAR	planting, pruning	OCT	light pruning
		NOV	planting
APR	feeding	DEC	rest
MAY	mulching		
JUN	flowering, deadheading		OTHER HYBRID MUSKS:
JULY	flowering, feeding		'Pax'
			'Penelope'
AUG	flowering, deadheading		'Camelia'
			'Francesca'

FLOWER CARPET AT A GLANCE

Flowers freely in full sunlight or light shade. Fully hardy to frost hardy.

JAN	rest	SEPT	flowering, deadheading
FEB	rest		
MAR	planting, light pruning	OCT	light pruning
		NOV	planting
APR	feeding	DEC	rest
MAY	mulching		
JUN	flowering, deadheading		OTHER FLOWER CARPET FORMS:
JULY	flowering, feeding		'White Flower Carpet'
			'Sunshine'
AUG	flowering, deadheading		

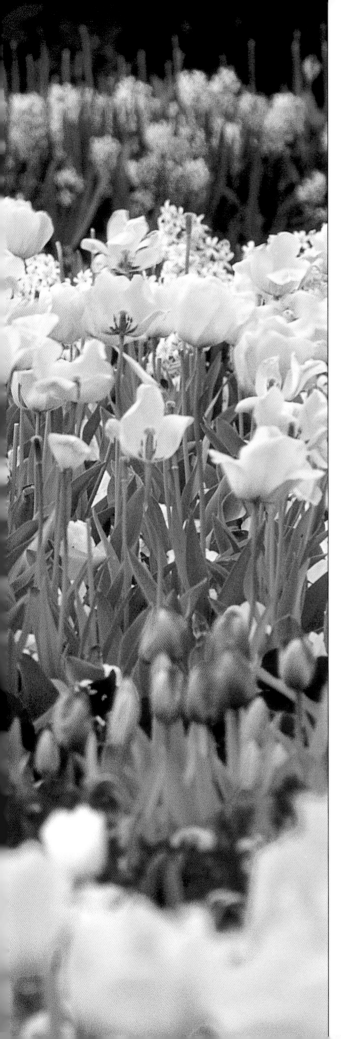

GROWING BULBS

Bulbs are the easiest of plants to grow – probably no other plant group gives as much variety and pleasure to the gardener with so little effort. Even people without gardens can enjoy bulbs as there are so many that make excellent container plants.

Most people think of bulbs as an essential part of spring, but spring is by no means their only season – there are bulbs that flower through the summer, autumn and even through the depths of the winter. They are usually very easy to look after, and many types will go on giving pleasure for years with the minimum of attention.

ABOVE: These parrot tulips just breaking from their buds already show the typical ruffled petals and colour streaking.

LEFT: Deepest blue hyacinths make a wonderful foil for the bright yellow tulips in this landscape planting.

BULBS, CORMS, TUBERS AND RHIZOMES

What most people know as bulbs covers a whole range of plants with some kind of underground storage organ that allows their survival over their dormant season, which may be winter or summer. They include true bulbs and plants with corms, tubers and rhizomes.

• True bulbs are made up of a bud enclosed by modified leaves or fleshy scales from which roots and shoots emerge. The shoots grow out of the pointed top and the roots from the other end. Most, such as onions, daffodils, and hyacinths, have an outer papery cover or tunic: lilies, which are bulbs, too, have a bulb of swollen leaf bases but lack the protective tunic.

• Corms are bulb-like structures formed by the enlargement of an underground stem base. They do not have the 'rings' of true bulbs, but stems grow out of the top and roots from the base in the same way. Freesias, gladioli and crocuses all grow from corms.

• Tubers are swollen underground parts of roots or stems. Dahlias grow from buds at the ends of tubers.

• Rhizomes may grow underground or along the soil surface. They are fleshy, tuberous roots with new growth emerging from the end. Some irises grow from rhizomes (other irises are bulbs). Some bulbous plants described as having rhizomes or tubers appear to have little more than a small crown from which the roots emerge.

For convenience, all the above groups are discussed throughout this book as bulbs.

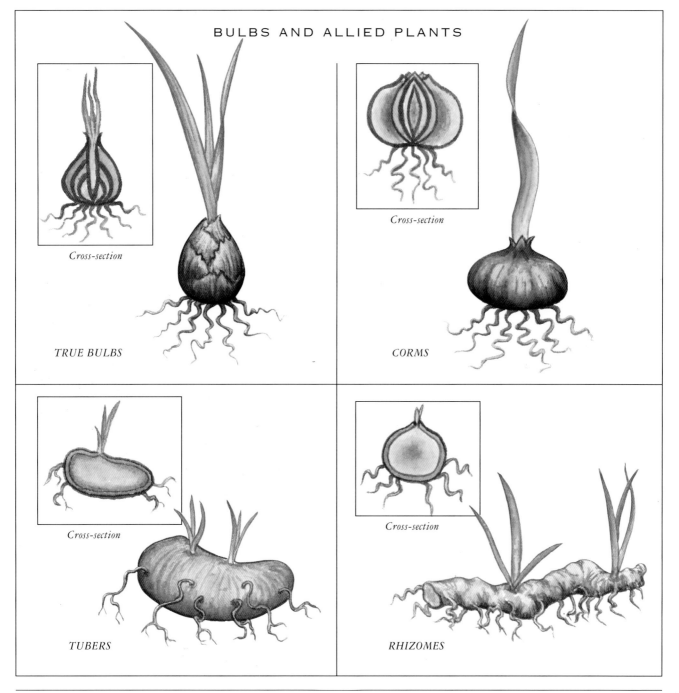

BULBS AND ALLIED PLANTS

Cross-section

TRUE BULBS

Cross-section

CORMS

Cross-section

TUBERS

Cross-section

RHIZOMES

TENDER BULBS

Indoors or out?

Some bulbs are not suitable for growing outdoors in our climate, and must be grown in a greenhouse or conservatory, or in the home, to produce good results. In many cases, bulbs can be started into growth under protection and brought outside later in the season when the weather has warmed up: when grown in containers, these look good on patios or even positioned amongst other flowering plants in borders so that the container is hidden. Other bulbs, however, need to be grown under protection throughout their lives, as their flowers would be spoiled outdoors.

Which bulbs must be considered tender enough for indoor cultivation often depends on the area in which you live, and the situation of your own garden. Species that can be grown successfully outside in the mild South-west of the country would often fail in cold, exposed Northern gardens, but even in mild regions a garden may be exposed to chilly, windy weather that makes it unsuitable for the more tender plants.

Experience is often the only way to gain an accurate picture of which plants are hardy enough for your conditions, but when growing dubiously hardy bulbs, always play safe and overwinter one or two specimens under cover in case an unexpectedly cold winter destroys your outdoor stock. Protect slightly tender bulbs by heaping straw, dry leaves or bracken over the planting site once the foliage has died down in autumn: this helps to prevent frost penetrating to the bulbs below ground. Deep planting is also recommended for extra protection.

The table below gives a guide to the plants that need indoor conditions, and those that are risky outdoors in all but the most favoured areas of the country. It is often adequate to bring tender bulbs under cover for the winter only:

THE TUBEROUS ROOTS of dahlias can be left in the ground in some areas, but are better lifted and stored in a frost-free place.

TENDER BULBS

BULBS FOR THE HOUSE, GREENHOUSE OR CONSERVATORY ONLY

- Achimenes
- Clivia
- Gloriosa
- Hippeastrum
- Lachenalia
- Sinningia

BULBS NEEDING PROTECTION OR OVERWINTERING UNDER COVER IN COLD AREAS

- Agapanthus
- Amaryllis
- Canna
- Crinum
- Cyrtanthus
- Dierama
- Eremurus
- Eucomis
- Gladiolus callianthus
- Hedychium
- Hymenocallis
- Ixia
- Nerine
- Polianthes
- Romulea
- Schizostylis
- Sparaxis
- Sprekelia
- Tigridia
- Tritonia
- Zantedeschia
- Zephyranthes

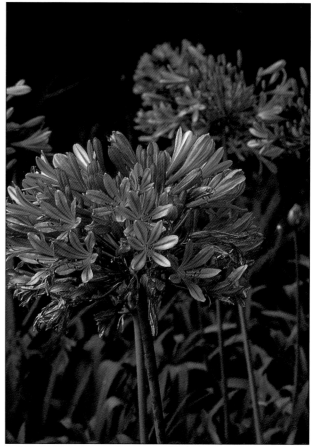

AGAPANTHUS PLANTS are suitable for leaving outdoors over winter in warmer areas of the country only.

STRONGLY CONTRASTING white and rich crimson tulips are mass planted under a silver birch tree in this lovely garden. The tulip planting is brilliantly set off by the wide, sweeping border of purple Virginian stock.

CHOOSING BULBS

What do you want from your plants?

There are so many bulbs, in such a range of colours, sizes and forms, that it is all too easy to get carried away when buying them. Their appeal is instantaneous: here they are, ready packaged, just needing to be popped into the soil – and within a short time, with no further effort, you can expect to be enjoying the brilliant flowers pictured on the display units at garden centres.

Perhaps one of their greatest virtues is that the bulk of bulbs appear for sale at just the time when summer is finally drawing to a close. The summer flowers are nearly over, trees will soon be shedding their leaves and the days growing shorter and more gloomy; the cold, wet, miserable weeks of winter stretch out ahead. No wonder we are so pleased to see the arrival of bulbs, with their promise of the spring to come!

But in order to achieve the best possible results from your bulbs, you should plan for them more carefully. Consider the type of garden in which they are to be grown; whether it is mild and sheltered or cold and exposed. Where in the garden are the bulbs to grow? Is there space on a rock garden or in a border? Do you have an area of lawn where bulbs could be naturalised, and if so, are you prepared for the grass to be untidy while the bulb foliage is dying down? Do you want all your bulbs to flower in spring, or would a longer flowering season be more appropriate? Do you want bulbs in pots for growing on the patio, or varieties that will flower out of season to brighten up the home in the middle of winter? If you have a good idea of what you want from your bulbs *before* you go out to buy them, it could save you making some expensive mistakes.

Choose for colour

Consider the colour schemes of your bulb planting as you would any other item, either inside your home or outside it. Do you want strong contrasts in colour, gradations of a single colour or colours that complement each other? Do you want to create a bright, warm, active look or do you want to give a cooler, calmer impression? Warm, active colours are red, yellow, orange and bright pink, while blue, lavender, white, cream, pale pink and pale yellow are cooler colours.

Blue and white spring-flowering bulbs include spring star flower, grape hyacinth, bluebell and hyacinth, all of which would team well with white or cream daffodils. Some of the brightest bulbs in the 'hot' colour range are ranunculus and harlequin flowers (sparaxis). Both these are more commonly available in mixed colours but sometimes you can find a supplier who is able to sell them as single colours. Anemones also come in strong colours and these too can be purchased in single colours. Greater impact is generally achieved by planting blocks of single colours rather than mixtures. Try bulbs in blocks of red, orange and yellow for a tremendous impact, or if you want a quieter look, plant groups of two shades of pink and white.

Many bulbous plants, such as daffodils, come in a wide range of varieties but a fairly limited colour range: they also look their best if planted in groups of one variety. Corn lily is another good example. Although there is a wide colour range available and corn lilies can be purchased in mixtures, these flowers look best if planted in blocks of one colour. They can, of course, be planted as mixtures, especially in an informal garden setting, but in nature they would be more likely to grow in blocks of one colour.

Consider flowering time

Some gardeners prefer one huge display over three or four weeks in spring while others may find more interest in spreading the season over several months of the year. For instance, with crocus alone, different varieties provide blooms from late autumn right through to mid-spring. There is some form of bulbous plant to give a display in every month of the year if that is what you require.

It can be hard to give precise information on exactly when different species will be in bloom, as the time can vary from one district to another and even from one garden to another because of variation in microclimates. However, if you spend some time noting the times when bulbs flower in your garden, in future seasons you will be able to plan to have a succession of bulbs in flower during many months of the year.

BUYING BULBS

There are several different ways in which you can buy bulbs. Most garden centres, and several other stores, sell bulbs in perforated plastic bags backed by a card giving planting details, along with a picture of the bulb in flower. Bulbs are also available in small netting sacks with attached pictures and growing instructions. Most garden centres and nurseries sell bulbs in bulk in the main planting season, and you can make your own selection from large bins. Another option is to send away for catalogues from bulb-growing nurseries and order bulbs by mail – these growers advertise in popular gardening magazines. The range of bulbs available from specialist nurseries is generally very much more extensive than what is on offer at your local garden centre. Mail order is a good option if you want some of the more unusual varieties, and if you want to order a lot of bulbs as it can be a good deal cheaper, though you need to take postal charges into account. When planning to buy by mail order, remember that you need to order well in advance of the planting date; if you leave it until bulbs are starting to appear in the shops, the specialist suppliers are likely to have sold out of many of the less common varieties. Once you are on the mailing list of mail order suppliers, they will send you their catalogues in plenty of time in future years.

When buying bulbs at a garden centre, try to buy them as soon as possible after they have been delivered, as they tend to deteriorate in the warm conditions, and will soon become bruised as other buyers sort through them to make their choice. Select plump, firm, well-rounded bulbs and make sure there are no soft spots or patches of mould. Especially avoid buying any bulbs that are starting to shoot and showing signs

HYACINTH BULBS will be on sale from early autumn. Select yours early to be sure of getting the best available.

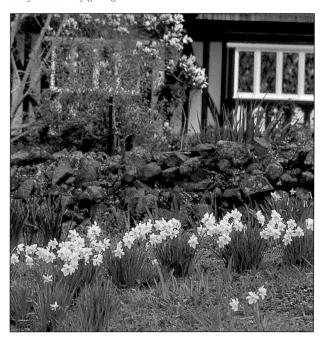

GOLDEN DAFFODILS planted in sweeping drifts beneath a fine magnolia tree show to advantage against an old stone wall.

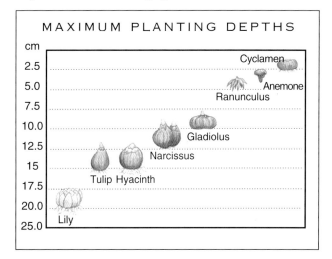

MAXIMUM PLANTING DEPTHS

cm
2.5 — Cyclamen
5.0 — Anemone
Ranunculus
7.5
10.0 — Gladiolus
12.5 — Narcissus
15 — Tulip Hyacinth
17.5
20.0
25.0 — Lily

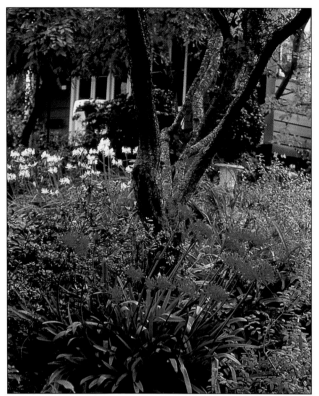

GROUPS OF BRIGHT PINK, autumn-flowering nerines provide showy splashes of colour as summer flowers fade.

BLUEBELLS, TULIPS and daffodils are here planted informally in a lovely woodland setting beside a tiny stream.

of growth. Unless there is just the tiniest shoot appearing and you know you can plant the bulbs at once, these bulbs will be a bad buy as they will not thrive. Some chain stores and supermarkets sell bulbs and continue to display them long after they should have been planted out or discarded. If you see long pale shoots emerging from bulbs definitely don't buy them. These bulbs have been stored for too long in poor conditions. They are badly stressed and have used up a great deal of their stored reserves of energy and growing capacity so that they may fail completely or do very poorly. Try to make your selection early in the season so that you have a choice of the best on offer.

Bulbs are best planted as soon as possible once you get them home, but if you are forced to delay planting for a short while, store the bulbs in paper bags or nets – not plastic bags – and keep them in a cool, dry, airy place. If the weather is very warm, the crisper drawer of a refrigerator can be a good place to keep bulbs in good condition, but do not put them in the main part of the refrigerator as this will dry them out.

PLANTING BULBS

Choosing a site

For the majority of bulbs, choose an open planting site where they will receive sun for at least half a day. There are a few bulbs that will grow well in shade but most like at least some sun. Even woodland species such as bluebell and wood anemone grow as understorey plants in deciduous woodlands and so receive some sun during their early growing and flowering period, before the trees are fully in leaf.

The vast majority of bulbs need well-drained soil or they will rot. If there is any doubt about the drainage, plant bulbs

in raised beds or mix sharp sand or grit with the soil in the planting area. Bulbs like a fairly rich, fertile soil. At least a month before planting, incorporate a generous amount of well-rotted manure or garden compost into the planting area.

Positioning the bulbs

Your bulbs will look more natural if you plant them in clumps or groups, not in straight lines. The depth depends on the size of the bulb but it is usually two or three times its diameter (see diagram on page 9). Details of planting depths are given in the individual entries for each bulb, and refer to the depth of soil above the tip of the bulb. Spacing between bulbs is also dependent on size. Larger bulbs are usually set out about 8cm (3in) apart and smaller ones 2–5cm (1–2in) apart, but they can be crowded together for effect.

Be sure to plant the bulbs the right way up. Usually the pointed part points upwards, but there are exceptions to this rule: ranunculus and anemone have the claws or points facing down into the soil and some lilies and crown imperials are sometimes planted on their sides to avoid moisture collecting between the scales, which can lead to rotting.

In dry conditions, bulbs may need to be watered in after planting, but it is usually not necessary to water again at least until leaf shoots have appeared.

Planting under trees

Mass planting of bulbs that flower through winter and early spring under deciduous trees can turn what might otherwise be a somewhat dull area of the garden into a lovely feature. Although it is sometimes difficult to dig and plant in these areas as the soil is hard and full of matted roots, the result can be well worth the effort. The leaves that fall from the trees in autumn break down into leafmould which provides ideal growing conditions for the bulbs.

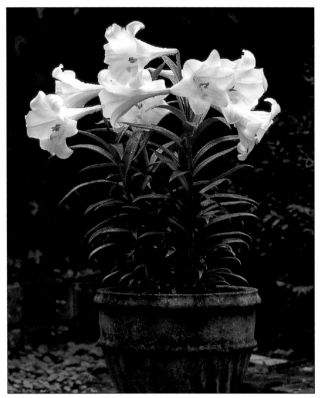

MAJESTIC WHITE LILIES grown in a large ceramic container make a stunning decoration for a courtyard.

INCREASING YOUR STOCK OF BULBS

Left to themselves, many bulbs will multiply of their own accord, but there are a number of ways in which you can help the process along.

Separation
Many bulbs produce offsets or bulblets that can be gently broken away from the mother bulb when the bulbs are lifted, and planted separately. Most first-year bulblets will reach flowering size in two or three years if they are planted separately, but some are slower to flower. When separating clumps of dahlia tubers, make sure each tuber has an 'eye' attached or it will not sprout and flower.

PROPAGATING DAHLIAS

DAHLIAS are propagated by dividing the tuber clump, but only tubers with a bud or 'eye' at the top will grow.

THREE WAYS TO PROPAGATE LILIES

1 DETACHING SCALES

THE LILY BULB consists of lots of scales. Remove the outer scales.

PUSH the individual scales, right way up, into a box of moist peat.

BULBLETS will appear at the base of each scale.

POT UP the scales when the new bulblets appear.

2. DETACHING AERIAL BULBILS

BULBILS grow in the leaf axis of some species. Collect them and pot them up.

3. DETACHING BULBLETS

OFFSETS on the base of some lilies can be detached and planted out.

LIFTING BULBS

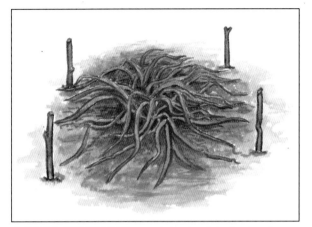

1. PUT A FEW STAKES around the edge of the clump so that you know where to dig when the leaves have died down.

2. AFTER THE LEAVES have died down, use a spade to outline the area of the clump.

3. LIFT THE CLUMP UP with a fork and shake off as much soil as possible.

4. SEPARATE THE BULBS from the clump, clean them and then store them in a dry, airy place or replant them.

Scoring and scooping

Cut a V-shape into the base plate of a mature bulb at planting time, taking care not to damage the growth bud of the bulb. This should result in many small offsets being produced by the end of the growing season. Or score through the basal plate of the bulb at right angles with a sharp knife to produce the same result. Depending on species these small offsets should produce bulbs of flowering size in two to four years.

With a sharp-sided teaspoon or curved knife, you can scoop out the entire basal plate and bulblets will form around the rim of the scooped out area. Wear gloves if you are treating hyacinths as the sap can sometimes irritate the skin.

Lilies

These techniques are not suitable for lilies, which are propagated by other methods.
• A mature lily bulb is composed of numerous individual scales. The individual scales can be carefully removed and planted upright in a coarse, free-draining mixture such as three parts coarse washed sand and one part peatmoss or peat substitute. The scales should produce bulblets at their bases.

• Some lilies produce aerial bulbils in the axis of the leaf and these can be collected as they are about to fall. Potted into pots or trays they should produce leaves by the following spring and reach flowering size in two or three years.
• Other lilies produce bulblets just below the soil surface, around the base of the stem. If these are carefully dug out from among the roots they can be potted up and will form flowering plants in two or three years.

CARING FOR GROWING BULBS

Once planted, bulbs need little maintenance. Once the plants are actively growing, the soil should be kept moist, but never soggy. Bulbs do not usually need feeding before they flower. They are fed after blooming, when they are storing food for the following season's growth. Special instructions for feeding and watering are included in the entries for individual plants where appropriate.

AFTER FLOWERING

• After flowers have finished, cut off the spent flower stems but do not cut back the foliage. If you cut off the leaves before they have died down naturally, the bulb will not have the reserves to grow and flower the following season.

• After flowering, feed the plants with a liquid or granular balanced fertiliser and continue to water in dry conditions until the leaves begin to die off naturally. This may take about two or three months.

• If bulbs have been planted in clumps, you may be able to plant annuals between the clumps, using either seed or seedlings. Quick growers such as Virginian stock will provide a pretty distraction from the dying bulb foliage. You could also put in summer-flowering annuals or perennials that will be ready to take over the display once the bulbs have truly died down. Or you can, of course, purchase some 'potted colour' – annuals that are already in bloom.

• Bulbs do not usually need to be lifted every season. Most are left in the ground and lifted only every two or three years, or in a number of cases only every four or five years. Many bulbs flower well when they are crowded and then it is only necessary to lift and divide clumps when the flower numbers or quality drop off.

• Take care when you lift bulbs that you do not cut or damage

TALL WHITE RANUNCULUS dominate this white border, formed of plants with contrasting shapes, textures and sizes.

A CARPET OF COLOUR has been created in this garden bed by combining white tulips with violas and anemones in a range of colours. To achieve such a pleasing effect, careful planning before planting is necessary.

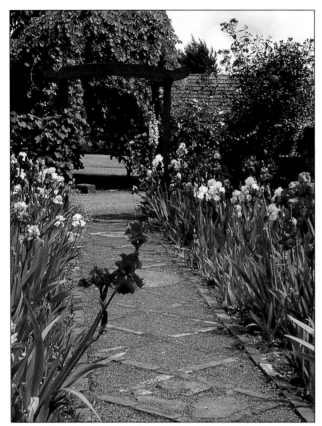

TALL BEARDED IRIS make an elegant border for this attractive garden path. Irises come in a rich array of colours.

ZEPHYR LILY, with its starry white flowers and deep green glossy foliage, makes an ideal edging plant. Here it grows with portulacas.

them – it is easy to slice into them with a spade or spear them with a fork. Discard damaged, soft or rotted bulbs immediately. Place the sound bulbs to dry in a cool, airy spot, brush off excess soil and then store them in nets, old stockings or in single layers in cardboard boxes. Ideally, bulbs should be stored so that they do not touch each other: they can be kept separate with shredded paper or something similar.

• Because lilies have no protective outer sheath on their bulbs, they must be lifted, the clumps divided if necessary and the bulbs replanted at once. They can be stored for short periods in damp sphagnum moss but take care that they don't dry out.

• Some bulbous plants, such as freesias, produce quite a lot of seed if the spent flower stems are not cut off. You can collect these seeds when they are ripe or allow them to self-sow. Seedlings may take two to five years to reach flowering size, depending on the type of bulb, and they will probably not be true to type. The results can, however, be interesting as you never know quite what to expect. Particularly good seedlings should be marked at flowering time so that the bulbs can be propagated at the end of the season.

MAKING THE MOST OF BULBS IN THE GARDEN

You may wish to plant groups of bulbs under deciduous trees or in other permanent places in the garden but there are many other options. Bulbs mix well with many herbaceous perennials as the new growth of the perennials tends to camouflage the not-so-attractive foliage of the bulbs as it yellows and dies off. Bulbs in this situation can usually be left in the ground for several years before they need to be lifted and divided.

Many bulbs can be treated like annuals for a seasonal display, then lifted and stored for use the following season. This, of course, creates more work but the results can be well worth the effort, allowing you to create different displays each year. You can have a delightful show of bulbs on their own but consider the possibility of planting bulbs and spring bedding plants together for a really stunning spring display. As well as forming an attractive association, the bedding plants help to mask the dying foliage of the bulbs, which must be left to die down naturally if the bulbs are to flower well next season. Autumn-sown hardy annuals will also serve the same purpose. Plant your bulbs and bedding plants at the same time, placing a bulb between each of the plants. For best effect, planting should be quite dense. You can experiment with colour combinations or opt for tried and tested associations such as yellow lily-flowered tulips and blue forget-me-nots.

• An early-flowering bedding plant such as white primula could be interplanted with cream or yellow narcissi, or deep blue anemones for a vivid contrast.

• White, yellow-centred primulas would team well with blue *Anemone blanda* and the dwarf narcissus 'Tête-à-Tête'.

• Other spring-flowering plants to combine with bulbs include polyanthus, wallflowers and forget-me-nots.

Dwarf bulbs are ideal for growing on a rockery, usually providing colour and interest before the other alpine plants come into their own. Suitable bulbs include alliums, chionodoxa, crocus, cyclamen, iris, muscari, narcissus, oxalis and rhodohypoxis, among others.

IF YOU WANT show quality tuberous begonias, grow them under cover. Here they grow in a conservatory, where they can also be placed on raised benches so the flowers are more easily admired.

NATURALISING BULBS IN GRASS

Bulbs naturalised in grass make a very attractive feature in gardens. However, you need to remember that the bulb foliage must be allowed to die down naturally if the bulbs are to perform well in future years, and that means that the grass cannot be mown for several weeks after the bulbs have finished flowering. This can look rather untidy, so a position for naturalised bulbs needs to be chosen with some care. Popular sites are the perimeters of lawns or under deciduous trees. In a small garden with a limited area of lawn used for many purposes, naturalising in turf may not be a practical idea.

Choose bulbs that will flower at an appropriate period; early spring is convenient because the grass can then be mown from late spring onwards. Some summer-flowering bulbs are good in a wildflower meadow, and autumn-flowering bulbs such as colchicum also grow well in grass. You can either lift a square of turf, plant a group of bulbs and replace the cut turf, or you can plant larger bulbs individually, using a trowel or bulb-planting tool to cut a hole in the turf. Place the bulb in the bottom of the hole and replace the plug of soil and turf. Give a good watering after planting, both to settle the bulbs and to help the turf re-establish.

After the bulbs have bloomed, give the plants an application of balanced fertiliser and water the area regularly if conditions are dry. Once the bulb foliage has yellowed and died off mowing can be resumed – this usually takes some six weeks after flowering.

MINIATURE PINK NERINES and other small bulbous plants grow between paving stones where they benefit from the sharp drainage.

GROWING BULBS IN CONTAINERS

Many bulbs make lovely container plants. Pots full of bulbs are ideal for balcony gardens and patios, and for instant colour, pots of bulbs in bud or in flower can be plunged into garden beds throughout the growing season.

Use a good quality potting compost, and make sure the base of the container is crocked for good drainage. Plant the bulbs at the same depth as you would in the soil, crowding them into the container for a good flowering display. Keep the compost moist at all times; regular watering will be needed.

Growing bulbs indoors

'Prepared' bulbs are specially treated to flower early – often in time for Christmas. Plant them in a shallow pot or bowl of moist potting compost and put them in a cold place such as a garden shed, keeping them dark by placing them in a black plastic bag. Leave them for 8–12 weeks; when shoots begin to appear, move them into a bright, cool room. Once flower buds begin to show colour, move the bulbs to their flowering position in the home.

The bunch-flowered narcissus 'Paperwhite' is unusual in that it doesn't need a cold, dark period after planting; bulbs can be left on a cool, light

A POT OF JACOBEAN LILIES can be brought to the fore when they flower.

POTTING NARCISSI FOR INDOOR USE

1. CHOOSE A POT at least twice as tall as the bulbs.

2. HALF FILL the pot with a good soilless potting compost.

3. POSITION THE BULBS with their tops level with the top of the pot and a small gap between each and around the edge of the pot.

4. COVER THE BULBS with the compost and gently firm it down. Water, drain and place in a cold – 4°C (40°F) – position in total darkness. A cold, dark period of 8–12 weeks is necessary.

5. WHEN SHOOTS appear, move the pot into a bright, cool position at about 10°C (50°F).

6. WHEN BUDS appear, move the pot into its flowering position, still in bright light.

WHAT CAN GO WRONG?

There are relatively few pest and disease problems that regularly beset the home gardener growing bulbs. Bulbs that fail to come up at all have usually been planted too deep or have rotted through disease or waterlogging, especially in clay based soils. Yellowing foliage early in the growing season may also be caused by waterlogging. More serious pests of bulbs are often associated with storage conditions and it is wise to examine bulbs for damage, decay or insect pests such as aphids before planting. Diseases specific to certain bulbs are mentioned in the text under individual entries.

Failure to flower

This may be due to a number of reasons, including:
• natural offsets are not sufficiently mature to flower.
• foliage has been cut off prematurely the previous season.
• insufficient sunlight or lack of water while the foliage is still green.
• congestion of bulbs.
• 'blindness' – a condition that occurs especially with daffodils and tulips. The flower bud forms but gives up trying to continue on to bloom. It may be due to incorrect storage temperature, lack of chilling or fluctuating temperatures as the flower bud emerges from the bulb.

Leaf scorch

• This fungal disease affects bulbs of daffodils and narcissi, and others including hippeastrum, crinum and belladonna lilies. It is worse in wet seasons, and occurs at the top of the bulb scales so that emerging leaves are infected. The leaf tips are reddish and scorched, and later on brown spots appear further down the leaf. Eventually the tissue around these damaged areas goes yellow. Remove and destroy the worst affected leaves and spray with a suitable fungicide if symptoms persist.

Bulb rots

• These may be caused by a number of bacteria or fungi, and lead to rotting and decay of the bulbs either in store or in the ground. They are made worse by poor drainage and overwet soil conditions. Damaged bulbs are particularly prone to infection, so take care when handling or lifting bulbs and discard damaged ones.

Grey mould (botrytis species)

• Grey mould attacks an enormous range of plants. It may manifest itself initially by spotting on leaves or stems, followed by breakdown of the tissue and the typical furry grey growth. Poor air circulation, overcrowding, overwatering and cool, humid weather conditions are favourable to its spread. Improve growing conditions and spray if necessary with a suitable fungicide.

Bulb flies

• Bulb flies lay their eggs in the soil near the bulb neck; the maggots tunnel into the bulb to feed. Affected plants produce sparse, yellow foliage and fail to flower. If you are not lifting the bulbs in autumn, pull soil up round their necks to fill the holes left by the leaves dying down.

Thrips

• Gladioli are very susceptible to attack by thrips, or thunderflies. These tiny winged insects cause silver streaking and flecking of both foliage and flowers; in a bad attack, the display can be ruined. The pest is worst in hot, dry conditions. Affected plants can be sprayed with a contact insecticide. Thrips overwinter on the corms, so after an attack, dust the corms with HCH dust after lifting and again before planting out in spring.

Lily beetle

• These small, scarlet beetles can be a serious pest of lilies and other plants such as fritillaries. Both larvae and adults feed on the leaves and stems of plants, often causing considerable damage. They are quite conspicuous and should be picked off by hand and destroyed whenever they are noticed; bad infestations can be sprayed with a contact insecticide. Beetles overwinter on weeds and plant debris, so clean up round the planting area in autumn.

Aphids

• These may attack a range of bulbous plants and should be sprayed or hosed off as they can carry virus diseases. A bad infestation disfigures flowers and foliage.

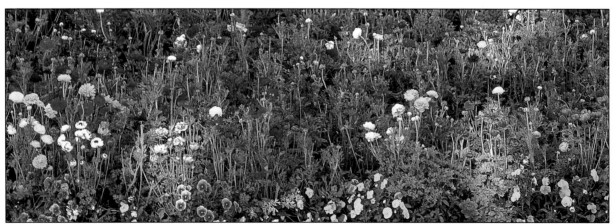

MULTI-COLOURED RANUNCULUS and anemone are crowded together to produce this bright springtime scene.

windowsill directly after planting and flowers will appear in about six weeks. Plant mid-November for Christmas blooms.

Normally, non-prepared bulbs will flower at their normal period. They should be planted and left out in a sheltered position in the garden in their containers until flower buds are showing, when they can be brought into the house.

After flowering
If after flowering the whole plant and bulb are planted out into the garden, there is some chance of the bulb flowering the following year. Bulbs that stay in their pots until they have died down will in most cases not reflower the following year. When the foliage on these bulbs has died down, lift the bulbs, store them and replant them in the garden at the right time the following season. They may not flower that year but should do so the next. They are not suitable for growing as indoor-flowering plants again.

BULBS AS CUT FLOWERS

Many bulbous plants produce flowers that are ideal for cutting for the house. Most are best picked before they are fully open. For longer vase life, change the water daily or add a few drops of household bleach, or a proprietary cut flower food to the water.

FRAGRANT FREESIAS come in a glorious range of colours to epitomise the joy of the spring garden.

THIS RUSTIC BASKET of choice hyacinth blooms could not fail to lift the spirits, appearing as they do just when winter draws to a close.

TULIPS MAKE ideal cut flowers and several colourful bunches are here shown to perfection against the terracotta of the containers.

ALLIUM
Ornamental onion

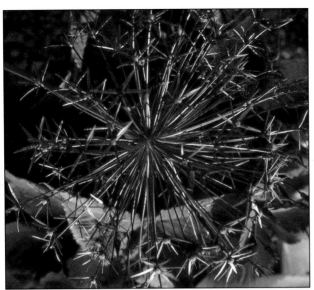

LARGE ROUNDED HEADS are typical of alliums and the star-burst effect of this one looks stunning in the garden.

THE PURPLE-PINK FLOWERS of Allium oreophilum *(also known as* A. ostrowskianum*) brighten up the early summer garden.*

FEATURES

There are a large number of *Allium* species, including edible onions, garlic and chives as well as many ornamental plants. Typically, they produce rounded heads of flowers, often in rosy purple shades, but there are also yellow and white-flowered species. Some are small-growing and suitable for the rock garden, while others make excellent plants for the middle or back of borders. *A. giganteum* produces its eye-catching heads of mauve-pink, starry flowers on stems 1m (3ft) or more high, while *A. moly* grows to only 20cm (8in) and has loose clusters of golden yellow blooms. Many alliums make excellent cut flowers. They are usually long lasting in water, and the dried inflorescence which remains after the blooms have fallen can be used successfully in dried arrangements, too.

ALLIUM AT A GLANCE

Versatile and varied bulbs with usually rounded heads of starry flowers in spring and early summer.

		RECOMMENDED SPECIES
JAN	/	
FEB	/	*Allium albopilosum*
MAR	/	*A. beesianum*
APR	flowering	*A. caeruleum*
MAY	flowering	*A. giganteum*
JUN	flowering	*A. karataviense*
JULY	flowering	*A. moly* 'Jeannine'
AUG	/	*A. neopolitanum*
SEPT	plant	*A. oreophilum*
OCT	plant	*A. schubertii*
NOV	/	*A. siculum*
DEC	/	

CONDITIONS

Aspect Best in full sun but will tolerate light shade.
Site Alliums in borders should be positioned where other plants will help to hide their often untidy foliage. Smaller species are suitable for rock gardens. The soil must be well drained and should contain plenty of well-decayed manure or compost. Add a dressing of lime to acid soils before planting.

GROWING METHOD

Planting Plant in autumn. Planting depth varies according to the size of the bulb: cover bulbs with soil to three times their height.
Feeding Apply a high potash liquid fertiliser as buds form. Water during dry spells, but never allow the soil to become sodden. After flowering, stop watering altogether.
Problems Plants may suffer from the fungal disease rust, causing orange pustules on the foliage: destroy affected specimens. Feeding with high potash fertiliser may increase resistance to attacks.

FLOWERING

Season Flowers in late spring and summer.
Cutting Cut alliums when about half the flowers are fully open.

AFTER FLOWERING

Requirements Foliage starts to die down before blooming is complete. Cut off the spent flower stems if required. Overcrowded clumps can be divided in autumn, replanting immediately.

ALSTROEMERIA
Peruvian lily

THE FLOWERS of alstroemeria are very delicately marked when viewed close-up, and have an almost orchid-like appearance.

SUMMER BORDERS are brightened by these colourful, long-lasting flowers which are also excellent for cutting for the home.

FEATURES

These exotic-looking plants are prolific flowerers which can be spectacular in borders. The open-faced flowers are carried in clusters at the top of 90cm (3ft) stems; the sword-like foliage is dark green. The plants may take a year to become established and produce flowers, but once they have settled in, flowering is profuse. Container-grown plants become established more quickly. The colour range includes yellow, cream, orange, red, salmon and pink. The Princess series contains dwarf varieties that represent a major breeding breakthrough. Alstroemerias are from South America and are not always reliably hardy; Ligtu hybrids are among the hardiest types.

ALSTROEMERIA AT A GLANCE

Once established, these plants produce a profusion of colourful, attractively marked summer flowers on tall stems.

		RECOMMENDED VARIETIES
JAN	/	
FEB	/	
MAR	plant	Ligtu hybrids
APR	plant	Princess series
MAY	/	
JUN	flowering	
JULY	flowering	
AUG	flowering	
SEPT	/	
OCT	/	
NOV	/	
DEC	/	

CONDITIONS

Aspect Full sun or partial shade.

Site Alstroemerias do well in a sheltered border and are very effective mixed with herbaceous perennials. They require free-draining soil.

GROWING METHOD

Planting Plant the fleshy tubers 15cm (6in) deep in spring, as soon as you obtain them. Handle them carefully, as they are usually brittle and break easily. Do not let them dry out before planting. You can also obtain alstroemerias as container-grown plants in summer.

Feeding Add a balanced granular fertiliser to the soil before planting. Water plants in very dry conditions, but never allow the soil to become waterlogged.

Problems Plants may fail to flower in their first season after planting. Once established, however, they can be very invasive, and should be planted where their spread can be kept in check. Slugs find them attractive, and should be controlled with slug pellets where necessary.

FLOWERING

Season Flowers in mid-summer.

Cutting Alstroemerias last very well in water, and should be cut as the buds start to open.

AFTER FLOWERING

Requirements Remove dead heads. Once the foliage has died down, protect the crowns with a mulch of dry straw or leaves through the winter. Crowded clumps can be split in spring.

AMARYLLIS BELLADONNA
Belladonna lily

THESE TALL FLOWER STEMS appear before the leaves, which is why belladonna lilies are also known as 'naked ladies'.

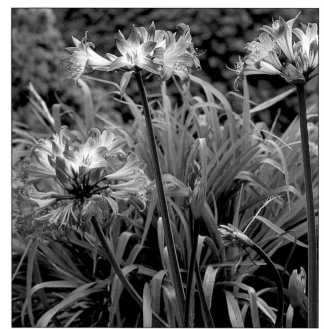

BRIGHT PINK BELLADONNA LILIES brighten the late summer and autumn garden. The foliage here is from a clump of daylilies.

FEATURES

This lovely South African bulb produces its multiple and sweetly perfumed blooms on sturdy purple-green stems 60cm (24in) or more high. The funnel-shaped flowers may be various shades of pink or white and the flowering stem appears before the leaves, giving the plant its alternative common name of naked lady. This bulb is a great asset in the garden as the flowering period is autumn, while the glossy strap-like leaves look good throughout winter and early spring. It makes an excellent cut flower. Best flowering comes from clumps that are left undisturbed for several years.

AMARYLLIS AT A GLANCE

A tall plant producing its stems of fragrant, funnel-shaped flowers in autumn. Needs a warm, sheltered, sunny position.

		RECOMMENDED VARIETIES
JAN	/	
FEB	/	'Johannesburg'
MAR	/	'Kimberley'
APR	/	'Major'
MAY	/	
JUN	plant	
JULY	plant	
AUG	/	
SEPT	flowering	
OCT	flowering	
NOV	/	
DEC	/	

CONDITIONS

Aspect   Prefers a warm, sheltered spot in full sun – the bulbs need a good summer baking to produce the best flowers.

Site   A good plant for a flower bed under a south-facing wall. *Amaryllis belladonna* can also be grown in containers, planting the large bulbs singly in 20cm (8in) pots. Well-drained soil is required: poor soil is tolerated but best results are achieved by digging in decayed organic matter a month or more before planting.

GROWING METHOD

Planting   Plant bulbs with their necks just at ground level and 20–30cm (8–12in) apart in early to mid-summer.

Feeding   Apply a balanced fertiliser after flowering, as the leaves appear. Water in dry periods while the plant is in growth.

Problems   It is rarely troubled by any problems.

FLOWERING

Season   Flowers in very late summer and autumn.

Cutting   A good cut flower for large arrangements.

AFTER FLOWERING

Requirements   Remove spent flower stems. Protect the crowns with a mulch of peat over winter. Leave bulbs undisturbed for several years. If lifting and dividing, do so in early summer.

ANEMONE
Windflower

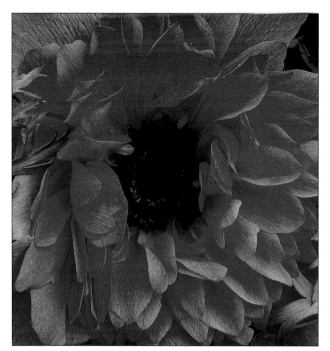

THE DARK CENTRES, *deep blue or black, of* Anemone coronaria *make a stunning contrast to the rich colours of the petals.*

THIS MIXED PLANTING *of* Anemone coronaria *shows some of the range of colour and form available from this lovely plant.*

FEATURES

Anemones, also known as windflowers, form a large and versatile group of plants, the most commonly grown species being *A. coronaria*, *A. blanda* and *A. nemorosa*. *Anemone coronaria* grows from a hard little tuber, *A. blanda* from hard tuberous roots and *A. nemorosa* from very brittle, creeping rhizomes. The flowers are often very colourful, and can be daisy-like with lots of petals, or cup-shaped, rather like poppies. Anemones flower in spring; *A. coronaria* will also flower in summer, depending on the planting time. They are excellent for cutting.

ANEMONE AT A GLANCE

Low-growing, hardy plants which form a colourful carpet of spring or summer flowers.

JAN	/	
FEB	flowering	
MAR	flower /plant *	**RECOMMENDED VARIETIES**
APR	flower /plant *	*Anemone blanda:*
MAY	/	'Atrocaerulea'
JUN	flowering	'White Splendour'
JULY	flowering	'Radar'
AUG	flowering	*Anemone coronaria:*
SEPT	plant **	'Mona Lisa'
OCT	plant **	'Mister Fokker'
NOV	/	*Anemone nemorosa:*
DEC	/	'Alba Plena'
		'Purity'
		'Robinsoniana'
		'Vestal'

* summer flowering **spring flowering

TYPES

A. coronaria Reaching 15–20cm (6–8in) high, *A. coronaria* is available in a lovely range of clear colours including red, white, blue, violet, cerise and pink, all with a black to deep navy blue centre. The most popular strains are 'de Caen', with single poppy-like flowers, and 'St Brigid', with semi-double to double flowers. There are many named cultivars in both these strains. They can be planted in single blocks of colour or mixed at random, and they can be grown in containers as well as making an excellent garden display.

A. blanda This native of Greece and Turkey bears daisy-like flowers, usually in shades of blue, although white and pink forms are available. One of spring's early bloomers, its flowers are carried on stems some 15–25cm (6–10in) high above ferny, divided leaves. A variety of cultivars is available now and some of these are grown as potted plants. This species seeds readily and can be naturalised under trees.

A. nemorosa The wood anemone, *A. nemorosa*, likes a cool, moist climate and is often grown massed under deciduous trees, imitating its natural habitat. Here, its starry, white (sometimes lavender blue), single flowers, with their central boss of golden stamens, make a glorious showing in late spring and into early summer. The wood anemone's mid-green foliage is deeply cut. Growth may be from 10–20cm (4–8in) high. This species increases rapidly where it finds the growing conditions suitable, and plants will eventually increase to carpet the ground.

THE BRIGHT, DAISY-LIKE flowers of Anemone blanda *brighten up the garden in late winter or very early spring.*

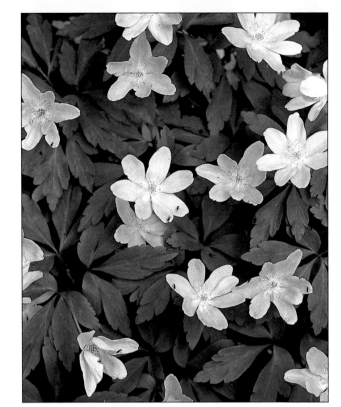

*WOODLAND ANEMONE (*Anemone nemorosa*) makes a pretty groundcover in a cool, moist climate where it naturalises readily.*

CONDITIONS

Aspect   All anemones prefer some protection from strong wind. *A. coronaria* is best in full sun, while *A. nemorosa* prefers to be grown in dappled sunlight or with morning sun and afternoon shade. *A. blanda* comes from exposed sites in mountainous districts and so will tolerate full sun or part shade.

Site   *A. blanda* and *A. nemorosa* grow well under deciduous trees, or on a rock garden, while *A. coronaria* provides bright colour towards the front of beds and borders. Soil must be well drained or tubers and roots will rot. All anemone species prefer a soil rich in organic matter although *A. blanda* is happy to grow in fairly poor soils as long as drainage is good. Plenty of well-decayed compost or manure should be dug into the ground about a month before planting the bulbs.

GROWING METHOD

Planting   Plant tubers of *A. coronaria* 5cm (2in) deep and 10–15cm (4–6in) apart in September and October for spring flowers, or in March and April to bloom in summer. *A. blanda* and *A. nemorosa* should be planted 5–7.5cm (2–3in) deep and 10cm (4in) apart in early autumn. Take care not to damage brittle roots; soaking the tubers or rhizomes overnight before planting will help them to get established quickly. After planting, mulch soil with bark chips or leafmould.

Feeding   A balanced fertiliser can be applied after flowering, but feeding is not usually necessary in reasonably fertile soils.
Water in after planting if the soil is dry, and ensure the soil is kept moist but not waterlogged once the flower buds start to form.

Problems   Mosaic virus can cause distortion and mottling of the leaves and eventual death of plants. Control aphids, which spread the virus.

FLOWERING

Season   *A. coronaria* will bloom from late winter until mid-spring, or in mid-summer, depending on planting time. *A. blanda* flowers in early spring while *A. nemorosa* flowers later in spring and into early summer.

Cutting   *A. coronaria* makes an excellent cut flower. Cut rather than pull flowers from the plant. The flowers of *A. blanda* and *A. nemorosa* may last a few days in the vase but these anemones make a much better showing in the ground. Leaving the flowers on the plants allows seed to form to increase your stock.

AFTER FLOWERING

Requirements   If dry, continue to water plants until the foliage dies down. Cut off spent flowerheads unless you require seeds to form. Tubers of *A. coronaria* can be lifted, cleaned and stored in a dry, airy place until the following autumn, or left in the ground as long as drainage is good. The other species are best left in the ground to form large colonies. Lift, divide and replant in autumn if required.

BEGONIA
Begonia

EXQUISITE FORM and beautiful colour shadings make this tuberous begonia a show stopper. It's worth the effort to produce blooms like this.

THE LARGE, many-petalled flowers of some begonia hybrids are reminiscent of camellias. This variety is 'Roy Hartley'.

FEATURES

Tuberous begonias result from the breeding and selection of several South American species and many are grown by specialists for exhibition. *Begonia tuberhybrida* is the most commonly grown type; the hybrid 'Non-Stop' strain is particularly popular for its prolonged flowering. Begonias make excellent house plants, but can also be grown in containers on patios or in beds outdoors; pendulous varieties are especially suitable for hanging baskets. Flowers can take many forms, including single or double, camellia-flowered or carnation-flowered – some are very simple while others are heavily ruffled. Flowers appear in threes, with the large, central male flower being the showpiece; the small female flowers are usually removed as they develop. The colour range includes many shades of red, pink, yellow, cream and white, with some bicolours. Plants grow some 25–45cm (10–18in) high.

BEGONIA AT A GLANCE

Very large, showy flowers are carried throughout the summer. Plants are frost-tender.

		RECOMMENDED VARIETIES
JAN	/	
FEB	/	'Billie Langdon'
MAR	plant (under cover)	'Can-Can'
APR	plant (under cover)	'Fairylight'
MAY	plant (under cover)	'Orange Cascade'
JUN	plant (outside)	'Roy Hartley'
JULY	flowering	'Sugar Candy'
AUG	flowering	
SEPT	flowering	
OCT	/	
NOV	/	
DEC	/	

CONDITIONS

Aspect   Begonias prefer dappled sun or light shade, and need shelter from wind.

Site   Grow the plants in the house or conservatory, or in pots or flowerbeds outdoors once all risk of frost has passed. Soil should be rich and moisture retentive, with plenty of organic matter such as well-rotted garden compost.

GROWING METHOD

Planting   Dormant tubers can be started off in pots of moist peat or compost under cover in spring, pressing the tuber into the soil with the dished side up. Spray the top of the tuber once only with a fine mist of water, and keep the compost just moist. Pot-grown plants can also be bought in leaf later in the spring. Plant out when all risk of frost is over, 23–30cm (9–12in) apart.

Feeding   Apply high potash liquid fertiliser every 14 days throughout the growing period. Keep the plants moist at all times, but do not allow the soil to become waterlogged.

Problems   Powdery mildew may be a problem, especially in hot, dry weather. If this occurs, try to improve air circulation round the plants and use a suitable fungicide if necessary.

FLOWERING

Season   From early summer right through to autumn.

Cutting   Flowers are unsuitable for cutting.

AFTER FLOWERING

Requirements Lift tubers as the stems die down in autumn. Store them in dry peat in a cool, frost-free place until the following spring.

CAMASSIA
Quamash

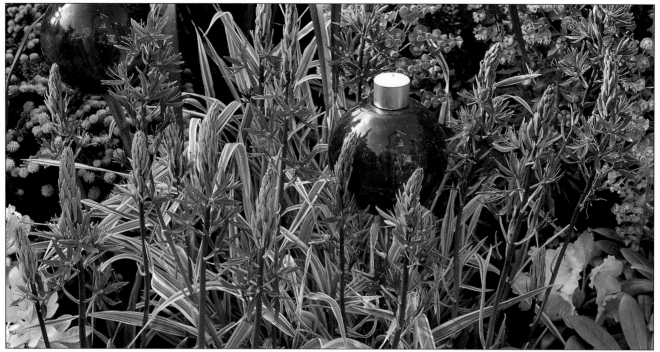

The intense blue flower spikes of Camassia leichtlinii make a striking group amongst other border plants. A moisture-retentive soil is needed for best results – regular watering is likely to be necessary if the weather is dry. Camassias can cope with heavier soil conditions than many other bulbs.

FEATURES

The botanical name of this plant is derived from that given to it by American Indians, who grew the bulbs for food. It is relatively unusual among bulbous plants in preferring moist, heavy soils. The tall, graceful flower stems carry dense spires of starry blue flowers. *Camassia leichtlinii* is very reliable, with 1m (3ft) flowering stems: *C. quamash (C. esculenta)* is a little shorter and has flowers varying from white, through pale blue to deep purple. *C. cusickii* produces its 1.2m (4ft) pale lavender flower spikes in late spring.

CAMASSIA AT A GLANCE

Tall, stately spikes of blue, starry flowers provide valuable colour in the perennial border in early summer.

		RECOMMENDED VARIETIES
JAN	/	
FEB	/	*Camassia cusickii*
MAR	/	
APR	/	
MAY	flowering	*Camassia leichtlinii:*
		'Electra'
JUN	flowering	'Blue Danube'
JULY	flowering	'Semiplena'
AUG	flowering	
SEPT	plant	*Camassia quamash*
OCT	plant	
NOV	/	
DEC	/	

CONDITIONS

Aspect   Full sun or light, dappled shade will suit these bulbs.

Site   Camassias make excellent border plants, valuable for early summer colour. A moisture-retentive, fertile soil is preferred, though they will also grow adequately in free-draining conditions.

GROWING METHOD

Planting   Plant the bulbs in early to mid-autumn, 7.5–10cm (3–4in) deep. Space them about 15cm (6in) apart.

Feeding   Feeding is not usually necessary, but an application of a balanced, granular fertiliser can be made in spring, especially on poor soils. Water thoroughly in dry conditions and on free-draining soil.

Problems   Camassias are usually trouble free.

FLOWERING

Season   Flowers from late spring through early summer.

Cutting   Stems can be cut as the lowest buds on the spike begin to open.

AFTER FLOWERING

Requirements Cut down the flowering spikes once the flowers have faded. Do not disturb the bulbs until they become overcrowded, when they can be lifted and divided in autumn.

CHIONODOXA

Glory of the snow

'PINK GIANT', a variety of Chionodoxa siehei, *has relatively large blooms in a pale, purplish pink shade.*

THE BRIGHT BLUE flowers of chionodoxa, with their prominent central white eye, make a cheerful sight in the early spring months.

FEATURES

This dainty little bulb is ideal for rock gardens or raised beds, with its mass of open, star-shaped blue flowers with white centres. They are carried on short spikes of up to a dozen or so flowers per spike. The strap-shaped leaves form loose, rather untidy rosettes.
Chionodoxa luciliae (C. gigantea) grows to 10cm (4in) tall with clear blue, white-eyed flowers some 4cm (1½in) or more across. *Chionodoxa siehei*, which used to be known as *C. luciliae*, and is sometimes listed as *C. forbesii*, reaches 10–25cm (4–10in), with slightly smaller flowers which are available in pale blue, white or purplish pink forms. The flowers have a distinct white eye and a central boss of stamens, tipped with gold. *C. sardensis* has flowers of a striking gentian blue with a tiny white centre that is almost unnoticeable.

CHIONODOXA AT A GLANCE

A low-growing bulb producing plenty of bright blue flowers in early spring.

		RECOMMENDED VARIETIES
JAN	/	
FEB	flowering 🌸	*Chionodoxa siehei:*
MAR	flowering 🌸	'Alba'
APR	flowering 🌸	'Pink Giant'
MAY	/	'Rosea'
JUN	/	
JULY	/	
AUG	/	
SEPT	plant 🖐	
OCT	/	
NOV	/	
DEC	/	

CONDITIONS

Aspect Full sun or dappled shade is suitable, though they grow best in an open, sunny position..

Site Chionodoxa is suitable for window boxes, rock gardens, raised beds, the front of borders or naturalised in grass. Soil should be free draining, but otherwise these bulbs are not fussy about their growing conditions.

GROWING METHOD

Planting Plant the bulbs in groups about 7.5cm (3in) deep and 7.5cm (3in) apart in early autumn.

Feeding A balanced granular fertiliser can be sprinkled over the soil surface in spring, but plants usually grow well without supplementary feeding, except in very poor, thin soils. Watering is necessary only in very dry conditions.

Problems Apart from occasional slug damage, plants are generally trouble free.

FLOWERING

Season Chionodoxa flowers in early spring, sometimes appearing as the snow is thawing to live up to its common name.

Cutting Flowers can be cut when they begin to open. They are valuable for cutting when few other flowers are available in the garden.

AFTER FLOWERING

Requirements Lift and divide overcrowded plants when the foliage dies down in early summer after flowering, otherwise little attention is needed.

CLIVIA MINIATA
Kaffir lily

CLIVIAS MAKE SHOWY and colourful house plants, and will bloom for many years if they are given a winter rest.

THE PALE creamy yellow flowers of Clivia miniata citrina *make this unusual plant worth seeking out.*

FEATURES

This evergreen forms a striking house or conservatory plant, with long, deep green, strap-shaped leaves which overlap at the base rather like a leek. In spring or summer, a stout stem pushes between the leaf bases and grows to around 45cm (18in), carrying a head of 20 or so bright orange, bell-shaped flowers. These are marked with yellow in the throat and have prominent golden anthers.

Selected hybrids have larger flowers in various rich orange shades: a beautiful yellow-flowered variety, *C. miniata citrina*, has been developed but to date these plants are scarce and expensive, as are cultivars with cream striped foliage.

CLIVIA AT A GLANCE

A striking house plant with large heads of orange, bell-shaped flowers on stout stems. Minimum temperature 10°C.

		RECOMMENDED VARIETIES
JAN	/	
FEB	flowering 🌿	*Clivia miniata citrina*
MAR	flowering 🌿	'Striata'
APR	flowering 🌿	
MAY	transplant 👆	
JUN	/	
JULY	/	
AUG	/	
SEPT	/	
OCT	/	
NOV	/	
DEC	/	

CONDITIONS

Aspect   Clivia prefers a reasonably bright position in the home, but not one in direct sun, which will scorch the foliage. Provide shading in a greenhouse or conservatory

Site   Grow as a room plant while it is flowering; during the summer the container can be placed in a sheltered position outdoors. Use a loam-based or soilless potting compost.

GROWING METHOD

Planting   Clivias are usually bought as house plants in growth.

Feeding   Give a high potash liquid feed every two or three weeks from early spring through the summer. Keep the compost thoroughly moist from spring to autumn, then keep the plant cool and water it very sparingly in winter.

Problems   Mealy bugs can appear as fluffy white blobs between the leaf bases; use a systemic insecticide to control them.

FLOWERING

Season   Flowers may be carried any time between late winter and early summer

Cutting   Not suitable for cutting.

AFTER FLOWERING

Requirements   Remove spent flower stalks. Repot only when essential; crowded plants tend to flower more reliably.

COLCHICUM AUTUMNALE

Autumn crocus, meadow saffron

THE DELICATE COLOUR and form of meadow saffron flowers are particularly prominent, as they appear long before the leaves. They are very welcome as they appear in autumn when the garden is often looking rather untidy and faded after its summer exuberance.

FEATURES

This is another lovely plant to brighten and lift the garden in autumn. It is unusual in that the 15–23cm (6–9in) high flowers emerge directly from the neck of the corm, the leaves not appearing until months later, in spring. Although the flowers look similar to crocuses, the plants are not related. Up to a dozen rose-pink to pale lilac, goblet-shaped flowers emerge from each corm. There is a pure white form, 'Alba', and a glorious double form known as 'Waterlily', which has a profusion of rose-lilac petals. Always plant in fairly large groups for the best effect.

This easy-care bulb gives great rewards. It has a long history of use in herbal medicine but all parts of the plant are poisonous.

COLCHICUM AT A GLANCE

A crocus-like plant valuable for its autumn flowers held on delicate stems.

		RECOMMENDED VARIETIES
JAN	/	
FEB	/	
MAR	/	'Alboplenum'
APR	/	'Album'
MAY	/	'Pleniflorum'
JUN	/	'The Giant'
JULY	plant	'Waterlily'
AUG	plant	
SEPT	flowering	
OCT	flowering	
NOV	flowering	
DEC	/	

CONDITIONS

Aspect   Colchicum grows in full sun or very light shade.

Site   Suitable for rock gardens, borders or for naturalising in grassed areas or in light shade under trees. For best results grow this plant in well-drained soil to which organic matter has been added.

GROWING METHOD

Planting   Corms should be planted in late summer, 7.5cm (3in) deep and 10–15cm (4–6in) apart, in groups. Established clumps are best divided at this time, too.

Feeding   Apply a generous mulch of decayed organic matter in winter. Further feeding is not usually necessary. Water in dry spells once the leaves appear in spring, and throughout their growing period.

Problems   No specific pest or disease problems are common for this plant.

FLOWERING

Season   Flowers spring out of the ground in autumn.

Cutting   Cut flowers for the vase when the goblet shape is fully formed but before it opens out. Flowers last about a week in the vase.

AFTER FLOWERING

Requirements   Spent flowers may be cut off or left on the ground. Dead foliage may need tidying up at the end of the season.

CONVALLARIA MAJALIS
Lily-of-the-valley

LONG A FAVOURITE with spring brides, fragrant lily-of-the-valley is an easy and rewarding bulb to grow.

IDEAL FOR EDGING a shady garden, these lovely plants are also completely reliable, increasing and flowering every year.

FEATURES

This is a tough little plant with a dainty appearance that belies its ease of growth. It is ideal for naturalising in shady spots in the garden and also under trees where it can grow undisturbed. The dainty little white bell flowers are borne in spring; they are delightfully scented and last well in the vase. Flower stems may be 20–25cm (8–10in) high, just topping the broadish, furled leaves which clasp the flower stems in pairs. There are several named cultivars but the straight species is by far the most popular. Previously used in folk medicine, the plant is now known to contain several poisonous substances although research continues on its potential medical use. The fleshy rhizomes with their growth shoots are known as 'pips'.

CONVALLARIA AT A GLANCE

A low-growing plant with very fragrant, dainty white bells on arching stems in late spring. Ideal for light shade.

		RECOMMENDED VARIETIES
JAN	/	
FEB	/	'Albostriata'
MAR	/	'Fortin's Giant'
APR	flowering	'Flore Pleno'
MAY	flowering	'Prolificans'
JUN	/	*Convallaria majalis rosea*
JULY	/	
AUG	/	
SEPT	/	
OCT	plant	
NOV	plant	
DEC	plant	

CONDITIONS

Aspect Prefers to grow in partial shade; ideal under deciduous trees.

Site A good ground cover plant; also suitable for mixed beds and borders. Soil should be free draining but moisture retentive, containing large amounts of decayed organic matter.

GROWING METHOD

Planting The pips are planted in late autumn about 2.5cm (1in) deep and 10cm (4in) apart. Congested clumps can be divided in autumn or winter.

Feeding In early winter apply a generous mulch of decayed manure or compost, or pile on the decaying leaves of deciduous trees. Keep soil moist throughout the growing season, giving a thorough soaking when necessary.

Problems Few problems are encountered but poor drainage may rot the root system.

FLOWERING

Season Flowers appear from mid-spring

Cutting This lovely cut flower perfumes a whole room. Pull the stems from the plant. It is traditional to use the foliage to wrap around the bunch.

AFTER FLOWERING

Requirements If possible, leave the plants undisturbed for several years. If clumps are extremely dense and flowering poor, lift and divide sections during autumn or early winter.

CRINUM
Swamp lily

LIGHT PERFUME is an added reason to grow these pretty pink crinums. They are a good choice for a sheltered border.

VERY TALL STEMS carry the white flowers of Crinum x powellii *well clear of the leaves so that the blooms are always well displayed.*

FEATURES

There are over 100 species of crinum, but *C. x powellii* and the more tender *C. moorei* are the two most commonly grown. Both bear large, scented, lily-like flowers in pale pink or white on stems up to 1m (3ft) high; plants have long, strap-shaped, light-green leaves. The flowers appear from middle to late summer and sometimes into autumn.

The bulbs can grow very large indeed, up to 15cm (6in) or more across, and can be very weighty. In time very large clumps are formed and they require considerable physical effort to lift and divide. Crinums need a sheltered position to do well. In cool areas they can also be grown quite successfully in containers which can be moved under cover in autumn.

CRINUM AT A GLANCE

Large, scented, lily-like flowers in late summer and autumn. This plant needs a sheltered, sunny position to thrive.

Month		RECOMMENDED VARIETIES
JAN	/	
FEB	/	*Crinum* x *powellii:*
MAR	/	'Album'
APR	plant	'Roseum'
MAY	plant	
JUN	/	*Crinum moorei*
JULY	/	
AUG	flowering	
SEPT	flowering	*Crinum bulbispermum:*
OCT	/	'Album'
NOV	/	
DEC	/	

CONDITIONS

Aspect Grow crinum in a sunny, south-facing, sheltered position. *C. moorei* is best grown in a pot in a conservatory.

Site Suitable for borders or as a specimen plant in a container on a patio or similar. Soil must be free draining but moisture retentive.

GROWING METHOD

Planting Plant in spring, which is also the best time to divide existing clumps. *C. x powellii* should have the neck of the bulb above soil level, while *C. moorei* should be planted with the nose of the bulb at the level of the soil.

Feeding Balanced fertiliser may be applied as new growth starts in spring. Keep the soil moist while the plants are in growth. Water plants in containers regularly.

Problems Not generally susceptible to disease or pests but snails love to eat the foliage and flowers.

FLOWERING

Season Flowers appear during summer and into the autumn months.

Cutting It is possible to cut blooms for the house but they last longer on the plant.

AFTER FLOWERING

Requirements Cut off the flowering stalk once the flowers are over. Protect the crowns with a mulch of peat over winter, or move plants under cover. Disturb established plants as little as possible.

CROCOSMIA
Montbretia

THE VIBRANT COLOUR of crocosmia flowers gives great decorative value but is matched by vigorous growth that may need to be controlled.

THE CLEAR, GOLDEN YELLOW flowers of 'Citronella' make a pleasant change from the intense orange-reds of other varieties.

FEATURES

Also known as montbretia, some types of crocosmia are extremely vigorous and can become invasive in warm areas. It will often survive in old, neglected gardens where virtually everything else has disappeared. The foliage is slender, sword-shaped, and upright or slightly arching. The flowers are carried on double-sided spikes which also arch gracefully, reaching some 60–90cm (2–3ft) tall. Most types have eye-catching bright reddish-orange flowers which open progressively from the base of the spike. In cold areas, plants should be protected with a mulch of dry leaves over winter, and should be planted in a reasonably sheltered position.

CROCOSMIA AT A GLANCE

A vigorous plant with sword-shaped leaves and brightly coloured spikes of flowers through the summer.

		RECOMMENDED VARIETIES
JAN	/	
FEB	/	'Bressingham Blaze'
MAR	plant	'Canary Bird'
APR	plant	'Citronella'
MAY	/	'Emily McKenzie'
JUN	/	'Jackanapes'
JULY	flowering	'Lucifer'
AUG	flowering	'Solfaterre'
SEPT	flowering	
OCT	/	
NOV	/	
DEC	/	

CONDITIONS

Aspect   Grows best in a fully open, sunny position.
Site   Good in beds or borders in well-drained soil.

GROWING METHOD

Planting   Plant corms in spring, 7.5cm (3in) deep and about 15cm (6in) apart. Pot-grown specimens can be planted throughout the spring and summer, even when in flower. It usually becomes necessary to thin out clumps every few years.

Feeding   A balanced fertiliser can be applied in early summer, but feeding is not generally necessary.

Problems   There are no pests or diseases that commonly attack crocosmia.

FLOWERING

Season   There is a long flowering period all through summer. Congested clumps often seem to produce more blooms.

Cutting   Flowers are not suitable for cutting and are better appreciated in the garden.

AFTER FLOWERING

Requirements   Cut off spent flower stems as soon as the blooms have faded to avoid seed setting and plants spreading. Once the leaves have died down, protect the corms with a mulch of straw or dry leaves in all but very warm, sheltered gardens.

CROCUS
Crocus

SAFFRON CROCUS (Crocus sativus) displays branched bright orange stigmas, the source of saffron, the costly spice used in cooking.

CROCUS CHRYSANTHUS 'ARD SCHENK' – one of the most popular species – pushes up white goblet-shaped flowers in spring

FEATURES

There are over 80 species of crocus, mainly late winter and spring flowering, but there are some autumn bloomers, too. Crocus are among the earliest flowers to appear in spring, often pushing their flowers up through the snow. In some species flowers appear some weeks before the leaves. Crocus are mostly native to the countries around the Mediterranean Sea where they usually grow at high altitudes. They do, however, extend as far east as Afghanistan.

Appearance
Crocus foliage is short, rather sparse and looks like a broad-leaf grass. The lovely little goblet-shaped flowers are borne on short stems 6–12cm (2–5in) high. Most are blue, violet, white, yellow or cream but some species have pink flowers. Many have deeper coloured stripes or feathering on the petals.

Uses
Although unsuitable for cutting, these little bulbous plants are one of the greatest delights of the garden. They are often mass planted in garden beds, especially at the front of borders. They can be naturalised in lawns or grouped together under deciduous trees. Crocuses are excellent plants for rock gardens and they make good container plants, being especially suitable for winter and early spring window-boxes. The floral display of some individual species in the garden can be short, but by growing a selection of species you can enjoy these charming flowers over an extended period, from early autumn virtually right through to late spring.

POPULAR SPECIES

Spring
Some of the most popular spring-flowering species are *C. biflorus, C. chrysanthus, C. flavus, C. minimus, C. tommasinianus* and *C. vernus*. Cultivars of a number of these species are available, with the many and varied cultivars of *C. chrysanthus* being especially popular, although each of these species have their admirers. *C. ancyrensis* is particularly early flowering, appearing in January and February.

Autumn
Autumn-flowering species include *C. kotschyanus, C. niveus, C. laevigatus, C. longiflorus, C. nudiflorus, C. sativus* (the saffron crocus), *C. serotinus* (also known as *C. salzmannii*) and *C. speciosus. Crocus sativus* is well known as the source of the costliest of all herbs and spices. Native to temperate Eurasia and widely grown in Mediterranean regions, saffron crocus needs a very specific climate to flourish and is an extremely labour-intensive crop to harvest. Saffron comes only from the stigmas of the flowers and 154,000 flowers are needed to make up a kilogram of pure saffron.

CONDITIONS

Aspect
Prefers an open, sunny position but may be grown in light shade.

Site
Good for rock gardens, raised beds, the fronts of borders or naturalised in grass. Soil must be well drained, preferably containing plenty of well-rotted organic matter.

AUTUMN-BLOOMING Crocus serotinus *here displays its lovely pale lilac flowers and stiff, grass-like foliage. All crocus look best when planted like this, in a random fashion that mimics their natural growth.*

GROWING METHOD

Planting   Plant new corms about 5cm (2in) deep and 5–10cm (2–4in) apart. Spring-flowering varieties should be planted in autumn, from September to November, while autumn-flowering species should be planted in July and August. The corms of some species become quite large over time; lift and plant them further apart as it becomes necessary.

Feeding   Apply a light dressing of balanced fertiliser after flowering, particularly in poor soil conditions. Watering is necessary only if conditions are very dry: however, autumn-flowering types are likely to need watering after planting in summer.

Problems   Few problems are encountered when crocuses are grown in the right aspect and soil. However, birds can sometimes damage flowers. Some birds, particularly sparrows, seem to be attracted by the shape or colour of flowers and can peck them to pieces. If this occurs you will have to place a frame covered in wire netting over the plants.

FLOWERING

Season   Flowering depends on the species; some varieties begin flowering in late winter to very early spring, others slightly later in spring. Autumn-flowering species flower between September and early December, and may overlap with the earliest of the winter-flowering species growing against a warm wall.

Cutting   Crocuses are not good cut flowers although they may last a few days in the vase.

AFTER FLOWERING

Requirements It is essential not to remove crocus leaves before they have yellowed as they are important in building up the corms and, therefore, next season's flowering potential. Plantings may need lifting and dividing every 3–4 years, but they can be left until corms start to push their way to the surface.

CROCUS AT A GLANCE

Low-growing bulbs valuable for their early spring flowers in a range of colours. Good for containers.

		RECOMMENDED VARIETIES
JAN	flowering*	*Crocus chrysanthus:*
FEB	flowering*	'Cream Beauty'
MAR	flowering*	'Ladykiller'
APR	flowering*	'Snow Bunting'
MAY	/	*Crocus tommasinianus:*
JUN	/	'Ruby Giant'
JULY	plant**	*Crocus vernus:*
AUG	plant**	'Little Dorrit'
SEPT	**/ *	'Queen of the Blues'
OCT	**/ *	'Vanguard'
NOV	**/ *	
DEC	flowering **	

* spring flowering species   ** autumn flowering species

CYCLAMEN
Cyclamen

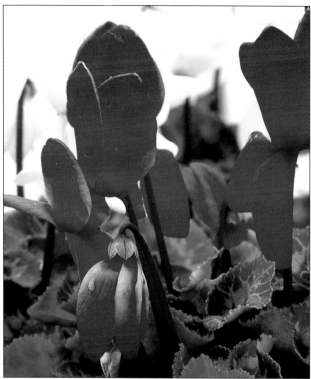

LOVELY UPSWEPT PETALS and a range of glorious colours ensures the lasting popularity of florist's cyclamen as house plants.

NEAPOLITAN CYCLAMEN (Cyclamen hederifolium) provides weeks of flowers and many months of decorative foliage.

FEATURES

Cyclamen form an enchanting group of plants admired for their attractive, mostly marbled foliage and distinctive flowers with swept back, slightly twisted petals. Some, such as the florists' cyclamen, have large showy flowers, while many of the species have small flowers growing only 7.5–10cm (3–4in) high. Some cyclamen flower in autumn or winter, while others flower in late winter and spring. Native to parts of Europe and countries around the Mediterranean, all share a similar need to be kept rather dry during their dormant period. Plants growing in good conditions can remain undisturbed for many years. The original tubers will increase greatly in size and many new plants will come from self-sown seed.

Uses
The smaller varieties make a great show when planted in masses or drifts. The floral display is quite long lasting and even out of flower the marbled leaves make a good groundcover for many months of the year. Cyclamen can be grown in light shade under trees, in rock gardens and in containers.

Potted plants of *C. persicum* hybrids in bloom make excellent house plants and are available from late summer right through the winter. The flowers may be delicately scented. In warm rooms in the home it can be difficult to keep these plants in good condition, and they are sometimes best considered as short-term floral decoration.

TYPES

Florists'
Florists' cyclamen (*C. persicum*) is usually seen as a flowering potted plant for indoor use, and many hybrids are available, including very fragrant miniature types. The beautifully marbled foliage and spectacular flowers make this a very showy plant. The flowers with their swept back petals come in every shade of pink and red, purple, cerise, white and bicolours, and there are some fancy frilled or ruffled kinds. This species came originally from the eastern Mediterranean but many of the modern hybrids grown bear little resemblance to the original species.

Garden
The most easily grown garden cyclamen is the Neapolitan cyclamen (*C. hederifolium*) which flowers during autumn. It can be grown more successfully in warmer areas than most of the other species. *C. hederifolium* has beautifully marbled foliage about 7.5–10cm (3–4in) high, with the small, clear pink flowers held above the leaves. There is also a pure white form of this species. *C. coum* flowers from late winter into spring and has larger, very deep pink flowers on short stems. Again, there is a white form of this species available. *C. repandum*, another spring bloomer, has probably the largest flowers of all the species cyclamens but none of these have flowers that are the size of the florists' cyclamen. The foliage on *C. repandum* is noted for its reddish undersides.

THESE CYCLAMEN COUM are thriving in an alpine-type sink garden: when they are allowed to self-seed, they soon form dense colonies. The marbled leaves are attractive, as well as the dainty, pale pink and purple flowers with their upswept petals.

CONDITIONS

Aspect   The ideal situation for hardy cyclamen is beneath deciduous trees where there is some winter sun but dappled sunlight for the rest of the year. In the home, florists' cyclamen need a cool, bright position.

Site   Hardy cyclamen can be grown on rock gardens, under trees and shrubs, and in borders. The soil must be well drained with a high organic content. Indoors, choose a bright, cool windowsill or a conservatory.

GROWING METHOD

Planting   The flattened tubers (often wrongly referred to as corms) should be planted with their tops just below the soil surface. Plant in late summer and early autumn at about 15cm (6in) intervals. Pot-grown seedlings are easier to establish than dry tubers, and can be obtained from garden centres and specialist nurseries.

Feeding   If soil is poor, a sprinkling of balanced fertiliser can be given when growth begins and again after flowering. Florists' cyclamen should be given high potash liquid fertiliser every 14 days from when the flower buds appear until flowering is over. Water carefully from the base to avoid splashing the top of the tuber; never leave the pots standing in water.

Problems   Florists' cyclamen grown indoors often succumb to overwatering, drying out, and a dry, overwarm atmosphere. Vine weevils are attracted to the tubers and may cause the sudden collapse of the plant: use a soil insecticide if they are caught in time.

CYCLAMEN AT A GLANCE

Characteristic, upswept petals on a mound-forming plant with attractive marbled foliage. Suitable for outdoors or as pot plants.

		RECOMMENDED VARIETIES
JAN	flowering	*Cyclamen cilicium album*
FEB	flowering	*Cyclamen coum album*
MAR	flowering	*Cyclamen hederifolium*
APR	flowering	'Bowles' Apollo'
MAY	/	'Silver Cloud'
JUN	/	*Cyclamen libanoticum*
JULY	plant	*Cyclamen pseudibericum*
AUG	plant	*Cyclamen purpurascens*
SEPT	flowering	*Cyclamen repandum*
OCT	flowering	*Cyclamen persicum*: many
NOV	flowering	hybrids available
DEC	flowering	

FLOWERING

Season   *C. persicum* flowers through winter into spring. *C. hederifolium* has a long flowering period in autumn, while *C. coum* and *C. repandum* flower betwen late winter and spring.

Cutting   Pull flowers from the plant with a rolling motion and cut off the thin base of the stalk.

AFTER FLOWERING

Requirements   Outdoors, leave spent flowering stems to set seed and do not disturb tubers. After flowering, allow pot plants to die down and keep dry over summer. Start into growth again in August.

CYRTANTHUS ELATUS
Vallota, Scarborough lily

SCARLET FLOWERS with a flared, trumpet-like shape make Scarborough lily a most striking plant.

IN WARM AREAS Scarborough lily can be grown outdoors, but it is more reliable as a pot plant for the conservatory or greenhouse.

FEATURES

Still more commonly known under its earlier botanical name of *Vallota*, this old favourite should be more widely grown. Four or more brilliant scarlet, open trumpet-shaped blooms are held on a sturdy stem some 45cm (18in) tall among dark green, strappy leaves. The plant originates from South Africa, and unfortunately, is not hardy enough to try outdoors except in the most favoured, warmest areas of the country. However, it makes a good pot plant for a cool greenhouse or conservatory, or it can be grown indoors on a sunny windowsill. During the summer, the pots can be taken outside to decorate the patio. The Scarborough lily is not difficult to cultivate, and deserves to be more popular.

CYRTANTHUS AT A GLANCE

A tender bulb with large, trumpet-shaped flowers in summer – an excellent house or greenhouse plant. Min 7°C (45°F)

		RECOMMENDED VARIETIES
JAN	/	'Pink Diamond
FEB	/	
MAR	/	
APR	/	
MAY	/	
JUN	plant	
JULY	flowering	
AUG	flowering	
SEPT	flowering	
OCT	/	
NOV	/	
DEC	/	

CONDITIONS

Aspect   Grows best in a bright, sunny position.
Site   Must be grown as a house or greenhouse plant in all but the very warmest areas of the country.

GROWING METHOD

Planting   Plant bulbs in summer with the tip of the bulb just at or above soil level. Set one bulb in a 12.5cm (5in) pot.

Feeding   Apply liquid fertiliser every 14 days as soon as growth appears. Keep the plant well watered throughout the spring and summer, but reduce watering after flowering.

Problems   No specific pest or disease problems are known for this plant.

FLOWERING

Season   Flowers usually appear in mid-summer.
Cutting   Flowers will last well when cut but probably give better decorative value if they are left on the plant.

AFTER FLOWERING

Requirements Cut off the spent flower stems. Reduce watering and allow the compost to dry out completely between late winter and mid-spring. Do not repot for several years as the plants flower best when the pot is crowded. Offsets are produced freely, and some of these may be removed to pot up and grow on to flowering size in two or three years.

DAHLIA
Dahlia

THE RICH PINK of this freshly opened dahlia will gradually lighten to a delicate pale pink as the flower ages.

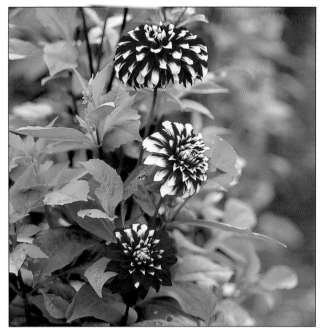

BICOLOURED DAHLIAS have always had a strong following, whether in small, neat forms or dinner-plate sized blooms.

FEATURES

Dahlias come in many different flower forms and in a huge range of colours. Flower sizes range from tiny pompoms less than 5cm (2in) across to huge blooms 30cm (12in) or more wide, and they may be single, double or semi-double. Most home gardeners are content to have a lovely garden display but there are many enthusiasts who grow dahlias for showing.

Dahlias are grouped into different classes according to the shape and form of their flowers, and classes include single, anemone-flowered, collerette, waterlily, decorative, ball, pompon, cactus and semi-cactus. There is also a miscellaneous group for any other type not covered by these classes. Plants can be anywhere from 30cm (12in) to nearly 1.5m (5ft) high. They have a long flowering season from mid to late summer right through the autumn. An ever-increasing range of bedding dahlias can be grown from seed; they form tubers which can be lifted and stored in the normal way in autumn. Bedding varieties can also be bought as growing plants in spring.

CONDITIONS

Aspect
Dahlias prefer full sun all day with protection from strong wind. The taller varieties need staking.

Site
Dahlias are especially suitable for the herbaceous or mixed border, where they provide very welcome late summer colour, but they can also be grown as bedding plants or the smaller varieties can be grown in containers. Soil must be well drained and heavily enriched with manure or compost. Dahlias give best results in rich soil and are heavy feeders.

GROWING METHOD

Planting
The tuberous roots should be planted 10–15cm (4–6in) deep with the neck containing the sprouting eyes pointing up, in middle to late spring. Spacing between plants depends on variety – set small growers about 30cm (12in) apart, very large growers 75–100cm (30–40in) apart. The stakes and labels should be put in at planting time to avoid damaging tubers later.

Dahlia tubers can also be potted up in moist compost in a warm greenhouse in early spring, and cuttings taken of the shoots that arise from the tubers. These can be potted up individually and planted out in the garden once the risk of frost has passed. This is a good way to increase your stock of a particularly prized variety.

Feeding
Once flowering has begun, feed dahlias monthly with balanced fertiliser, or apply a high potash liquid feed every 14 days from when the flower buds begin to form. Applying a mulch of well-rotted garden compost will also help to retain soil moisture. Water well after planting tubers if the soil is dry, but further watering is usually unnecessary until after growth begins. During the growing and flowering season, it is important to make sure the plants never go short of water.

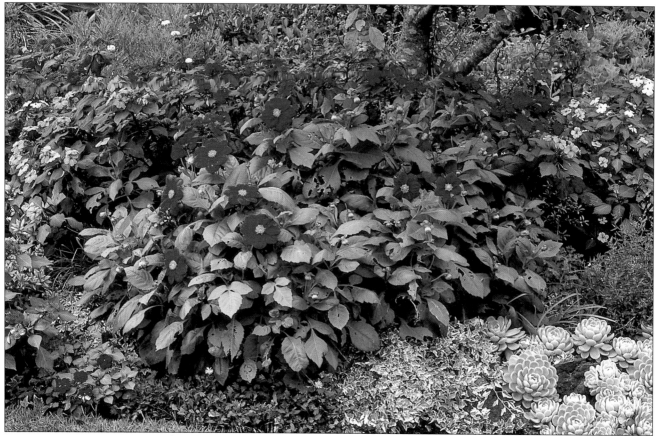

THIS SHRUB-LIKE DAHLIA with its clear, scarlet flowers will give many months of colour in the garden if dead blooms are regularly removed. Dahlias prefer a sunny corner of the garden where they are protected from the wind.

Problems Dahlias are affected by a number of viruses, notably dahlia mosaic virus, which causes yellowing foliage and sometimes stunted plants. It is transmitted by aphids. Spotted wilt virus causes spots and rings on leaves; it is carried by thrips and affects a range of plants. Watch for thrips and aphids early in the season and spray if necessary. Snails love dahlia foliage and flowers so take care to control them. They will climb up into the plant and stay there: if plants are being damaged, search for snails on and under the leaves and destroy them, or use slug bait, making sure it is positioned out of the reach of pets and wildlife. Earwigs can also damage blooms, feeding mainly at night and causing ragged holes in petals or distorted blooms. During the day they can be trapped in upturned pots stuffed with straw positioned on stakes amongst the plants.

FLOWERING

Season The long flowering period lasts from mid-summer to the first frosts. Deadhead the plants regularly to prolong blooming.

Cutting Cut flowers early in the day, remove lower leaves and scald stems for 10–15 seconds before arranging them. They are very long lasting in a vase.

AFTER FLOWERING

Requirements Tubers may survive in the ground for several years if the soil is well drained, but in heavy soils and in cold areas, they are better lifted in late autumn. Cut off the stem 15–20cm (6–8in) above ground, dig up the clump carefully and shake off excess soil. Stand upside down to drain moisture from the stem, then store in a cool, airy place such as a garden shed, lightly covered with sand, soil or peat, for replanting next spring. Tubers can be divided, but make sure that each section has a portion of stem with a visible bud or 'eye' – the tuberous root portion on its own cannot grow.

DAHLIAS AT A GLANCE

Spectacular flowering plants giving four months of bloom. Perfect for cutting, showing or garden decoration.

		RECOMMENDED VARIETIES
JAN	/	
FEB	/	'Bishop of Llandaff'
MAR	/	'Daleko Jupiter'
APR	plant	'Firebird'
MAY	plant	'Glorie van Heemstede'
JUN	/	'Grenidor Pastelle'
JULY	flowering	'Hamari Gold'
AUG	flowering	'Jescot Julie'
SEPT	flowering	'Kenora Fireball'
OCT	flowering	'Wootton Cupid'
NOV	/	
DEC	/	

DIERAMA PULCHERRIMUM
Fairy fishing rods, wandflower

SILKY FLOWERS in two shades of pink are suspended from the fine stems of this lovely South African plant.

AN ESTABLISHED CLUMP of fairy fishing rods produces many flowering stems. It is easy to see how the plant gained its common name.

FEATURES

The slender, arching stems of this highly desirable South African plant carry numerous bell-shaped, pendulous flowers and rise out of stiff, evergreen, sword-shaped leaves. Flowers are a rich silvery pink in the species but there are a number of named cultivars in shades of pink, lilac and even white.

Dense clumps of established plants produce many flowering stems, which sway in the slightest breeze to give a delightful effect. A mass planting creates a striking feature in the garden and it is often placed near water where the reflections increase its impact. Foliage grows 50cm (20in) or so high but the flowering stems may be almost 2m (6ft) long in the right conditions.

DIERAMA AT A GLANCE

A perennial with graceful, slender, arching stems carrying dainty pink blooms in summer. Needs moist soil to thrive.

		RECOMMENDED VARIETIES
JAN	/	
FEB	/	'Blackbird'
MAR	/	'Peregrine'
APR	/	'Slieve Donard Hybrids'
MAY	/	
JUN	/	
JULY	flowering	
AUG	flowering	
SEPT	flowering	
OCT	plant	
NOV	plant	
DEC	/	

CONDITIONS

Aspect Needs full sun all day.
Site Dierama fits well in the herbaceous border. This plant needs well-drained but moisture-retentive, fertile soil containing plenty of well-rotted organic matter such as garden compost or animal manure.

GROWING METHOD

Planting Plant in mid to late autumn, 7.5cm (3in) deep and 30cm (12in) apart.
Feeding A balanced fertiliser can be applied annually in early spring or after flowering. Water during late spring and summer if conditions are dry; the soil should remain moist throughout the growing season.
Problems There are no specific pest or disease problems normally experienced with this plant.

FLOWERING

Season Dierama bears its flowers from mid to late summer.
Cutting Not suitable for cutting.

AFTER FLOWERING

Requirements Once spent, flower stems can be cut off at ground level, although they can be left to set seed if required. Dierama resents root disturbance, so corms should not be lifted unless it is essential. Self-sown seedlings can often be transplanted successfully to increase your stock of this plant.

ERANTHIS
Winter aconite

THE GLOSSY, *golden buttercups of winter aconites, backed by their green leafy ruffs, give a welcome show of colour in early spring.*

FEATURES

The glossy yellow flowers of this tuber are a welcome sight in early spring. They are backed by a bract that forms a green leafy ruff, giving the flowers a Jack-in-the-green appearance. The true winter aconite is *Eranthis hyemalis*, with divided, pale green leaves and buttercup-yellow blooms: it seeds itself freely and soon spreads to form a carpet. *Eranthis* x *tubergenii* is a more vigorous hybrid, with larger, slightly later flowers. Both types grow to around 10cm (4in). Another type is sometimes sold as the Cilicica form of *E. hyemalis*, sometimes as a separate species, *E. cilicica*. It has deep yellow flowers, carried in March, backed by bronzy green, very finely cut foliage, and it grows to 5–7.5cm (2–3in) tall.

ERANTHIS AT A GLANCE

A low-growing plant, welcome for its bright golden-yellow flowers in late winter and early spring.

		RECOMMENDED VARIETIES
JAN	/	
FEB	flowering ✿	'Guinea Gold'
MAR	flowering ✿	
APR	plant ✿ flowering ✿	
MAY	/	
JUN	/	
JULY	/	
AUG	/	
SEPT	plant ✿ (tubers)	
OCT	/	
NOV	/	
DEC	/	

'GUINEA GOLD', *a variety of* Eranthis x tubergenii, *has particularly large, showy flowers.*

CONDITIONS

Aspect   Full sun or light shade are acceptable.

Site   Winter aconites are perfect for rock gardens, the fronts of borders, or beneath deciduous trees, which allow sufficient light to the plants during their spring growing period. They prefer a free-draining but moisture-retentive soil.

GROWING METHOD

Planting   Plant the tubers in September, as soon as they are obtained – if they dry out before planting they are difficult to establish. They should be planted 2.5–5cm (1–2in) deep and 7.5–10cm (3–4in) apart. Eranthis are also available freshly lifted, like snowdrops, in spring, when they establish more readily.

Feeding   Ensure the soil is kept moist during the spring, especially where the plants are growing under trees or shrubs. Supplementary feeding is not normally necessary.

Problems   Plants can become invasive where conditions suit them as they seed freely; otherwise no specific problems are generally experienced.

FLOWERING

Season   Flowers from early February to mid-March or into April.

Cutting   Flowers can be cut just as the buds are opening.

AFTER FLOWERING

Requirements Divide crowded clumps after flowering, replanting the tubers immediately.

EREMURUS
Foxtail lily

THE STATELY yellow spikes of bloom of Eremurus stenophyllus *make this border plant certain to attract attention.*

THE TALLEST member of the group is Eremurus robustus, *its salmon-pink flower spikes towering up to 3m (10ft).*

FEATURES

These stately plants produces tall spires of numerous, star-shaped flowers, giving a very impressive display and making good focal points in the garden. Their foliage is pale green and strap shaped; the flowering spikes tower above the leaves, reaching as much as 3m (10ft) or more in some species. *Eremurus robustus* is among the tallest, with 2.6–3m (8–10ft) spikes of salmon-pink blooms: *E. stenophyllus (E. bungei)* grows to around 1.2m (4ft) with orange-yellow flowers. Probably most popular are some of the hybrid varieties at around 2m (6ft), which bear flowers in a range of yellow, orange and pink shades. Because of their height, plants need a position sheltered from wind.

EREMURUS AT A GLANCE

Tall, stately plants with large, showy flower spikes made up of masses of individual starry flowers.

		RECOMMENDED VARIETIES
JAN	/	
FEB	/	'Shelford Hybrids'
MAR	/	'Ruiter Hybrids'
APR	/	'Moneymaker'
MAY	/	
JUN	flowering	
JULY	flowering	
AUG	/	
SEPT	plant	
OCT	plant	
NOV	/	
DEC	/	

CONDITIONS

Aspect   Eremurus are reasonably hardy but demand a sheltered position in full sun.

Site   These are excellent plants for a place at the back of a border, or plant a foxtail lily at the end of a path for a dramatic focal point. Taller varieties usually need staking. Soil must be rich and fertile but free draining; dig some sharp sand into the site at planting time to improve drainage if necessary.

GROWING METHOD

Planting   In early to mid-autumn, set the roots 10–15cm (4–6in) deep and 60–90cm (2–3ft) apart.

Feeding   Keep the soil moist at all times. A dressing of balanced granular fertiliser can be made over the site in early spring, or high potash liquid feed can be given occasionally during the growing season.

Problems   Normally, no problems are experienced. The young foliage is vulnerable to frost damage and may need protection in early spring when shoots first appear through the soil.

FLOWERING

Season   Flowers in early to mid summer.

Cutting   Flower spikes may be cut as the first flowers are opening. They last well in water.

AFTER FLOWERING

Requirements   Cut down flower stems once the flowers fade. Protect the crowns from frost with a mulch of sand or dry leaves over winter. When overcrowded, divide the clumps in autumn.

ERYTHRONIUM
Dog's tooth violet

'PAGODA' IS DESERVEDLY one of the most popular erythronium hybrids, with its tall stems of graceful, nodding, yellow flowers.

THE DOG'S TOOTH VIOLET, E. dens-canis, has beautifully mottled foliage as well as attractive little rose-pink flowers.

FEATURES

Plants of the dappled shade of woodlands, erythroniums have attractive spring flowers, star-shaped and generally nodding, with swept-back petals.

The dog's tooth violet (named after the shape of its tuber) is *E. dens-canis*, with pinkish purple flowers carried about 15cm (6in) above the attractively mottled leaves. Slightly taller is *Erythronium californicum*, with lush, mid-green, lightly mottled leaves and creamy flowers with bronze backs to the petals. *Erythronium revolutum* grows to 30cm (12in), with white, pink or purple mottled flowers, and has given rise to the popular hybrid 'Pagoda', with 6–10 pendent, graceful yellow flowers on a slender, 40cm (16in) flower stalk.

ERYTHRONIUM AT A GLANCE

Spring-flowering tubers with appealing, pendulous flowers in a range of heights and colours. Many also have attractive foliage.

		RECOMMENDED VARIETIES
JAN	/	
FEB	/	'Pagoda'
MAR	/	'Citronella'
APR	flowering	
MAY	flowering	*Erythronium californicum:*
JUN	/	'White Beauty'
JULY	/	
AUG	plant	*Erythronium dens-canis*
SEPT	plant	'Lilac Wonder'
OCT	/	'Rose Queen'
NOV	/	
DEC	/	

CONDITIONS

Aspect	As a woodland plant, erythronium thrives in cool conditions and light shade.
Site	Excellent under trees or among shrubs in beds and borders or on rock gardens. Fertile, moisture-retentive soil with plenty of organic matter will ensure good growth.

GROWING METHOD

Planting	Plant the tubers in groups, 7.5–15cm (3–6in) deep and 10–15cm (4–6in) apart in late summer or early autumn. Do not let the tubers dry out before planting or you will find it difficult to get the plants established: plant them as soon as possible after purchase.
Feeding	Feeding is not usually necessary. Moist soil is essential during the growing season, but the tubers must never become waterlogged. Water carefully during dry spells.
Problems	No specific pest or disease problems are usually experienced with this plant. Plants resent disturbance and may be difficult to re-establish if lifted and replanted.

FLOWERING

Season	Flowers in mid spring.
Cutting	The taller species can be cut successfully when the buds have opened.

AFTER FLOWERING

Requirements	Disturb the roots as little as possible. If clumps become so overcrowded that flowering is adversely affected, they can be lifted and divided in late summer, replanting the tubers immediately.

EUCOMIS COMOSA
Pineapple lily

THE TUFT on top of the flower spike does resemble a pineapple, but the pretty individual flowers below give a softer impression.

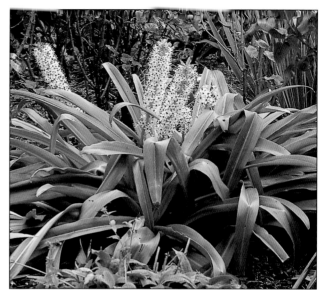

THE ROBUST GROWTH of this clump of pineapple lilies shows that the growing conditions in this spot are ideal.

FEATURES

This South African plant gets its common name from the pineapple-like flower spike with its topknot of tufted leaves. The greenish-white or white flowers, sometimes tinged with pink, are scented and packed tightly on to the spike; their weight can sometimes cause the stem to flop over. The broad, sword-shaped leaves are light green and attractively spotted with purple on the underside. This flower is always of interest, whether in the garden or as a potted plant: blooms are extremely long lasting when cut. Another species in cultivation is *E. bicolor,* with attractive green and purple flowers. Both species grow to about 60cm (24in). Pineapple lily grows from a fleshy bulbous rootstock and is dormant in winter.

EUCOMIS AT A GLANCE

A tall, striking bulb with a pineapple-like flower stem. A sunny, sheltered spot is required.

Jan	/	
Feb	/	
Mar	plant	**RECOMMENDED VARIETIES**
Apr	plant	
May	/	*Eucomis bicolor*
Jun	/	*E. b.* 'Alba'
July	flowering	*E. comosa*
Aug	flowering	*E. pole-evansii*
Sept	/	*E. zambesiaca*
Oct	/	
Nov	/	
Dec	/	

CONDITIONS

Aspect — Prefers full sun but tolerates light shade. Grows best in warm, sheltered areas, but can also be grown in colder gardens if the rootstock is protected or lifted for winter.

Site — Eucomis is good for the middle or back of the flower border. Needs well-drained soil enriched with decayed organic matter before planting time.

GROWING METHOD

Planting — Plant in spring, 5–10cm (2–4in) deep and 20–30cm (8–12in) apart.

Feeding — Apply complete plant food as new growth begins. Mulch around plants in summer with well-decayed compost or manure. Keep the soil moist while the plant is actively growing.

Problems — No specific problems are known.

FLOWERING

Season — Flowers during mid-summer.

Cutting — The pineapple lily is usually enjoyed as a specimen garden plant, but if there are enough blooms, or if the stems are broken by wind, the cut flowers may last for several weeks if the vase water is changed regularly.

AFTER FLOWERING

Requirements — Cut down the flowering stem once the flowers have passed their best. Either dig up the bulb and overwinter in a frost-free place, or in mild districts, mulch the planting area with peat or dry leaves to protect the bulb over winter.

FREESIA
Freesia species and hybrids

THE SPECIES Freesia alba (also known as F. refracta) *is the most heavily scented of all freesias, but can be difficult to find.*

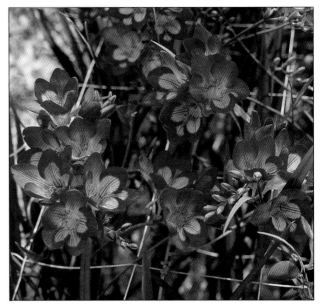

THERE ARE MANY hybrid varieties of freesia, some with strikingly bicoloured flowers like these. Most, but not all, are sweetly scented.

FEATURES

Freesias are loved for their strong perfume as well as their appearance. The wild species have yellow or white flowers and may grow about 30cm (12in) high: modern hybrids grow 45cm (18in) or more high and are available in a wide range of colours which includes blue, mauve, pink, red and purple. However, some of these large-flowered hybrids have no scent. The white-flowered *F. alba* (*F. refracta*) is generally considered to have the best perfume.

For growing outdoors, buy specially prepared freesias and plant them in a sheltered position; they will flower in summer. Other freesias should be planted in containers which are brought into the house and greenhouse in autumn for winter flowering.

FREESIA AT A GLANCE

Fragrant, tubular flowers in a wide range of colours are held on delicate spikes. Grow indoors or outside in a sheltered position.

		RECOMMENDED VARIETIES
JAN	flowering** 🌸	'Diana'
FEB	flowering** 🌸	'Fantasy'
MAR	flowering** 🌸	'Oberon'
APR	plant 🌱*	'Romany'
MAY	/	'White Swan'
JUN	/	'Yellow River'
JULY	plant 🌱**	
AUG	plant 🌱**/flowering 🌸*	
SEPT	flowering* 🌸	
OCT	flowering* 🌸	
NOV	/	
DEC	/	

** indoors   *outdoors

CONDITIONS

Aspect   Freesias prefer full sun but tolerate very light shade for part of the day.

Site   Grow outdoors in a sheltered border. For winter flowers, plant in pots in summer, standing the pots in a sheltered position outside until autumn, then bring them into a cool greenhouse or conservatory to flower. Use free-draining, John Innes or soilless potting compost.

GROWING METHOD

Planting   Outdoors, plant 5cm (2in) deep and the same distance apart in mid-spring. For pot culture, plant 5cm (2in) deep, six to a 12.5cm (5in) pot in July.

Feeding   Apply a high potash liquid fertiliser every 14 days through the growing season. Keep the compost just moist at all times.

Problems   Aphids may attack the flower stems. Control with a contact insecticide when necessary.

FLOWERING

Season   From middle to late winter through to mid-spring indoors, late summer outside.

Cutting   Cut when the lowest flower on the spike is fully open and other buds are well developed.

AFTER FLOWERING

Requirements   Remove spent flower stems. When the foliage dies down, lift corms and store them in dry peat until it is time for replanting.

FRITILLARIA
Crown imperial, snake's head fritillary

THE FLOWERS of snake's head fritillary bear a distinctive, intricately checkered pattern that looks a bit like a game board.

SNAKE'S HEAD FRITILLARY is probably the easiest fritillary to grow and is ideal for damp meadows or woodlands.

FEATURES

The name fritillary comes from the Latin word *fritillus*, meaning 'dice-box', as the checkered patterns on the flowers of some of the species resemble the checkerboards associated with many games played with dice. There are about 100 species of this striking bulbous plant, which is related to the lilies, but only a relatively small number are in general cultivation. The form and colour of the flowers varies considerably from one species to another, and some are fascinating rather than beautiful. The flowers are generally pendent and bell shaped, carried on leafy stems; their height varies considerably, from low-growing rock garden plants such as the 10–15cm (4–6in) *Fritillaria michailovskyi*, to the stately and imposing crown imperials (*F. imperialis*), which can reach well over 1m (3ft) tall. Many fritillaries, especially crown imperial, have a strong 'foxy' scent to them which some people find unpleasant. All parts of the plant, including the bulbs, possess this scent, which can be quite penetrating.

Uses These plants, especially crown imperial, deserve a prominent place in the spring garden. They are sometimes seen taking pride of place in a bulb garden but are more often included in a mixed border planting with other bulbs and perennials. To show them to their best advantage, plant several of the same type together as individual plants will not have the same impact. Those that multiply readily, such as the snake's head fritillary, can be naturalised in dappled shade. All species can be grown in containers but most are easier to grow in the open ground.

Availability Crown imperials and snake's head fritillaries are readily available from garden centres, but some of the other species may have to be obtained from mail order bulb specialists.

TYPES

F. imperialis The best known fritillary is the majestic crown imperial, *F. imperialis*, which has a cluster of orange, yellow or red bell-shaped flowers hanging below a crown of green leaves on a stem 50–100cm (20–39in) high.

F. meleagris The snake's head fritillary or checkered lily, *F. meleagris*, occurs in the wild in meadows throughout Europe and is one of the easiest to cultivate. The checkered flowers occur in shades of green, purple, magenta or white.

Others Among the many other species worth growing are *F. acmopetala*, with bell-shaped green and brown flowers; *F. biflora* 'Martha Roderick', with brown-streaked cream flowers, *F. camschatcensis*, with very deep purple, almost black flowers; *F. michailovskyi*, with yellow-tipped purple bells, *F. pallidiflora*, with soft yellow flowers veined lime-green or burgundy; *F. persica* with deep purple flowers; *F. pontica* with greenish bells; and *F. pyrenaica*, a deep burgundy purple, spotted green outside while the inside is purple-checked green.

CROWN IMPERIAL (Fritillaria imperialis) is an exciting fritillary that takes pride of place in many keen bulb growers' gardens. The 'crown' referred to in the common name is the topknot of leaves from which the bell-shaped flowers are suspended.

CONDITIONS

Aspect   Fritillary grows best in light shade or with morning sun and afternoon shade. Some species take full sun. All are best with protection from strong wind.

Site   Fritillaries can be grown in beds and borders, on rockeries, or in containers, according to species. *F. meleagris* can be naturalised in grass. Soil for fritillaries must be well drained but should contain plenty of well-rotted compost or manure. The area around the plants should be well mulched, too. *F. meleagris* prefers a more moisture-retentive soil than some of the other species.

FRITILLARIA AT A GLANCE

Unusual bulbs in a wide range of sizes and flower forms, with striking, pendent, bell-shaped blooms.

		RECOMMENDED VARIETIES
JAN	/	
FEB	/	
MAR	/	*Fritillaria biflora:*
APR	flowering	'Martha Roderick'
MAY	flowering	
JUN	/	*Fritillaria imperialis:*
JULY	/	'Lutea'
AUG	/	'Rubra Maxima'
SEPT	plant	'Prolifera'
OCT	plant	'The Premier'
NOV	plant	
DEC	/	*Fritillaria persica:*
		'Adiyaman'

GROWING METHOD

Planting   The lily-like bulbs can dry out quickly and should be planted as soon as they are available. Planting depth varies between 5–20cm (2–8in) depending on species. Plant the large bulbs of crown imperials on their sides on a layer of sand so that water does not collect in the hollow centre.

Feeding   Apply a general fertiliser after flowering or a high potash fertiliser in early spring as growth starts. Water in dry spells during the growing season, especially before flowering.

Problems   Bulbs may rot in badly drained soil.

FLOWERING

Season   Flowers appear from mid-spring to early summer.

Cutting   Despite being fairly long-lasting as a cut flower, blooms are rarely used this way because of the unpleasant smell of some flowers. Unfortunately crown imperial is one of these. However, they are so striking in the garden that they are best enjoyed there.

AFTER FLOWERING

Requirements   Once flowers have faded, flowering stems can be cut down, but leave the flowerheads on snake's head fritillaries to set seed. Bulbs are best left undisturbed, but if necessary clumps can be divided in summer and replanted immediately.

GALANTHUS
Snowdrop

TRUE HARBINGERS of spring, snowdrops are among the first bulbs to appear in late winter, often pushing up through the snow.

THE DOUBLE SNOWDROP, Galanthus nivalis 'Flore Pleno', is an easily grown, vigorous and reliable variety.

FEATURES

The snowdrop (*G. nivalis*) is well loved for flowering in late winter while conditions are still very bleak. Most of the dozen or so species flower in late winter to early spring although there is one autumn-flowering species (*G. reginae-olgae*). *G. elwesii* and *G. caucasicus* are also very early bloomers. There are named varieties of several species available. *G. nivalis* grows only 10–12.5cm (4–5in) high, but taller varieties such as *G. elwesii* can grow up to 25cm (10in). The nodding flowers have three long, pure white petals and three shorter ones marked with a bright green horseshoe shape. The dark green foliage may be matt or glossy but is normally shorter than the flowers.

GALANTHUS AT A GLANCE

A small, dainty bulb popular for its late winter and early spring flowers. Very hardy.

JAN flowering	RECOMMENDED VARIETIES
FEB flowering	'Atkinsii'
MAR flowering / plant 'in	'Cordelia'
the green	'Sam Arnott'
APR /	*Galanthus lutescens:*
MAY /	'Magnet'
JUN /	*Galanthus nivalis:*
JULY /	'Flore Pleno'
AUG /	'Lady Elphinstone'
SEPT plant	'Lutescens'
OCT plant	'Pusey Green Tip'
NOV /	'Scharlockii'
DEC flowering	'Viridapicis'

CONDITIONS

Aspect Grows best in shade or dappled sunlight.
Site Ideal for rockeries, the fronts of beds and borders or naturalising under deciduous trees. Soil must contain plenty of decayed organic matter to prevent excessive drying out in summer. Mulching in autumn with old manure, compost or leafmould is beneficial.

GROWING METHOD

Planting Plant bulbs in autumn 8–10cm (3–4in) deep (deeper in light soils) and about the same apart. Do not allow the bulbs to dry out before planting. Snowdrops are much more reliable when transplanted while in growth, after flowering – known as planting 'in the green'. Plants are available from specialist suppliers in late winter or early spring.
Feeding Mulch during autumn with decayed organic matter. Watering is not usually necessary.
Problems No specific problems are known.

FLOWERING

Season Flowering is from winter through to spring, depending on species.
Cutting Flowers can be cut for indoor decoration.

AFTER FLOWERING

Requirements Existing clumps can be lifted, divided and replanted as soon as the flowers have faded. Do not leave the plants out of the soil any longer than necessary.

GLADIOLUS CALLIANTHUS
Acidanthera

EACH BLOOM carries an attractive central, deep purple blotch, and has a slightly uneven, star-like shape.

THE SWEETLY-SCENTED white blooms of acidanthera appear late in the summer, when many other bulbs are over.

FEATURES

Although this plant is now classified as a species of gladiolus, many gardeners still know it better under its previous botanical name of *Acidanthera murielae*. The pure white, slightly drooping blooms have a dark purple central blotch, and are sweetly scented; their similarity to a gladiolus flower is obvious, but they are more delicate and graceful. The leaves are erect and sword shaped, growing to about 60cm (2ft). The flowers – up to a dozen per corm – are held on slender stems above the tips of the leaves, and appear in late summer. This is not a plant for cold, exposed gardens, requiring a warm, sunny position to do well. In cold regions it can be grown successfully as a conservatory or cool greenhouse plant.

G. CALLIANTHUS AT A GLANCE

A late summer flowering plant with attractive, white, scented blooms. Suitable for growing outdoors in mild areas only.

		RECOMMENDED VARIETIES
JAN	/	'Murieliae'
FEB	/	
MAR	plant (indoors) 🖔	
APR	plant (outdoors) 🖔	
MAY	/	
JUN	/	
JULY	/	
AUG	flowering �௹	
SEPT	flowering 🌿	
OCT	/	
NOV	/	
DEC	/	

CONDITIONS

Aspect   These plants require full sun.

Site   Acidantheras can be grown in a sheltered, sunny spot outside in mild areas: otherwise grow the corms in pots in a greenhouse or conservatory, moving the pots on to a sheltered patio or similar position in midsummer. Light, free-draining soil is required. In pots, use soilless or John Innes potting compost.

GROWING METHOD

Planting   Plant in late spring, 10cm (4in) deep and 20–25cm (8–10in) apart.

Feeding   Give an occasional application of high potash liquid fertiliser (such as rose or tomato feed) during the growing season. Pot-grown plants should be fed every 10–14 days. Watering is not necessary for plants in the open ground except in very dry conditions; water pot-grown plants sufficiently to keep the compost just moist.

Problems   Plants may fail to flower in cold, exposed gardens. Corms may rot in heavy, clay soils.

FLOWERING

Season   Flowers in late summer – mid August through September.

Cutting   Pick the stems when the buds are showing white at their tips.

AFTER FLOWERING

Requirements   Allow the foliage to die down, then lift the corms before the first frosts. Allow them to dry, brush off soil and store in dry, cool, frost-free conditions until the following spring.

GLADIOLUS HYBRIDS
Gladiolus, sword lily

THE STRIKING red and yellow flowers of Gladiolus dalenii *ensure this species will always stand out in a crowd.*

A POPULAR hybrid gladiolus, 'Green Woodpecker' is much sought after by flower arrangers because of its unusual colouring.

FEATURES

The gladiolus with which we are most familiar comes from South Africa as do many other species, but other species originated in the Mediterranean regions and western Asia. There are around 300 species of gladiolus, many of them well worth seeking out for your garden, but the modern garden gladiolus is a hybrid. The stiff, sword-shaped leaves surround a flower spike that appears in spring and may be 1m (39in) or more high, but there are dwarf forms less than half this height. Flower spikes carry numerous individual blooms, usually densely packed on the stem and of a characteristic, irregular trumpet shape. The colour range is extensive, including various shades of pink, red, yellow, orange, mauve, maroon, white and green: flowers are often bicoloured.

Special types A great range of species and cultivars is now available to add to the familiar hybrids. Baby gladiolus or painted ladies, *G. x colvillei*, (sometimes wrongly known as *G. nanus*) grows 30–40cm (12–16in) high and comes in a range of colours, including many with contrasting markings. Green and white 'The Bride' is perhaps the best known. Other species worth seeking out include *G. tristis*, with pale creamy yellow flowers; *G. dalenii* (syn. *G. natalensis*) with red to yellow flowers; *G. carneus*, with pink flowers; *G. cardinalis*, with rich red flowers marked in white; and *G. communis byzantinus*, hardy in warmer parts of the country and producing spikes of purple-pink flowers in early summer.

Uses Gladiolus makes a great garden display and cut flower. Dwarf forms make good pot plants.

CONDITIONS

Aspect Grows best in full sun with some shelter from strong wind.

Site Gladiolus can be difficult to place, as their stiff, upright form, which usually requires staking, is very formal. They are often grown in the vegetable garden and used as cut flowers, but with care they can be grown in beds and borders. Soil should be well drained with a high organic content. Dig in well-rotted manure or compost a month or more before planting.

GROWING METHOD

Planting Corms should be planted 7.5–10cm (3–4in) deep and about 15cm (6in) apart. Plant hybrid varieties in spring; stagger planting between March and May to give a succession of blooms. Spring-flowering species should be planted in autumn; in colder areas of the country they are best overwintered in a cool greenhouse.

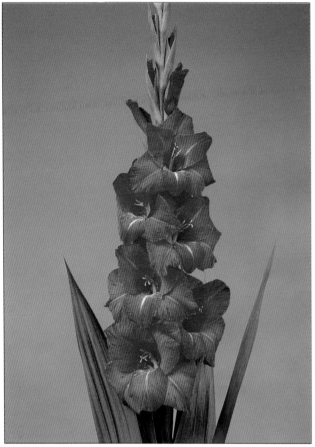

THE GLOWING red blooms of 'Victor Borge' make a brilliant splash of colour in any garden setting.

THE PURE WHITE of these gladiolus appears even whiter against the blue forget-me-nots. The blooms will last longer in cool areas.

Feeding   In soils enriched with organic matter supplementary feeding should not be necessary. In poor soils apply a balanced fertiliser to the soil before planting. In dry weather, water regularly throughout the growing season.

Problems   Thrips, which rasp and suck sap from foliage and flowers, are a perennial problem in some areas. Deep coloured flowers, such as reds and maroons, show their damage more readily than paler ones, with light-coloured flecks spoiling their appearance. The summer months are the worst time for attacks, but the pest may overwinter on corms in store. Dust the corms with a suitable insecticide before storing and again before planting. At planting time, discard corms with dark or soft spots, which may be infected with various fungal rots.

FLOWERING

Season   Hybrids planted in spring will produce flowers through summer into early autumn. Autumn-planted species will flower in early summer.

Cutting   Cut spikes for indoor decoration when the second flower on the spike is opening. Cut the flower stem without removing the leaves if that is possible. Change the water in the vase daily and remove lower blooms from the spike as they fade.

AFTER FLOWERING

Requirements   Lift corms carefully as soon as foliage begins to yellow. Cut off old leaves close to the corm. Dry corms in a warm, airy place for 2–3 weeks and clean them by removing old roots and the outer sheath of corm. To increase your stock of gladiolus, remove the small cormlets from the parent bulb and store them separately. These cormlets should produce full flowering size corms in the second year. If you have had problems with thrips in previous seasons, treat corms with insecticide dust before storing.

GLADIOLUS AT A GLANCE

Popular hybrid varieties have tall, stiff spikes, packed with large, colourful flowers; more delicate species flower in spring.

		RECOMMENDED VARIETIES
JAN	/	
FEB	/	*Hybrids:*
MAR	plant	'Amsterdam'
APR	plant	'Christabel'
MAY	flowering */plant	'Esta Bonita'
JUN	flowering *	'Green Woodpecker'
JULY	flowering	'Hunting Song'
AUG	flowering	'Lady Godiva'
SEPT	flowering plant *	'Victor Borge'
OCT	/	
NOV	/	*G.* x *colvillei:*
DEC	/	'Amanda Mahy'
		'The Bride'

*autumn planted species

GLORIOSA
Glory lily

FLUTED RECURVED PETALS give these flowers an airy, floating effect. Plants grow rapidly in warm, humid conditions.

THESE GLORIOSA LILIES at various stages of development display a fascinating range of colours and shapes.

FEATURES

This climber is always sure to attract attention. It grows from elongated, finger-like tubers, and needs greenhouse or conservatory conditions. A plant will grow up to 2.4m (8ft) in the right conditions, its long, slender stems twining their way through netting or wooden trellis supports by means of tendrils at the tips of the lance-shaped leaves. The unusual lily-like flowers are crimson and yellow, with their wavy-edged petals strongly recurved to show the prominent, curving stamens.

Gloriosa has a long flowering period through summer and autumn and usually gives a spectacular display. It is worth growing in a prominent position where it can be admired, but it is not hardy enough to grow outdoors.

GLORIOSA AT A GLANCE

A greenhouse climber with spectacular summer flowers.
Minimum temperature 10°C (50°F).

JAN	plant	
FEB	plant	
MAR	plant	
APR	/	
MAY	/	
JUN	/	
JULY	flowering	
AUG	flowering	
SEPT	flowering	
OCT	/	
NOV	/	
DEC	/	

RECOMMENDED VARIETIES

Gloriosa superba:
'Rothschildiana'
'Lutea'

CONDITIONS

Aspect   Grow in a greenhouse or conservatory, in bright light but shaded from direct summer sun.

Site   Use either soilless or John Innes potting compost.

GROWING METHOD

Planting   The tubers are planted out in late winter or early spring about 5cm (2in) deep, placing one tuber in a 15cm (6in) pot of moist compost. Take care not to injure the tips of the tubers.

Feeding   Apply high potash liquid fertiliser every 14 days during the growing season. Water sparingly until growth commences, more freely during active growth but never allow the soil to become waterlogged.

Problems   Slugs may attack the tubers, and poor drainage or overwatering will rot them.

FLOWERING

Season   Flowers throughout the summer.
Cutting   Flowers last well when picked.

AFTER FLOWERING

Requirements   Snap off flowers as they fade. Reduce watering when flowering has finished and allow the tubers to dry out for the winter. Store them dry in their pots or in dry peat in a minimum temperature of 10°C (50°F) and replant in spring.

HEDYCHIUM
Ginger lily

LONG RED STAMENS contrast nicely with the clear yellow flowers on this kahili ginger. The flowers have a strong perfume.

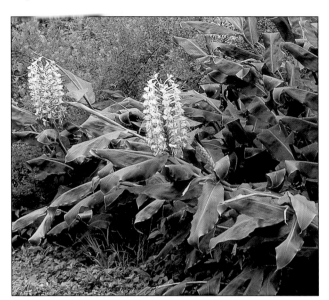

THIS GINGER LILY needs room to spread out and show off its strong lines. It is a useful landscaping plant.

FEATURES

There are over 40 species of ginger lily although not many species are in cultivation. These plants are strong growers, mostly to about 1.8m (6ft), their growth originating from sturdy rhizomes. They can be bedded out in borders for the summer, or grown in tubs as a patio or greenhouse and conservatory plant. Mid-green leaves are lance shaped.

The tall, showy heads of flowers are carried in late summer. White ginger or garland flower, *H. coronarium*, has white and yellow, very fragrant flowers while scarlet or red ginger lily, *H. coccineum*, has faintly scented but most attractive blooms in various shades of red, pink or salmon. Also heavily scented is kahili ginger, *H. gardnerianum*, with large, clear yellow flowers and prominent red stamens.

HEDYCHIUM AT A GLANCE

Large, showy leaves are topped by striking heads of many flowers, often scented. Needs a minimum temperature of 7°C (45°F).

		RECOMMENDED VARIETIES
JAN	/	
FEB	/	*Hedychium coccineum*
MAR	plant 🖏	*aurantiacum*
APR	plant 🖏	*Hedychium coccineum:*
MAY	/	'Tara'
JUN	/	*H. coronarium*
JULY	flowering 🌼	*H. densiflorum:*
AUG	flowering 🌼	'Assam Orange'
SEPT	flowering 🌼	*H. gardnerianum*
OCT	/	
NOV	/	
DEC	/	

CONDITIONS

Aspect Needs a bright, sunny spot.
Site In cold areas, grow in a greenhouse or conservatory; otherwise grow in a sheltered border outside. Rich, moisture-retentive soil is necessary; add well-rotted organic matter before planting time.

GROWING METHOD

Planting Plant in spring, with the tip of the rhizome just buried below the soil surface. Space rhizomes about 60cm (24in) apart.
Feeding A balanced fertiliser can be applied as growth begins in spring. Keep the soil moist throughout the growing season.
Problems There are generally no particular problems experienced.

FLOWERING

Season Flowers in mid to late summer and early autumn.
Cutting Flowers can be cut for indoor decoration but they will last very much longer on the plant.

AFTER FLOWERING

Requirements Cut flower stems down to the ground once the flowers have faded. Lift the rhizomes when the foliage has died down and overwinter in dry peat in a frost-free place, replanting the following spring. Pot plants can be left in their pots over winter. Rhizomes may be divided in spring to increase your stock.

HIPPEASTRUM
Hippeastrum, amaryllis

'APPLE BLOSSOM' is a cultivar with unusual soft, pastel flowers. Most hippeastrums have very strongly coloured flowers in the red range.

BIG, SHOWY TRUMPET FLOWERS on stout stems are a hall-mark of hippeastrums.

FEATURES

There are many species of hippeastrum but the most familiar plants, with their very large, trumpet-shaped flowers, are cultivars or hybrids of a number of species. They are popular winter-flowering house plants; between two and six large flowers are carried on thick stems that are generally over 50cm (20in) high. Blooms appear all the more spectacular because they appear ahead of the leaves or just as the leaves are emerging. There are many cultivars available but most flowers are in various shades of red, pink or white, separately or in combination. Because of the very large size of the bulb it is normal to use only one bulb per 18cm (7in) pot. The bulbs should be allowed to rest during summer if they are to be brought into bloom again.

HIPPEASTRUM AT A GLANCE

A windowsill plant with very showy, large, trumpet-shaped flowers on tall stems in winter and spring. Minimum 13°C.

		RECOMMENDED VARIETIES
JAN	flowering	'Apple Blossom'
FEB	flowering	'Bouquet'
MAR	flowering	'Lady Jane'
APR	flowering	'Lucky Strike'
MAY	/	'Mont Blanc'
JUN	/	'Flower Record'
JULY	/	'Oscar'
AUG	/	'Picotee'
SEPT	/	'Star of Holland'
OCT	plant	
NOV	plant	
DEC	plant	

CONDITIONS

Aspect Needs full sun and bright conditions.
Site Grow as a pot plant in the home or greenhouse. Use soilless potting compost.

GROWING METHOD

Planting Plant with about half to one-third of the bulb above soil level in a pot just large enough to hold the bulb comfortably. Bulbs can be planted any time between October and March. Use 'prepared' bulbs for Christmas and early winter flowers.

Feeding Apply a high potash liquid feed every 10–14 days once the bulb starts into growth. Water sparingly until the bud appears, then more freely until the foliage begins to die down.

Problems No problems usually, but overwatering can cause the bulb to rot.

FLOWERING

Season Showy flowers appear in about eight weeks after planting, between late December and late spring.

Cutting With frequent water changes flowers can last well, but are usually best left on the plant.

AFTER FLOWERING

Requirements Remove spent flower stems, continue to water and feed until foliage starts to yellow and die down. Allow the bulbs to dry off in a cool place, repot in fresh compost and resume watering in autumn to start them into growth.

HYACINTHOIDES
Bluebell

AN ALL-TIME FAVOURITE, clear sky-blue bluebells don't need a lot of attention to produce a lovely display year after year.

NATURALISED UNDER TREES, these Spanish bluebells revel in the moist soil formed from the decaying leaf litter.

FEATURES

This is the ideal bulb for naturalising under deciduous trees or for planting in large drifts in the garden. The delicately scented blue flowers are a great foil for many spring-flowering shrubs which have pink or white flowers: there is a white and a pink form but the blue is undoubtedly the most popular. The botanical names of these plants have undergone several changes in recent years, and they are sometimes listed under endymion and scilla as well as hyacinthoides. The Spanish bluebell (*H. hispanica*) is a little larger, up to 30cm (12in) high, and more upright in growth than the English bluebell (*H. non-scripta*). Bluebells multiply rapidly and can be very invasive. They can also be grown in containers.

HYACINTHOIDES AT A GLANCE

Well-known and loved blue flowers in mid to late spring, ideal for naturalising under deciduous trees.

Month		RECOMMENDED VARIETIES
JAN	/	
FEB	/	*Hyacinthoides hispanica:*
MAR	/	'Danube'
APR	flowering	'Queen of the Pinks'
MAY	flowering	'White City'
JUN	/	
JULY	/	*Hyacinthoides non-scripta:*
AUG	plant	'Pink Form'
SEPT	plant	'White Form'
OCT	plant	
NOV	/	
DEC	/	

CONDITIONS

Aspect
These woodland plants prefer dappled sunlight or places where they receive some morning sun with shade later in the day.

Site
Perfect when naturalised under deciduous trees; bluebells also grow well in borders but don't let them smother delicate plants. A moisture-retentive soil with plenty of organic matter suits them best.

GROWING METHOD

Planting
Plant bulbs 5cm (2in) deep and about 8–10cm (3–4in) apart in late summer or early autumn. The white bulbs are fleshy and brittle; take care not to damage them when planting.

Feeding
Not normally required.

Problems
No specific problems are usually experienced.

FLOWERING

Season
Flowers from middle to late spring, with a long display in cool seasons. Flowers do not last as well if sudden high spring temperatures are experienced.

Cutting
Not suitable for cutting.

AFTER FLOWERING

Requirements
Remove spent flower stems unless you require plants to seed themselves. Keep the soil moist until the foliage dies down. The bulbs are best left undisturbed, but overcrowded clumps can be lifted and divided in late summer and replanted immediately.

HYACINTHUS ORIENTALIS
Hyacinth

WELL-ROUNDED FLOWER SPIKES are characteristic of the fine hyacinth cultivars available today. They make excellent pot plants.

HYACINTHS, with cool white flowers and dark green foliage, combine with a silvery groundcover to make a pretty garden picture.

FEATURES

Sweet-scented hyacinths are favourites in the garden or as potted plants. In the garden they look their best mass planted in blocks of one colour. They are widely grown commercially both for cut flowers and as potted flowering plants. Flower stems may be from 15–30cm (6–12in) high and the colour range includes various shades of blue, pink and rose, plus white, cream and yellow. Individual flowers are densely crowded onto the stem, making a solid-looking flowerhead. Bulbs usually flower best in their first year, the second and subsequent years producing fewer, looser blooms. Some people with sensitive skin can get a reaction from handling hyacinth bulbs, so wear gloves if you think you may be affected.

Types The most popular hyacinths are the so-called Dutch hybrids; many varieties are available from garden centres and mail order bulb suppliers. Blues range from deep violet to pale china blue: the rose range includes deep rosy red, salmon and light pink. As well as white varieties, there are those with cream and clear yellow flowers. Some varieties have flowers with a lighter eye or a deeper coloured stripe on the petals, giving a two-tone effect. Roman hyacinths – *H. orientalis albulus* – have smaller flowers loosely arranged on the stems: Multiflora varieties have been treated so that they produce several loosely packed flower spikes from each bulb, and have a delicate appearance which makes them ideal for growing in pots.
Cynthella hyacinths are miniatures growing to about 15cm (6in), usually sold in colour mixtures.

CONDITIONS

Aspect Does well in sun or partial shade but does not like heavy shade.
Site Grow hyacinths in pots and bowls indoors; pots and tubs outside and in flower borders. Soil must be well drained.

GROWING METHOD

Planting Plant bulbs 15cm (6in) deep and 20cm (8in) apart in early to mid-autumn. Apply compost or rotted manure as a mulch after planting.
Feeding Apply a balanced general fertiliser after flowering. Watering is not usually necessary in beds and borders, but bulbs in containers must be kept just moist during the growing season.
Problems Hyacinths are not generally susceptible to pest and disease problems, though bulbs will rot if soil conditions are too wet. Forced bulbs indoors often fail to flower if they have not had the correct cold, dark period after planting.

FLOWERING

Season Flowers appear from late winter to mid-spring. 'Prepared' bulbs should be used for Christmas flowering, and must be planted in September.
Cutting Blooms may be cut for the vase where they will last about a week if the water is changed daily.

AFTER FLOWERING

Requirements Remove spent flower stems and continue to water and feed the plants until the foliage starts to yellow and die down.

BLUE AND WHITE are always an effective combination, a proposition amply demonstrated by this formal garden in which deep violet-blue hyacinths stud a bed of white pansies. Although they are often grown in pots, hyacinths are at their most beautiful in a setting such as this.

POTTED HYACINTHS

Features   Potted hyacinths in bloom make a lovely cut flower substitute and are ideal as gifts. They can be grown to flower in midwinter when their colour and fragrance are most welcome.

Outdoors   If growing hyacinths outdoors choose a container at least 15cm (6in) deep so that you can place a layer of potting compost in the base of the pot before planting. Bury the bulbs 10cm (4in) below the surface of the compost. Water to moisten the compost thoroughly after planting and place the pot where it will receive sun for at least half a day. Don't water again until the compost is feeling dry or until the shoots appear. When the flower buds are showing colour, move the pots indoors. Once blooms have faded, cut off spent stems and water as needed until the foliage dies down.

Indoors   If growing hyacinths indoors, choose a container 10–15cm (4–6in) deep but plant the bulbs just below the surface of the compost. (In pots without drainage holes, bulb fibre can be used intead of compost.) Water after planting, allow to drain and then transfer the pot to a cool, dark position. The pots can be placed inside a black plastic bag and put into a shed, cold frame or similar place with a temperature of around 4ºC (40ºF). Check from time to time to see if shoots have emerged. Once shoots emerge (this usually takes around 10–12 weeks) and reach 2.5–5cm (1–2in) in height, bring the pot into the light, gradually increasing the amount of light as the shoots green up. As buds appear, give them as much sunlight as possible.

In glass   Hyacinths can also be grown in a glass or ceramic container that has a narrow neck. Sometimes you can buy a purpose-built container, usually plastic, that has the top cut into segments so that the bulb sits neatly on it. Fill the container with water to just below the rim. Choose a good-sized bulb, then rest it on top of the rim of the container so that the base of the bulb is in water. Place the container in a cool, dark place and leave it there until large numbers of roots have formed and the flower bud is starting to emerge, when they can be brought into the light. These bulbs are unlikely to regrow and may be discarded after flowering.

HYACINTHUS AT A GLANCE

Sweetly scented, densely packed flower spikes, ideal for growing indoors or outside. Frost hardy.

		RECOMMENDED VARIETIES
JAN	flowering	'Amsterdam'
FEB	flowering	'Anna Marie'
MAR	flowering	'Blue Giant'
APR	flowering	'City of Haarlem'
MAY	/	'Delft Blue'
JUN	/	'Gipsy Queen'
JULY	/	'Jan Bos'
AUG	/	'L'Innocence'
SEPT	plant	'Lord Balfour'
OCT	plant	'Mont Blanc'
NOV	/	'Queen of the Pinks'
DEC	flowering	

1.

2.

4.

5.

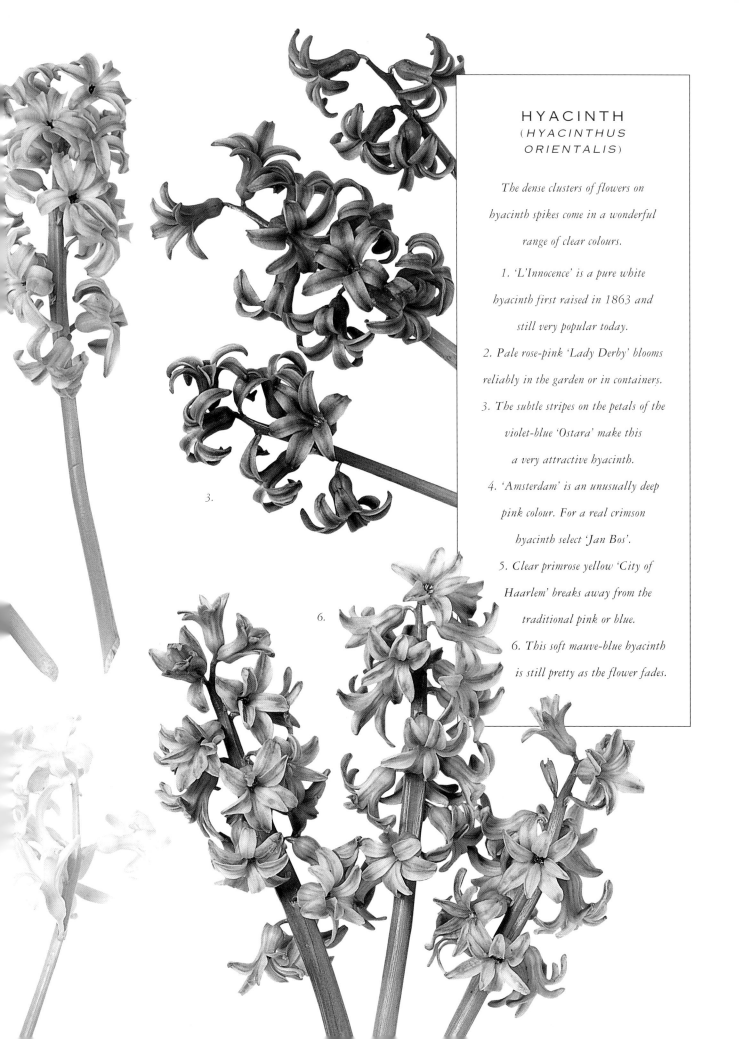

HYACINTH
(*HYACINTHUS ORIENTALIS*)

The dense clusters of flowers on hyacinth spikes come in a wonderful range of clear colours.

1. 'L'Innocence' is a pure white hyacinth first raised in 1863 and still very popular today.

2. Pale rose-pink 'Lady Derby' blooms reliably in the garden or in containers.

3. The subtle stripes on the petals of the violet-blue 'Ostara' make this a very attractive hyacinth.

4. 'Amsterdam' is an unusually deep pink colour. For a real crimson hyacinth select 'Jan Bos'.

5. Clear primrose yellow 'City of Haarlem' breaks away from the traditional pink or blue.

6. This soft mauve-blue hyacinth is still pretty as the flower fades.

3.

6.

HYMENOCALLIS
Spider lily, Peruvian daffodil

THE WHITE *or cream flowers of spider lilies are something like an exotic daffodil, with an attractive fragrance.*

HYMENOCALLIS CAN *be grown outside in reasonably sheltered gardens, but the bulbs should be lifted in autumn to ensure survival.*

FEATURES

Spider lilies are native to various parts of North and South America. They produce broad, strap-shaped, deep green leaves and fascinating, lightly fragrant flowers which are carried on a stout stem. The flower has a trumpet-shaped central cup with long, narrow, petal-like segments surrounding it; flowers are usually white but can be yellow or cream. Hymenocallis can be grown in a sheltered, sunny position outside, but is often treated as a greenhouse or conservatory plant. All spider lilies can be container grown. *H.* x *festalis, H. narcissiflora* and the cultivar 'Sulphur Queen' are the deciduous varieties most often grown, while the more difficult to find *H. littoralis* and *H. speciosa* are the most popular of the evergreen species. Hymenocallis is sometimes also listed as ismene.

HYMENOCALLIS AT A GLANCE

A rather tender bulb bearing unusual fragrant blooms like exotic daffodils. Can also be grown as a conservatory plant.

		RECOMMENDED VARIETIES
JAN	/	
FEB	/	'Advance'
MAR	plant (indoors)	'Sulphur Queen'
APR	/	
MAY	(outdoors)/flowering	*Hymenocallis* x *festalis:*
JUN	flowering	'Zwanenburg'
JULY	/	
AUG	flowering	
SEPT	/	
OCT	/	
NOV	/	
DEC	/	

CONDITIONS

Aspect	Grows in full sun or light shade with shelter from strong wind.
Site	In sheltered gardens hymenocallis can be grown outside in beds and borders or containers. In cold areas, it is best grown as a greenhouse or conservatory plant. Soil must be free draining. Use soilless potting compost for pots.

GROWING METHOD

Planting	For growing in containers, plant bulbs in spring with the neck of the bulb just below the soil surface, using one of the large bulbs per 15cm (6in) pot. Outdoors, plant in May, burying the bulbs 12.5cm (5in) deep.
Feeding	High potash liquid fertiliser can be applied as buds form. Mulching around plants with well-rotted organic matter also supplies nutrients. Water sparingly until the shoots show, then water regularly through the growing season.
Problems	No specific problems are usually experienced.

FLOWERING

Season	The fragrant spider lilies are produced in early summer indoors, mid to late summer outside.
Cutting	Makes a delightful and unusual cut flower.

AFTER FLOWERING

Requirements	Allow the foliage to die down after flowering; lift outdoor bulbs and store in dry peat in a frost-free place over winter. Leave potted plants dry in their containers over winter and repot the following spring.

IPHEION UNIFLORUM
Spring star flower

SPRING STAR FLOWER is an ideal edging plant for a sunny garden and it can be left undisturbed for several years.

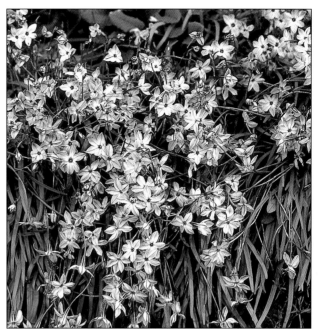

THE SOFT LILAC of the flowers makes spring star flower very versatile as it blends into most garden colour schemes.

FEATURES

This low-growing plant makes an ideal edging but should be planted in large drifts wherever it is grown to produce its best effect. Tolerant of rather tough growing conditions, it is most suitable for filling pockets in a rockery or growing towards the front of a herbaceous border. It also makes a good container plant. It has grey-green, narrow, strappy leaves which smell strongly of onions when crushed; the pale blue, starry, lightly scented flowers are carried on stems 15cm (6in) or so high. There are several varieties available with flowers ranging in colour from white to deep violet-blue.

IPHEION AT A GLANCE

A low-growing bulb with a profusion of starry blue or white flowers in spring.

		RECOMMENDED VARIETIES
JAN	/	
FEB	/	'Album'
MAR	flowering	'Alberto Castello'
APR	flowering	'Froyle Mill'
MAY	flowering	'Rolf Fiedler'
JUN	/	'Wisley Blue'
JULY	/	
AUG	/	
SEPT	plant	
OCT	plant	
NOV	/	
DEC	/	

CONDITIONS

Aspect   Grows best in full sun but tolerates light shade for part of the day.

Site   Good for a rockery, border or container. Ipheion needs well-drained soil. It will grow on fairly poor soils but growth will be better on soils enriched with organic matter.

GROWING METHOD

Planting   Plant bulbs 5cm (2in) deep and the same distance apart in autumn.

Feeding   Apply some balanced fertiliser after flowers have finished. Water regularly during dry spells while plants are in leaf and bloom.

Problems   No specific problems are usually experienced with this bulb.

FLOWERING

Season   The starry flowers appear from early spring to mid-spring.

Cutting   Flowers are too short to cut for all but a miniature vase but they may last a few days in water.

AFTER FLOWERING

Requirements   Shear off spent flower stems and remove the old foliage once it has died down. If clumps become overcrowded and fail to flower well, they can be lifted in autumn, divided, and replanted immediately.

IRIS – BULBOUS TYPES
Irises

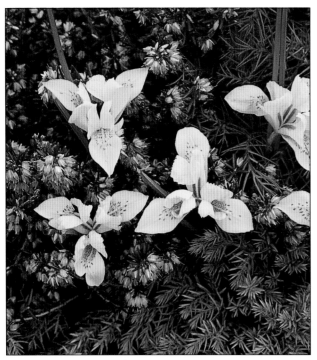

THE LOW-GROWING flowers of Iris danfordiae *appear very early in the year – usually February or March.*

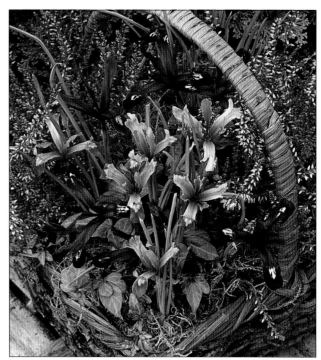

SEVERAL DIFFERENT cultivars of Iris reticulata *are available, in varying shades of blue with yellow markings.*

FEATURES

There are many species of these irises, which have true bulbs as storage organs, unlike the creeping rhizomes of their larger cousins. The leaves are not arranged in the typical fan of sword shapes like rhizomatous irises, but are usually narrow and lance shaped, or rolled. The flowers have the typical iris form with six petals, three inner ones (standards), and three outer ones (falls). The falls are often brightly marked or veined. Many species and varieties are blue with yellow markings on the falls; some types are yellow with brown or green speckling on the falls and others are white with yellow markings. The blue varieties come in many shades, from deep violet and purple through to pale China blue.

Many bulbous irises are early-flowering dwarf forms suitable for growing on rockeries or at the front of beds: they also excellent for shallow pots ('pans') in the greenhouse or alpine house. Other types are taller and flower in summer; they are valuable for herbaceous and mixed borders, and are particularly good for cutting for flower arrangements. There are also some spring-flowering irises which are far less commonly grown than the other groups.

POPULAR SPECIES

Bulbous irises can be split into three main groups: Reticulata irises, Xiphium irises and Juno irises.

Reticulata These irises have bulbs with a netted tunic around them which gives them their group name. They are dwarf, growing to around 15cm (6in) high, and the flowers appear early in the year, usually in February and March. *I. danfordiae* has lightly fragrant flowers whose yellow petals are speckled with greenish brown. *I. reticulata* also has fragrant flowers: the petals are thinner than those of *I. danfordiae* and are blue or purple with yellow markings. Several different cultivars are available. The flowers of *I. histriodes* and its cultivars are larger and have short stems; they are deep to light blue, with dark blue, white and yellow markings. The flowers open before the leaves reach their full height.

Xiphium This group of summer-flowering irises is popular and easily grown. It consists of Dutch irises, flowering in early summer, in white, yellow or blue with contrasting markings; English irises, flowering in early to mid-summer in shades of white, blue or purple; and Spanish irises, flowering in mid-summer in various shades of white, blue, purple and yellow.

Juno The Juno irises are not as well-known as the other bulbous types, probably because they are more difficult to grow well. The group includes *I. bucharica*, bearing yellow or white flowers with yellow falls, and *I. graeberiana*, which has lavender flowers with a white crest on the falls. These two are among the easiest Juno irises to grow: others include *I. fosteriana*, *I. magnifica* and *I. rosenbachiana*, which do best in an alpine house.

WHEN EXAMINED closely, the lightly fragrant flowers of Iris danfordiae *can been seen to have attractive freckling in the throat.*

'KATHERINE HODGKIN', a cultivar of Iris histrioides, *is perhaps the most sought-after of all the dwarf irises.*

CONDITIONS

Aspect
Site
All bulbous irises like open, sunny, positions. Reticulatas are good for rock gardens, raised beds, or containers: Xiphiums and Junos for sunny, sheltered borders. Soil needs to be well drained; Juno irises require a soil containing plenty of well-rotted organic matter.

GROWING METHOD

Planting
Plant Reticulatas 7.5cm (3in) deep and 10cm (4in) apart. Xiphiums are planted 10–15cm (4–6in) deep and 15cm (6in) apart, and Juno irises are planted 5cm (2in) deep and 20cm (8in) apart, taking care not to damage the brittle, fleshy roots. They are all planted in autumn, in September or October.

Feeding
Supplementary feeding is not normally necessary.

Problems
Bulbs may rot in overwet soil. Bulbous irises in warmer areas of the country may be affected by iris ink disease, causing black streaks on the bulb and yellow blotches on the leaves. Destroy affected bulbs.

FLOWERING

Season
Reticulata irises flower in February and March, Junos in April and May, and Xiphiums in June and July.

Cutting
The Xiphiums make excellent, long-lasting cut flowers.

AFTER FLOWERING

Requirements Remove faded flowers. Most bulbous irises are best left undisturbed for as long as possible; they can be increased by lifting and dividing the bulbs after flowering when necessary. Juno irises should not be divided until the foliage has died down, and must be handled very carefully. Spanish irises of the Xiphium group benefit from being lifted when the foliage has died down and replanted in September; this helps the bulbs to ripen.

BULBOUS IRIS AT A GLANCE

A varied group of plants with colourful flowers in early spring or in summer. Good for a range of situations.

JAN	flowering	
FEB	flowering	
MAR	flowering	
APR	flowering	
MAY	flowering	
JUN	flowering	
JULY	flowering	
AUG	/	
SEPT	plant	
OCT	plant	
NOV	/	
DEC	/	

RECOMMENDED VARIETIES

Reticulata group:
I. *danfordiae*
I. *reticulata* 'Katharine Hodgkin'
I. *histrioides* 'Major'

Xiphium group:
'Bronze Queen'
'Excelsior'
'Ideal'

Juno group:
I. *bucharica*
I. *graeberiana*

IRIS – RHIZOMATOUS TYPES

IRIS WAS THE Greek god of the the rainbow, and this plant is aptly named as there are irises in every colour of the spectrum.

WATER IRIS (Iris pseudoacorus) is a tall grower that needs to be planted in water or permanently wet soil.

FEATURES

Irises comprise a very large plant group of over 200 species. Some grow from bulbs (see the previous two pages): those covered here grow from rhizomes. They have stiff, sword-shaped leaves and carry their colourful flowers on tall, stiff stems in spring and early summer. Iris flowers have six petals; three inner, vertical ones, (standards), and three outer ones, which curve outwards (falls). The colour range is very varied, covering blue, purple, lavender, yellow, rose and white; many of the flowers are bicoloured, and attractively marked. Rhizomatous irises contain several different groups, the most popular of which are bearded, Japanese and Siberian irises. **Bearded irises** have large, very showy flowers with a short, bristly 'beard' on the falls; dwarf cultivars are also available. **Japanese irises** have unusual

RHIZOMATOUS IRIS AT A GLANCE

Stately border plants with fans of sword-shaped leaves and tall, attractively marked flowers in summer.

		RECOMMENDED VARIETIES
JAN	/	
FEB	/	*Bearded irises:*
MAR	/	'Black Swan'
APR	/	'Rocket'
MAY	flowering	'White City'
JUN	flowering	*Siberian irises:*
JULY	flowering	'Sparkling Rose'
AUG	/	'Caesar'
SEPT	plant	'Perry's Blue'
OCT	/	*Japanese irises:*
NOV	/	'Rose Queen'
DEC	/	'Moonlight Waves'

flat-faced flowers, and **Siberian irises** have delicate flowers with finer petals.

CONDITIONS

Aspect   Rhizomatous irises like a position in full sun, but with protection from strong winds.

Site   Excellent plants for the middle to back of a mixed or herbaceous border. Bearded irises like a slightly alkaline, well-drained soil: Japanese and Siberian irises need moisture-retentive, humus-rich loam.

GROWING METHOD

Planting   Usually sold as container-grown plants in growth. Plant shallowly, with the rhizome barely covered, in late summer.

Feeding   Supplementary feeding is rarely necessary. Ensure moisture-loving types are never allowed to dry out during the growing season.

Problems   Slugs and snails can be troublesome. Use covered slug bait where necessary, or hand pick the pests after dark.

FLOWERING

Season   Flowers are carried in early summer.

Cutting   Make lovely cut flowers.

AFTER FLOWERING

Requirements Cut off spent flower stems. Every few years, lift the rhizomes after flowering, cut them into sections each containing a strong, healthy fan of leaves, and replant, discarding the old, woody, worn out portions of rhizome.

IRIS UNGUICULARIS

Winter iris, Algerian iris

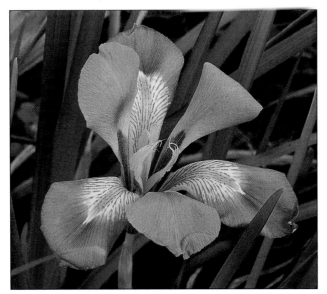

THE FULL BEAUTY *of this iris can be seen in close up. Many iris have fine veining or feathering on their petals.*

A LARGE PATCH *of Algerian iris gives a great lift to the garden in winter. Even if flowers come singly their appearance is still a joy.*

FEATURES

This beardless, rhizomatous iris is different to all others in its group because it flowers throughout the winter. The lovely little fragrant flowers rarely exceed 20cm (8in) in height and may be hidden by the stiff, grassy foliage. They are ideal for cutting and taking indoors, where their sweet scent may be almost overpowering at times.

The flowers of the species are deep lavender with creamy yellow centres deeply veined in violet. There are some cultivars available, including a white form, one or two varieties in particularly deep shades of blue, one in a pale silvery lilac, and a dwarf form. A large single clump of this iris is effective but in the right position it could be mass planted to good effect.

I. UNGUICULARIS AT A GLANCE

A low-growing iris valuable for its sweetly scented flowers which appear throughout the winter.

JAN	flowering	
FEB	flowering	
MAR	plant	
APR	/	
MAY	/	
JUN	/	
JULY	/	
AUG	/	
SEPT	/	
OCT	/	
NOV	flowering	
DEC	flowering	

RECOMMENDED VARIETIES

'Abington Purple'
'Alba'
'Bob Thompson'
'Mary Barnard'
'Oxford Dwarf'
'Walter Butt'

CONDITIONS

Aspect Needs a reasonably sheltered position because of its flowering time. The rhizomes must be exposed to a summer baking if plants are to flower well, so a position in full sun is essential.

Site Grow in beds or borders where it will be able to spread – plants can be invasive. Soil must be well drained. If it is very poor, dig in quantities of well-decayed manure or compost ahead of planting time.

GROWING METHOD

Planting Plant rhizomes in spring with the top at or just below soil level. Container-grown plants in growth can also be bought and planted virtually year round in suitable weather.

Feeding Supplementary feeding is generally unnecessary. Water the plants in spring and autumn if conditions are dry, but do not water in summer.

Problems Slugs and snails will often attack the flowers. Use slug pellets if necessary.

FLOWERING

Season Flowers are produced any time from late autumn through winter.

Cutting The flowers make a lovely indoor decoration.

AFTER FLOWERING

Requirements Cut off spent flowers and tidy up foliage when necessary. Little other attention is required. Crowded plants can be divided in spring.

IXIA
Corn lily

EACH TALL SPIKE of corn lily produces dozens of flowers. These are still producing blooms despite the many fading and falling ones.

PALEST TURQUOISE FLOWERS make this lovely corn lily (Ixia viridiflora) a favourite although its corms are not always easy to buy.

FEATURES

This plant produces starry flowers in a stunning range of colours including white, cream, yellow, orange, red, cerise and magenta. Hybrid varieties are the most popular, but the sought-after *I. viridiflora* has duck-egg blue flowers with a dark centre. The narrow, grass-like foliage may be 30–50cm (12–20in) high while the wiry-stemmed flower spikes stand clear of the leaves. Corn lilies are a great addition to the garden. Being fairly tall they should be planted towards the back of a bed or among other bulbs and perennials. Although colours can be mixed, a better effect is obtained by planting blocks of one colour.

IXIA AT A GLANCE

A rather tender plant with masses of colourful, starry flowers on slender stems.

JAN	/	
FEB	/	
MAR	plant	
APR	plant	
MAY	flowering	
JUN	flowering	
JULY	flowering	
AUG	/	
SEPT	/	
OCT	plant (indoors)	
NOV	/	
DEC	/	

RECOMMENDED VARIETIES

'Blue Bird'
'Mabel'
'Rose Emperor'
'Venus'

CONDITIONS

Aspect Prefers full sun all day but with shelter from strong wind.
Site A good border plant in reasonably mild districts. In colder areas it can be grown in containers on a sheltered patio or in a conservatory. Needs well-drained soil.

GROWING METHOD

Planting Plant corms in the open garden in spring, about 5cm (2in) deep and 8–10cm (3–4in) apart. Plant in pots for the conservatory in autumn.
Fertilising Apply balanced liquid fertiliser in early spring to increase the size of the blooms. In dry conditions, water if necessary in spring once the shoots are growing strongly.
Problems No specific pest or disease problems are usually experienced, though corms may rot in overwet soil.

FLOWERING

Season Flowers from late spring to mid-summer.
Cutting Flowers can be cut for the vase but will probably give better value in the garden.

AFTER FLOWERING

Requirements In all but the mildest gardens, lift the corms once the foliage has died down and store them in a dry place for replanting in spring.

LACHENALIA ALOIDES
Cape cowslip

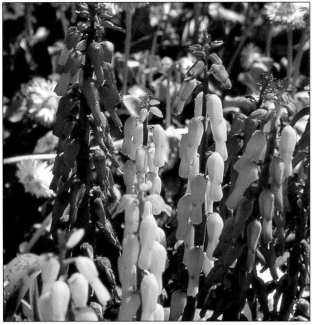

STIFF FLOWER SPIKES of yellow and red tubular bells are the hallmark of Lachenalia aloides.

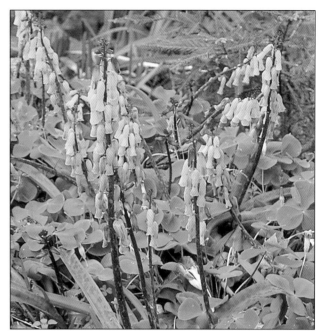

CAPE COWSLIPS need a cool room to grow well. In the right conditions they make excellent winter-flowering house plants.

FEATURES

Also known as 'soldier boys' because of its upright, neat and orderly habit, this bulb is grown as a house plant to produce its colourful bell-like flowers in midwinter. The rather stiff leaves grow to about 15cm (6in) high and are dark green, often spotted with purple. The 20–30cm (8–12in) spikes of 20 or so tubular flowers stand well above the foliage and remain colourful for several weeks. Individual blooms are yellow or orange-red, marked with red, green or purple; they are often a deeper colour in bud, becoming paler as the flowers open. There are several different varieties with subtly varying shades to the flowers.

LACHENALIA AT A GLANCE

A tender bulb grown as a house or greenhouse plant for its spikes of yellow or orange tubular flowers in winter.

JAN	flowering	
FEB	flowering	
MAR	flowering	
APR	/	
MAY	/	
JUN	/	
JULY	/	
AUG	plant	
SEPT	plant	
OCT	/	
NOV	/	
DEC	/	

RECOMMENDED VARIETIES

Lachenalia aloides:
  'Aurea'
  'Lutea'
  'Nelsonii'
  'Quadricolor'

Lachenalia bulbifera:
  'George'

CONDITIONS

Aspect   Needs a very brightly lit spot; will stand direct sun for part of the day.
Site   Grow on a bright windowsill in a cool room, or in a cool greenhouse or conservatory. Lachenalia does not like centrally heated rooms.

GROWING METHOD

Planting   Plant bulbs in late summer or early autumn, growing six to a 12.5cm (5in.) pot. Set them just below the surface of the compost.
Feeding   Apply high potash liquid fertiliser every 14 days or so from when the buds appear. Water regularly while plants are in flower.
Problems   Overwatering or poorly drained compost will cause the bulbs to rot.

FLOWERING

Season   Flowers appear between midwinter and early spring.
Cutting   Not suitable for cutting.

AFTER FLOWERING

Requirements Cut off spent lachenalia flower stems. Continue to water until early summer, then gradually stop watering and allow the pot to dry out until the following autumn, when the bulbs can be shaken out and repotted in fresh compost.

LEUCOJUM
Snowflake

THE WHITE BELLS with their fresh green dots at the end of each petal make Leucojum vernum *particularly evocative of spring.*

PREFERRING SHADE and moist soil, spring snowflake is one of the easiest bulbs to grow. This plant is typical of an established clump.

FEATURES

Easily grown snowflakes have clusters of white, bell-shaped flowers, each petal bearing a bright green spot on its tip. Foliage is a rich, deep green and bulbs multiply readily to form good sized clumps in a few years.

There are three types of snowflake; spring snowflake (*Leucojum vernum*), summer snowflake (*L. aestivum*) and autumn snowflake (*L. autumnale*). The spring snowflake flowers in February or March, while the summer snowflake, despite its name, usually flowers in late spring. Spring snowflake reaches a height of around 20cm (8in); summer snowflake up to 60cm (24in) and autumn snowflake 15cm (6in), with very fine, narrow foliage. The flowers have a passing resemblance to snowdrops, but are easily distinguished by their rounded, bell shape and taller growth.

LEUCOJUM AT A GLANCE

Delicate looking plants with white bells tipped with green, appearing in spring or early autumn. Hardy.

		RECOMMENDED VARIETIES
JAN	/	
FEB	flowering 🌱	*Leucojum aestivum:*
MAR	flowering 🌱	'Gravetye Giant'
APR	flowering 🌱	
MAY	flowering 🌱	*Leucojum autumnale:*
JUN	/	'Cobb's Variety'
JULY	/	'Pulchellum'
AUG	/	
SEPT	plant 🌱 / flower 🌱	*Leucojum vernum:*
OCT	plant 🌱	'Carpathicum'
NOV	/	'Vagneri'
DEC	/	

CONDITIONS

Aspect
Grows well in sun but also happy in shade or in dappled sunlight. Autumn snowflakes prefer an open, sunny position.

Site
Low-growing species are excellent for rock gardens or the front of borders; taller summer snowflakes towards the middle of a border. Spring and summer snowflakes prefer a moisture-retentive soil enriched with organic matter: autumn snowflake needs light, free-draining soil.

GROWING METHOD

Planting
Plant bulbs 7.5cm (3in) deep and 10–20cm (4–8in) apart in late summer or early autumn.

Feeding
An annual mulching with decayed manure or compost after bulbs have died down should provide adequate nutrients. Keep the soil for spring and summer snowflakes moist throughout the growing season.

Problems
No specific problems are known.

FLOWERING

Season
Spring snowflake flowers between midwinter and early spring; summer snowflake mid to late spring and autumn snowflake in September.

Cutting
Best enjoyed in the garden.

AFTER FLOWERING

Requirements
Remove spent flower stems. Divide crowded clumps when the foliage dies down, and replant immediately.

LILIUM
Lily

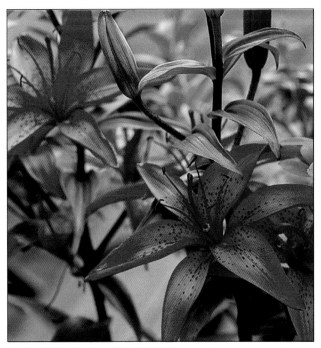

THIS BURNT ORANGE HYBRID shows the characteristic dark spotting in its throat. Lilies make excellent cut flowers.

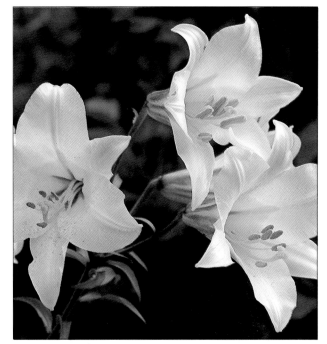

WHITE LILIES are traditionally symbols of purity. Lilium regale is one of the most popular species, and its flowers are very strongly scented.

FEATURES

Lilies are tall, stately plants that carry a number of large, trumpet-shaped blooms on each flowering stem. Flowering stems may be anywhere from about 60cm (2ft) to over 2m (6ft) high. There are 80–90 species of lily and many hundreds of cultivars, so it is difficult to outline their requirements concisely. Lily flowers are often fragrant and the main colour range includes white, yellow, pink, red and orange – many have spotted or streaked petals. A fairly small range of lily bulbs is usually available in garden centres in autumn and these should be planted as soon as possible after their arrival: lily bulbs have no tunic or outer covering and so can dry out unless they are carefully handled. For a greater range of species and hybrids you will need to contact specialist growers and mail order suppliers. Many lily enthusiasts belong to societies devoted to learning more about the enormous range of types available and their cultivation.

Types   Some of the more popular species grown are *L. auratum*, golden-rayed lily, which has white petals with gold bands; *L. candidum*, Madonna lily, which is pure white; *L. martagon*, Turk's cap lily, with fully recurved, dark red petals with dark spots; *L. regale,* the regal lily, with white flowers which have purple backs to the petals and a yellow base; *L. speciosum* which has white petals with a deep pink centre and reddish spots; and *L. tigrinum*, tiger lily, dark orange with black spots and revurving petals. As well as the species, many hybrid varieties are grown, which are classified into a number of groups. Among the most popular are the Asiatic hybrids, short to medium height, with upward-facing flowers produced early in the season; and the Oriental hybrids, which are taller and more refined, with nodding, strongly scented blooms. Asiatic hybrids are ideal for pots and are available pot grown throughout the summer.

CONDITIONS

Aspect   The ideal situation is a sunny position with a little dappled shade during part of the day. They need protection from strong wind.

Site   Lilies grow well when mixed with other plants that will shade their roots, in a bed or border, or in containers. Plant them where their perfume can be appreciated. Soil must be well drained with a high organic content. Dig in copious amounts of well-rotted manure or compost a month or so before planting.

GROWING METHOD

Planting   Plant 10–23cm (4–9in) deep and 23–38cm (9–15in) or so apart in autumn or early spring. Bulbs must not be bruised or allowed to dry out, and they should be planted as soon as possible after purchase. Apply a layer of compost or manure to the soil surface as a mulch after planting. Your stock of lilies can be increased by bulb scales, bulbils or offsets, according to type:

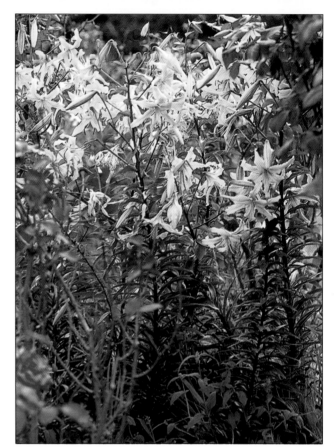

THE GOLDEN-RAYED lily of Japan, Lilium auratum, *carries its attractively speckled, reflexing flowers late in the summer.*

MASSES OF BLOOMS, with buds still to open, make this yellow lily a great asset for the summer garden.

Feeding   If the soil contains plenty of organic matter these plants should not need a lot of feeding. Apply a slow-release granular fertiliser as growth starts and after flowering. Water regularly during dry spells but avoid overwatering which may rot the bulbs.

Problems   Most problems with lilies result from poor cultivation or unsuitable growing conditions. Grey mould (botrytis) can be a problem in cool, humid conditions, especially if plants are overwatered or if air circulation is poor. The small, bright red lily beetle and their larvae can cause a lot of damage in some areas:

control them with a contact insecticide and clear away plant debris in which the adults overwinter.

FLOWERING

Season   Lilies flower some time between early summer and autumn with many flowering in middle to late summer. Flowering time depends on the species and, to some extent, the conditions.

Cutting   Lilies make wonderful and very long lasting cut flowers. Cut them when flowers are just open or all buds are rounded and fully coloured. Don't cut right to the bottom of the stem – retain some leaves on the lower part. Change water frequently and cut off spent flowers from the cluster to allow the other buds to develop fully.

AFTER FLOWERING

Requirements   Remove spent flower stems as they finish blooming. Remove only the flowering stem and leave as much foliage as possible. Don't be in a hurry to cut back yellowing growth too soon: allow the plant to die back naturally and mulch with chipped bark for the winter. Bulbs are best left in the ground for several years. When they are lifted they must be divided and replanted at once, as having no tunic on the bulb means they dry out very quickly. If they can't be planted at once, store them in damp sphagnum moss or peat.

LILIUM AT A GLANCE

Stately plants with trumpet-shaped, usually intensely fragrant flowers on tall spikes.

		RECOMMENDED VARIETIES
JAN	/	
FEB	/	'Apollo'
MAR	/	'Barcelona'
APR	/	'Casa Blanca'
MAY	/	'Corsage'
JUN	flowering	'Enchantment'
JULY	flowering	'Green Dragon'
AUG	flowering /plant	'Mrs R. O. Backhouse'
SEPT	flowering /plant	'Orange Triumph'
OCT	plant	'Shuksan'
NOV	plant	'Tamara'
DEC	/	

MORAEA
Peacock iris, butterfly iris

IT IS EASY to see how this pretty bulb got its common name of peacock iris. Iridescent blue spots are sharply defined against the white petals.

THE FOLIAGE of peacock iris looks unpromising, as it is sparse and grass-like, but the 'floating' flowers are worth waiting for.

FEATURES

Of the 120 species of *Moraea*, most come from South Africa with others native to tropical Africa and Madagascar. Few are in cultivation but it is worth seeking out this unusual plant from specialist bulb growers. All grow from corms and some, such as *M. spathulata*, grow only a single leaf, which may be 20–50cm (8–20in) high.

Flowers are like those of irises, with three showy outer petals and three smaller, rather insignificant inner ones. The commonest species is *M. spathulata*, with bright yellow, summer flowers on 60cm (2ft) stems. *Moraea aristata* has white flowers with a large blue blotch at the base of the outer petals, while *M. villosa* bears flowers in a range of colours with a blue blotch on the petals.

Plant peacock iris in groups for the best effect.

MORAEA AT A GLANCE

An uncommon bulb with iris-like flowers, often strikingly marked. Needs a warm, sunny position.

JAN	/	
FEB	/	
MAR	/	
APR	plant	
MAY	/	
JUN	flowering	
JULY	flowering	
AUG	flowering	
SEPT	/	
OCT	/	
NOV	/	
DEC	/	

RECOMMENDED SPECIES

Moraea aristata
M. bellendenii
M. gawleri
M. spathulata

CONDITIONS

Aspect Moraea needs full sun all day.

Site A warm, sunny and sheltered position is necessary. This corm needs well-drained soil with plenty of decayed organic matter incorporated into it before planting. Moraea also makes an attractive plant for the conservatory or home when grown in containers. Use John Innes or soilless potting compost.

GROWING METHOD

Planting Plant corms 5cm (2in) deep and 20cm (8in) apart in spring.

Feeding Performance is improved by applying a balanced fertiliser as flower buds appear. Container-grown plants should be liquid fed every three weeks or so through the growing season. Water in dry conditions, but take care not to make the soil too wet or the corms will be liable to rot.

Problems No specific pest or disease problems are known for this plant.

FLOWERING

Season Flowers throughout the summer.

Cutting Not suitable for cutting.

AFTER FLOWERING

Requirements Cut off spent flower stems unless you want to obtain seed from them. In autumn, lift the corms and store them in a dry place over winter, ready for replanting the following spring.

MUSCARI
Grape hyacinth

THE FEATHERY *violet heads of* Muscari comosum *'Plumosum'* *make this showy variety quite different from other grape hyacinths.*

ROYAL BLUE *grape hyacinths here border a garden of daffodils and pop up from among the groundcover of snow-in-summer.*

FEATURES

Vigorous and easy to grow, grape hyacinths have blue flowers of varying intensity. There are several species and named varieties available, including the double 'Blue Spike' and the feathery 'Plumosum'. *Muscari aucheri* (*M. tubergenianum*) is known as 'Oxford and Cambridge' because it has pale blue flowers at the top of the spike and dark blue at the base. Grape hyacinths are a great foil for other bright spring-flowering bulbs such as tulips or ranunculus. Flowers are lightly scented and are carried on a stem about 10–20cm (4–8in) tall. This plant gives the most impact when planted in drifts: in large gardens where there is space it can easily be naturalised in grass or under deciduous trees.

MUSCARI AT A GLANCE

Pretty, easy-to-grow, little bulbs with short spikes of intense blue bells in spring.

		RECOMMENDED VARIETIES
JAN	/	
FEB	/	*Muscari armeniacum:*
MAR	flowering	'Blue Spike'
APR	flowering	'Early Giant'
MAY	flowering	
JUN	/	*Muscari azureum:*
JULY	/	'Album'
AUG	/	
SEPT	plant	*Muscari comosum:*
OCT	plant	'Plumosum'
NOV	/	
DEC	/	

CONDITIONS

Aspect Best in full sun or dappled sunlight such as is found under deciduous trees.

Site Useful on rockeries, in the front of borders and for naturalising under trees, but the plants can be invasive. Muscari needs well-drained soil, preferably with plenty of organic matter incorporated before planting.

GROWING METHOD

Planting Plant the bulbs about 7.5cm (3in) deep and 10cm (4in) apart in late summer or early autumn.

Feeding Supplementary feeding is not normally necessary, but a light sprinkling of general fertiliser after flowering helps to ensure good growth. Watering is not normally necessary unless the weather is exceptionally dry.

Problems No specific problems are known.

FLOWERING

Season Flowers appear in early to mid-spring.

Cutting Although not often used as a cut flower, it lasts in water quite well if picked when half the flowers on the stem are open.

AFTER FLOWERING

Requirements Remove spent flower stems if required. Bulbs can be divided every 3–4 years in autumn, replanting immediately. The foliage appears in the winter, long before the flowers.

NARCISSUS
Daffodil and narcissus

MODERN HYBRID DAFFODILS *come in a wide range of forms, including double-flowered varieties and varieties with split coronas.*

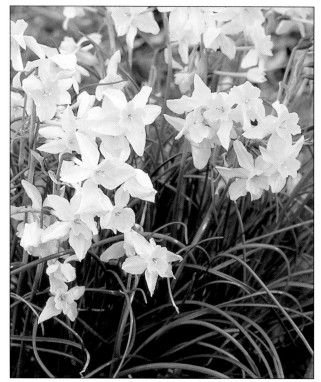

SUNSHINE YELLOW, *this group of smaller growing daffodil cultivars lights up the late winter garden.*

FEATURES

Daffodils are probably the best known and most widely grown of all bulbs and to many they are the true indicator of spring. They look wonderful mass planted in the garden or naturalised in grass, but they also make great pot plants and excellent cut flowers. The best-known colour is yellow, but there are also flowers in shades of white, cream, orange and pink. The trumpet, or cup, is often a different colour to the petals and may be bicoloured. There are many species and cultivars and the genus *Narcissus* has been divided into 12 different groups, depending on the form and size of the flowers. The height varies from 7.5–50cm (3–20in), depending on variety.

Trumpet   The trumpet (cup) is at least as long as the petals, and there is one flower per stem.

Large cupped   Cup is shorter than, but at least one-third of, the length of the petals. One flower per stem.

Small cupped   The cup is less than one-third of the length of the petals; flowers usually carried singly.

Double   Double or semi-double flowers carried single or in small groups. The whole flower may be double, or just the cup.

Triandrus   Two to six pendant flowers with reflexed petals per stem.

Cyclamineus   Slightly pendant flowers with long trumpets and strongly reflexed petals, usually one per stem.

Jonquilla   Several flowers per stem, with short cups. Sweetly scented.

Tazetta   Half hardy. Very fragrant flowers in clusters of 10 or more per stem. Early flowering.

Poeticus   Small red or orange cup and broad white petals, usually one or two per stem. Often strongly fragrant. Late flowering.

Wild   A varied group containing the species and natural varieties found in the wild.

Split cupped   The cup is split to varying degrees for at least one-third to half its length.

Miscellaneous   Hybrids which do not fit into any of the other divisions.

CONDITIONS

Aspect   These bulbs grow best in a sunny spot or under deciduous trees where they will receive sun in the early spring.

Site   Grow narcissi in beds and borders, on rockeries, or in containers for the patio or in the home. Soil must be well drained, ideally with some well-rotted organic matter dug in a month or so before planting.

GROWING METHOD

Planting   Planting depth will vary greatly according to the size of the bulb. Plant so that the nose is covered to twice the height of the bulb, in September or October. Plant as early as possible for the best results.

DAFFODILS

There are many daffodil cultivars with wonderful variety in form and colour. Yellow is most common colour but some have white or pinkish petals or cups.

1. 'Flower Record' displays the characteristics of N. poeticus, *which is in its breeding.*

2. Bright, clear yellow 'Meeting' is a fine example of modern double daffodils.

3. 'E. E. Morbey', dating from the 1930s, has a particularly pretty centre to its orange cup.

4. 'Ice Follies' has white petals. The flared lemon cup fades as it ages.

5. Simplicity of form and white purity make 'Mount Hood' a classic variety.

6. Reddish-orange inner petals on double-flowered 'Tahiti' make it a very showy addition to the garden.

7. The yellow and white centre of 'White Lion' demonstrates another style of double daffodil.

8. Soft, pretty 'Mrs Oscar Ronalds' has a long pink cup and white petals.

9. 'King Alfred', raised about 1890, is possibly the most widely grown of all yellow daffodils.

THE ESSENCE OF SPRING BEAUTY is captured in this drift of mixed daffodils and delicate white blossom. As the planting has been kept to the edge of the lawn, the grass can be mown while still allowing the bulb foliage to die down naturally.

Feeding   Feed with a balanced fertiliser in early spring. Plants can be given a liquid feed after the flowers have faded. Watering may be necessary in very dry spells, particularly once flowering has finished.

Problems   Basal rot can occur in storage; destroy bulbs with any sign of softening or rot at planting time. Similar symptoms can be caused by stem eelworm; these bulbs should also be destroyed by burning. Narcissus fly lays eggs near the necks of the bulbs; these hatch into larvae that tunnel into the bulb and weaken or destroy it. Bulbs in light shade are less susceptible to attack. Pull soil up round the necks of the bulbs after flowering to discourage egg laying.

FLOWERING

Season   Depending on area and variety, flowers may be carried anywhere from midwinter to early summer. Bulbs indoors may be brought into flower for Christmas or earlier; specially treated bulbs are available to ensure early flowering.

Cutting   This excellent cut flower should last a week with frequent water changes, or with the use of proprietary cut flower additives. For longest vase life pick daffodils when the buds are about to burst open or as soon as they are fully open. Cut, don't pull, the stems as low as possible. Cut off any white section at the base of the stem. Don't mix daffodils with other flowers until they have spent a day in a vase on their own as their slimy sap may reduce the vase life of other blooms.

AFTER FLOWERING

Requirements   Spent flowers should be removed before they set seed. Allow foliage to die down naturally; do not tie the leaves in clumps. Where bulbs are naturalised in grass, do not mow the grass until at least six weeks after the flowers have faded. Premature removal of leaves will have a detrimental effect on growth and flowering the following season.

If drainage is good, bulbs may be left in the ground and clumps can be divided after flowering every three years or so. Bulbs grown indoors in pots can be planted out in the garden after flowering, where they should recover in a season or two.

NARCISSUS AT A GLANCE

Well-known spring-flowering bulbs in a wide variety of flower forms and sizes. Most types are very hardy.

			RECOMMENDED VARIETIES
JAN	flowering	🌱	
FEB	flowering	🌱	'Carlton'
MAR	flowering	🌱	'Cheerfulness'
APR	flowering	🌱	'February Gold'
MAY	flowering	🌱	'Irene Copeland'
JUN	/		'King Alfred'
JULY	/		'Minnow'
AUG	plant	🌿	'Peeping Tom'
SEPT	plant	🌿	'Pipit'
OCT	plant	🌿	'Thalia'
NOV	/		*N. bulbocodium*
DEC	/		*N. canaliculatus*

NERINE
Nerine, Guernsey lily

THE GUERNSEY LILY, Nerine sarniensis, *needs to be grown in a conservatory or greenhouse except in very mild areas.*

TALL AND ELEGANT, these bright pink nerines appear as the summer garden fades away in autumn.

FEATURES

Nerine bowdenii brightens the autumn garden, producing its heads of bright pink flowers before the leaves appear. It is easy to grow and flowers last well when cut. Bulbs should be planted where they can be left undisturbed for several years; they flower best when crowded and after a dry summer. They can also be grown in containers. Flower stems grow 30–45cm (12–18in) high and the deep green, strappy leaves from 20–30cm (8–12in) long. The Guernsey lily (*N. sarniensis*) has bright red flowers, and other species and cultivars of nerines may be red, white, pink or apricot, but only *N. bowdenii* is hardy enough to grow outdoors in this country.

NERINE AT A GLANCE

Heads of funnel-shaped pink flowers appear on leafless stalks in autumn. Needs a warm, sheltered position.

JAN	/	
FEB	sow	🖐
MAR	sow	🖐
APR	plant	🖐
MAY	/	
JUN	/	
JULY	/	
AUG	plant	🖐
SEPT	flowering	🌼
OCT	flowering	🌼
NOV	flowering	🌼
DEC	/	

RECOMMENDED VARIETIES

Nerine bowdenii alba
Nerine bowdenii:
  'Mark Fenwick'
  'Pink Triumph'
  'Wellsii'

N. 'Corusca Major'
N. 'Fothergillii Major'
N. *undulata*

CONDITIONS

Aspect Nerines require full sun and a warm, sheltered spot.

Site A useful plant for borders, especially under the shelter of a south-facing wall. The soil should be free-draining and moderately fertile. In cold areas and with the more tender species, grow bulbs in pots of John Innes potting compost.

GROWING METHOD

Planting Plant in middle to late summer or in mid-spring, 10cm (4in) deep and 15cm (6in) apart. In containers, plant with the neck of the bulb at or just below soil level.

Feeding Can be grown successfully without supplementary fertiliser. However, if you wish, you can give weak liquid fertiliser every couple of weeks once flower buds appear until growth slows down. Water regularly while in active growth but keep the bulbs dry during the dormant period.

Problems No specific problems are known.

FLOWERING

Season Flowers appear during early autumn.

Cutting Nerines last well as cut flowers with frequent water changes.

AFTER FLOWERING

Requirements Cut off spent flower stems. Outdoors, mulch the planting site for winter protection.

POLIANTHES TUBEROSA
Tuberose

'THE PEARL', a double-flowered cultivar, is the variety most often available to home gardeners.

PINK-TINGED BUDS open to the heavy-textured cream flowers, so prized for their characteristic strong perfume.

FEATURES

Tuberose is known for its heavily perfumed flowers – tuberose oil is used in perfume production. A double form known as 'The Pearl' is the most widely grown. It can be grown in a sunny, sheltered border, but is often more reliable when grown as a conservatory or house plant, especially in cooler areas. The scent can more easily be appreciated under cover.

A flower spike 60cm (2ft) or more high appears from the basal leaves in summer and early autumn. The waxy flowers have a heavy texture and are white with a pinkish tinge at the base. Tubers that have bloomed once will not reflower the following season – new tubers must be planted each year.

POLIANTHES AT A GLANCE

Valued for its intensely fragrant, creamy white flowers which are carried on tall spikes in late summer.

		RECOMMENDED VARIETIES
JAN	/	*Polianthes tuberosa:*
FEB	/	'The Pearl'
MAR	plant	
APR	/	
MAY	/	
JUN	/	
JULY	/	
AUG	flowering	
SEPT	flowering	
OCT	flowering	
NOV	/	
DEC	/	

CONDITIONS

Aspect Prefers full sun and shelter from strong wind.
Site Grow in a warm, sheltered border, or in containers for the conservatory, house or greenhouse. Use either John Innes or soilless potting compost.

GROWING METHOD

Planting Plant 5cm (2in) deep, or 2.5cm (1in) deep in containers.
Feeding Once growth appears, liquid feed with a balanced fertiliser every 14 days through the growing season. Water sparingly to start with, but keep the plant moist at all times when in growth.
Problems No particular problems are known.

FLOWERING

Season Flowers should appear during late summer or in early autumn.
Cutting Makes an excellent cut flower. Cut spikes for the vase when two or three of the lower blooms are fully open. Removing spent flowers from the spike as they fade will help to prolong the vase life.

AFTER FLOWERING

Requirements Tubers are usually discarded at the end of the season. Offsets are produced, and these may sometimes be grown on to flower in two years or so, but they are often disappointing.

RANUNCULUS ASIATICUS

Ranunculus, Persian buttercup

TAFFETA-LIKE PETALS are ruffled and folded closely together around the dark eye of this vibrant scarlet ranunculus.

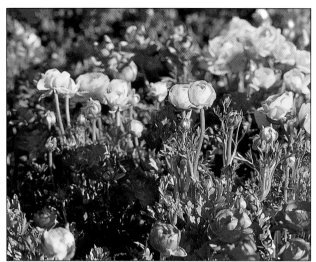

RANUNCULUS FLOWERS last well in a sheltered, sunny garden and close planting will produce a wonderfully colourful display.

FEATURES

One of the brightest and most colourful of all spring-flowering bulbs, ranunculus can be massed in mixed colours or blocks of single colour in the garden or in containers. Left in the ground they may give several seasons, although they are often treated as annuals. However, the woody, oddly shaped tubers can be lifted and stored like other bulbs.

The many-petalled flowers of ranunculus come in bright yellow, cream, white, reds and pinks, and stems of some strains may reach 45cm (18in) in height. Although there are single flowered varieties, double or semi-double types are by far the most popular. They are usually sold as colour mixtures, but separate red and yellow forms are sometimes available from specialist suppliers.

Ranunculus blooms make very good cut flowers, lasting well in the vase.

RANUNCULUS AT A GLANCE

Brightly coloured, many-petalled, poppy-like flowers are carried above attractive ferny foliage in summer.

		RECOMMENDED VARIETIES
JAN	/	
FEB	/	'Red form'
MAR	planting	'Yellow form'
APR	planting	'Accolade'
MAY	/	
JUN	flowering	
JULY	flowering	
AUG	flowering	
SEPT	/	
OCT	/	
NOV	/	
DEC	/	

CONDITIONS

Aspect Prefers full sun all day with shelter from very strong wind.

Site Ideal for beds, borders and containers, where they will make a colourful display. The soil should be well drained, ideally with plenty of compost or manure dug in a month or so before planting.

GROWING METHOD

Planting Plant the woody, tuberous roots 3–5cm (1–2in) deep and about 15cm (6in) apart, with the claws pointing down, in early spring. Soaking the tubers in water for a few hours before planting gets them off to a good start.

Feeding Liquid feed with a balanced fertiliser every two weeks from when the flower buds start to appear. Keep the soil moist once the ferny leaves appear, particularly during bud formation and flowering.

Problems Usually trouble free, though powdery mildew may occur in hot, dry seasons. Spray with a general fungicide if necessary.

FLOWERING

Season Flowers throughout the summer.

Cutting Cut flowers early in the morning and change the water frequently to prolong vase life.

AFTER FLOWERING

Requirements Cut off spent flower stems. When the foliage has died down completely, tubers can be lifted, cleaned and stored in dry peat in a frost-free place until the following spring. After three seasons tubers are best replaced.

SCHIZOSTYLIS COCCINEA
Kaffir lily

THE EXTENDED FLOWER spikes give the appearance of a small gladiolus, thought the individual flowers are more delicate.

THE RICH ROSE flowers of Schizostylis 'Tambara' are displayed to great effect against evergreen shrubs in the late autumn garden.

FEATURES

The lovely, scarlet or pink, gladiolus-like flowers of schizostylis add a very welcome splash of colour to autumn borders, coming as they do right at the end of the season. The tall, grassy leaves form a clump from which 60–90cm (2–3ft) spikes of flowers arise, bearing some 8–10 open, star-shaped blooms. There are several named varieties in a range of pink and red shades: 'Major' has large, deep red flowers, 'Viscountess Byng' is a delicate pink, and 'Tambara' is a rich, rosy pink. 'November Cheer' is one of the latest-flowering varieties.

Schizostylis is not suitable for cold, exposed gardens, but grows and spreads rapidly where conditions suit it.

SCHIZOSTYLIS AT A GLANCE

A valuable late autumn-flowering plant for the border, with colourful scarlet or pink, gladiolus-like flower spikes.

		RECOMMENDED VARIETIES
JAN	/	
FEB	/	'Jennifer'
MAR	plant	'Mrs Hegarty'
APR	plant	'November Cheer'
MAY	/	'Sunrise'
JUN	/	'Tambara'
JULY	/	'Viscountess Byng'
AUG	/	
SEPT	flowering	
OCT	flowering	
NOV	flowering	
DEC	/	

CONDITIONS

Aspect A sheltered spot in full sun or light shade suits this plant.

Site Suitable for the middle of the flower border; in cold districts they do well as pot plants in a conservatory or greenhouse. Moisture-retentive, fertile soil is required.

GROWING METHOD

Planting Plant in spring, 5cm (2in) deep and 30cm (12in) apart. Pot-grown plants are available for planting in summer and autumn. Rhizomes can also be planted in 20cm (8in) pots of soilless or John Innes compost in a sheltered position outdoors, being brought into a cool conservatory or greenhouse before the first frosts for flowering inside.

Feeding Keep the soil moist at all times. Feed pot-grown plants with high potash liquid fertiliser every 14 days from early summer until flower buds form.

Problems No specific problems are generally experienced.

FLOWERING

Season Flowers from late September into November.

Cutting The flower spikes are excellent for cutting, lasting well in water. Pick them when the buds start to show colour.

AFTER FLOWERING

Requirements Cut down faded flower stems. Protect the crowns with a mulch of chipped bark, straw or dry leaves over winter. Overcrowded plants can be divided in autumn.

SCILLA
Squill

A STARBURST of bright blue flowers topped with golden stamens makes up the pretty inflorescence of Scilla peruviana, *the Cuban lily.*

THE SIBERIAN SQUILL, Scilla siberica, *makes its appearance in early spring. 'Atrocoerulea' has particularly rich blue flowers.*

FEATURES

The most familiar scillas are the dwarf varieties that flower in early spring. They include *Scilla siberica* (Siberian squill), which has clusters of nodding blue bells about 15cm (6in) high, and *Scilla mischtschenkoana* (*S. tubergeniana*), which has starry, pale blue flowers with a deeper blue stripe on the petals. This species grows only 5–10cm (2–4in) high. *S. bifolia* grows 5–15cm (2–6in), with a spike of 15 or more star-shaped flowers in blue, pink or white. Leaves of all these species are elongated and strap shaped. *Scilla peruviana*, the Cuban lily, is quite different – a tall, early summer-flowering bulb with densely packed, conical heads of purple-blue flowers.

SCILLA AT A GLANCE

Mainly dwarf bulbs with starry or bell-shaped blue or white flowers in early spring.

JAN	/	
FEB	flowering	
MAR	flowering	
APR	flowering	
MAY	flowering	
JUN	flowering	
JULY	/	
AUG	plant	
SEPT	plant	
OCT	plant	
NOV	/	
DEC	/	

RECOMMENDED VARIETIES

Scilla bifolia:
'Rosea'
Scilla siberica:
'Alba'
'Spring Beauty'
Scilla peruviana:
'Alba'
Scilla peruviana elegans
S. p. venusta

CONDITIONS

Aspect   Tolerates full sun but the flowers will have better, longer lasting colour if they are grown in semi-shade.

Site   Grow in beds and borders, in almost any kind of soil as long as it drains well. Soils enriched with organic matter will give better results.

GROWING METHOD

Planting   Plant the bulbs about 5–10cm (2–4in) deep and 15–20cm (6–8in) apart in late summer or early autumn.

Feeding   Apply a balanced fertiliser after flowering in early summer. Water during dry spells before and during the flowering season.

Problems   No specific pest or disease problems are known for this plant.

FLOWERING

Season   The flower spikes appear during late spring and early summer.

Cutting   Flowers can be cut successfully for indoor decoration.

AFTER FLOWERING

Requirements   Faded flower spikes should be cut off just above ground level. Clumps will usually need to be lifted only every 4–5 years unless they are very congested. Divide crowded clumps in late summer, replanting immediately to avoid drying out of the bulbs.

SINNINGIA
Gloxinia

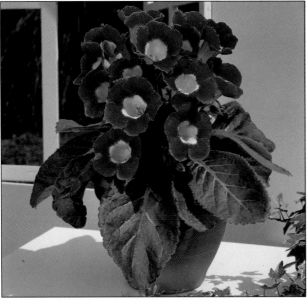

THE VELVETY texture of trumpet-shaped gloxinia flowers shows up well here on the variety 'Blanche de Meru'.

'GREGOR MENDEL' is one of several fully double-flowered varieties. The heavy heads of bloom may need supporting with thin canes.

FEATURES

Gloxinias are tender plants suitable for growing in the home, greenhouse or conservatory, where they will make an impressive, colourful display. The large, showy, brilliantly coloured flowers are trumpet shaped, often with speckled throats. Both flowers and leaves have a velvety feel and appearance: the large leaves are mid-green and oval.

Flowers are produced in abundance on well-grown plants, and are available in many colours, from white through pink and red to deepest blue and violet. The edges of the petals may be ruffled, or frilled with a contrasting colour; there are several double-flowered varieties.

SINNINGIA AT A GLANCE

A showy house plant with colourful, velvety-textured flowers. Minimum temperature 15°C (60°F).

		RECOMMENDED VARIETIES
JAN	plant	'Blanche de Meru'
FEB	plant	'Mont Blanc'
MAR	plant	'Princess Elizabeth'
APR	/	'Gregor Mendel'
MAY	/	
JUN	flowering	
JULY	flowering	
AUG	flowering	
SEPT	/	
OCT	/	
NOV	/	
DEC	/	

CONDITIONS

Aspect   Choose a bright position, but not one which is in direct sun or the foliage will be scorched.

Site   Gloxinias are house plants requiring average warmth; they dislike hot, dry air and benefit from standing on a dish of moist pebbles for increased humidity. Moisture-retentive soilless potting compost should be used.

GROWING METHOD

Planting   Start the tubers off in moist peat or compost in a frost-free position in spring, potting them up individually once the shoots start to grow. Tubers must be planted with the dished side up, level with the surface of the compost – not buried.

Feeding   Apply high potash liquid fertiliser every 14 days during the growing season. Keep the compost only just moist until growth has started, then water more freely. Take care to keep water splashes off the leaves and flowers, and never waterlog the compost.

Problems   Hot, dry air causes the leaves to shrivel and flower buds to fall before opening. Overwatering leads to rotting of the roots.

FLOWERING

Season   Flowers throughout the summer.

Cutting   Not suitable for cutting

AFTER FLOWERING

Requirements   Gradually reduce watering until the leaves have died back, then store the tubers in dry compost in a cool but frost-free place. Repot in fresh potting compost in spring.

SPARAXIS TRICOLOR
Harlequin flower

HARLEQUIN FLOWERS come in a veritable kaleidoscope of colours, with the patterned throat revealing yet more colours and patterns.

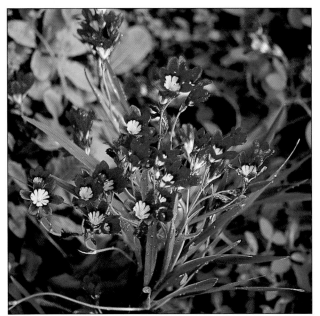

THE STRONG, BRIGHT COLOURS of harlequin flowers are shown to best advantage when they are planted in an open, sunny spot.

FEATURES

This showy, easy-care plant has bright flowers of yellow, red, pink, orange or purple carried on stems that can be anywhere from 15–45cm (6–18in) high. Many of the brightly coloured flowers have a darker purple or deep red area in the centre and a yellow throat. Harlequin flowers hybridise readily, often producing seedlings that have interesting colour variations. These are bulbs that thrive in dry, warm areas of the garden. They look their best when mass planted but can also be grown in containers, where they should be crowded together for best effect. The flowers cut well for indoor decoration. Harlequin flower bulbs increase rapidly by offsets.

SPARAXIS AT A GLANCE

Very brightly coloured, star-shaped flowers are carried on slender stems in early summer. Not suitable for cold, exposed gardens.

Month		RECOMMENDED VARIETIES
JAN	/	Usually supplied as a colour mixture
FEB	/	
MAR	/	
APR	/	
MAY	flowering	
JUN	flowering	
JULY	/	
AUG	/	
SEPT	/	
OCT	/	
NOV	plant	
DEC	/	

CONDITIONS

Aspect Needs full sun all day for best results.
Site Sparaxis needs a sheltered spot in a reasonably mild area to do well; in cold gardens it is best grown in containers under cover. Soil must be well-drained and moderately fertile.

GROWING METHOD

Planting Corms should be planted 7.5cm (3in) deep and 7.5–10cm (3–4in) apart in mid-autumn. Mulch the planting area with chipped bark or leafmould for winter protection.
Feeding In very poor soil apply a balanced fertiliser in early summer after flowering. Mulch the soil in late winter with well-rotted organic matter. In dry seasons, water when the foliage emerges and as buds and flowers develop if necessary.
Problems No specific problems are known.

FLOWERING

Season Flowering should be abundant in late spring and early summer.
Cutting Sparaxis makes a good cut flower for the home and should last well in water.

AFTER FLOWERING

Requirements Allow foliage to die down naturally, then lift the corms and dry them off until it is time to replant in autumn. Any cormlets that have formed can be removed when the corms are lifted and replanted separately.

SPREKELIA FORMOSISSIMA
Jacobean lily

THE SCULPTURED LINES of Jacobean lilies need to be appreciated at close quarters. Growing them in containers is a perfect solution.

THE DARK CRIMSON of the flowers tends to recede into the deep green foliage but still gives a lovely rich glow.

FEATURES

The rich crimson flowers of Jacobean lily are carried singly on stems 30–45cm (12–18in) high and the foliage, which is about the same height, appears with or just before the flowers. This plant is sometimes called the Aztec lily and is in fact native to Mexico where it occurs in open, sunny places, often in poor soil. The unusual shape of the flower gives rise to another common name, orchid amaryllis, and the exotic-looking flower could easily be mistaken for an orchid. Unfortunately it is suitable for gardens in mild areas only; in less favoured climates it must be grown as a greenhouse or conservatory plant. Formerly much more widely grown than it is today, it deserves to become more popular.

SPREKELIA AT A GLANCE

An exotic-looking, rather tender plant which needs greenhouse conditions in cooler areas. Minimum temperature 10°C (45°F).

		RECOMMENDED VARIETIES
JAN	/	Only the straight species is grown – no cultivars or varieties of this plant are available.
FEB	/	
MAR	/	
APR	plant 🖑	
MAY	/	
JUN	flowering 🌿	
JULY	/	
AUG	/	
SEPT	/	
OCT	/	
NOV	/	
DEC	/	

CONDITIONS

Aspect Grows best in full sun with wind protection. Indoors it likes a bright position.

Site Suitable for a sheltered border in mild areas, or containers in a greenhouse or conservatory. Outdoors, soil must be well drained and enriched with compost or manure. Use John Innes potting compost for containers.

GROWING METHOD

Planting Plant bulbs in spring, 5cm (2in) deep and 20cm (8in) apart. In containers, plant with the neck of the bulb just above the compost surface.

Feeding Give a high potash liquid feed every two or three weeks throughout the growing season. Water container plants regularly until the foliage starts to die down.

Problems No specific problems are known.

FLOWERING

Season The showy flowers appear in early summer.

Cutting Can be cut for the vase but usually better enjoyed on the plant.

AFTER FLOWERING

Requirements When the leaves die down, lift outdoor bulbs and keep them in a cool, dry place. For container-grown plants, allow the compost to dry out when the leaves die down, then keep the bulb dry in its pot until spring when watering will start it into growth again.

STERNBERGIA LUTEA
Autumn daffodil, lily-of-the-field

MOST SCHOLARS *today believe* Sternbergia lutea *is the plant referred to in the Bible as 'the lily of the field'.*

SHORT IN STATURE *but big on impact, lily-of-the-field is one of the most delightful of bulbs, especially so as it blooms in autumn.*

FEATURES

Clear, bright yellow flowers, rather like crocuses, appear on 15cm (6in) stems from their surround of shorter, dark green, strappy leaves. The foliage persists until spring when it dies down to remain dormant until the following autumn. Ideal for the rock garden, these plants also show to advantage when planted in the garden in good-sized groups where they can be left to multiply. This is a bulb that could be naturalised in turf but the area would have to be well marked to avoid cutting off the emerging growth in autumn, and the grass could not be mown for several months. Lily-of-the-field can be grown in containers but they are more successful in the open ground.

STERNBERGIA AT A GLANCE

A crocus-like bulb with flowers appearing in late summer and autumn. Needs very well-drained soil to thrive.

		RECOMMENDED VARIETIES
JAN	/	
FEB	/	*Sternbergia lutea:*
MAR	/	Angustifolia Group
APR	/	
MAY	/	*Sternbergia clusiana*
JUN	/	
JULY	plant 🖐	*Sternbergia sicula*
AUG	plant 🖐	
SEPT	flowering 🌸	
OCT	flowering 🌸	
NOV	/	
DEC	/	

CONDITIONS

Aspect   Prefers full sun: a summer baking of the dormant bulbs is necessary for good flowering in the autumn.

Site   Suitable for a rockery, raised bed, or a sunny, reasonably sheltered border. Very well-drained soil is essential for this plant. Well-rotted organic matter can be dug into the bed ahead of planting.

GROWING METHOD

Planting   Plant bulbs in summer about 12.5cm (5in) deep and the same distance apart.

Feeding   Supplementary fertiliser is generally not needed.

Problems   The main problem encountered is rotting of bulbs due to heavy or poorly drained soil. Improve drainage by incorporating sharp sand into the planting area.

FLOWERING

Season   The small, bright golden flowers appear in autumn.

Cutting   These flowers are not suitable for cutting.

AFTER FLOWERING

Requirements   Ensure the plants are allowed to remain dry once the foliage has died down in early summer. The site may need protection from excessive summer rain with a cloche or similar. Do not disturb established plants unless it is essential.

TRITELEIA
syn *Brodiaea laxa*

'QUEEN FABIOLA' is probably the most widely planted of the triteleias. The paler centre gives definition to the flower form.

BLUE FLOWERS are always a favourite, and the violet-blue, starry flowers of these triteleias fill a sheltered pocket in the garden.

FEATURES

These pretty bulbous plants are native to Oregon and California. There is some confusion over their correct name; they are often listed as brodiaea, with some species as dichelostemma. *T. laxa* is the most popular form. Flower stems may be 45–60cm(18–24in) or so high with the strappy leaves growing to about 30cm (12in). The starry flowers are carried in loose clusters and are pale or violet blue with the most popular cultivar, 'Queen Fabiola', producing deeper violet-blue blooms with a pale centre. The foliage dies back in spring while the plant is in bloom, and the corm remains dormant from mid-summer until winter.

TRITELEIA AT A GLANCE

Dainty clusters of tubular blue blooms are carried on slender stems in mid-summer. Well-drained soil is essential.

		RECOMMENDED VARIETIES
JAN	/	
FEB	/	*Triteleia hyacinthina*
MAR	/	
APR	/	*Triteleia ixioides*
MAY	flowering	
JUN	flowering	*Triteleia laxa:*
JULY	flowering	'Queen Fabiola'
AUG	/	
SEPT	plant	*Triteleia peduncularis*
OCT	/	
NOV	/	
DEC	/	

CONDITIONS

Aspect An open, sunny but sheltered site is necessary.
Site Grow this plant in the flower border or in containers. The soil must be light and very well drained; triteleia cannot stand waterlogging. It can be grown in containers of sandy potting compost where the garden soil is heavy.

GROWING METHOD

Planting Plant corms 7.5–10cm (3–4in) deep and 10–15cm (4–6in) apart in autumn.
Feeding A balanced or high potash fertiliser can be given when the flower buds appear, but normally no feeding is necessary. Plants in containers can be liquid fed fortnightly. Watering is not normally necessary; the soil should be allowed to dry out while the corm is dormant during the summer.
Problems There are no specific pest or disease problems known for this plant.

FLOWERING

Season Flowers appear from early to mid-summer.
Cutting Blooms last particularly well as a cut flower.

AFTER FLOWERING

Requirements Flowering stems can be cut off once they are past their peak, or left to set seed. Plants resent disturbance, so should be left alone once planted.

TULIPA
Tulip

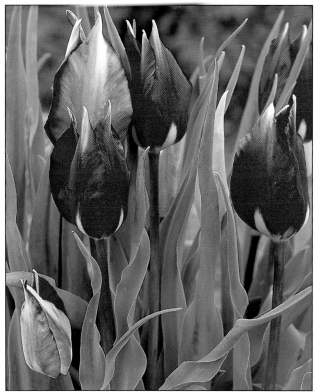

THE POINTED PETALS of these goblet-shaped, bright lipstick-pink tulips will open to form a starry shape.

A NATIVE of Crete, pale pink Tulipa saxatilis needs a sunny, warm position with perfectly drained soil in which to grow.

FEATURES

There are over 100 species of tulips and many hundreds of hybrids. Most modern garden tulips are the result of extensive breeding programmes that began in the late sixteenth century in Europe and are continuing to this day. Tulips were all the rage at that time as more and more species were introduced to Europe from Turkey, Iran and central Asia. Tulip species range in height from about 15–60cm (6–24in) but the greatest number of hybrids are probably in the range of 30–40cm (12–16in). Tulips look their best in mass plantings of one colour but they can, of course, be mixed. They make very good container plants and are delightful cut flowers. Some of the most charming are the dwarf types which do particularly well in rock gardens and are also very suitable for containers.

Tulip bulbs are widely available in garden centres in late summer and early autumn, but to get a wider choice it is often best to obtain catalogues from specialist bulb growers who run mail-order businesses. Many of the species tulips are only available from specialist growers. With careful selection it is possible to have a tulip in flower from early to very late spring.

Like daffodils, tulips are split into a number of divisions according to their flower form and time of flowering.

Single early	Cup-shaped single flowers, up to 40cm (16in) in early to mid-spring.
Double early	Fully double flowers up to 40cm (16in) in early to mid-spring.
Triumph	Conical then rounded, single flowers up to 50cm (20in) in mid to late spring.
Darwin hybrid	Large, single flowers of varying shape, up to 60cm (24in) in mid to late spring.
Single late	Single, blocky or square shaped flowers up to 75cm (30in) in late spring and early summer.
Lily-flowered	Single, waisted flowers with pointed petals, up to 60cm (24in) in late spring.
Fringed	Single flowers with very finely cut petal edges, up to 60cm (24in) in late spring.
Viridiflora	Single flowers with green bands or streaks on the outside, up to 50cm (20in) in late spring.
Rembrandt	Single flowers with a broken pattern of feathering or streaking caused by a virus. Up to 75cm (30in) in late spring.
Parrot	Single flowers with very strongly frilled and curled petals, up to 60cm (24in) in late spring.
Double late	Large, fully double flowers up to 60cm (24in) in late spring.
Kaufmanniana	Single, often bi-coloured flowers of a waterlily shape, up to 25cm (10in) in late spring. Leaves may be mottled.
Fosteriana	Large, single, wide-opening flowers up to 50cm (20in) in early to mid-spring.
Greigii	Large, single flowers up to 35cm (14in) in mid to late spring. Leaves streaked and mottled.
Miscellaneous	Any other species, varieties and hybrids.

1.

2.

3.

6.

7.

TULIPS
(*TULIPA*)

Tulips, with their wide range of forms and colours, are divided into fifteen horticultural groups.

1. From a crimson bud 'Leen van der Mark' opens to reveal a crystalline white centre.

2. A fully opened 'Bokassa Red' shows its deep scarlet petals tipped with gold.

3. 'Judith Lyster', a single late tulip, is rich cream merging to watermelon pink.

4. Goblet-shaped 'Bokassa Rose' is deep rose pink with a yellow centre.

5. 'Kees Nelis' is a bright, two-tone tulip in primary red and yellow.

6. No two parrot tulip flowers are identical as this flamboyant 'Flaming Parrot' proves.

7. 'Princess Victoria' is a heavy-textured tulip that is more weather resistant than some other varieties.

8. 'Angélique', a pale pink ruffled beauty, is best grown in pots so it can be protected from weather.

9. 'Monte Carlo' is a bright gold, fully double tulip with a light scent.

4.

5.

8.

9.

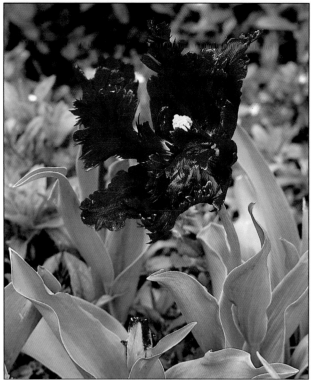

THE BIZARRE FORM of parrot tulips is exemplified by this dark crimson flower. People either love these forms or hate them.

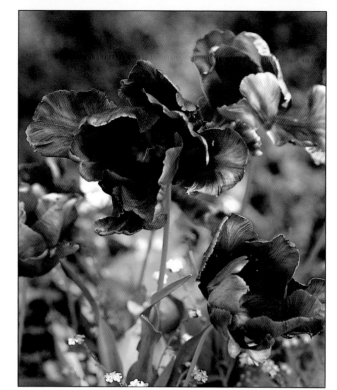

THE BURGUNDY of these full-blown tulips will appeal to lovers of the unusual but they may be hard to incorporate into the garden scheme.

CONDITIONS

Aspect Tulips need full sun for at least half the day, with some wind protection.

Site Grow tulips in beds and borders, on rockeries or in containers. Soil should be well drained with a high organic content. Add lime to acid soils.

GROWING METHOD

Planting Bulbs should be planted in late autumn. Planting depth varies according to the size of the bulbs; usually 15–20cm (6–8in) for the larger types and 10cm (4in) for the smaller species. Space them 10–20cm (4–8in) apart.

Feeding Apply liquid fertiliser as soon as buds appear and again after flowers have faded. Water regularly in dry spells, especially once the buds have appeared.

Problems Tulip breaking virus, causing streaking of the flowers, is carried by aphids. Remove affected plants and keep aphids under control. Tulip fire disease is a type of botrytis or grey mould. It causes small brown spots on flowers and leaves; stems may rot and grey furry growth may develop on the damaged areas. Destroy plants infected with this disease and avoid planting tulips in the same spot for a couple of years. Spraying with a general fungicide may control early infection.

FLOWERING

Season Tulips flower somewhere between late winter and late spring, depending on variety.

Cutting If cutting blooms for the house, choose those that are not fully open and cut them early in the morning. Change vase water frequently.

AFTER FLOWERING

Requirements Remove spent flower stems and dead foliage. Tulips may be left in the ground for two or three years, or the bulbs can be lifted once the foliage has died down, cleaned and stored in a cool, dry, airy place. Dwarf tulips tend to be left in the ground, but other varieties usually perform better if they are lifted and replanted every year. If you do not want to lift them annually, make sure the bulbs are planted deeply.

TULIPA AT A GLANCE

Well-known flowers in a very wide range of colours, sizes and forms, flowering between late winter and late spring.

		RECOMMENDED VARIETIES
JAN	/	
FEB	flowering	'Peach Blossom'
MAR	flowering	'Apeldoorn'
APR	flowering	'Clara Butt'
MAY	flowering	'China Pink'
JUN	/	'Burgundy Lace'
JULY	/	'Spring Green'
AUG	/	'Texas Gold'
SEPT	/	'Angelique'
OCT	/	'Ancilla'
NOV	plant	*Tulipa fosteriana*
DEC	plant	*Tulipa greigii*
		Tulipa tarda

WATSONIA
Watsonia

THE VIVID PINK FLOWERS *of watsonia make it a most desirable plant, but it is not commonly grown in gardens.*

WATSONIA FLOWERS *are displayed well clear of the upright foliage and so are ideal for planting at the back of a border.*

FEATURES

Although there are many species of watsonias in the wild, they are not commonly cultivated plants. The stiff, sword-shaped leaves are similar to those of a gladiolus: the flower spike, growing to over 1m (39in) carries tubular flowers in various shades of pink and red, violet, magenta and orange. Watsonia is ideally placed towards the back of a mixed border. In all but very warm districts the corms should be lifted in autumn and stored in a dry place until it is time to replant them the following spring.

The usual species offered is *W. pillansii* (also known as *W. beatricis*), which has orange-red flowers. The slightly more tender *W. borbonica* (*W. pyrimidata*) has rich pink blooms.

WATSONIA AT A GLANCE

An unusual bulb with tall, stately spikes of pink or red flowers, good for the back of the border.

		RECOMMENDED VARIETIES
JAN	/	
FEB	/	
MAR	/	
APR	plant	'Stanford Scarlet'
MAY	plant	'Tresco Dwarf Pink'
JUN	flowering	
JULY	flowering	*Watsonia borbonica ardernei*
AUG	flowering	
SEPT	plant (warm areas)	
OCT	/	
NOV	/	
DEC	/	

CONDITIONS

Aspect Watsonia needs full sun and a warm, sheltered position.

Site These tall plants are good for the back of a border. They can also be grown in pots in a greenhouse. Any well-drained soil is acceptable, but growth will be better if well-rotted organic matter is dug in before planting.

GROWING METHOD

Planting Plant corms in mid to late spring, 10cm (4in) deep and 30cm (12in) apart. In warm, sheltered areas, corms can be planted in autumn 15cm (6in) deep and mulched with chipped bark or dry leaves.

Feeding Apply a long-acting fertiliser such as general fertiliser in early summer. Watering is necessary only in prolonged dry spells.

Problems Generally free from pest or disease problems when grown in an open, sunny position.

FLOWERING

Season Watsonias flower in mid-summer.

Cutting Stems can be cut for the vase. They should last well with frequent water changes.

AFTER FLOWERING

Requirements Except in very warm areas, lift the corms after flowering, when the foliage starts to die down. Clean them, allow them to dry, and store in a cool, airy place until the following spring.

ZANTEDESCHIA
Arum lily, calla lily

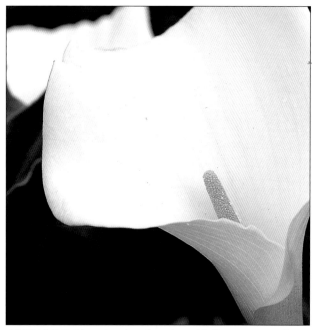

ARUM LILIES have long been favourites with flower arrangers for their texture and sculptural shape which adds form to an arrangement.

PURE WHITE FLOWERS and decorative leaves are features of arum, which are quite easy to grow in a variety of conditions.

FEATURES

Arum lilies are greatly prized for their beautiful waxy flowers, pure white with a golden central spadix. The arrow-shaped leaves are deep green, and the whole plant can grow up to 1m (39in) high. Several species are suitable for growing only in a greenhouse or conservatory, but *Z. aethiopica* can be grown outside in reasonably sheltered gardens. It likes moist, boggy conditions, and often grows best beside a pond or water feature: it can be grown as a marginal plant in up to 30cm (12in) of water. *Z. elliottiana*, the golden arum, and *Z. rehmannii*, the pink arum, are good greenhouse or conservatory plants.

ZANTEDESCHIA AT A GLANCE

A rhizomatous plant grown for its beautiful waxy white flower spathes. Needs greenhouse conditions in some areas.

JAN	/	**RECOMMENDED VARIETIES**
FEB	/	*Zantedeschia aethiopica:*
MAR	/	'Crowborough'
APR	plant	'Green Goddess'
MAY	/	
JUN	flowering	
JULY	flowering	
AUG	/	
SEPT	/	
OCT	/	
NOV	/	
DEC	/	

CONDITIONS

Aspect   Can be grown in full sun or light shade. It should be sheltered from strong wind.

Site   *Z. aethiopica* can be grown on the fringe of a pool or in a border in moist, humus-rich soil. Other arum species need rich but free-draining soil and are grown in a greenhouse or conservatory in containers.

GROWING METHOD

Planting   Plant rhizomes 15cm (6in) deep and 45cm (18in) apart in spring.

Feeding   Apply liquid fertiliser as buds appear and continue to feed every 14–21 days while plants are in bloom. Keep the soil moist at all times while the plants are in active growth during spring and summer.

Problems   Leaf spot can cause dark blotches on all parts of the plant and may cause premature leaf drop. It often occurs where conditions are too cool and damp. Destroy affected parts and spray with a suitable fungicide.

FLOWERING

Season   Flowers in early summer.

Cutting   Flowers are excellent for cutting.

AFTER FLOWERING

Requirements   Remove flower stems as they fade. Mulch outdoor plants with dry leaves for winter.

ZEPHYRANTHES

Zephyr lily, rainflower

ZEPHYR LILY shows how even the simplest of flowers can be very beautiful. The green throat and yellow stamens emphasise the purity.

A BROAD BORDER of zephyr lily gives a star-studded performance in the autumn garden.

FEATURES

With its starry white flowers and shiny green, grass-like foliage, zephyr lily is a bulb for mass planting in sheltered gardens. It is quite easy to grow and can remain undisturbed for years where conditions suit it. It can be planted in borders or on a rockery, and it can also be grown very successfully in containers. The crocus-like flowers are carried in late summer or autumn, especially after showers of rain, which accounts for its common name of rainflower.

Zephyranthes candida is the species suitable for growing outdoors in Britain; it generally reaches a height of 20–25cm (8–10in).

Z. grandiflora (also called *Z. rosea*) has lovely rosy pink flowers but is only suitable for cultivation in a greenhouse or conservatory, as is the yellow flowered *Z. citrina*.

ZEPHYRANTHES AT A GLANCE

An attractive, low-growing plant with crocus-like flowers in autumn.

		RECOMMENDED SPECIES
JAN	/	
FEB	/	*Zephyranthes candida*
MAR	/	
APR	plant 🖐	*Z. citrina*
MAY	/	
JUN	flowering 🌸 *	*Z. flavissima*
JULY	flowering 🌸 *	
AUG	/	*Z. grandiflora*
SEPT	flowering 🌸	
OCT	flowering 🌸	
NOV	/	
DEC	/	

* indoors

CONDITIONS

Aspect	Grows best in full sun.
Site	Grow in beds or borders or in pockets in a rockery. Needs a well-drained but moisture-retentive soil. Growth will be improved if soils contain some humus.

GROWING METHOD

Planting	Plant in spring, 5cm (2in) deep and 10cm (4in) apart. For greenhouse cultivation, plant 5 bulbs in a 12.5cm (5in) pot in loam-based potting compost.
Feeding	Supplementary fertiliser is generally not needed. Spread a mulch of well-decayed manure or compost around the bulbs in spring. Water in dry spells during spring, but stop watering when the foliage starts to die down.
Problems	No specific problems are usually experienced with this plant.

FLOWERING

Season	Flowers appear from late summer into autumn, or in mid-summer in the greenhouse.
Cutting	Flowers are not suitable for cutting.

AFTER FLOWERING

Requirements	Spent flower stems may be cut off but this is not essential. No special treatment is needed as the bulbs are best left undisturbed for several years. If you wish to lift and divide a clump this is best done in spring. Greenhouse plants should be allowed to dry out when the leaves die down, and started into growth again by plentiful watering the following spring.

INDEX

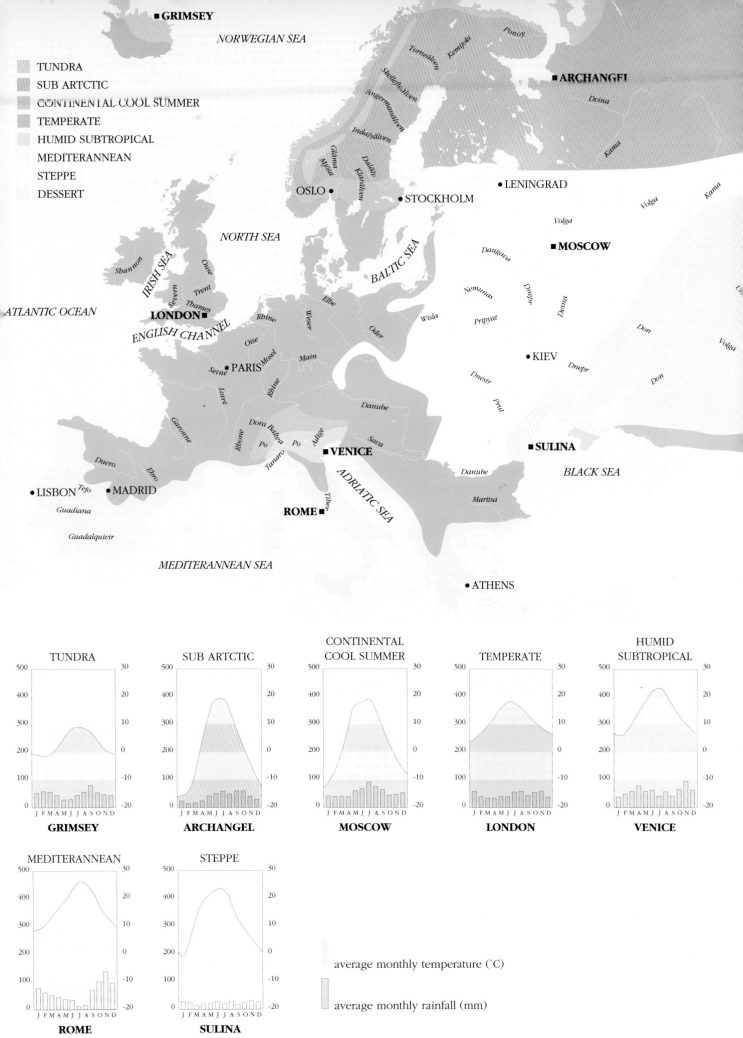

■ GRIMSEY

NORWEGIAN SEA

TUNDRA
SUB ARTCTIC
CONTINENTAL COOL SUMMER
TEMPERATE
HUMID SUBTROPICAL
MEDITERANNEAN
STEPPE
DESSERT

Torneälven *Kemijoki* *Ponoy*

■ ARCHANGEL

Dvina

Skellefteälven

Angermanälven

Kama

Indalsälven

• LENINGRAD

Glama *Dalälv*
Mjösa *Klarälven*

OSLO •

• STOCKHOLM

Volga

■ MOSCOW

NORTH SEA

BALTIC SEA

Daugava

Shannon

IRISH SEA *Oise*

Dnepr

ATLANTIC OCEAN

Severn *Trent*
Thames

LONDON ■

ENGLISH CHANNEL

Rhine

Elbe

Weser

Oder

Wisla

Nemunas

Pripyat

Desna

Don

Volga

Oise

Seine PARIS • *Mosel*
Rhine

Main

• KIEV

Dnepr

Loire

Garonne

Rhone

Dora Baltea

Danube

Dnestr

Prut

Don

Po *Po* *Adige*

Sava

■ SULINA

Duero

Tanaro

■ VENICE

Danube

BLACK SEA

• LISBON *Tejo* • MADRID

Ebro

Maritsa

ROME ■ *Tiber*

ADRIATIC SEA

Guadiana

Guadalquivir

MEDITERANNEAN SEA

• ATHENS

TUNDRA

GRIMSEY

SUB ARTCTIC

ARCHANGEL

CONTINENTAL COOL SUMMER

MOSCOW

TEMPERATE

LONDON

HUMID SUBTROPICAL

VENICE

MEDITERANNEAN

ROME

STEPPE

SULINA

average monthly temperature (°C)

average monthly rainfall (mm)

First published in 2000 by Merehurst Limited,
Ferry House, 51–57 Lacy Road, Putney, London, SW15 1PR

ISBN 1-85391-956 X

A catalogue record of this book is available from the British Library.

This work is a compilation of:
A Gardener's Guide to Annuals, A Gardener's Guide to Perennials
and A Gardener's Guide to Bulbs (Merehurst Editions)

COMMISSIONING EDITOR: Iain MacGregor
PROJECT EDITOR: Anna Nicholas
JACKET DESIGN: Axis Design
MAP DESIGN: Julian Osbaldstone
PRODUCTION MANAGER: Lucy Byrne
PUBLISHING MANAGER: Fia Fornari
CEO & PUBLISHER: Anne Wilson
UK SALES & MARKETING DIRECTOR: Kathryn Harvey
INTERNATIONAL SALES DIRECTOR: Kevin Lagden
GROUP GENERAL MANAGER: Mark Smith

Colour separation by Colourscan in Singapore
Printed in Hong Kong by Toppan Printing Pte Ltd